SILVER BURDETT music

TEACHER'S EDITION / 4

ELIZABETH CROOK
BENNETT REIMER
DAVID S. WALKER

SILVER BURDETT COMPANY
MORRISTOWN, NEW JERSEY • GLENVIEW, ILLINOIS
PALO ALTO • DALLAS • ATLANTA

SPECIAL CONTRIBUTORS

William M. Anderson (non-Western music), Aurora, Ohio

Kojo Fosu Baiden (music of Africa), Silver Springs, Maryland

Dulce B. Bohn (recorder), Wilmington, Delaware

Charles L. Boilès (music of Mexico), Bloomington, Indiana

Ian L. Bradley (Canadian music), Victoria, British Columbia, Canada

Gerald Burakoff (recorder), Levittown, New York

Henry Burnett (music of Japan), Flushing, Long Island, New York

Richard J. Colwell (testing and evaluation), Urbana, Illinois

Marilyn C. Davidson (music for Orff instruments), Bergenfield, New Jersey

Joan Davies (music of Canada and Japan), Charlottetown, P.E.I., Canada

Kay Hardesty (special education), Chautauqua, New York

James M. Harris (music in early childhood), San Francisco, California

Doris E. Hays (avant-garde music), New York City

Nazir A. Jairazbhoy (music of India), Windsor, Ontario, Canada

Maria Jordan (music of Greece), Hicksville, Long Island, New York

Robert A. Kauffman (music of Africa), Seattle, Washington

Edna Knock (music of Canada), Brandon, Manitoba, Canada

John Lidstone (visual arts), Brooklyn, New York

David McHugh (youth music), New York City

Alan P. Merriam (music of the North American Indians), Bloomington, Indiana

Lucille Mitchell (American folk songs), Alexandria, Virginia

María Luisa Muñoz (music of Puerto Rico), Houston, Texas

Lynn Freeman Olson (listening program), New York City

Mary E. Perrin (music in the inner city), Chicago, Illinois

Carmino Ravosa (children's song literature), Briarcliff Manor, New York

Joyce Bogusky-Reimer (avant-garde music), Wilmette, Illinois

Geraldine Slaughter (music of Africa), Washington, D.C.

Mark Slobin (music of the Near East), Middletown, Connecticut

Ruth Marie Stone (music of Africa), New York City

Leona B. Wilkins (music in the inner city), Evanston, Illinois

CONSULTANTS

Lynn Arizzi (levels 1 and 2), Reston, Virginia

Joy Browne (levels 5 and 6), Kansas City, Missouri

Nancy Crump, classroom teacher, Alexandria, Louisiana

Lyla Evans, classroom teacher, South Euclid, Ohio

Catherine Gallas, classroom teacher, Bridgeton, Missouri

Linda Haselton, classroom teacher, Westminster, California

Ruth A. Held, classroom teacher, Lancaster, Pennsylvania

Judy F. Jackson, classroom teacher, Franklin, Tennessee

Mary E. Justice, Auburn University, Auburn, Alabama

Jean Lembke (levels 3 and 4), Tonawanda, New York

Barbara Nelson, classroom teacher, Baytown, Texas

Terry Philips (youth music), New York City

Ruth Red, Director of Music Education, Houston, Texas

Mary Ann Shealy (levels 1 and 2), Florence, South Carolina

Beatrice Schattschneider (levels 1–6), Morristown, New Jersey

Paulette Schmalz, classroom teacher, Phoenix, Arizona

Sister Helen C. Schneider, Clarke College, Dubuque, Iowa

Merrill Staton (recordings), Alpine, New Jersey

ACKNOWLEDGMENTS

The authors and editors of SILVER BURDETT MUSIC acknowledge with gratitude the contributions of the following persons.

Marjorie Hahn, New York
Yoriko Kozumi, Japan
Ruth Merrill, Texas
Mary Ann Nelson, Texas
Bennie Mae Oliver, Texas
Joanne Ryan, New York
Helen Spiers, Virginia
Shirley Ventrone, Rhode Island
Avonelle Walker, New York

Credit and appreciation are due publishers and copyright owners for use of the following.

"Crossing" from *Letter from a Distant Land* by Philip Booth. Copyright 1953 by Philip Booth. Originally appeared in *The New Yorker*. Reprinted by permission of Viking Penguin Inc.

"Geranium" by Mary Ellen Solt from *Flowers in Concrete* by Fine Arts Department, University of Indiana © 1966. Reprinted by permission of Mary Ellen Solt.

"Poem" from *The Dream Keeper and Other Poems* by Langston Hughes. Copyright 1932 and renewed 1960 by Langston Hughes. Reprinted by permission of Alfred A. Knopf, Inc.

"Roll, Roll, Tootsie Roll" and "See a Pin and Pick It Up" from *Lore and Language of School Children* by Iona and Peter Opie. © 1959 Iona and Peter Opie. Reprinted by permission of Oxford University Press.

"Slowly" from *The Wandering Moon* by James Reeves. Used by permission of the publisher, William Heinemann Ltd.

"Swift Things Are Beautiful" from *Away Goes Sally* by Elizabeth Coatsworth. Copyright 1934 by Macmillan Publishing Co., Inc., renewed 1962 by Elizabeth Coatsworth Beston. Reprinted by permission of Macmillan Publishing Co., Inc., and Blackie and Son Limited, Scotland.

"Tom and Joe" from *Away and Ago* by David McCord. Copyright © 1968, 1971, 1972, 1973, 1974 by David McCord. Reprinted by permission of Little, Brown and Co.

"Windy Winter Rain . . ." by Shisei-Jo, from *Japanese Haiku*, p. 57. Copyright © 1955 Peter Pauper Press, Inc. Reprinted by permission.

CONTENTS

Also available from the publisher are
• Student Response spirit masters for the *What Do You Hear?* lessons
• Competency Tests, three for each level, 1–6

INTRODUCTION

The first edition of SILVER BURDETT MUSIC heralded a new age for music education. SILVER BURDETT MUSIC was based firmly in the long history and strong traditions of school music; its organization reflected newly gained understanding of how children can best be helped to learn; and its philosophy captured the emerging focus on aesthetic education. The first edition was accepted enthusiastically and used successfully by teachers and students in all sections of the country.

Those responsible for SILVER BURDETT MUSIC, however, were determined that it not be allowed to rest on its success, but that it be studied conscientiously for ways to improve it. A major effort was launched to study scientifically what was being learned by children using the materials, what levels of success they were achieving, what tasks in the materials were too easy or too difficult, what examples were effective in enhancing musical perception and what examples were less so, what lessons needed reorganization, what possible changes would make every learning event as powerful as

---

MODULE
The module is the organizing unit of the program. A module is a single lesson or a cluster of lessons that can stand alone as an entity.

OBJECTIVES
Beginning on page *xi*, objectives for the modules are presented in chart form.

SUBJECT
...the subject of the module and the number of the lesson.

MATERIALS
...a list of the records, pupils' pages, instruments, and equipment needed to teach the lesson.

VOCABULARY
...a list of the terms used in this lesson.

IDEAS FOR TEACHING
...ideas for introducing the material and presenting it effectively.

ESSENTIAL ACTIVITY
The heavy black line identifies the Essential Activity in the lesson. If time permits, use of the additional suggestions is recommended.

ACCOMPANIMENT
...indicates the page number of the accompaniment. Accompaniments are for piano. Some songs have Orff-Instrument accompaniments also.

RECORDING
...indicates the location of the selection in the record package.

MODULE 13

OBJECTIVES, p. XIII

RHYTHM PATTERNS 2 • Lesson 1

MATERIALS
Record 6, "The Mosquito"; Mozart: *Variations on "Ah, vous dirai-je, Maman?"; Din Don;* Pupil's Book, pp. 142 and 143; percussion instruments (maracas, bongos, claves); wood block, finger cymbals, recorders or bells

VOCABULARY
triplet, fermata

IDEAS FOR TEACHING
Note: Through singing, listening, and playing instruments, children have experienced rhythm patterns that have the beat divided into two equal sounds [♫]. In each phrase of "The Mosquito," they will encounter this rhythm along with the triplet, the beat divided into three equal sounds [♪♪♪]. The triplet was introduced in "Island Hopping," p. 118.

1. As they listen to the recording of "The Mosquito," have children follow the notation on p. 142. Help them observe that the rhythm of the first phrase (*I went to the Sierra Blanca*) is repeated throughout the song.

2. When children know "The Mosquito," ask them to sing with the recording. Have them take turns playing the rhythm of the melody on an appropriate percussion instrument (e.g., maracas, bongos, claves). <u>Note</u>: Thinking the words will help children play the rhythm accurately.

→

RHYTHM PATTERNS 2

Notice the triplet ♪♪♪ in each phrase as you sing this song.

How many triplets can you find?

THE MOSQUITO
FOLK SONG FROM COLOMBIA   ENGLISH WORDS BY MARGARET MARKS

Piano acc., p. 294

1. I went to the Sie - rra Blan - ca   To hunt with my dog, Pe - rri - to,
When sud - den - ly I en - count - ered   a great o - ver - grown mos - qui - to.
I dropped to my knees and fired, ___   And star - tled by that ex - plo - sion,
The an - i - mal lost his bal - ance   And tum - bled in - to the o - cean.

2. So huge was this big mosquito,
A tidal wave swelled the water,
His head lay in Cádiz harbor,
His feet lay across Gibraltar.
And then the ordeal was over,
The bug ceased to make a motion,
I called for a crane and derrick,
You've never seen such commotion.

3. They made from his hide ten thou
High boots of the finest leather,
And just from the bits left over,
A hundred or so umbrellas;
And even now, ten years later,
Though nothing could seem absu
The whole of the Spanish Army
Is eating mosquito-burger!

Can you hear triplets in this piece for piano?

Mozart: *Variations on "Ah, vous dirai-je, Maman?"*

142 MODULE 13: Rhythm Patterns 2

TRY THIS
Children can add an accompaniment for "The Mosquito" by plucking the A and (either high or low) E strings of a guitar. The following diagram shows which strings to pluck. The notation shows the order and rhythm for playing the tones. <u>Note</u>: Children begin playing on the first strong beat of the song, on the word *went.*

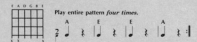

OPTIONAL PARTS FOR ORFF INSTRUMENTS OR BELLS

(Melody begins)
Introduction

Alto Gl.

Alto Met.

Bass Xyl. or Met.

(Alto Gl. = Alto Glockenspiel; Alto Met. = Alto Metallophone; Bass Xyl. = Bass Xylophone)

experience and research could lead it to be. This research effort is described in more detail on page ix, "Testing Musical Competencies."

The result of all this work is the present edition of SILVER BURDETT MUSIC. It contains many of the improvements the studies suggested could be made, including more songs in each grade, greatly revised teachers' editions giving highly detailed suggestions for teaching, a clearer format (see below), more effective graphics, and reorganization of certain learning sequences. Virtually every change was based on hard evidence

that the change would indeed improve children's learning. SILVER BURDETT MUSIC offers the flexibility of being usable as a coherent curriculum in and of itself, or serving as a source of materials for use within an alternative curriculum. However used, the materials of SILVER BURDETT MUSIC embody "state of the art" principles from education in general combined with the best available knowledge about effective music education in particular. The authors and editors believe the series provides a model for what a good music curriculum should be. (Continued on p. vi.)

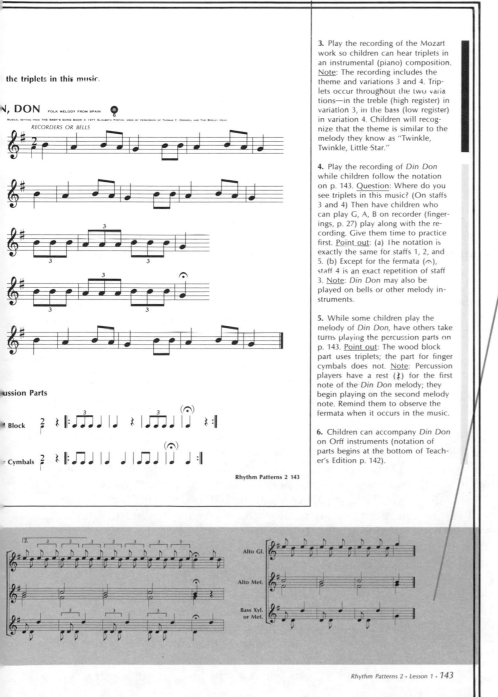

the triplets in this music.

N, DON FOLK MELODY FROM SPAIN

MUSICAL SETTING FROM THE BABY'S SONG BOOK © 1971 ELIZABETH POSTON. USED BY PERMISSION OF THOMAS Y. CROWELL AND THE BODLEY HEAD.

RECORDERS OR BELLS

ussion Parts

Block

Cymbals

Rhythm Patterns 2 143

3. Play the recording of the Mozart work so children can hear triplets in an instrumental (piano) composition. Note: The recording includes the theme and variations 3 and 4. Triplets occur throughout the two variations—in the treble (high register) in variation 3, in the bass (low register) in variation 4. Children will recognize that the theme is similar to the melody they know as "Twinkle, Twinkle, Little Star."

4. Play the recording of Din Don while children follow the notation on p. 143. Question: Where do you see triplets in this music? (On staffs 3 and 4) Then have children who can play G, A, B on recorder (fingerings, p. 27) play along with the recording. Give them time to practice first. Point out: (a) The notation is exactly the same for staffs 1, 2, and 5. (b) Except for the fermata (⌒), staff 4 is an exact repetition of staff 3. Note: Din Don may also be played on bells or other melody instruments.

5. While some children play the melody of Din Don, have others take turns playing the percussion parts on p. 143. Point out: The wood block part uses triplets; the part for finger cymbals does not. Note: Percussion players have a rest (𝄽) for the first note of the Din Don melody; they begin playing on the second melody note. Remind them to observe the fermata when it occurs in the music.

6. Children can accompany Din Don on Orff instruments (notation of parts begins at the bottom of Teacher's Edition p. 142).

Alto Gl.

Alto Met.

Bass Xyl. or Met.

Rhythm Patterns 2 · Lesson 1 · 143

BLUE PANEL MATERIAL
Various kinds of materials are presented in the blue panel.

- Dance Directions

- Instrumental Parts

- Orff-instrument accompaniments; short ostinatos are notated on page. Longer arrangements are in the accompaniment section.

- Music Reading: Suggestions for developing music reading skills are frequently independent of the main emphasis of the lesson.

- Try This: The suggestions under this heading represent a wide variety of materials and approaches to teaching. Often they provide a challenge for gifted students. They are optional.

- Teacher Information: This historical, biographical, or procedural information enhances or expands upon the subject of the lesson. It may be shared with the students at your discretion.

- Mainstreaming: Suggestions for adapting the materials for mainstreamed classes are given, as well as references to adaptations in *Silver Burdett Music for Special Education.*

- Competency Tests: When the appropriate amount of material has been covered, a note reminds you that a certain test should be given at that time.

- Language Arts and Social Studies Correlation: Suggestions for language arts and social studies correlation are made when appropriate.

In addition to the teaching aids found on page, other helps are provided in the back of the Teacher's Edition.

- The Kodály Guide categorizes the song material in terms of the basic melody patterns used in the Kodály approach.

- The Note Reading Index categorizes the songs according to note values, rhythm patterns, and pitches.

- Classified Index

- Instructions for tuning the Autoharp

THE ORGANIZATION OF
Silver Burdett Music

MODULES AND LESSONS. In Silver Burdett Music, the organizing unit is the module. A module is a single lesson or a cluster of lessons that can stand alone as an entity. The modules are the building blocks from which the teacher structures the curriculum. They are interchangeable and can be arranged in a great variety of sequences depending on particular circumstances.

A lesson is a single teaching-learning event that involves children in music through a variety of activities. Each lesson is designed to serve a twofold function:

1. A complete learning episode in itself

2. One of a set of lessons making up a module

The final lesson in many of the modules is called *What Do You Hear?* This kind of lesson requires the children to demonstrate what they have learned by responding to the instructions on the recording. These lessons give the children and the teacher a concrete assessment of progress toward increased musical discernment.

Each book in the series is part of a cyclical movement from obvious to subtle that extends from early childhood through Grade 8. From lesson, to module, to book, to series of nine books, each level is both complete in itself and a structural part of a larger whole. This cyclical, or "spiral," organization ensures a high level of consistency and a maximum of efficiency. It takes the child through a nine-year period of progressively deeper experiences with music. At the same time, it allows a newcomer to the program to begin at any point and be drawn into the spiral from that point on.

The spiral mode of organization is consistent with learning theory. The developmental nature of human learning has been well established. Silver Burdett Music provides opportunities for gradual, progressive, consistent growth—constantly building upon and widening previous learnings, consistently challenging each musical behavior while providing a high level of success, and focusing activities in a specific direction while allowing for and encouraging individual freedom of movement within the general organization.

USING
Silver Burdett Music

THE BASIC PROGRAM. The quantity of materials provided in Silver Burdett Music is so great that it is unlikely that any particular class could cover the complete contents of a given book in a year's time. For this reason, the lessons constituting the Basic Program have been identified. These lessons form the basis for a year's work. The Basic Program includes the material evaluated in the *Silver Burdett Music Competency Tests,* available from the publisher.

THE EXTENDED PROGRAM. The lessons in the Extended Program reinforce or extend the learning provided in the basic lessons. In many instances, a specific extended lesson can be substituted for a basic lesson if the song or listening selection in the extended lesson is more appropriate for a particular teaching situation, and if the concept taught is the same.

Identification of whether a lesson is part of the Basic Program or the Extended Program is provided in the Progress Chart, page xvi.

PROGRESSING THROUGH THE PROGRAM. A simple and effective way to progress through Silver Burdett Music is consecutively from beginning to end. The sequence of lessons and modules has been arranged so that a majority of children will be likely to encounter a maximum of unity and diversity as they move from page to page. The teacher using a book for the first time may well find it advantageous to follow the book's outline progressively.

However, a high level of choice is built into the books. The lessons in each module can be taken in sequence until the module is finished. Depending upon the response of the children, a switch can be made at any time to a new module or to a previously unfinished module. The rule to follow is that in switching from module to module *the lessons within each module be covered in numerical sequence.* This procedure applies whether all lessons in a module are used or only the lessons in the Basic Program. In choosing lesson sequences, the teacher will be sensitive to

(1) the amount of time available,
(2) the children's attention span,
(3) a spontaneous interest in a new concept,
(4) the desire to explore a particular concept further, and
(5) the need to explore a wide variety of concepts.

The progression of learnings can be tailored to each situation with full confidence. The cyclical organization of the lessons ensures that learnings will not be diffuse or unrelated. Freedom and structure are basic and compatible features of Silver Burdett Music.

PROGRESS CHART. The Progress Chart on p. xvi is provided to help teachers plan their program and to record class progress through the materials. When a lesson is completed, it can be checked off on the chart.

THE PHILOSOPHY OF
Silver Burdett Music

The Silver Burdett Music program is aesthetic education in action. Its major goal is to increase the sensitivity of all children to the power of music as an art—to develop their abilities to perceive the art of music keenly and respond to it deeply. Nonartistic values—the social, psychological, physical, and other benefits of involvement in music—are recognized and included. They are treated as contributory to the main purpose.

Musical aesthetic experience consists of the following:
(1) Perceiving the expressive qualities in a piece of music;
(2) Responding to those qualities in a feelingful way. Each such musical experience has two important values: it is satisfying for its own, immediate sake; and it whets the appetite for more of such experience in the future. Opportunities for immediate aesthetic satisfaction and future aesthetic growth are built into every learning episode.

If musical experience is to be powerful, it must involve both the mind and feelings. Materials that overemphasize intellectual learnings can lead to a bloodless, clinical atmosphere, which leaves the whole person untouched. On the other hand, materials that cater only to immediate pleasure can lead to superficiality and a stagnation of growth. To balance musical challenges with musical satisfactions is a delicate task. Every effort has been made to do so in SILVER BURDETT MUSIC.

Challenges to understanding and perception are present in abundance. But equally abundant are opportunities for success and pleasure. Each lesson includes both perceptual problems to be grappled with and musical experiences to be enjoyed, one reinforcing the other. As perception deepens, enjoyment deepens. And as children's feelings are moved by the power of music, their ability and desire to perceive increase. Thinking and feeling become inseparable as both are exercised in the experience of music.

To be effective, aesthetic education must be active education. Passive learning will not generate the intellectual and emotional excitement that helps bring people and art together. In SILVER BURDETT MUSIC children are involved wholeheartedly in a variety of activities designed to make music come alive for them. But activities for the simple sake of keeping children busy are avoided. Involvement must never be mindless and unfocused. SILVER BURDETT MUSIC requires energy—of students and of teachers. But it carefully channels this energy toward a larger goal—the ever-increasing ability to share the aesthetic power of music.

THE REPERTORY OF SILVER BURDETT MUSIC

MUSIC LITERATURE. The music in SILVER BURDETT MUSIC offers a wide variety of styles, types, and mediums. At most grade levels, music is included that may seem quite adventurous for children of that age. In regard to the introduction of unfamiliar music, the general principle guiding this program is "better sooner than later."

A great deal of evidence points to the receptivity of young children to musical experiences of great diversity. If musical tastes are to be broadened rather than narrowed, the wide world of music must be sampled and enjoyed at every step of the way. If an attitude of adventure is adopted, if no one assumes that every piece must be immediately "liked," and if the commitment of the music educator is to be honest as to what music really consists of in the world outside the classroom, then at every grade level the materials presented will contain as wide a variety of music as is feasible.

When teaching for deeper perception of a particular musical quality, one should present examples of that quality as it appears in music of many different types and levels of complexity. The quality must be obvious enough to be perceived by most children studying it, yet subtle enough to expand their perceptivity. These conditions are present in each module. By focusing on a particular musical quality, examples can be chosen from many segments of music literature. This broadens the familiarity of children with many kinds of music while helping them become involved in the pieces as much as they can for their present level of development.

SONGS. The songs in SILVER BURDETT MUSIC are

(1) of high musical quality,

(2) attractive to children,

(3) notated in vocal ranges appropriate for particular age groups, according to current research,

(4) representative of a wide variety of types, styles, and ethnic origins, and

(5) helpful in developing musical perception.

Songs are used in the modules to illustrate concepts. They have also been chosen because each of the other conditions has been met.

THE ARTS. While the basic purpose of SILVER BURDETT MUSIC is to offer an aesthetic education in the art of music, children should recognize that music is a member of a larger community that includes all the arts. Developing sensitivity to other modes of aesthetic expression is valuable in and of itself, and it also gives children a broad view of music as one of several ways to explore and understand feeling.

Each book contains several lessons on the arts. Each lesson explores a particular aesthetic quality or process that exists in several arts. The purpose of the lesson is to show how that quality or process operates distinctively in each art. The focus is always on the unique way each art uses that particular aesthetic quality. The impression that "all arts are the same" is avoided. Indeed, it is the *differences* among arts—the characteristics that make them unique—that are explored. The more sensitive a child becomes to the expressiveness of painting *as* painting, of poetry *as* poetry, of dance *as* dance, of music *as* music, the more deeply can that child share the characteristic way each fulfills its goal of capturing and displaying a sense of human subjectivity. At the same time, the child comes to recognize that all the arts share that same goal.

MUSIC STYLES. The style lessons in each book are integrative experiences. They pull together previous learnings and focus them on the characteristic musical style of a specific composition. Children can respond to style characteristics with great success even in the primary grades. It is essential that style-expectations be cultivated from the very start of music education so that children can develop the ability to share and enjoy a rich variety of music styles.

MUSIC READING IN SILVER BURDETT MUSIC

The ability to read music notation is considered an important means for exploring music and participating in its creation. Every child should be helped to learn to read music.

Most modules include an involvement with notation as an essential part of the learnings. Music reading is integrated in a variety of ways as an important means for perceiving, performing, analyzing, and conceptualizing. Reading skills are developed gradually but consistently, moving from simplified notation to traditional notation and to exploration of nontraditional notation. These learnings are fostered in the context of a rich involvement with musical experience itself, the notation being one of many means toward closer contact with the expressiveness of music.

To master the skill of sight-singing requires many hours of practice. However, in many situations, too little time is alloted in general music classes for students to acquire the kind of mastery that makes sight-singing truly functional. On the other hand, the ability to read music with the aid of a simple instrument is a practical goal for general music classes. For this reason, beginning in *Book 1,* notation is also studied in conjunction with instruments available in the classroom.

KODALY GUIDE and NOTE READING INDEX. The Kodály Guide indexes the songs in this volume according to basic melody patterns used in the Kodály approach to the teaching of sight-singing. In the Note Reading Index, the songs are indexed according to the note values, rhythm patterns, and pitches that are contained in the songs. This Guide and Index precede the Classified Index.

THE INDIVIDUAL AND
Silver Burdett Music

This program may be used in a large-group situation, or in a small-group situation, or it may be used by individual children. Used in conjunction with the accompanying recordings and classroom instruments, the Pupil's Book provides the materials the students need to gain considerable insight on their own. In an "open" classroom, small groups of children may be working on different parts of a learning module. In addition to saving time, such a plan allows for choice and for more concentration on specific details. Moreover, some parts of a module can be done by one or two children working independently or by several children, one of whom is given the responsibility of leadership.

As the students progress through the program, they will be given more and more opportunity to develop the skills needed to sing, to play an instrument, to read notation, and to create their own compositions. It is not necessary for every student to take part in all the options SILVER BURDETT MUSIC provides. Each individual should be encouraged to follow his or her own bent, but should also be encouraged to "stick with" a particular activity until a reasonable skill is developed.

When books, recordings, and classroom instruments are made available to each child through a media center, students can learn at home as well as in school. When students prepare assignments or performances outside the large-group situation, they should be given an opportunity to share their achievements with their classmates. Such sharing among members of a peer group is a powerful motivating force.

MAINSTREAMING AND
Silver Burdett Music

The needs of children in mainstreamed classes are as varied as the children themselves. SILVER BURDETT MUSIC helps to meet these needs by (1) providing lessons that encompass a range of learnings, from very simple to more complex; (2) suggesting ways that lesson materials can be adapted to special needs; (3) providing references to *Silver Burdett Music for Special Education* for further ideas about helping special children.

The following is a summary of some basic approaches to teaching that are *essential* in dealing with children who have been designated as requiring special education.

- Always communicate acceptance and respect for all students.
- Be consistent in rules and in dealing with groups and individuals.
- Stress positive rather than negative things about children: this will help forestall inappropriate behavior.

- Communicate openly with students concerning their feelings, expectations, and needs.
- Take time to talk with students, parents, and other teachers to promote a better understanding of disabilities and individual differences.
- Recognize and accept the fears and frustrations of your students, and help them find acceptable means of dealing with them.
- Avoid overprotecting special students. Do not lower your expectations for reasonable behavior.
- Offer assistance to disabled students, but never do things for them that they can do for themselves.
- Give students the opportunity to make choices and decisions, and to assume leadership roles.
- Evaluate *with* students rather than *for* them.
- Teach for transfer. Remind students of opportunities to use previously learned skills in new contexts.
- Avoid over-verbalizing. Involve students in activities *before* giving extensive directions or explanations.
- Allow adequate time for individuals to respond. Be patient.
- Be sensitive to those students for whom reading and writing tasks are difficult or impossible.
- Plan lessons that are socially appropriate. All children are quick to resent materials they consider "baby stuff."
- In teaching for concepts, use as many concrete means (teaching aids, manipulative materials, charts) as you possibly can.
- Use more than words to communicate—touch, show, move, manipulate, gesture, demonstrate.

THE RECORDINGS FOR
Silver Burdett Music

The recordings for SILVER BURDETT MUSIC are carefully coordinated with the text material in every module. In each module there is a variety of activities. In addition to providing for singing and listening, the recordings include music for improvising, dramatizing, echo clapping. Among the recorded materials are poems, direct teaching materials, evaluation tools, and play-along/sing-along accompaniments. (The songs in this book are recorded in the key of the printed version. However, the recording does not necessarily follow the same chord structure as the piano accompaniment.)

When played on a stereo phonograph, the *Pick-a-Track* recordings enable the teacher to highlight either the voices or the song accompaniments. When the voices are highlighted, the children can (1) focus on vocal quality and style, (2) learn parts quickly, and (3) perfect the pronunciation of foreign and English lyrics. When the instrumental accompaniments are highlighted, the children can (1) focus on identifying instrumental tone colors and (2) sing to professional accompaniments in the classroom and assembly or for special performances.

Sometimes a song has been recorded to serve as a listening experience only. This occurs when children can readily grasp and understand the musical intent, but because of limited vocal skill are unable to reproduce the correct sound and vocal style.

Musicians will readily agree that the music score is only a "skeleton of intent" for the performer. At best, a score is a mere approximation of the composer's musical ideas. Notated tempo, rhythm patterns, dynamics, and all the rest must, in performance, be made flexible in order to "bend" into a musical statement while still remaining true to the composer's wishes. The "bending of the notation" results in an artistic performance. In the SILVER BURDETT MUSIC recordings, the intent of the performances is not necessarily to duplicate the exact notation in all cases, but rather to create as powerful a musical experience as possible for children to hear and share. The teacher must bear this fact in mind when comparing the performances on the recordings with the notation in the book.

The recordings of the *What Do You Hear?* lessons give children an opportunity to make active choices about the qualities of music they are learning to perceive. These lessons use focused listening as a means to

(1) reinforce perception of a particular quality in familiar music,

(2) widen perception of a particular quality in unfamiliar music,

(3) develop habits of perceptive listening to music.

Each *What Do You Hear?* lesson, therefore, is an integral part of its module, bringing the varied activities in the module to a musical culmination. It should be used for its educational function rather than as a formal test. Even if all the lessons in a particular module are not used, the *What Do You Hear?* material should be included. If children are uncertain about the terms or instructions on the *What Do You Hear?* recording, explain them more fully. Work out an item or two at the chalkboard while the class watches. With familiarity, these lessons will become quite easily understood. (Spirit masters for these lessons are available from the publisher.)

ILLUSTRATIONS/ PHOTOGRAPHS

Throughout the series, photographs are used as a means of acquainting students immediately with the concepts and vocabulary presented within the lessons. Usually these visuals make use of environmental scenes, home, school, and playground activities, as well as common objects known to children. These visuals will help children progress from the known to the unknown and will provide a means for relating particular visual concepts with similar music concepts. Other visuals that teach show particular activities such as movement, correct playing positions for classroom instruments, and specific illustrations of orchestral, folk, and ethnic instruments. Each book shows photographs of children at the appropriate age level.

The *Silver Burdett Sound/Color Filmstrips,* available from the publisher, are a series of six experiences that expand on the concepts presented in the text materials. The filmstrips are cross-referenced in the Teacher's Notes when germane to the lesson.

TESTING MUSICAL COMPETENCIES

Throughout the long history of music education it has been assumed that involvement in musical activities— singing, playing, listening, moving, etc.—would improve children's abilities to discern what the sounds are actually doing in a piece of music. There was a lack of hard evidence as to precisely what children at each grade level were capable of perceiving. In planning SILVER BURDETT MUSIC, the authors and editors were determined to improve on the timeworn practice of teaching "by hunch and by hope."

The philosophy of SILVER BURDETT MUSIC suggests that aesthetic learnings occur when specific behaviors are cultivated—the behaviors discussed below under the heading "Objectives of SILVER BURDETT MUSIC." The central behavior—musical perception—is capable of being measured with a high degree of accuracy when children are asked to analyze and conceptualize what they notice as they listen to a musical example. This fact was the guideline for a history-making project to (1) assess the musical perceptual abilities of children at each grade level, 1 to 6, (2) develop a series of tests that could be used to measure students' musical perception at each grade level, and (3) produce teaching materials reflecting not just *opinion* as to what children are capable of learning in music, but *factual evidence* of what they can and cannot perceive.

Under the direction of Dr. Richard Colwell, data were collected from several thousand children in a carefully planned, step-by-step series of initial pilot testings. *What Do You Hear?* listening lessons from the first edition of SILVER BURDETT MUSIC were given extensive field trials. Then initial prototype tests were given in 30 school systems in 21 states; later, random-sample testing was administered in 54 communities representing all sections of the country. In all, some 26,000 children were involved in the study, representing small, medium, and large communities and diverse socioeconomic and cultural groupings in the United States. This project accumulated more information about how and what children learn about music than has ever before been available.

The results of this unprecedented project are the *Silver Burdett Music Competency Tests* and this edition of the SILVER BURDETT MUSIC text materials. Revision of the textbooks and recordings has been extensive. Effects of the massive research project on the instructional program include (1) a more gradual, step-by-step learning sequence for concepts that take more time to develop, (2) increased review and reinforcement of some concepts, and (3) additions and substitutions in the listening program.

Together, the SILVER BURDETT MUSIC text materials and the *Competency Tests* provide the most carefully researched and therefore the most realistic, most effective musical learning opportunities ever available to all children in the schools.

OBJECTIVES OF SILVER BURDETT MUSIC

The major goal of SILVER BURDETT MUSIC, as stated in the philosophy, is to increase the sensitivity of all children to the power of music as an art. This goal is fulfilled through the accomplishment of objectives stated in terms of seven behaviors:

(1) Perceiving

(2) Reacting

(3) Producing

(4) Conceptualizing

(5) Analyzing
(6) Evaluating
(7) Valuing

The first two of these behaviors—perceiving and reacting—are "ends." They constitute musical aesthetic experience. The next four behaviors—producing, conceptualizing, analyzing, and evaluating—are "means" to those ends. The seventh behavior—valuing—is an "outcome." It occurs as a result of effective development of the other six behaviors.

PERCEIVING. To perceive music aesthetically, one must notice or discern those qualities that make sound expressive. Works of art present conditions or qualities that must be perceived in order to be enjoyed. Most, if not all, works of art present a complex set of such qualities, requiring far more than casual attention if they are to be more fully perceived.

Silver Burdett Music is devoted to the cultivation of musical perception. The materials carefully, systematically, and progressively involve children in opportunities to perceive music more precisely. Each child demonstrates his or her perception through a variety of overt responses, ranging from simple body movements to written responses.

REACTING. Whereas perceiving requires *thinking*, reacting requires *feeling*. Aesthetic education has often been called the "education of feeling." For aesthetic experience to take place, one must *respond* to the expressive qualities one *perceives*.

Reaction is an intensely personal, subjective behavior. Silver Burdett Music never tells children what their individual feelings should be, nor does it invade their privacy by asking them to describe what they feel. The materials often suggest, however, that what is *heard* should also be *felt*.

Musical perception and musical reaction together equal musical experience. Such experience occurs through listening. Silver Burdett Music provides opportunities for active listening unprecedented in the history of music education. Whatever the particular activity of the moment—singing, playing, composing, and so forth—listening is present as an essential, active ingredient. And special, imaginative devices are used to help develop listening skills directly.

PRODUCING. In Silver Burdett Music, the term *producing* denotes singing, playing, composing, conducting, moving, and so forth. In the general music program, producing is a major means of experiencing musical sounds and how they work. Silver Burdett Music relies heavily on production activities to bring children and music together. Production activities are both means and ends. As ends, they need no discussion, for they have found an honored place in the music education curriculum for many years. As means, the production activities are powerful tools to aid in heightening musical perception, intensifying musical reaction, and encouraging musical creativity. Since the production activities are all observable behaviors, they can serve as a valuable means for assessing student progress.

CONCEPTUALIZING. A child conceptualizes about music when describing
(1) the inner workings of music (melody, rhythm, texture, form, tone color),

(2) the roles of music in human life,
(3) styles of music, or
(4) the relationship of music to the other arts.

Although these four concept categories form the organizational basis of Silver Burdett Music, they are not treated as ends in themselves. Conceptual development is a means for fostering deeper perception of the actual sounds being described. So verbal descriptions are always kept in direct contact with the experience of musical sounds.

ANALYZING. To analyze music is to explore its inner workings. Silver Burdett Music includes analysis in every learning event as a means of heightening musical discrimination. But a sterile kind of analysis, in which the examination of musical sounds is separated from actual involvement with those sounds, is useless for aesthetic education and is carefully avoided in Silver Burdett Music.

EVALUATING. As a basic objective, Silver Burdett Music seeks to help the child
(1) appraise the musical quality of a wide variety of pieces,
(2) recognize that appraisal is a tentative process, subject to change,
(3) become aware of the many problems inherent in judging the arts, and
(4) learn about his or her own tastes and preferences in the context of the tastes and preferences of others.

The materials avoid giving the impression that judging is the major thing one should do with music, or that one can judge a work immediately, or that one is always qualified to do so. Nevertheless, thoughtful evaluation is an important means toward the development of musical discrimination.

VALUING. As children are successful in developing the other six behaviors, it is hoped that they will come to value music and the arts as important, fulfilling aspects of their world. The materials openly show that music is valued highly by others, without imposing on the child any particular set of values about music or even asking the child to "like" the music. Rather, Silver Burdett Music shows the child that music can be valued by all who are willing to become involved with it.

The seven behaviors described above are cultivated at every grade level. They differ from grade to grade only in degree of sophistication, cyclically growing in breadth and depth throughout the program. At every level, the specific objectives, as stated in terms of the seven behaviors, serve a larger, more general goal—to increase each child's ability to participate in the aesthetic experience of music.

SCOPE AND SEQUENCE CHART

On the pages following, the objectives for this level of Silver Burdett Music are presented in chart form. Scanning the chart horizontally provides a review of the behaviors that are covered in a particular module. Scanning the chart vertically provides a survey of the cyclical development of particular behaviors. Thus the chart illustrates both the scope of the musical learnings and the sequence of learning events.

OBJECTIVES: SCOPE AND SEQUENCE

	Perceiving and Reacting	Producing	Conceptualizing	Analyzing	Evaluating	Integrative Learning
MODULE 1 pages 38–47	Different tempos, changes of tempo, use of hold	Dramatizing an athletic "play," singing, using gestures, chanting, conducting, creating accompaniments, playing instruments, dancing, moving, creating a chance composition—to aid in discrimination of tempo qualities	The speed, or tempo, of music is basic to the experience it gives • Music may be very fast, very slow, or anything in between • Some pieces change tempo by getting gradually faster or slower • Some music stops or "holds" the tempo for a while • Many pieces use a variety of tempos.	Examining the tempos of various pieces and the effect of different tempos on the same piece • Investigating complex uses of tempos and holds in a variety of pieces • Using words and notation to indicate tempos and holds	Assessing the appropriateness of tempo choices and accompaniment patterns for several songs	The experience of music includes perception of many qualities of sound going on at the same time • Even in a single quality of sound, such as tempo, music can offer a high degree of complexity.
MODULE 2 pages 48–49	The variety of ways that musical elements can be used to produce an effective performance	Singing a song—to determine the effects of performers' decisions about how it might be performed	Because composers and performers are rarely able to rehearse together, performers must make their own decisions as to tempo, phrasing, dynamics, etc., based on what they find in the score.	Comparing a variety of ways to use musical elements to enhance the performance of a composition	Comparing the class performance with a recorded one to determine the effects of decisions made about how the music might be performed	In executing a musical composition, the performer interprets musical elements to create a satisfying effect.
MODULE 3 pages 50–65	Upward and downward movement; melodic sequences and contours	Drawing, singing, playing instruments, using natural sound sources, reading poetry and song lyrics, creating accompaniments, interpreting and creating sound pieces—to emphasize melodic direction, contours, and sequences	The upward and downward movement of tones in a melody helps organize the melody into a coherent whole with a recognizable shape or contour • Different contours give different musical experiences • When a particular contour is repeated at different pitch levels, the result is a "sequence," which retains contour even though the highness and lowness of the actual pitches have changed.	Exploring direction and its unifying function in forming melodies • Using conventional notation and line drawings to investigate melodic organization		Melody is made up of direction, sequences, and contour, each of which adds to a unified experience of a melody as a whole.
MODULE 4 pages 66–67	Stylistic characteristics of two eras		Some poems have very different organizations than others: they are in a different style • Pieces of music also come in a variety of styles • It is possible to identify the qualities of a style—those parts that add up to a distinctive whole with its own flavor of expressiveness.	Exploring aesthetic qualities of poems and music in contrasting styles		The arts are not confined to a single kind of expressiveness: each art has many styles to experience.
MODULE 5 pages 68–81	Strong and weak beat, metrical organization	Using gestures, playing instruments, playing games, creating visuals, singing, chanting, moving, performing sound pieces, accompanying, dancing—to clarify strength of beat and metrical organization	Beats can be strong and weak • When beats are organized into sets, or groups, the result is "meter" • Music that uses a regular meter (a grouping of beats into 2, 3, 4, 5, and so forth) has a powerful feeling of rhythmic stability—"knowing what will happen next" as the music goes on • More complex organizations of beats give more complex rhythmic experiences.	Comparing strong- and weak-beat pieces • Defining how beat organization can contribute to the form of a piece • Matching conducting patterns to appropriate meters • Discussing meter signatures and their function	Judging the expressive effects of beat strengths in different pieces and within the same piece	A meter sets up an expectation that movement will continue as it began, with the same groupings of beats • This enables other musical qualities to work and is expressive in and of itself.

	Perceiving and Reacting	Producing	Conceptualizing	Analyzing	Evaluating	Integrative Learning
MODULE 6 pages 82–85	Differences and similarities between two styles of the same era		There are many modern styles of painting and music • Each style has special qualities, but all styles depend on some basic qualities.	Exploring specific aesthetic qualities in painting, poetry, and music that make different styles and recognizing those qualities that are universal from style to style • Matching pieces of music to each other according to style		Many things are different about different styles of art; some things remain the same.
MODULE 7 pages 86–93	Various dynamic levels and changes	Singing, chanting, reading poetry, using gestures, playing accompaniments, creating sound pieces—with a variety of uses of dynamics	Loudness and softness are basic qualities of sound • They are used in music in many subtle ways to create an experience of organized sound-events • While some pieces are mostly soft or mostly loud, others use several dynamic levels and many gradual changes of dynamics (< and >).	Recognizing loudness and softness as elements in musical organization and expression • Associating dynamics with words, letters, and notational symbols	Judging whether the performance of several pieces has an effective balance of loud and soft • Assessing the effects of decisions about the use of dynamics on the expressiveness of a composition	What might seem like a simple quality of sound—loudness and softness—is actually a complex and rich source of experiences in the art of music.
MODULE 8 pages 94–111	Use of forming procedures and overall form	Singing; moving; playing accompaniments; creating movements, a sound piece, and visuals; interpreting sound pieces—to clarify the formal organization of a variety of pieces	Repetitions and contrasts of ideas help give music a sense of structure • The formal organization of a piece is often an arrangement of sections that repeat or contrast.	Examining sectional repetitions and contrasts in a variety of settings • Using notational devices to depict forms • Associating melodic, harmonic, dynamic, and tone color qualities with their function in forming a piece	Judging the effect of tone color choices in enhancing repetitions and contrasts • Evaluating decisions as to how to realize a composition following contemporary notation	The ongoing experience of most pieces includes a recognition of what came before and its relation to what comes after—a perception of structure, or form.
MODULE 9 pages 112–115	The musical qualities used to create a stylistic whole		The same musical qualities can yield different musical results (styles) when they are used differently.	Discerning several musical qualities that have been used in different ways to produce different stylistic effects		In art, the same parts can add up to different wholes, yielding different styles.
MODULE 10 pages 116–129	Use of register and range	Creating a display, singing, playing accompaniments, playing a game, performing and creating a sound piece—to provide experience with a variety of registers and narrow and wide ranges	Register is the highness or lowness of tones • Music in a high register gives a different feeling than music in a low register • Many pieces use several registers • Range is the spread of pitches in a melody • A wide-range melody, encompassing many pitches, has a different musical effect than a narrow-range melody, which might have only a few pitches close together from its lowest to its highest.	Differentiating registral and range functions in music • Discovering that register can be used to add distinctive qualities to accompaniments and melodies and that the range of various melodies is a basic part of their character • Use of traditional and nontraditional notation that depicts various registers and ranges	Judging the effectiveness of student-created accompaniments	Highness and lowness (register) by themselves add to music's expressive possibilities • The spread between high and low (range) in a melody is another way that high and low work to make music interesting • These are two simple but basic uses of a complex phenomenon.
MODULE 11 pages 130–133	Use of repeated, varied, and contrasting qualities	Using gestures, singing, playing and creating accompaniments, making a bulletin board about the environment, to experi	Several arts use repeated ideas along with varied and contrasting ideas • Repeats with variations and contrasts make for challenging artistic experiences.	Recognizing a repeated idea in two compositions (ground) and use of repetition in two visuals • Discerning repetition and contrast of four rhythm patterns • Exploring the simultaneous use of variety and contrast in all of		Many works combine stability (an idea repeated over and over) with uncertainty (varied and contrasting ideas going on at the same

	Perceiving and Reacting	Producing	Conceptualizing	Analyzing	Evaluating	Integrative Learning
MODULE 12 pages 134–141	Durational values and rhythm patterns	Making a collage, singing, playing accompaniments, creating pattern patterns, chanting, clapping, snapping fingers, patting—to experience a variety of rhythm patterns	Longer and shorter sounds can be combined into recognizable patterns • Rhythm patterns of all sorts are expressive in and of themselves and add to a sense of what can be expected in a piece of music.	Using notation for quarter, eighth, sixteenth, and dotted notes	Judging the appropriateness of patterns used in a variety of functions and settings	A simple quality like long and short duration is, in music, a building block for an endless variety of more complex events.
MODULE 13 pages 142–155	Durational values and rhythm patterns	Singing, playing instruments, tapping, experimenting with different ways of performing a sound piece and creating one, chanting, playing rhythm pattern accompaniments, using gestures—to demonstrate recognition of rhythm patterns, including syncopation and rests	Longer and shorter sounds can be combined into recognizable patterns • Rests and dotted notes may be used in patterns to add special effects • Rhythm patterns of all sorts are expressive in and of themselves and add to a sense of what can be expected in a piece of music • Countermelodies can provide rhythmic as well as melodic contrast in a musical composition.	Using notation for triplets and rests, and graphic notation for various durations • Discerning the special feeling of syncopation, triplets, and dotted-note patterns	Judging appropriateness of patterns used in a variety of functions and settings	A simple quality like long and short duration is, in music, a building block for an endless variety of more complex events.
MODULE 14 pages 156–159	Use of pattern in the arts	Clapping, drawing lines, creating pattern pictures and movements—to illustrate the presence of patterns	Painting and music use patterns as a way of organization • In paintings, patterns are made by lines and arrangement of shapes, which the eye sees all at once • In music, patterns are made of rhythmic durations and pitches, and are heard one after the other.	Recognizing several recurring patterns in a painting and recurring rhythmic-melodic patterns in a song and a listening selection		Painting and music both use patterns, which are produced and experienced differently in each art.
MODULE 15 pages 160–185	Use of various tone colors	Singing, making a tape of voices of people students know, playing instruments, reading aloud a poem and song lyrics, performing a sound piece and creating one, making vocal and instrumental sound effects, creating percussion accompaniments and compositions, chanting, experimenting with different ways of picking and strumming the Autoharp, dancing—to explore differences in tone color	The voice and several groups of instruments (woodwinds, brass, strings, percussion, keyboard) all add distinctive sound qualities or "tone colors" to music • Because each tone color is different, the musical experience one gets from each is different.	Examining effects produced by different uses of the voice and different instruments		A piece is "the same piece" even when performed with a different tone color.

	Perceiving and Reacting	Producing	Conceptualizing	Analyzing	Evaluating	Integrative Learning
MODULE 16 pages 186-187	Stylistic characteristics of a particular type of music		Jazz is a style of music with a distinctive sound, but there are many kinds of jazz with much variety • Jazz can be soft, loud, fast, slow, played by a big band or small combo • Most jazz uses improvisation.	Searching for particular musical qualities in a variety of pieces, to discover that a style can contain different qualities and yet be cohesive		
MODULE 17 pages 188-199	Intervallic organization and relations	Playing accompaniments, singing, tracing contour lines, creating accompaniments, translating numbers into intervals to create a piece—to explore intervallic organization and relationships	Pitches may be very close together, wide apart, or anywhere in between • They may also repeat • The distance from one pitch to another is an "interval" • The intervals of a melody give it a shape, or contour • Each melody contour has its own expressiveness.	Examining intervals in a variety of pieces • Using line and traditional notation to depict intervals • Using intervals as building blocks for student-created pieces	Appraising the effectiveness of self-composed pieces and accompaniments	Intervals can be large or small • As the basis of melody, they can give an entire composition its special character.
MODULE 18 pages 200-205	Forming processes in the arts	Interpreting a sound piece through movement, creating a sound piece—to demonstrate comprehension of the contemporary forming process	Works of art are "formed"—put together—by using materials to create and extend events • Lines may do this with the help of a computer • Sounds may do this by any method of making something happen over a period of time.	Focusing on the sense of ongoing events created by various contemporary means		When someone forms sounds to be expressive, the result is music, whether traditional or nontraditional means are used.
MODULE 19 pages 206-213	Various metrical organizations and changes of meter	Performing a hand jive, clapping, patting, playing instruments, singing, playing a name game involving chanting—to clarify different meters	A meter can stay the same throughout a piece or it can change • Changes affect the feeling of expectation in a piece • Some music has constant changes of meter • Meter can be in groups of 2, 3, 4, or 5, or combinations of these • Sometimes sets of 3 are felt as one beat (or a beat is divided into three) • This gives a different feeling than when beats are divided into two.	Discovering metrical organizations in 2, 3, 4, or 5 compound meters • Use of notational symbols for meters and rhythm patterns • Use of accent to emphasize meter	Considering the musical effects of different metrical organizations	Musical movement can be regular, even if the regular groupings are of different lengths • Some music has irregular organizations of meters, giving a different feeling.
MODULE 20 pages 214-223	Phrase length and organization and use of cadences	Moving, dancing, singing, playing and creating accompaniments, making phrase diagrams, expanding a phrase into a composition—to employ a variety of phrase organizations	A phrase is a unit of a melody • Phrases help organize pieces • Some pieces have phrases of the same length; others have phrases of differing lengths • A cadence is the ending point of a phrase; some cadences are stronger than others.	Exploring same and different phrases (length and content) in a variety of settings • Characterizing cadences as weak or strong		Phrases and cadences give music a feeling of organization • When they are regular the feeling is different than when they are not regular.
MODULE 21 pages 224-227	Stylistic characteristics of one type of music	Singing, dancing, playing accompaniments—to experience the style of Polynesian music	Polynesian music has much variation from piece to piece, but the general sound, using words, chant, rhythm, and melody, is recognizable as a style • Often a story, or legend, is told by the music • Dance is also an important component of this music.	Examining the melodic, rhythmic, tone color, and textural aspects of Polynesian music		

	Perceiving and Reacting	Producing	Conceptualizing	Analyzing	Evaluating	Integrative Learning
MODULE 22 pages 228–237	General sound of tonality and atonality and use of specific arrangements of tone for each	Examining visuals, playing accompaniments, singing, dancing, composing a melody—to employ various linear pitch arrangements in tonal and atonal settings	Music that uses a strong pitch center, or focus, is "tonal". • Music that does not use this particular device is "atonal." • Both use arrangements of pitches—major, minor, pentatonic, whole-tone scales—and 12-tone row.	Examining overall effects and specific pitch organizations of music that is tonal (using major, minor, and pentatonic scales) and of music that lacks a strong tonal focus (using the whole-tone scale and 12-tone row)	Considering the different expressive effects of music using different scales	Music is not limited to just one- or two-pitch organizations or to a sound that depends on a strong pitch focus • The existence of many pitch possibilities gives music many expressive flavors.
MODULE 23 pages 238–239	Use of focus and no focus	Using flashlights, moving—to create an experience of focus and no focus	Music may have a home or key tone that provides a focus for the ear, or it may have no focal tone • Painting may have a strong center of interest or focus for the eye, or it may have none • Both arts are free to use both kinds of organization to create different ways of feeling.	Discerning presence and absence of focus in several pieces and paintings		
MODULE 24 pages 240–247	Various textures, thick and thin density	Singing, playing instruments, creating accompaniments, moving—to experience different textural organizations	Music can be organized by melody alone, melody with harmony, melody sung as a round, and melody with countermelody • When just one or two tones are heard at a time, the density is thin; adding more tones makes the density thicker.	Comparing and contrasting several textures and thicker and thinner densities	Considering the different musical effects caused by the use of various textures and densities	Music can have several layers of sound happening together • Different arrangements of these layers give different experiences.
MODULE 25 pages 248–249	Density in the arts	Creating a sound piece, examining visuals, creating accompaniments—to employ a variety of densities	In painting, density can be created by having more or less happening in a space • In music, thick and thin densities are created by the quantities of sound used at one time • Each art gives its special experience of density.	Discovering areas of thick and thin density in two paintings by the same artist and different densities of sound in two pieces by the same composer		

PROGRESS CHART

The PROGRESS CHART shows the Module/Lesson organization of this book—a module being a sequence of lessons, or a single lesson, that can stand alone as an entity. Although progressing through the modules consecutively from beginning to end is a simple and effective way to approach the material, it is possible to switch from one module (before finishing all of its lessons) to another module. It is important, however, that the lessons within a module be covered in numerical sequence. This procedure applies whether all lessons in a module are used or a selection of lessons. When a lesson is completed it can be checked off on the chart. Teachers with more than one class may duplicate this chart.

CONTENTS	PAGES	LESSONS											
Beginning Experiences	2–37												
Listening to Music	34–35	1 (34)											
The Arts: Active/Still	36–37	**1** (36)	Lessons identified by boldface numerals constitute the Basic Program. The Basic Program covers all the material evaluated in the *Silver Burdett Music Competency Tests*.* The Basic Program can be extended by adding lessons identified by lightface numerals. Numerals in parentheses are page numbers.										
MODULES													
1. Tempo	38–47	1 (38)	2 (39)	**3** (40)	4 (41)	**5** (42)	6 (44)	7 (46)	**8** (47)				
2. Things People Do with Music	48–49	1 (48)											
3. Direction	50–65	**1** (50)	2 (52)	**3** (54)	4 (55)	5 (56)	6 (58)	7 (59)	**8** (60)	9 (61)	**10** (62)	**11** (63)	12 (64)
													13 (65)
4. Style: Classic/Expressionistic	66–67	1 (66)											
5. Meter	68–81	**1** (68)	2 (70)	**3** (72)	4 (74)	5 (75)	6 (76)	7 (77)	**8** (78)	**9** (79)	10 (80)	11 (81)	
6. Modern Styles: Electronic, Folkloric	82–85	**1** (82)											
7. Dynamics	86–93	**1** (86)	2 (88)	3 (90)	**4** (91)	5 (92)	**6** (93)						
8. Form	94–111	**1** (94)	2 (96)	**3** (98)	4 (100)	**5** (102)	**6** (103)	7 (104)	**8** (105)	**9** (106)	10 (108)	**11** (110)	
										Silver Burdett Music Competency Test 1			
9. Style	112–115	**1** (112)											
10. Register—Range	116–129	1 (116)	**2** (118)	**3** (120)	4 (122)	**5** (123)	6 (124)	7 (126)	**8** (127)	**9** (128)	**10** (129)		
11. The Arts: Repetition with Variety and Contrast	130–133	**1** (130)											
12. Rhythm Patterns 1	134–141	1 (134)	**2** (136)	3 (138)	4 (139)	5 (140)	**6** (141)						
13. Rhythm Patterns 2	142–155	**1** (142)	**2** (144)	3 (145)	4 (146)	**5** (147)	6 (148)	7 (149)	8 (150)	9 (151)	**10** (152)	**11** (153)	**12** (154)
													13 (155)
14. The Arts: Pattern	156–159	1 (156)											
15. Tone Color	160–185	1 (160)	2 (161)	3 (162)	4 (164)	**5** (166)	6 (167)	7 (168)	8 (170)	**9** (172)	**10** (174)	**11** (176)	**12** (178)
									13 (180)	14 (182)	**15** (183)	16 (184)	17 (185)
16. Style: Jazz	186–187	1 (186)											
17. Melody	188–199	**1** (188)	**2** (190)	**3** (192)	4 (194)	5 (195)	6 (196)	7 (198)	**8** (199)				
18. The Arts: Contemporary Forming Process	200–205	1 (200)						*Silver Burdett Music Competency Test 2*					
19. Meter	206–213	**1** (206)	2 (208)	3 (209)	**4** (210)	5 (212)	6 (213)						
20. Phrases	214–223	**1** (214)	**2** (216)	3 (217)	**4** (218)	**5** (219)	6 (220)	7 (222)					
21. Style: Polynesian	224–227	1 (224)											
22. Tonality—Atonality	228–237	1 (228)	**2** (230)	3 (232)	**4** (233)	5 (234)	6 (235)	7 (236)	8 (237)				
23. The Arts: Focus, No Focus	238–239	1 (238)											
24. Texture	240–247	**1** (240)	**2** (242)	**3** (244)	**4** (245)	5 (246)	6 (247)						
25. The Arts: Density	248–249	**1** (249)					*Silver Burdett Music Competency Test 3*						

*The *Silver Burdett Music Competency Tests* are criterion-referenced to the series, and are available from the publisher. Test 1 should be administered after the completion of Module 8; Test 2 after completion of Module 18; and Test 3 after completion of Module 25. Use of the *Competency Tests* is optional.

The Piper

Piping down the valleys wild,
    Piping songs of pleasant glee,
On a cloud I saw a child,
    And he laughing said to me:

"Pipe a song about a Lamb!"
    So I piped with merry cheer.
"Piper, pipe that song again;"
    So I piped; he wept to hear.

"Drop thy pipe, thy happy pipe;
    Sing thy songs of happy cheer!"
So I sang the same again,
    While he wept with joy to hear.

"Piper, sit thee down and write
    In a book that all may read."
So he vanished from my sight;
    And I plucked a hollow reed.

And I made a rural pen,
    And I stained the water clear,
And I wrote my happy songs
    Every child may joy to hear.

William Blake

BEGINNING EXPERIENCES: Rhythm

MATERIALS
Record 1, *Run, Run, Run;* Pupil's Book, p. 2

VOCABULARY
steady beat

IDEAS FOR TEACHING
1. Have children look at the pictures on p. 2. The pictures show ways of moving to the steady beat—dancing, marching, doing a hand jive. Discuss these with children and encourage them to suggest other movements.

2. Play the recording and have children keep time to the steady beat any way they choose (clap hands, tap foot, pat lap, rock from one foot to the other). <u>Suggestion:</u> If space is limited, small groups can take turns moving while others try singing some of the words.

(Refrain)
Run, run, run through the sunlight,
Run, run, run through the snow.
Run, run, run, don't be uptight,
Run, run, run, Freedom, go.

(Verse)
If you're glad that you can
   use your legs, they're free;
If you're glad that you can
   use your eyes to see,
If you're glad the world has
   treasures you can find,
Go and run so fast your cares
   are left behind. (To *Refrain*)
            —Chris Dedrick
<u>Note:</u> The melody of "Run, Run, Run" is notated on p. 98.

BEGINNING EXPERIENCES

Show rhythm by moving.

🔵 *Run, Run, Run*

2 Beginning Experiences

TEACHER INFORMATION
<u>Mainstreaming Note:</u> Encourage motor-impaired, nonambulatory, and mentally retarded children to use the full range of movements they are capable of making, no matter how limited this may be (e.g., the ability only to nod the head). You might have them move on every other beat of the music, instead of on every beat. An adaptation for "Run, Run, Run" appears in *Silver Burdett Music for Special Education.*

The procedure suggested in Ideas for Teaching can be varied to suit individual needs. However, the activity indicated by a black line should always be done, since it high-lights a specific music learning.

The Beginning Experiences (pp. 2–37) are designed for children's immediate participation in singing, listening, moving, and playing instruments. For some children, the materials will serve as a review; for others, they will introduce the concepts for the first time.

Use as many of the Beginning Experiences as necessary for your class. However, be sure to cover the material on pp. 36 and 37, since this material is included in Test 1 of *Silver Burdett Music Competency Tests* for Book 4.

If you can move to the steady beat, you are ready to play the beat.

Steady beat:

Quarter notes:

Eighth notes:

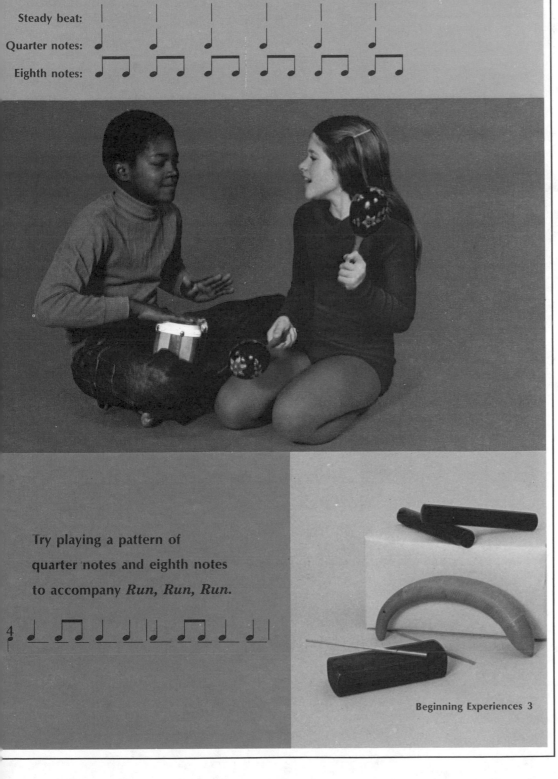

Try playing a pattern of
quarter notes and eighth notes
to accompany *Run, Run, Run.*

Beginning Experiences 3

MATERIALS
Record 1, *Run, Run, Run;* Pupil's
Book, p. 3; percussion instruments

VOCABULARY
steady beat, quarter notes, eighth
notes, rhythm pattern

IDEAS FOR TEACHING
1. Direct attention to the photographs on p. 3. The children in the picture are playing bongos and maracas. Other instruments shown are wood block, claves, and guiro.

2. Play the recording and have children take turns playing the steady beat while others sing. They may play one of the percussion instruments pictured, or a different one—tambourine, sandblocks, etc. Point out: The steady beat can be written using vertical lines (||) or quarter notes (♩ ♩). Call attention to the vertical lines and quarter notes on p. 3.

3. When children can play a steady beat to keep time with the music, ask them to try playing two equal sounds for each beat. They will be playing eighth notes (♫). Point out: Two eighth notes (two sounds for a beat) can take the place of one quarter note. Ask children to find the row of eighth notes on their page.

4. As the class sings "Run, Run, Run," have children take turns playing a rhythm pattern that combines the sound of the steady beat (♩) with the shorter eighth-note sounds (♫). It is found at the bottom of p. 3. Point out: The rhythm pattern is notated two ways—with quarter notes and eighth notes, and with line notation:
long short short long long

TRY THIS
Encourage children to combine quarter-note and eighth-note sounds in other ways to form their own rhythm patterns. Have them write their patterns, using line notation or quarter notes and eighth notes. To get them started, notate a few rhythm patterns on the chalkboard; for example:

1. _ _ _ _ _ _ _

2. _ _ _ _ _ _ _

3. _ _ _ _ _ _ _

TEACHER INFORMATION
It is important to repeat the activities in this lesson from time to time so that all children will have beginning experiences in rhythm through singing, playing, writing, and reading notation.

As in other subject areas, the teacher must be constantly aware of individual progress, as well as class progress. Although the large group completes some activities with ease, it takes time for an individual child to develop skill in accompanying on an instrument, making up a rhythm pattern, and writing notation.

BEGINNING EXPERIENCES: Rhythm

MATERIALS
Record 1, "Pay Me My Money Down"; Pupil's Book, pp. 4 and 5, 3; percussion instruments

VOCABULARY
steady beat, quarter notes, eighth notes, rhythm pattern

IDEAS FOR TEACHING

1. Play the recording and direct children's attention to the feeling of the steady beat (♩) by having them pretend to strum a guitar in time with the music.

2. Have some children play the steady beat on a percussion instrument. They may choose their instrument from the ones pictured on p. 3. Suggestion: As some children play instruments, others sing with the recording. At first, most children will be able to manage the parts that say *Pay me my money down*. The rest of the song will come as the activity is repeated. Have children follow the notation on p. 4 as they sing.

3. Have children take turns improvising a rhythm pattern to accompany the song. They begin to play on the first strong beat (on the word *thought*). Note: Some children will play patterns of quarter and eighth notes. Others may play patterns having more complicated rhythms. Since children do not have to notate their pattern, they are free to respond with whatever rhythm feels right. Suggestions: (a) Have two or more players perform their patterns at the same time for children to hear the sound of different patterns played simultaneously. (b) Repeat the activity with selected recordings that children bring to school. ⟶

Show rhythm by playing.

PAY ME MY MONEY DOWN

COLLECTED AND ADAPTED BY LYDIA A. PARRISH

SLAVE SONG FROM THE GEORGIA SEA ISLANDS

TRO—© COPYRIGHT 1942 AND RENEWED 1970 HOLLIS MUSIC, INC. New York, N.Y. Used by permission.

Orff-instrument acc., p. 336

Piano acc., p. 300

1. I thought I heard the cap-tain say,

"Pay me my mon-ey down,___

To-mor-row is our sail-ing day,___

Pay me my mon-ey down."___

REFRAIN

"Pay___ me,___ oh, pay___ me,___

Pay me my mon-ey down,___

Pay me or go to jail,___

Pay me my mon-ey down."___

4 Beginning Experiences

TEACHER INFORMATION

"Pay Me My Money Down" is accompanied by Orff instruments on the recording. The parts are notated on Teacher's Edition p. 336 so that children can play them in the classroom. If children are not yet ready to play them, they might play the parts that follow. Holding two mallets, one in each hand, they play notes with stems up (♩) with the right mallet, notes with stems down (♩) with the left. Note: The Orff-instrument accompaniments in Book 4 are included to enrich children's musical experience. They are optional, and should be presented by rote. If Orff instruments are not available, substitute keyboard instruments such as bells, xylophones, or piano.

(Optional Accompaniment for "Pay Me My Money Down")

(Alto Xyl. = Alto Xylophone; Alto Met. = Alto Metallophone)

Make up your own percussion accompaniment for this song. How many different rhythm patterns can you think of?

TRY THIS

1. Write four rhythm patterns like the following on the chalkboard. Choose a child to play one of them to accompany "Pay Me My Money Down." The other children try to identify the pattern.

2. One child plays a pattern of quarter and eighth notes to accompany "Pay Me My Money Down." Another child notates the pattern at the chalkboard, using quarter and eighth notes or line notation.

3. Make children aware that rhythm is present in their everyday experience in areas other than music. For example, there is rhythm in the chants they recite during jump rope and other playground activities. "Notate" chant a or b (see Playground Chants below) on the chalkboard. Then have someone play a steady beat on a percussion instrument while children take turns speaking the chant in rhythm.

4. Read chant c (see below) and have children try to notate the rhythm. They may use quarter notes and eighth notes or line notation.

2. As soon as the boat was clear of the bar,
   "Pay me my money down,"
   He knocked me down with the end of a spar,
   "Pay me my money down." *Refrain*

3. Well, I wish I was Mr. Steven's son,
   "Pay me my money down,"
   Sit on the bank and watch the work done,
   "Pay me my money down." *Refrain*

Beginning Experiences 5

PLAYGROUND CHANTS

a

Chew-ing gum, chew-ing gum,
Pen-ny per pack - et;
First you chew it, then you crack it,

Then you stick it in your jack - et,
Then your moth-er makes a rack - et;
Chew-ing gum, chew-ing gum,
Pen - ny per pack - et.

b

See a pin and pick it up,
All the day you'll have good luck;
See a pin and let it lay,
Bad luck you'll have all day.

c

Roll, roll, toot-sie roll,
Roll, mar-ble, in the hole.

BEGINNING EXPERIENCES: Rhythm

MATERIALS
Record 1, "Scratch, Scratch"; Pupil's Book, p. 6; percussion instruments

VOCABULARY
steady beat, rhythm pattern, rests

IDEAS FOR TEACHING

1. Play the recording and ask children to keep the steady beat by patting their lap during the verse (section A) and clapping hands during the part that begins *Scratch, scratch me back* (refrain, or section B). <u>Note:</u> Since children are not following the notation, some may pat and clap the beat as a pattern of half notes (♩), while others may pat and clap a faster beat—a pattern of quarter notes (♩). Either response is acceptable.

2. Have children keep the beat once more. As they clap during section B, help them hear that on some of the beats (claps) there is silence in the melody (after the word *back* each time, and after *fact*).

3. Have children take turns making scratching sounds to fill in the silences (after *back* and *fact*) in section B as others sing the song (p. 6). <u>Note:</u> Notched sticks, a guiro, or fingernails scraped across a drumhead all produce scratching sounds.

4. Make children aware that notes and rests can be combined to form rhythm patterns. Have them take turns playing a pattern (see below) throughout section B as others sing. "Thinking" the words *Scratch, scratch me back* as they play will help them keep the pattern. <u>Point out:</u> In notation, notes stand for sound; rests stand for silence.

SCRATCH, SCRATCH
WORDS AND MUSIC BY HARRY BELAFONTE AND LORD BURGESS

Piano acc., p. 310

Ⓐ VERSE

1. Oh, we went out to a par - ty,

It was me and Ben and Mac,

And be - fore I knew what hap - pened,

I got an itch - in' on my back.

Ⓑ REFRAIN

Scratch, scratch me back, Scratch, scratch me back.

It real - ly is a fact,___

The less I itch, the more I scratch.

2. Well, I was quite embarrassed,
Till my two friends I did see,
Well, they were madly itching,
And they were screaming louder than me.
Refrain

3. Now, this scratching was contagiou[s]
And it didn't take very long,
Ev'rybody there was itching,
As they joined me in this song.
Refrain

6 Beginning Experiences

SECTION B RHYTHM PATTERN

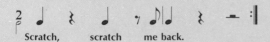

TRY THIS
Children can perform the following movement pattern throughout section B of "Scratch, Scratch." When the directions say *upper,* they pretend to scratch their right upper back with the right hand, then their left upper back with the left hand. For *lower,* they touch their lower back with the *back* of the right hand, then with the *back* of the left hand. Right and left hands alternate throughout.

Section B Movement Pattern (as developed by Liz McIntire) Perform entire pattern *two times.*

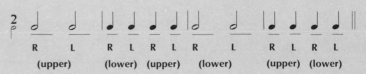

(R—right hand; L—left hand; upper—upper back; lower—lower back)

Use sticks to play beats grouped in twos.

AND GAME SONG   AMERICAN INDIAN SONG

FROM THE RED BOOK OF SINGING GAMES AND DANCES BY JANET E. TOBITT, COPYRIGHT ©, 1960 BY SUMMY-BIRCHARD CO. ALL RIGHTS RESERVED. USED BY PERMISSION.

Ha   a   a ho - e tha a, Ha   a   a ho - e tha a

Ha   a   a ho - e tha a, Ha   a   ho - e tha,

Ha   a   a ho - e tha a, Ha   a___ a ho - e tha a,

Ha   a___ a ho - e tha.

Try playing a different pattern.

Beginning Experiences 7

MATERIALS
Record 1, "Hand Game Song"; Pupil's Book, p. 7; sticks, bead

VOCABULARY
beats grouped in twos, meter

IDEAS FOR TEACHING
1. Play the recording and have children respond to the steady beat by patting their lap, alternately using the left hand, then the right hand. Note: The left-right pattern will help children feel the beats grouped in sets of two.

2. To reinforce the feeling of meter in 2 (beats grouped in twos), have children practice the quarter-note stick pattern at the top of p. 7. Sitting on the floor and holding one stick in each hand, they tap the floor with the left stick for all notes with stems pointing down (♩), with the right stick for all notes with stems pointing up (♩). The pattern alternates left, right, left, right throughout. Have them play the pattern to accompany the recording. Suggestion: Call attention to the bar lines that separate the beats into sets of two.

3. When children can play the quarter-note pattern at the top of p. 7, have them try the pattern of quarter notes and eighth notes at the bottom of the page.

4. Children can play a bead-passing game with "Hand Game Song" (see below for directions).

GAME DIRECTIONS
Two rows of children—a "stick" row and a "bead" row—sit on the floor, facing each other. One child in each row is designated the row's leader. The children in the "stick" row tap sticks on the floor in time with the music, while those in the "bead" row pass a bead from one to the other, trying not to let the "stick" row see where the bead is. When the song ends, the children in the "stick" row shout "Hi-i," and their leader points to the person he or she thinks has the bead. If the guess is right, the "stick" row earns a point and takes over the bead. The game then begins again, with the two rows reversing activities. If the guess is wrong, the "bead" row receives a point and the game is repeated as before. Before playing the game, children decide how many points win. Suggestions: (a) To keep the bead from being seen, children might pass it behind them along the row, or, with hands in front, they might all pretend to pass it throughout the song. (b) When they can, children should sing with the recording.

BEGINNING EXPERIENCES: Meter

MATERIALS
Record 1, Scruggs: *String Bender;*
Joplin: *Bethena;* Pupil's Book, p. 8.

VOCABULARY
meter in 2, meter in 3, steady beat,
quarter note, bar line

IDEAS FOR TEACHING

1. Play the recording of *String Bender.*
As children listen, have them keep
the beat by alternately clapping
hands twice to the left, then twice to
the right. Note: Alternating the directions of the claps will help children
feel the beats grouped in sets of two
(meter in 2).

2. To reinforce the feeling of meter
in 2, have children keep the beat by
performing a hand jive (see below).

3. Play the recording of *Bethena* and
have children keep the beat by alternately clapping hands three times to
the left, then three times to the right.
Note: Alternating the directions of
the claps will help children feel the
beats grouped in sets of three (meter
in 3).

4. Have children try to perform the
hand jive (see below) in time with
the steady beat of *Bethena.* Note:
Since the motions of the hand jive
are grouped in twos, children will
discover that the pattern does not fit
the music. Question: How can we
make the hand jive fit the beats in
this music? (By doing each motion
three times instead of two) Have
children perform the hand jive (each
motion three times) to accompany
Bethena.

Try doing a hand jive with this music.

Scruggs: *String Bender*   Joplin: *Bethena*

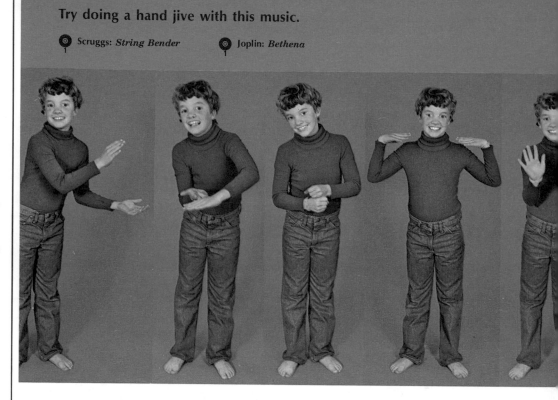

Can you hear the difference between meter in 2 and meter in 3?

HERE I GO ROUND

"Here I go, sure and slow,"

Says the tur - tle down be - low.

"Not so I, swift - ly fly," says the bird on high.

8 Beginning Experiences

HAND JIVE
(Notice that each motion is performed two times. After
completing step 8 of the pattern, go back to step 1 without missing a beat. Keep repeating the entire pattern until
the music ends. The pictures on p. 8 illustrate the hand-
jive motions.)

1. Clap hands twice to the left.
2. Clap hands twice to the right.
3. Brush right hand over left hand twice.
4. Brush left hand over right hand twice.
5. Pound right fist on left fist twice.

6. Pound left fist on right fist twice.
7. Tap both shoulders twice.
8. With palms at shoulder level and facing outward, pat
"air" in front twice.

TRY THIS
Some children may wish to make up their own motions
for a hand jive. Have them perform it with both recordings.

WHEN IS A DOOR?

WORDS AND MUSIC BY GEORGE F. ROOT

I. When is a door not a door? Give it up?

II. When is a door not a door? Let me see. Ah,

III. yes, when it is a - jar. _____

SANDY McNAB

ROUND

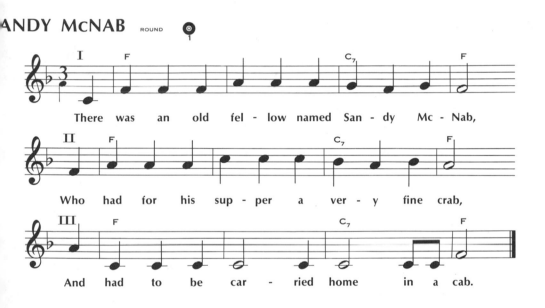

I. There was an old fel - low named San - dy Mc - Nab,

II. Who had for his sup - per a ver - y fine crab,

III. And had to be car - ried home in a cab.

Beginning Experiences 9

MATERIALS
Record 1, "Here I Go"; "When Is a Door?"; "Sandy McNab"; Pupil's Book, pp. 8 and 9; bells

VOCABULARY
beat, meter in 2, meter in 3

IDEAS FOR TEACHING
1. Play the recording of "Here I Go." As children listen, ask them to decide whether the beats are grouped in twos or in threes. (In twos)

2. To show they feel the meter in 2, children take turns alternately playing the low-G and high-G bells with the recording (see bell pattern *a* below). Others sing when they can (song notation, p. 8).

3. Play the recording of "When Is a Door?" When children can feel the meter in 3, they take turns playing the low-C and high-C bells with the recording (see bell pattern *b*). Others sing when they can (notation, p. 9). Question: How is this bell part different from the one for "Here I Go"? (The high bell is played twice each time.)

4. Play the recording of "Sandy McNab." Children decide how the beats are grouped. (In threes) Question: Which bell part will you play for this song—the one in two meter, or the one in three meter? (The one in three meter) Suggestion: Some children may be able to play a pattern of quarter and eighth notes (see bell pattern *c*). Give children time to experiment with patterns of their own. Note: The first note of the song is an upbeat. The bell part begins on the second note (on the word *was*).

BELL PATTERNS

TEACHER INFORMATION
The songs in this lesson are rounds. Have children sing with the recorded voices that begin the round (part I) until they are able to sing in parts.

TRY THIS
As someone plays a steady beat on a wood block, children chant this rhyme in two meter:

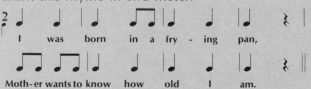

I was born in a fry - ing pan,

Moth-er wants to know how old I am.

One child then counts to his or her age in sets of two—ONE, two, THREE, four, etc.—or in sets of three—ONE, two, three, FOUR, five, six, etc.—stressing the first number in each set. Others identify the meter of the counting.

MATERIALS
Record 1, "Hear the Rooster," Version 1; Pupil's Book, pp. 10 and 11; bells

VOCABULARY
meter in 2, bar line, measure, meter signature, half note, interval, octave, leaps, steps, repeated tones

IDEAS FOR TEACHING

1. Play the recording and have children determine the meter. (Meter in 2) Note: To do this, children might perform the hand-jive pattern (p. 8).

2. When children can feel the beats grouped in twos, have them take turns alternately playing the low- and high-G bells with the recording (see bell pattern *a* below).

3. Write bell pattern *b* (see below) on the chalkboard. Point out: (a) In notation, bar lines group beats into sets called measures. (b) The meter signature ($^2_4$) at the beginning of the bell part has a number at the top and a note at the bottom. The number tells how many beats are in each measure. The note shows what kind of note receives one beat. When the meter signature is $^2_4$, there are two beats in each measure, and each quarter note receives one beat. (c) The notes in measures 2 and 4 are half notes ($\downarrow$). Each half note lasts as long as two quarter notes—two beats.

4. Have children take turns playing pattern *b* as others sing with the recording (song notation, p. 10).

5. Call attention to the differences between the two G's children have played: one has a low sound, the

→

Play low G and high G on the bells to accompany this song.

Will the meter be in 2, or in 3? In 2

HEAR THE ROOSTER *Kum bahur* FOLK SONG FROM ISRAEL ENGLISH WORDS BY ROSEMARY JACQUES

I
Hear the roost-er crow-ing, it's time to start the day,
Kum ba-hur a-tzel_____ v'-tzei la-a-vo-da,

Hear the roost-er crow-ing, it's time to start the day.
Kum ba-hur a-tzel_____ v'-tzei la-a-vo-da.

II
Wake, wake,_____ get up with-out de-lay,
Kum, kum,_____ v'-tzei la-a-vo-da,

Wake, wake,_____ get up with-out de-lay.
Kum, kum,_____ v'-tzei la-a-vo-da.

III
Ku-ku-ri-ku, ku-ku-ri-ku, let's be on our way,
Ku-ku-ri-ku, ku-ku-ri-ku, tar-n'-gol ka-ra,

Ku-ku-ri-ku, ku-ku-ri-ku, let's be on our way.
Ku-ku-ri-ku, ku-ku-ri-ku, tar-n'-gol ka-ra.

10 Beginning Experiences

BELL PATTERNS

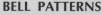

TEACHER INFORMATION
Like the songs on pp. 8 and 9, "Hear the Rooster" is a round. Be certain that children know the melody before they try to sing in parts.

The Hebrew words in "Hear the Rooster" literally say, "Get up, you lazy young man, and go out to work. The rooster is crowing, 'Kukuriku'." They are pronounced as follows:

Kum ba-hur a-tzel v'-tzei la-a-vo-da,
koom bah-hoor ah-tsel vuh-tsay lah-ah-voh-dah
Kum, kum v'-tzei la-a-vo-da,
koom koom vuh-tsay lah-ah-voh-dah
Ku-ku-ri-ku, ku-ku-ri-ku, Tar-n'-gol ka-ra.
koo-koo-ree-koo koo-koo-ree-koo tahr-n(uh)-gohl kah-rah

Note: The sound of an unfamiliar language is "caught," not taught. As children work with the recording, they will gradually be able to sing the Hebrew words as well as the English ones.

Find the repeated tones. Find the leaps.

Play 6 times.   high C

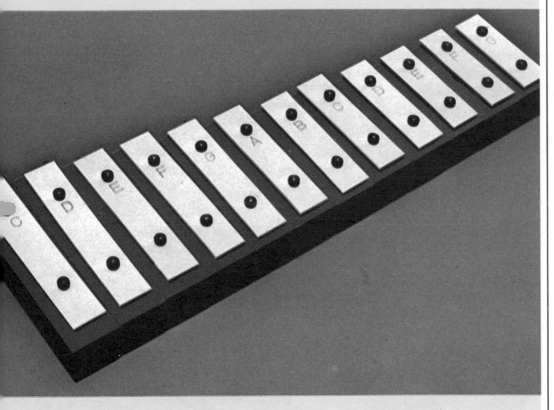

Find the tones that leap. Find the tones that step.

Play 2 times.

G E   D C

Beginning Experiences 11

other a high sound; the bell for low G is long, the one for high G is short. Refer to the chalkboard notation and point out the distance (interval) between the two G's. Call the low-G line "one," then count each space and line above it, ending with the high-G space. Help children conclude that low G and high G are eight lines and spaces, or an octave, apart. <u>Point out</u>: When children played low and high G and low and high C with the songs on pp. 8 and 9, they were playing octave leaps.

6. Direct attention to the bell part at the top of p. 11. <u>Questions</u>: Will you play octave leaps in any measure of this bell part? (No) Where will you play leaps that are smaller than an octave? (Between measures 2 and 3, low C to G; between measures 3 and 4, G to high C) Where will you play repeated tones? (In measures 1, 2, 3)

7. Have children take turns playing the bell part as others sing with the recording. They will have to play the pattern six times to fit the song. Remind them that the half note in measure 4 receives two beats.

8. Direct attention to the bell part at the bottom of p. 11. <u>Questions</u>: In which measures will you play small leaps? (Measures 1 and 2) In which measure will you play tones that move by step? (3) A tone that lasts for two beats? (4)

9. Provide time for children to practice the bell part on their own. Some children may discover that it has the same melody as section III of the song. <u>Note:</u> The leaps in measures 1 and 2 might be played with two mallets (right playing G, left E). Measures 3 and 4 are easier to play with one mallet.

TRY THIS

Put it all together. As children sing "Hear the Rooster" with the recording, one child accompanies with octave leaps during section I, alternately playing the low- and high-G bells throughout the section. A second child plays the bell part at the top of p. 11 (two times instead of six) during section II. A third child plays the bell part at the bottom of p. 11 during section III. <u>Suggestions</u>: Have children use three sets of bells or a combination of three keyboard instruments such as bells, xylophones, Orff instruments, and piano. If three instruments are not available,

children can share one set of bells, with each player taking over immediately as the one before him or her finishes. Before they play, children can refer to the picture of the bells on p. 11 to find where their part begins. <u>Mainstreaming Note</u>: Children who are visually impaired can readily play the octave leaps during section I of the song.

BEGINNING EXPERIENCES: Melody

MATERIALS
Record 1, "When Is a Door?"; "Sandy McNab"; "Here I Go"; Pupil's Book, pp. 12 and 13; bells (or other keyboard instruments—xylophone, Orff instruments, piano)

VOCABULARY
melody, steps, leaps, repeated tones, round, countermelody, interval, octave

IDEAS FOR TEACHING
1. Ask children to look at the notation for melody 1 on p. 12 to discover the meter. (Meter in 3) Questions: Which bells are needed to play melody 1? (F and C) Does the melody have mostly steps, leaps, or repeated tones? (Mostly repeated tones)

2. Lead children to compare the second melody with the first. Questions: Is the meter the same, or different? (The same—meter in 3) Which additional bell is needed to play the second melody? (A) Does the second melody have mostly repeated tones, or do the tones move mostly by leap or by step? (The melody has mostly repeated tones.)

3. Help children determine the ways in which the third melody is different from the other two. (The meter is in 2; the bells needed to play it are E, G, high C.) Point out: Melody 3 also uses mostly repeated tones. There are small leaps in all three melodies—F down to C (melody 1), C to F (1 and 2), G to high C and E to G (3)—and larger leaps (A down to C, high C down to E) in melodies 2 and 3. There is no movement by step in any of the melodies. ⟶

These melodies are endings of songs you know.

Can you name the songs?

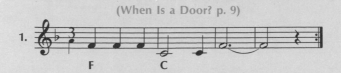
(When Is a Door? p. 9)

1.

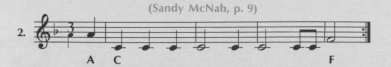
(Sandy McNab, p. 9)

2.

(Here I Go, p. 8)

3.

Can you find things that remind you of steps, leaps, and repeats in these pictures?

12 Beginning Experiences

TEACHER INFORMATION
The photographs on pp. 12 and 13 illustrate steps, leaps, and repeats in line, shape, and color. Provide time for children to find things in the room that show these qualities. Encourage them to collect pictures that suggest steps, leaps, and repeats for a bulletin-board display.

Some children may be able to design their own collage of lines, shapes, and colors to represent steps, leaps, and repeats. Make them aware that in their artwork they *see* these qualities; in music they *hear* them. Mainstreaming Suggestion: You might have children emboss their collages by gluing a textured material onto the shapes and lines. This will enable children who have visual or neurological impairment, as well as those who are mentally retarded, to discern the relationship between steps, leaps, and repeats by touch rather than by sight alone.

Here are three countermelodies to play with "Here I Go."

Which countermelody steps mostly downward? 1

Which one uses an octave leap? 2

Which one has mostly repeated tones? 3

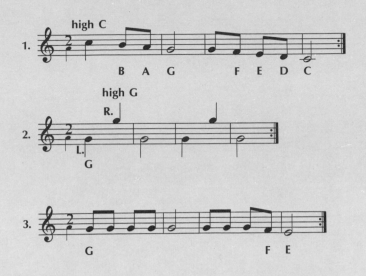

4. Make each child responsible for selecting one of the melodies to practice and then play while others sing the song. <u>Note:</u> (a) Each melody on p. 12 is actually the entire third section of the round from which it is taken. In order to fit the song, the child playing bells will have to play the melody three times. (b) This activity will extend over a period of time. Individual involvement of this type may best be implemented at times other than during the formal music class.

5. Direct children's attention to the countermelodies on p. 13. Each one can be played throughout the round "Here I Go." <u>Questions:</u> Which countermelody uses a quarter note, eighth notes, and half notes? (The first one) What kinds of notes does countermelody 2 use? (Quarter notes and half notes) Countermelody 3? (Eighth notes and half notes) In which countermelody do tones move mostly downward by step? (1) Which countermelody uses the interval of an octave? (2) Do the tones in countermelody 3 move mostly by step, or by leap, or do they mostly repeat? (They mostly repeat.)

6. Assign individual children to each of the countermelodies on p. 13. Give them time to practice. Then let them take turns playing their countermelody on bells as others sing "Here I Go." <u>Note:</u> Countermelody 2 should be played with two mallets; countermelodies 1 and 3 are easier to play with one mallet.

TRY THIS
Put it all together. As some children sing "Here I Go," have one child play melody 3 on p. 12, while others play the countermelodies on p. 13. Players may use any available keyboard instruments for their ensemble—bells, xylophone, Orff instruments, piano. <u>Suggestions:</u> (a) Some children may be able to play the entire melody of "Here I Go" (notation, p. 8) as part of the ensemble. Help them discover that the tones in sections I and II move mostly by step, while the tones in section III mostly repeat. (b) Encourage players to choose the part with which they can be successful. This will free them not only to perceive what is happening in the melody they are playing, but also to be aware of the melodies that others are playing. (c) Encourage children who are part of the ensemble to work together to create a blend of sound. Make them aware that the "Here I Go" melody must be heard at all times, and that the countermelodies must be played in a way that (1) does not drown out the melody, and (2) creates a blend in which they all sound equally important, with no one countermelody standing out from the rest.

BEGINNING EXPERIENCES: Direction

MATERIALS
Record 1, "Hand Me Down"; Pupil's Book, p. 14

VOCABULARY
melody, step, repeated tones, upward direction, downward direction, octave

IDEAS FOR TEACHING

1. Direct children's attention to staff 1 at the top of p. 14. Question: Does the melody move in an upward direction, or a downward direction? (In a downward direction)

2. Play the recording and have children sing melody 1 each time it occurs in the song. Point out: Melody 1 is made up of repeated tones and tones that move downward mostly by step.

3. Ask children to compare melody 2 with melody 1. Point out: Melody 2 is made up of repeated tones and tones that move upward by step.

4. Play the recording and have some children sing melody 2 while others sing melody 1 each time the melodies occur together in the song. Note: Staff 3 shows melodies 1 and 2 notated together. Encourage children to follow the notation as they sing. Some children may observe that the beginning note for melody 2 (C) is an octave lower than the beginning note for melody 1 (high C). Point out: One way to create harmony is to simultaneously perform melodies that move in contrasting directions.

Which melody moves in an upward direction? 2

In a downward direction? 1

What does staff 3 show? Both melodies together

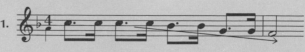

1. Hand me down my sil - ver trum-pet, Lord.

2. Hand me down my sil - ver trum-pet, Lord.

3. Hand me down my sil - ver trum-pet, Lord.

Find the places in "Hand Me Down" where upward

and downward directions are sung at the same time.

HAND ME DOWN BLACK SPIRITUAL

© COPYRIGHT: EDWARD B. MARKS MUSIC CORPORATION. USED BY PERMISSION. Piano acc., p. 282

SOLO C₇ F

Oh, hand me down, Hand me down,

CHORUS F C₇

Hand me down my sil - ver trum - pet, Ga - briel.

14 Beginning Experiences

TEACHER INFORMATION
To involve children with music reading, help them analyze the melodies on p. 14 in greater detail. Point out: (a) In addition to repeated tones (high C, B^b, G) and tones that move by step (high C down to B^b, G down to F), melody 1 also contains a leap (B^b down to G). (b) In melody 1, sets of repeated tones move in a downward direction; in melody 2, sets of repeated tones move in an upward direction. (c) Although melodies 1 and 2 begin an octave apart, they both end on the same tone, F.

Music-reading skills are developed gradually but consistently throughout Book 4. Parts with which most children can be successful are isolated and built into the development of the whole lesson. Notation is one of many means for encouraging later musical involvement and continual musical growth.

SOLO

Hand me down, throw it down, An-y way to get it down,

CHORUS

Fine

Hand me down my sil - ver trum - pet, Lord.

SOLO

Oh, Mo - ses had a lot to do,___

CHORUS

Hand me down my sil - ver trum - pet, Ga - briel,

SOLO

When he led the chil - dren of Is - ra - el through,

CHORUS

D.C. al Fine

Hand me down my sil - ver trum - pet, Lord.

D.C. al Fine (Da Capo al Fine—Dah Kah'-poh ahl Fee'-nay) means

"repeat from the beginning and continue to the word *Fine*."

Beginning Experiences 15

BEGINNING EXPERIENCES: Form

MATERIALS
Record 1, "Hand Me Down"; Pupil's Book, pp. 14 and 15

VOCABULARY
solo, chorus, call-and-response form

IDEAS FOR TEACHING
1. Play the recording and have children sing the parts marked "chorus" in the music (pp. 14 and 15). Note: Divide children into two groups for the chorus parts that are sung in harmony.

2. Have children take turns singing the solo parts as others sing the chorus parts. Question: Are the chorus parts the same as the solo parts, or different? (Different; they provide a contrast.) Point out: Songs with solo and chorus parts are said to have call-and-response form. Much music is written in call-and-response form.

TRY THIS
Reinforce the idea of contrast between solo and chorus parts as follows. (a) Have children play this pattern on a tambourine during each chorus part:

(strike)   (shake)

(b) Assign one child to sing the solo parts, the rest of the group to sing the chorus parts. If a stereo record player is available, use the Pick-a-Track technique. Adjust the balance-control knob to de-emphasize the voice on the recording during each solo part. Another time, de-emphasize the recorded voices during each chorus part.

TEACHER INFORMATION
As an aid to music reading, help children observe how the solo parts and chorus parts contrast. Point out: In staffs 1 and 2, the solo part moves upward and downward by step and by leap; the chorus part has mostly repeated tones. In staffs 3 and 4, 7 and 8, the solo part has repeated tones and tones that leap; the chorus part has repeated tones and tones that move mostly by step. In staffs 5 and 6, the solo part has tones that move mostly by step, then repeated tones at the end; the chorus part has repeated tones at the beginning, then tones that leap.

The repetition of the first part of "Hand Me Down" is indicated by D. C. al Fine (Da Capo al Fine—Dah Kah'-poh ahl Fee'-nay), which means "repeat from the beginning and continue to the word *Fine*."

As children work with the music materials in Book 4, you may wish to use the Pick-a-Track technique in other ways. By adjusting the balance-control knob on a stereo record player, you can highlight the instrumental accompaniment for children to sing with, or you can highlight the vocal track so that children can focus attention on the melody and words of the song.

BEGINNING EXPERIENCES: Form

MATERIALS
Record 1, "Sourwood Mountain";
Pupil's Book, pp. 16 and 17

VOCABULARY
chorus, solo, call-and-response form

IDEAS FOR TEACHING
1. Play the recording. Ask children to join in singing the chorus parts when they can. <u>Question</u>: Is each chorus part the same as the solo that comes before it, or different? (Different)

2. Have children take turns singing the solo parts while the rest of the group sings the chorus parts (p. 16).

3. Have children show the contrast between solo and chorus parts by performing this stamp-clap pattern during each solo part:

and by clapping the rhythm of each chorus part:

<u>Note</u>: Singing as they clap will help children perform the rhythm correctly.

4. Children can perform a square dance (see below) to the music of "Sourwood Mountain." Help them form sets like the one pictured on p. 17. In each couple, the boy stands to the girl's left. The couple whose back is to the music is the head couple. The other couples are positioned in relation to the head couple—couple 2 to the right, couple 3 opposite, couple 4 to the left. ⟶

SOURWOOD MOUNTAIN
AMERICAN FOLK SONG

Piano acc., p. 314

1. Chick - en crowin' on Sour - wood Moun - tain,
2. My true love's a blue - eyed dai - sy,

Hey de - ing dang did - dle al - ly day.

So man - y pret - ty girls, I can't count 'em,
If I don't get her, I'll go cra - zy,

Hey de - ing dang did - dle al - ly day.

My true love, she lives in Letch - er,
Big dog bark and little one bite you,

Hey de - ing dang did - dle al - ly day.

She won't come and I won't fetch her,
Big girl court and little one slight you,

Hey de - ing dang did - dle al - ly day.

16

SQUARE DANCE
(In the directions, the numbers stand for phrases. Each dance motion lasts for one phrase [4 beats] of the music.)

1 Dancers bow to their partner.
2 Dancers turn away from their partner and bow to their corner (the member of the next couple standing closest to them).
3 Dancers change places with their partner.
4 Dancers return to original position.
5 Boys take 4 steps to the center.
6 Boys take 4 steps back to their place.

7 Girls take 4 steps to the center.
8 Girls take 4 steps back to their place.

<u>Note</u>: The motions above can be performed each time the "Sourwood Mountain" melody occurs on the recording (6 times), or the dance can be extended as follows.

Second Time
1 Head couple moves to couple 2. They all join hands and circle left halfway around.
2 Couple 2 raises inside joined hands (boy's right, girl's left) to form an arch. Head couple goes under arch, dropping hands with couple 2. ⟶

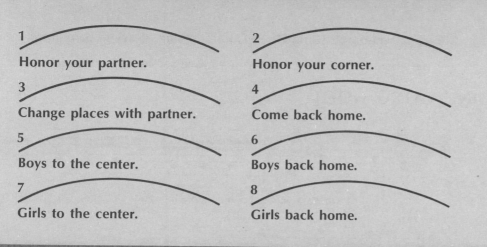

1		2	
Honor your partner.		Honor your corner.	
3		4	
Change places with partner.		Come back home.	
5		6	
Boys to the center.		Boys back home.	
7		8	
Girls to the center.		Girls back home.	

Couple 3

Couple 2

Couple 4

Head Couple

Beginning Experiences 17.

TRY THIS

Some of the children may be studying violin. Ask one of them to play this violin melody during each chorus part as everyone sings "Sourwood Mountain."

(on D string)   1st   3rd   3rd 2nd 1st
finger

Note: Make the addition of the violin part a special event. Enlist the aid of the instrumental teacher in tuning the violin before class begins. Ask the performer to share what he or she knows about the violin and the way it is played. Suggestion: If no one in the group plays violin, invite an older child to visit during music time and add the violin melody to the children's performance.

TEACHER INFORMATION

There are many countermelodies and ostinato parts throughout Book 4 that can be played on orchestral instruments.

Mainstreaming Note: An adaptation for "Sourwood Mountain" appears in *Silver Burdett Music for Special Education.*

3–4 Head couple moves on to couple 3, repeating the motions for phrases 1–2.

5–6 Head couple moves on to couple 4, repeating the motions for phrases 1–2.

7 Head couple returns home (to original position).

8 All couples swing once around in place.

Third–Fifth Time

Repeat pattern for "Second Time" with couple 2, then 3, then 4 as leaders.

Sixth Time

1–8 Partners join hands and walk around the set (promenade) in a large circle, moving counterclockwise.

When they get back home, they swing, stopping when the music ends.

Suggestions: (a) If space is limited, have eight children (one set) dance at a time. Others can sing, perform the stamp-clap and clapping patterns, and perhaps add the violin melody (see Try This). (b) One child might "call" the motions for the dance. The calls for the first eight phrases are given on p. 17. Help the caller decide on short calls for the rest of the dance—"Head and 2 circle left"; "Head goes under"; "Head and 3 circle left"; etc. The caller might practice with the recording to learn to fit in the calls at the beginning of the phrases.

BEGINNING EXPERIENCES: Form

MATERIALS
Record 1, "Ging Gong Gooli"; Pupil's Book, pp. 18 and 19; wood block, drum, tambourine

VOCABULARY
section A, section B, contrast, AB form, accent, harmony, repeat sign

IDEAS FOR TEACHING

1. Ask children to look at the notation for "Ging Gong Gooli" on pp. 18 and 19. Page 18 shows the melody for the first section of the song, section A; p. 19 shows the melody for the second section, section B. Question: Is the melody the same for both sections of the song, or is the melody for section B different from the melody for section A? (The melody for section B is different.) Point out: When the sections of a song have different melodies, the sections are said to contrast. A song with two contrasting sections—A and B—is said to have AB form.

2. Play the recording and ask children to listen for some of the things that make section B a contrast of section A. Have them follow the notation in their book as they listen. (Possibilities: Melody B starts on a higher tone than melody A. The rhythm of section B is different from that of section A. Section B has accents (sudden loud sounds, indicated by > in the notation); section A has no accents. Section B is sung in harmony; section A is not.) Note: Many children have difficulty focusing on more than one or two musical qualities at a time. Play the recording more than once so each child has an opportunity to hear several of the contrasts between sections A and B.

→

Choose a section of "Ging Gong Gooli" to sing or accompany on a percussion instrument. Will you choose section A, or section B?

GING GONG GOOLI
FOLK SONG FROM BRITISH GUIANA
Piano acc., p. 321

Ging gong goo-li goo-li goo-li goo-li wat-cha,

Ging gong goo, ging gong goo.

Ging gong goo-li goo-li goo-li goo-li wat-cha,

Ging gong goo, ging gong goo.

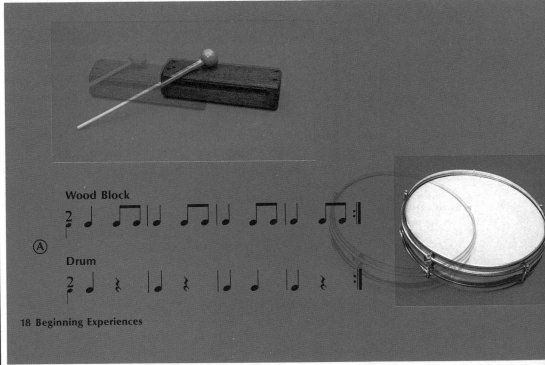

Wood Block

Drum

18 Beginning Experiences

TRY THIS
1. Children who have difficulty playing the percussion parts notated in their book can play easier parts instead (see Percussion Patterns a, Teacher's Edition p. 19). Suggestion: Write the percussion parts on a large chart or on the chalkboard so that children can follow the notation as they play.

2. Children who need a challenge may be able to play more difficult percussion parts (see Percussion Patterns b, Teacher's Edition p. 19).

3. Invite a group of older children to sing the harmony part during section B when the class performs "Ging Gong Gooli."

TEACHER INFORMATION
Mainstreaming Note: An adaptation for "Ging Gong Gooli" appears in *Silver Burdett Music for Special Education.*

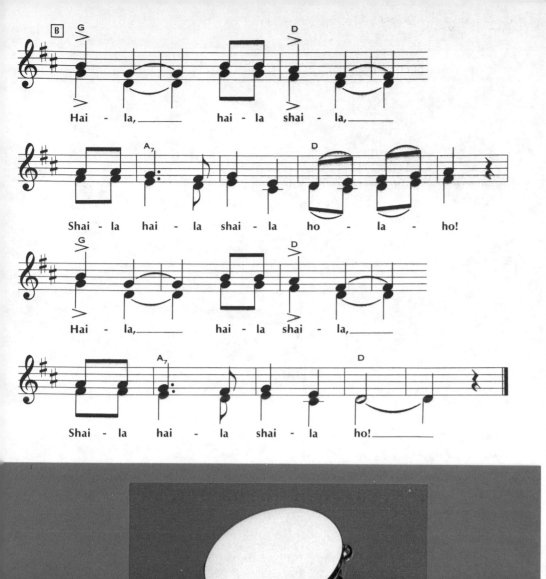

B   **G**   **D**

Hai - la,_____ hai - la shai - la,_____

A₇   **D**

Shai - la hai - la shai - la ho - la - ho!

G   **D**

Hai - la,_____ hai - la shai - la,_____

A₇   **D**

Shai - la hai - la shai - la ho!_____

B

Tambourine   (shake)

Beginning Experiences 19

3. Have children choose one of the sections—A or B—to sing with the recording. <u>Note:</u> Children who choose section B should all sing the melody (upper notes). The recorded voices will provide the harmony (lower notes).

4. Reinforce the concept of AB form by having children play the percussion parts notated in their book. Adding the tone colors of the wood block and drum during section A and that of the tambourine during section B will provide further contrast between the sections. <u>Note:</u> (a) The percussion parts for section A begin on the strong beat—on *goo* of the first *gooli*. (b) The repeat sign (:‖) at the end of each part indicates that when the player reaches the end, he or she should immediately play the part again from the beginning. <u>Suggestion:</u> Select children to practice the percussion part(s) for each section. Provide time for them to work out the parts on their own, away from the rest of the group. When they are ready, have them add the percussion parts as others sing with the recording. Then repeat the experience, having different children play the percussion parts. Children who practiced the parts can teach them to the new players.

PERCUSSION PATTERNS

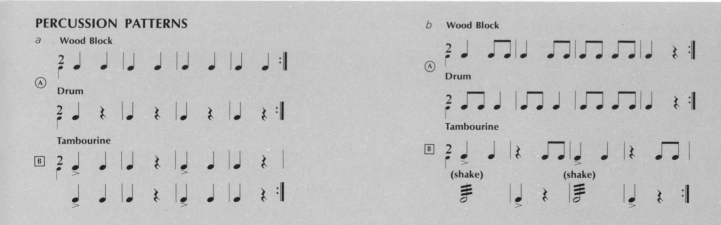

a   **Wood Block**

Ⓐ **Drum**

Tambourine

B

b   **Wood Block**

Ⓐ **Drum**

Tambourine

B   (shake)   (shake)

BEGINNING EXPERIENCES: Tone Color

MATERIALS
Record 1, "The Wise Man Built His House," Versions 1 and 2; Pupil's Book, pp. 20 and 21; Autoharp

VOCABULARY
Autoharp, tone color

IDEAS FOR TEACHING
1. Direct children's attention to the picture of the child playing the Autoharp on p. 20. <u>Questions:</u> Which hand is the child using to press the chord buttons? (Left) Which hand is strumming the strings? (Right) <u>Point out:</u> The right hand crosses over the left to strum the strings.

2. Play the recording (Version 1) and focus children's attention on the tone color of the Autoharp that is accompanying the singing.

3. Play the recording (Version 1) and lead children in softly clapping the steady beat (four beats per measure). <u>Question:</u> Is there an Autoharp strum on every beat of the song? (No, the strums occur on every other beat.) <u>Point out:</u> The Autoharp is playing a pattern of half notes (♩ ♩), with each strum lasting for two beats.

4. Have children read the directions for playing the Autoharp accompaniment on p. 20. Then provide time for them to practice it, following the chord-pattern notation on their page. <u>Suggestion:</u> Before children practice at the instrument, you might have everyone practice at their desk, using the diagram in the back of their book. Playing the recording (Version 1) while children pretend to play the →

LOOK

LISTEN

1 *The Wise Man Built His House*

PLAY

- **Place your left index finger on the button marked F.**
- **Place your left middle finger on the button marked C₇.**
- **Look at the chord pattern below. It shows when to press each button.**
- **As you press the buttons, use your right hand to strum the strings.**
- **Make each strum last for two beats.**
- **Follow the chord pattern to play as others sing "The Wise Man Built His House." You will be playing half notes.**

$$F \qquad C_7 \qquad C_7 \qquad F$$

20 Beginning Experiences

TEACHER INFORMATION
A child who is left-handed may find it easier to press the chord buttons with the right hand while strumming with the left. In that case, the child places the right ring finger on the F button, the right middle finger on C₇. The hands do not cross.

TRY THIS
Have children take turns playing the Autoharp accompaniments on Teacher's Edition p. 21 as others sing the songs. <u>Note:</u> (a) The accompaniment for "Hand Me Down" uses the same chords as the one for "The Wise Man Built His House"—F and C₇. The other accompaniments use the chords C and G₇. To play them, children place their index finger on the C button, their middle finger on G₇. (b) To keep the rhythm in "Pay Me My Money Down" and "Here I Go," children play long strums for the half notes (♩), short strums for the quarter notes (♩). (c) The patterns for "Hand Me Down" and "Pay Me My Money Down" begin on the strong beat—on the words *hand* and *thought*, respectively. <u>Suggestion:</u> Write the chord patterns on charts or on index cards so that children can practice them on their own.

THE WISE MAN BUILT HIS HOUSE

ORIGIN UNKNOWN

Piano acc., p. 324

1. Oh, the wise man built his house up-on the rock,
2. Oh, the rains came down and the floods came up,

Oh, the wise man built his house up-on the rock,
Oh, the rains came down and the floods came up,

Oh, the wise man built his house up-on the rock,
Oh, the rains came down and the floods came up,

And the rains came tum-bling down.
But the house on the rock stood firm.

3. Oh, the silly man built his house upon the sand, (*3 times*)
And the rains came tumbling down.

4. Oh, the rains came down and the floods came up, (*3 times*)
And the house on the sand went swisssssssssssh.

Beginning Experiences 21

Autoharp will help them coordinate their pressing and strumming motions with the changes in chord sounds. <u>Point out</u>: (a) Whenever a chord is played twice or more in succession, the player firmly presses the chord button (e.g., F), then keeps it depressed while strumming the required number of times for that chord. The player releases the button only when it is time to press a different chord button (e.g., C₇). (b) To accompany "The Wise Man Built His House," the player strums from lowest (longest) string to highest (shortest), making each strum last for two beats. The player begins to strum on the first strong beat of the song—on the word *wise*.

5. Have children take turns playing the Autoharp accompaniment as others sing the first verse of the song (notation, p. 21). If the Autoharp is in tune with the recording, use Version 1 as children sing and play. <u>Note</u>: Directions for tuning the Autoharp can be found on Teacher's Edition p. 350.

6. Play Version 2 of "The Wise Man Built His House" and have children sing and play the Autoharp (if it and the recording are in tune) for all four verses. Call attention to the variety of tone colors heard in the instrumental accompaniment. <u>Note</u>: Refer to the record jacket for the specific instruments used in Version 2. <u>Suggestion</u>: Have a different child play for each verse of the song. Choose and assign the players ahead of time. Caution them to be ready to immediately "take over" playing the Autoharp when the verse before theirs ends.

AUTOHARP ACCOMPANIMENTS
"Hand Me Down," p. 14

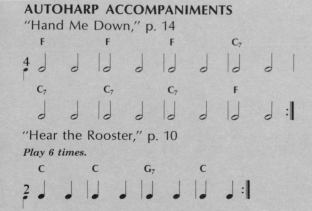

"Hear the Rooster," p. 10
Play 6 times.

"Pay Me My Money Down," p. 4

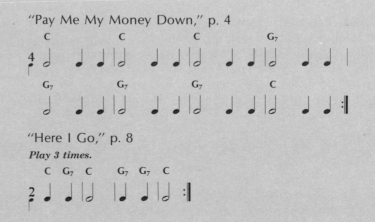

"Here I Go," p. 8
Play 3 times.

BEGINNING EXPERIENCES: Tone Color

MATERIALS
Record 1, "Sambalele"; Pupil's Book, pp. 22 and 23; Autoharp, castanets or maraca, bongos, cowbell, bells

VOCABULARY
accent, upstem, downstem, counter-melody

IDEAS FOR TEACHING
Here is another song for children to accompany on the Autoharp. It uses the same chords as "The Wise Man Built His House" (p. 21)—F and C₇.

1. Play the recording. As children listen with book closed, have them signal each time they hear a chord change in the Autoharp accompaniment.

2. As children listen to the recording, have them follow the notation for the Autoharp part on p. 22. Help them discover that this chord pattern is repeated throughout the song. Suggestion: Have children keep the steady beat by pretending to strum the Autoharp with the recording.

3. Select children to practice the Autoharp part. When they are ready, have them play it as others sing (song notation, pp. 22 and 23). Suggestions: (a) Make the recording available so that children can use it when they practice. Be certain that the Autoharp is in tune with the recording (see Teacher's Edition p. 350). (b) When children accompany the class's singing, use the Pick-a-Track technique to de-emphasize the instrumental track on the recording.

4. Direct children's attention to the ⟶

Play this chord pattern on the Autoharp to accompany "Sambalele."

SAMBALELE FOLK SONG FROM BRAZIL WORDS BY RUTH AND THOMAS MARTIN

Piano acc., p. 308

VERSE

1. Hear how the mu-sic is play-ing,
2. Dance while the drum-beat is pound-ing,

Dance to its light-heart-ed mea-sures,
Mel-low gui-tars soft-ly strum-ming,

Clap-ping and stamp-ing and sway-ing,
And cas-ta-nets clear-ly sound-ing,

Join in the car-ni-val plea-sures.
Join in the whis-tling and hum-ming.

Add a percussion accompaniment for section A.

Castanets
or Maraca
(struck against
palm of hand)

22 Beginning Experiences

TEACHER INFORMATION
Mainstreaming Note: Children with visual impairment can play the Autoharp with little difficulty. At first their fingers must be placed on the chord buttons. After considerable experience, however, some children will memorize the arrangement of the chord buttons and be able to play unassisted.

Sam - ba, sam - ba, sam - ba - la - le - le,

While we are danc - ing and sing - ing so gai - ly,

Sam - ba, sam - ba, sam - ba - la - le - le,

While we are danc - ing and sing - ing so gai - ly.

Add a percussion accompaniment for section B.

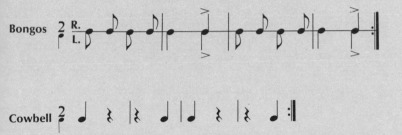

Bongos

Cowbell

Here is a countermelody to sing or play throughout section A or B,

or throughout the entire song.

C A B♭ G B♭ G A F
Sam-ba, sam-ba, sam - ba; Sam-ba, sam-ba, sam - ba.

Beginning Experiences 23

---

percussion parts on pp. 22 and 23. Questions: Which part uses eighth notes and quarter notes? (The part for bongos) Which part uses sound and silence? (The part for cowbell) Point out: Some notes in the bongos part have accents (>). The accented notes are played louder than the others. In the bongos part, the accented notes have two stems—an upstem (♩) and a downstem (♩)—indicating that they are played with both hands together. Suggestion: Have children take turns playing one of the percussion parts as others sing the song. When they are ready, have them create an accompaniment that includes the Autoharp part and as many of the percussion parts as they can manage successfully.

5. Have children look at the countermelody on p. 23. Questions: The countermelody has the same rhythm as one of the percussion parts. Which one? (The part for bongos) Does the countermelody begin lower, or higher, than the melody of "Sambalele"? (Higher) Point out: The countermelody also uses accents.

6. Have children take turns playing the countermelody on bells as others sing "Sambalele." Invite a small group of children to sing the countermelody when they can. Ask them to decide whether they will perform the countermelody during section A, during section B, or throughout the song.

TRY THIS
1. Divide the class into groups and have them each plan a way to perform "Sambalele." They may use any or all of the parts on pp. 22 and 23; for example:
    Section A—Voice, Autoharp, castanets
    Section B—Voice, Autoharp, bongos, countermelody

2. Play the recording and have children compare sections A and B of "Sambalele" to determine how they are different. (Possibilities: The melody and rhythm are different for each section. On the recording, different percussion instruments play during each section.)

MATERIALS

Record 1, "Oh, Won't You Sit Down?"; Pupil's Book, pp. 24 and 25; Autoharp, tambourine, wood block, bells (optional)

VOCABULARY

D. C. al Fine, ostinato, repeat signs

IDEAS FOR TEACHING

1. Have children add the tone color of their voice to those on the recording. Play the recording and lead children in singing the melody pattern at the top of p. 24 throughout section A. <u>Note:</u> The melody pattern is an *ostinato* (ah-sti-nah'-toh), a short melody or rhythm pattern that is repeated over and over as an accompaniment to a song. The ostinato begins on the first strong beat of the song—on the word *sit*. Questions: Do the tones of the melody pattern move mostly by step, or by leap, or do they mostly repeat? (They move mostly by step.) Do the tones move mostly upward, or mostly downward? (Mostly downward)

2. Have some children sing the ostinato pattern while others sing section A with the recording. Everyone listens during section B. <u>Suggestion:</u> If children seem insecure singing the ostinato, have someone play the bells (G, F#, E, D) to support their singing.

3. Direct children's attention to the melody pattern for section B on p. 25. Help them discover that this ostinato uses the same tones as the one for section A, but that each tone is repeated three times before the next tone down is sung. ⟶

Sing this part throughout section A.

Sit down, Broth-er. Sit down, Broth-er.

OH, WON'T YOU SIT DOWN? BLACK SPIRITUAL

Orff-instrument acc., p. 334   Piano acc., p. 316

Oh, won't you sit down?__ Lord, I can't sit down.__

Oh, won't you sit down?__ Lord, I can't sit down.__

Oh, won't you sit down?__ Lord, I can't sit down.__

'Cause I just got to Heav-en, gon-na look a-round.__

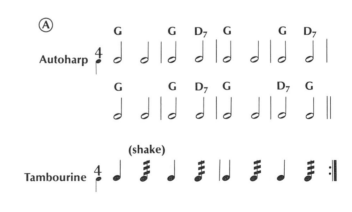

Sing this part throughout section B.

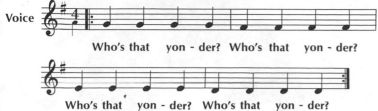

Voice

Who's that yon - der? Who's that yon - der?

Who's that yon - der? Who's that yon - der?

B VERSE

SOLO
G

1. Who's that yon - der dressed in red?__

CHORUS
G   D₇   G

Must be the chil-dren that__ Mo - ses led.__

SOLO
G

Who's that yon - der dressed in white?__

CHORUS
G   D₇   G   D.C. al Fine

Must be the chil - dren of the Is - rael - ite.___

2. Who's that yonder dressed in blue?

Must be the children that are comin' through.

Who's that yonder dressed in black?

Must be the hypocrites a-turnin' back. *Refrain*

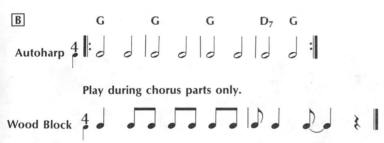

B   G   G   G   D₇   G

Autoharp

Play during chorus parts only.

Wood Block

Beginning Experiences 25

---

4. Have some children sing the osti- nato for section B as others sing the song with the recording. Note: Some children may be able to determine that the form of the song is ABA. Point out: The direction *D. C. al Fine* (Da Capo al Fine—Dah Kah'-poh ahl Fee'-nay) above the last phrase of section B indicates that the song re- peats from the beginning, then ends at the word *Fine* (end of Section A).

5. Give some children time to prac- tice the Autoharp chord pattern for section A, and let others practice the pattern for section B. When they are ready, have them take turns adding the tone color of the Autoharp to the singing. Mainstreaming Sugges- tion: Color-code the Autoharp chords and the corresponding chord buttons for children with sight or neurological impairment. Note: The chords G and D₇ are used to accom- pany both sections. The strumming pattern—long strums that each last for two beats—is the same through- out the song. For section A, players begin strumming on the strong beat—on the word *sit*. Remind chil- dren that the repeat signs (‖: :‖) in- dicate that the pattern for section B must be played twice.

6. Children can add the tone color of percussion instruments when they sing "Oh, Won't You Sit Down?". Have some of them play the tam- bourine pattern (p. 24) throughout section A; others, the wood-block part (p. 25) for section B. Note: The tambourine part begins on the strong beat—on *sit*. The player keeps the steady beat by alternately striking and shaking the instrument through- out the section. The wood-block part has the same rhythm as the chorus parts in section B of the song.

TRY THIS

Put it all together. Select some children to sing the solo parts in "Oh, Won't You Sit Down?", others to sing the chorus parts; some to sing the ostinato for section A, oth- ers, the one for section B. Have children add the tone col- ors of the Autoharp, wood block, and tambourine to their singing. Note: When children participate in an ensemble experience such as this, remind them that they must work together to create a blend of sound. The melody of the song is most important, and must be heard. The accompa- niment parts should be performed in such a way that they can all be heard without any part sounding louder than

the rest. Make children aware of how loud or soft they should play to create a blend that they and you are satis- fied with.

TEACHER INFORMATION

Mainstreaming Note: An adaptation for "Oh, Won't You Sit Down?" appears in *Silver Burdett Music for Special Educa- tion*.

BEGINNING EXPERIENCES: Tone Color

MATERIALS
Record 1, Widmann: *Margaretha;* *Hear the Rooster,* Version 2; "Ging Gong Gooli"; Pupil's Book, pp. 26 and 27; recorders

VOCABULARY
consort, mouthpiece, soprano recorder, fingering chart

IDEAS FOR TEACHING
1. Ask children to look at the picture of the child playing the recorder on p. 26. Question: What is the child doing to play a sound on the recorder? (Blowing into the mouthpiece, and using fingers to cover some of the holes)

2. Have children listen to the recording of *Margaretha* to hear the tone color of a recorder *consort* (kahn'-sort, a small ensemble of instruments). Point out: The recording provides an excellent example of ensemble playing. The tone colors of the individual instruments blend together to produce the total sound.

3. Play the recording of *Hear the Rooster* and have children listen to the melody played on a soprano recorder.

4. Play the recording of *Hear the Rooster* and ask children to accompany the melody by playing the tone G over and over on their recorder. Encourage them to make up their own rhythm patterns as they play. Note: (a) Have children hold their recorder with the left hand above the right as shown on p. 26. The recorder should be placed between the →

LOOK

LISTEN

Listen to the tone color of a group of recorders, called a consort.

 Widmann, Erasmus: *Margaretha*

26 Beginning Experiences

TEACHER INFORMATION
Just as all children should be given an opportunity to play the Autoharp and percussion instruments, every child should experience playing the recorder. This lesson provides an initial experience. For children who wish to continue with the recorder, a developmental program is presented throughout Book 4. Children who do not wish to continue with the recorder can play the recorder parts on bells or other melody instruments.

TRY THIS
Use sets of boxes like the following to give children more practice playing G, A, and B.

B	•		
A		•	
G			•

Each vertical column of boxes represents one beat. The columns are read from left to right. Children play a sound for each dot they see. The position of the dot (top box—B; →

PLAY

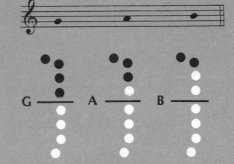

G

How to Play G

1. Using your left hand, cover the holes shown in the diagram.

   Press just hard enough so the holes make a light mark on your fingers.

2. Cover the tip of the mouthpiece with your lips. Blow gently

   as you whisper "daah."

Play G throughout a song you know.

Hear the Rooster, Version 2

Now try playing G, A, and B.

Your recorder notes look like this.

Your fingers should cover these holes.

G   A   B

Play a recorder part for "Ging Gong Gooli." It uses G, A, B.

Ⓐ

A   G

Ⓑ

B

---

lips and in front of the teeth. The teeth should not touch the instrument. (b) The fingering chart for the tone G and instructions for playing are given on p. 27. The black circles in the fingering chart indicate holes that are covered with the fingers; the white circles indicate holes that remain uncovered. Circles above the horizontal line indicate the left hand; circles below the line, the right hand. (Mainstreaming Suggestion: Place tape over the appropriate holes of recorders of children who are unable to use their fingers to cover the holes.) (c) Another song that children can accompany with the tone G is "Pay Me My Money Down" (p. 4).

5. When children are ready, have them learn the fingerings for the tones A and B (fingering chart, p. 27). Then they will be able to play the countermelody for "Ging Gong Gooli" on p. 27. Point out: (a) Each section of the countermelody is repeated. (h) For the tied notes at the end of section B, children play the half note and make the sound last for the value of the half note plus the value of the quarter note—three beats. Note: This activity can be accomplished over a period of time. Make the recording available for children to work on their own outside of class. When they are ready, have small groups perform for the class.

---

middle—A; bottom—G) in the column tells children which pitch to play.

Use more sets of boxes for a longer sound piece:

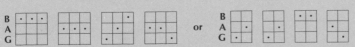

Children play from one set to the next without missing a beat. Have them decide whether to play at a fast tempo or at a slow tempo.

Encourage children to make up their own sound pieces and notate them for others to play. When they feel secure with the activity, they might try making the rhythm more interesting. For example, they might write two dots in some boxes (to be played as two equal sounds to the beat) or leave some columns empty (to indicate a silent beat, or rest).

BEGINNING EXPERIENCES: Tone Color

MATERIALS
Record 1, "Oh, Won't You Sit Down?"; Pupil's Book, pp. 28 and 29, 24 and 25; recorders or bells, Orff (or other keyboard) instruments, tambourine, wood block, Autoharp

VOCABULARY
whole note, countermelody

IDEAS FOR TEACHING
Help children see how B, A, and G are used in the melodies on p. 28. Sometimes tones are repeated; sometimes they move upward or downward by step; sometimes there is a small leap from G to B.

1. Have children look at the notation on p. 28. Questions: Which tones are used in all three melodies? (B, A, G) Which melodies use quarter notes, eighth notes, and half notes? ("Hot Cross Buns," "Merrily We Roll Along") <u>Note:</u> Call attention to the whole note (𝅝) in measures 4 and 8 of "At Pierrot's Door." A whole note lasts as long as four quarter notes—four beats.

2. Have children try to play each melody on recorder. <u>Suggestions:</u> (a) Children can also play the melodies on bells. (b) While some children learn to play the melodies on p. 28, have others practice parts to play on Orff instruments or on other keyboard instruments (see below). When they are ready, put the parts together with the melody for an ensemble.

REVIEW/REINFORCEMENT
1. Direct attention to the recorder parts for "Oh, Won't You Sit Down?" →

Practice playing some melodies that use B, A, G on the recorder.

HOT CROSS BUNS TRADITIONAL

AT PIERROT'S DOOR FOLK MELODY FROM FRANCE

MERRILY WE ROLL ALONG TRADITIONAL

28 Beginning Experiences

OPTIONAL PARTS FOR ORFF INSTRUMENTS

Hot Cross Buns (Arranged by Marilyn Davidson)

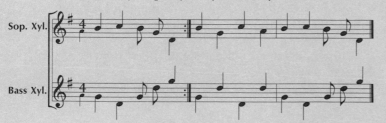

(Sop. Xyl. = Soprano Xylophone; Bass Xyl. = Bass Xylophone)

At Pierrot's Door (Arranged by Marilyn Davidson)

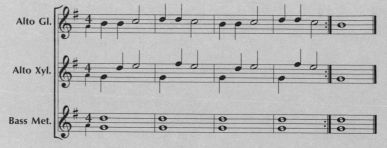

(Alto Gl. = Alto Glockenspiel; Alto Xyl. = Alto Xylophone; Bass Met. = Bass Metallophone) →

Playing an instrument in a group is one of the most pleasant kinds of music making. Try adding the recorder parts below to the percussion and Autoharp parts on pages 24 and 25.

Play this recorder countermelody during section A of "Oh, Won't You Sit Down?" It uses B, A, G.

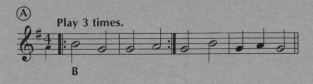

Here is a countermelody to play during section B.

It also uses B, A, G.

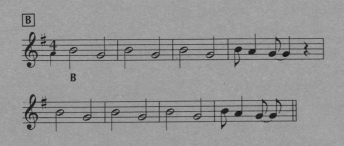

Beginning Experiences 29

on p. 29. There is a part for section A, and one for section B. <u>Note:</u> In the part for section B, the last measure of each staff has the same notes as the melody. Thinking the words *Moses led* or *Israelite* as they occur in the song will help children play the rhythm correctly.

2. Give children time to practice, then put it all together by having them add the recorder countermelodies to the "Oh, Won't You Sit Down?" ensemble on pp. 24 and 25. <u>Note:</u> The countermelody for section A begins on the first strong beat—on the word *sit.*

TRY THIS

1. Children can play these ear-training games, using B, A, G.
(a) Using a recorder or a keyboard instrument, a child plays one of the following:
    Tones moving upward or downward by step (e.g., G-A-B)
    Tones that leap upward or downward (e.g., B-G-B)
    Repeated tones (e.g., A-A-A)
Another child "sings back" what has been played, using letter names.
(b) As the class follows the notation, a child plays one of the melodies on p. 28, substituting a silence (rest) for one of the notes. The class indicates which note has been omitted.
(c) A child plays one of the melodies on p. 28, ending on the tone A or B instead of G. The class identifies the ending tone.

2. Children who have begun playing the Autoharp can develop skill by practicing the parts notated below. When they are ready, they play the parts to accompany the melodies on p. 28.

BEGINNING EXPERIENCES: Texture

MATERIALS
Record 1, "Michael Finnegan"; Pupil's Book, pp. 30 and 31; percussion instruments having contrasting sounds, recorders or bells

VOCABULARY
melody, harmony

IDEAS FOR TEACHING
1. Play the recording and have children follow the notation on p. 30. When they can, they sing the rhyming words at the end of the phrases.

2. When children know the song, use the Pick-a-Track technique (see Teacher Information, p. 15) to de-emphasize the instrumental track on the recording, and have them sing the melody with the recorded voices. Point out: (a) A melody has a special feeling when it is sung or played without harmony. (b) The first drawing on p. 31 shows the symbol for melody without harmony ($\sim$). Suggestion: As children sing without the recorded accompaniment, have individuals play the rhythm of the words on percussion instruments. They play everything but the rhyming words on one instrument (e.g., sticks); they play the rhyming words on a different-sounding instrument (e.g., tambourine). Point out: Using nonpitched percussion instruments does not add harmony to the singing.

3. Give children experience singing other songs without harmony; for example: "Ging Gong Gooli" (p. 18) and "The Wise Man Built His House" (p. 21). Have children who play recorder perform the melodies on p. 28 without harmony.

MICHAEL FINNEGAN CHILDREN'S GAME SONG

Orff-instrument acc., p. 341   Piano acc., p. 284

1.-2. There was an old man named Mi-chael Fin-ne-gan,

He had whis-kers on his chin-ne-gan,
He went fish-ing with a pin-ne-gan,

He pulled them out but they grew in a-gain,
He caught a fish but dropped it in a-gain,

Poor old Mi-chael Fin-ne-gan. Be-gin a-gain.

3. There was an old man named Michael Finnegan,
Climbed a tree and barked his shinnegan,
He lost about a yard of skinnegan,
Poor old Michael Finnegan. Begin again.

4. There was an old man named Michael Finnegan,
He grew fat and then grew thinnegan,
Then he died and that's the endegan,
Poor old Michael Finnegan. Begin again.

TRY THIS
1. Encourage children to make up their own verses for "Michael Finnegan"; for example:
    There was an old man named Michael Finnegan,
    He had wrinkles on his skinnegan,
    He washed them out, but they dried back in again,
    Poor old Michael Finnegan. Begin again.

2. Without the recording, children sing everything but the rhyming words at the end of phrases. Individuals take turns singing the rhyming words. Help children notice that each solo voice has a tone color of its own.

3. Children choose a partner and perform the following patting and clapping pattern throughout "Michael Finnegan." For the ♫ rhythm at the end of the pattern, they may clap their own hands, or their partner's hands.

Pat left leg. | Pat right leg. | Partners clap left hands together. | Partners clap right hands together. | Pat left leg. | Pat right leg. | Clap hands.

When you sing a melody alone, there is no harmony.

This drawing shows a melody alone.

When you play chords to accompany a melody, there is harmony.

This drawing shows a melody with chords.

Play chords to accompany "Michael Finnegan."

MATERIALS

Record 1, "Michael Finnegan"; Pupil's Book, pp. 30 and 31; Autoharp

VOCABULARY

chords, texture, harmony

IDEAS FOR TEACHING

1. Direct children's attention to the drawing on p. 31 that shows the symbol for a melody with chords (≣). Point out: A melody has a special feeling when sung or played with chord accompaniment. Chords add harmony to a melody. The texture of a melody with chords is different from that of a melody alone.

2. As the group sings "Michael Finnegan" (p. 30), have individuals add harmony by playing the Autoharp part on p. 31. Note: The strumming pattern matches the steady beat of the song. Players begin strumming on the first strong beat—on the word *was*.

TRY THIS

For a challenge, have children practice a different strumming pattern for "Michael Finnegan" (see below). When they are ready, have them use it to accompany the song. Note: Players strum with a motion away from them (from longest string to shortest) for notes with stems pointing up, and with a motion toward them (from shortest string to longest) for notes with stems pointing down. Point out: The pattern shows the rhythm of phrase 4, measure 1 of the song. Thinking the words for that measure—*poor old Michael*—will help them strum the rhythm correctly.

AUTOHARP PATTERN

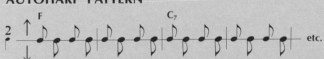

TEACHER INFORMATION

Children have experienced melody with chord accompaniment from the beginning of Book 4. Take time to review some of the following songs, giving children as many chances as possible to develop the skill of playing chords on the Autoharp. Strumming patterns (SP) that appear only in the Teacher's Edition (TE) can be written on the chalkboard or on a chart for children to follow.

- At Pierrot's Door, p. 28 (SP, p. 29 TE)
- Hand Me Down, p. 14 (SP, p. 21 TE)
- Hear the Rooster, p. 10 (SP, p. 21 TE)
- Here I Go, p. 8 (SP, p. 21 TE)
- Hot Cross Buns, p. 28 (SP, p. 29 TE)
- Merrily We Roll Along, p. 28 (SP, p. 29 TE)
- Oh, Won't You Sit Down? p. 24 (SP, pp. 24 and 25)
- Pay Me My Money Down, p. 4 (SP, p. 21 TE)
- The Wise Man Built His House, p. 21 (SP, p. 20)

BEGINNING EXPERIENCES: Texture

MATERIALS
Record 1, "Michael Finnegan"; Pupil's Book, pp. 31 and 32, 30

VOCABULARY
melody, harmony, countermelody, texture

IDEAS FOR TEACHING
1. Have children compare the drawings on p. 32 with those on p. 31 to try to determine what the symbol ⌣ stands for. (Two melodies together) Point out: A melody can be accompanied by chords (𝄚𝄚). A melody can also be accompanied by another melody (⌣). Both of these produce harmony.

2. Call attention to the "Michael Finnegan" countermelody on p. 32, and help children analyze it. Point out: (a) Measures 1, 2, 5, and 6 all use the same downward pattern. (b) Measures 3 and 4 use a different downward pattern. (c) The melody moves in a different way for measures 7 and 8.

3. When children know the countermelody, have a small group sing it while others sing the song "Michael Finnegan" (p. 30). Note: If the recording is used, have children sing with the voice track highlighted so they can hear the two melodies fit together to make harmony. Suggestion: Provide an opportunity for every child to participate by (a) singing the melody, (b) singing the countermelody, and (c) listening as others perform melody and countermelody together. Point out: The texture of a melody with countermelody is different from that of a melody with chords or a melody alone. Each texture has its own special feeling.

You know that when chords accompany a melody there is harmony.

Two melodies that fit together also make harmony.

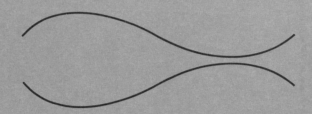

Here is a countermelody that can be sung with "Michael Finnegan."

32 Beginning Experiences

TEACHER INFORMATION
As an aid to music reading, ask questions like the following about the "Michael Finnegan" countermelody:
(a) In which measures do the tones move mostly downward? (Measures 1–6)
(b) Which measures begin with tones that move downward by step? (1, 2, 5, 6)
(c) Which measures begin with a downward leap? (3 and 4)
(d) Which measure has an upward leap? (7)
(e) How do the tones move in measure 8? (They repeat.)

WHAT DO YOU HEAR? 1: TEXTURE ◉

Listen to these pieces.

For each one, choose the symbol that best describes the texture.

If you hear melody alone, choose  .

If you hear melody with chords, choose  .

If you hear two or more melodies together, choose  .

1.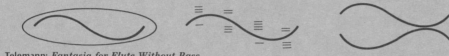
Telemann: *Fantasia for Flute Without Bass*

2.
Sourwood Mountain

3.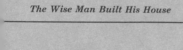
The Wise Man Built His House

4.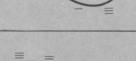
German Folk Melody

5.
Angelina

Beginning Experiences 33

BEGINNING EXPERIENCES: Texture

MATERIALS
Record 1, *What Do You Hear? 1: Texture;* spirit master

VOCABULARY
melody alone, melody with chords, two or more melodies together

TEACHER INFORMATION
The last part of the Beginning Experiences section and of many of the modules in this book will be a What Do You Hear? evaluation. This kind of activity requires the children to demonstrate what they have learned by responding to the instructions on the recording. It also gives the children and the teacher a concrete assessment of progress toward increased musical perception.

The What Do You Hear? evaluations can be done with a large group in a classroom situation or with a small group using earphones. Spirit masters are available so that each child can respond individually.

Sometimes it may be feasible to write the items on the chalkboard so that the group can answer the questions together. Children can take turns circling the correct answers. Mainstreaming Suggestion: For children with visual impairment, construct textured response cards as follows: Draw each of the symbols on a separate sheet of cardboard. Then trace the lines you have drawn with a thin layer of glue. Sprinkle with sand before the glue dries.

TRY THIS
Children can make up a What Do You Hear? of their own. Have small groups each choose five examples from the Beginning Experiences materials (pp. 2–32) to illustrate the three textures—melody alone, melody with chords, two or more melodies together. As each group performs its examples, the other children identify the texture of each one. Note: Unaccompanied singing of the melody of any songs in the Beginning Experiences will illustrate melody alone. Performing any of the melodies with Autoharp accompaniment will illustrate melody with chords. Songs that illustrate two melodies together include the following.

- Ging Gong Gooli, p. 18 (when performed with the countermelody, p. 27)
- Here I Go, p. 8 (first two phrases when performed with melody 3, p. 12; or all three phrases when performed with melody 1 or 3, p. 13)
- Michael Finnegan, p. 30 (when performed with the countermelody, p. 32)
- Oh, Won't You Sit Down? p. 24 (section A when performed with the countermelody, p. 29)
- Sandy McNab, p. 9 (first two phrases when performed with melody 2, p. 12)

BEGINNING EXPERIENCES: Listening to Music

MATERIALS
Record 1, *Call Chart 1: Listening to Music*; Pupil's Book, pp. 34 and 35

VOCABULARY
theme, orchestra, strings, wood-winds, variation, accompaniment, coda

IDEAS FOR TEACHING
1. Play the recording, stopping the music at the end of the theme (when the voice on the recording calls "Two"). Then ask the following questions.
(a) When you listen to music, what part of you lets you hear the sounds? (Discuss with children that our *ears* receive the sounds. If we try listening with eyes closed, our ears still hear the sounds. Explain that sound waves move from the outer ear into the inner ear, where sound vibrations are changed into impulses or signals that are sent to the brain.)
(b) What does your brain—or mind—do with the sounds that reach it? (Discuss the fact that the mind sorts out the sounds so that they "make sense." It lets us hear the sounds as being related to one another, as going somewhere, as having qualities that we can recognize.)

2. Play the recording and have children follow the chart on p. 35 as they listen. Point out: Each time a number is called on the recording, children find the number in the chart. Next to it are words that describe what they are hearing.

3. Discuss with children what happens in the music at each "call" number. Be certain they know that

→

What part of you lets you hear the sounds of this music? Ears

TEACHER INFORMATION
Georges Bizet (French, 1838–1875) *L'Arlésienne Suite No. 1*, Overture: This composer was also a gifted pianist and organist. His compositions include numerous symphonic and dramatic works as well as compositions for piano and voice. Among his most famous works are the opera *Carmen* and two orchestral suites based on his incidental music to Daudet's play *L'Arlésienne*.

Mainstreaming Note: For children who are visually impaired or who are nonreaders, an alternative method of using the Call Charts must be devised. Each nonreading child can be paired with a reader who can read or describe the events softly as the numbers are called. If the nonreaders can be grouped without stigma, one reader can read the events for the group. The one advantage of the latter method is that it reduces the amount of speaking during the playing of the music.

CALL CHART 1: LISTENING TO MUSIC 🔊

As your ears hear sounds, your mind tells you what the sounds are doing.

How many of these things is your mind aware of? The numbers will help you listen carefully.

Bizet: *L'Arlésienne Suite No. 1*, Overture

1. *THEME:* **Strings play together.**

2. *VARIATION 1:* **Soft; woodwinds play.**

3. *VARIATION 2:* **Gets louder and softer.**

4. *VARIATION 3:* **Slower; theme smooth; accompaniment has short tones.**

5. *VARIATION 4:* **Like a march; drums play.**

6. *CODA (ending section):* **Loud, soft, ends softly.**

The more *sounds* your *ears hear*, and the more sounds your *mind* is *aware* of, the more your *feelings* can *respond*.

An orchestra is making the sounds of this music.

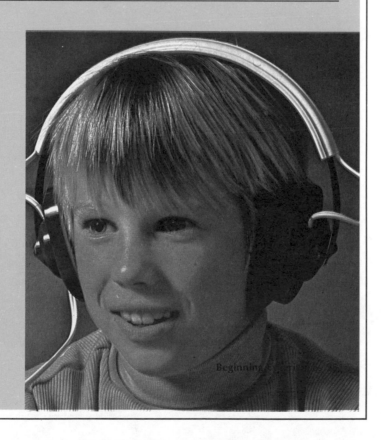

in music the word *theme* means "the main melody"; the word *variation* means "the main melody, but with some things changed, or varied."
<u>Note:</u> Be certain to play the music over and over to illustrate and aid the discussion.

4. Help children summarize the listening process as follows.
Listening requires:
  (a) sounds to hear
  (b) ears to receive the sounds
  (c) mind to make sense out of the sounds
  (d) feelings to "get involved" so that the sounds "matter" to us—are enjoyed
Emphasize that the more our minds can make sense of sounds, the more we can enjoy, be touched by, get involved with what we hear. This is why we study how music works.

TRY THIS
1. Use other listening selections in Book 4 to reinforce the ideas of this lesson. Have children choose a piece to listen to. Then review the components of the listening process—sounds, ears, mind, feelings—in relation to the music they have selected.

2. Apply the ideas of this lesson to performance. Have children sing a song. Then ask if they were able to hear it *as they sang.* Point out that the ears, mind, and feelings are involved in listening even when we are making the sounds ourselves. Whether music is made by oneself or by others, it is always "heard" with the ears, mind, and feelings.

BEGINNING EXPERIENCES: The Arts—Active, Still

MATERIALS
Record 2, Gershwin: *An American in Paris;* Ives: *The Pond;* Pupil's Book, pp. 36 and 37

VOCABULARY
active, still

IDEAS FOR TEACHING
1. Through questioning and discussion, establish the idea of action and stillness. Use examples from the children's experience; for example: *active*—running a race, playing a game of basketball, riding a bicycle, cleaning their room; *still*—taking a nap, reading a book, working a crossword puzzle. Emphasize that both action and stillness have movement, but that action involves more and faster movements.

2. Give children time to look at the paintings on pp. 36 and 37. Ask the following questions.
(a) What makes the picture on p. 36 seem so active?
(By questioning and discussing, help children discover the following features. There are short jagged lines covering the entire space. The shapes made by the lines are very jerky, awkward, and irregular. There is a jumble of colors banging up against each other. The lines and shapes go in every direction, changing direction all the time.)
(b) What makes the picture on p. 37 seem so still?
(By questioning and discussing, help children discover the following features. There is a wide-open space of yellow with "nothing" in it. There are just two smooth lines, one mov- →

36 Beginning Experiences

TEACHER INFORMATION
Joseph Stella (Italian, 1877–1946) *Battle of Lights:* Stella's fascination with the visual energy of America's expanding cities in the early 20th century is reflected in his paintings. The colors are luminous, the detail intricate, the shapes jumbled, yet carefully constructed.

Jules Olitsky (Russian, 1922–   ) *High A Yellow:* Olitsky's paintings show his concern for color above all else. They have few shapes, lines, or objects in them. But in their subtle blendings and contrastings of colors in space, they have a fascination that allows us to see more every time we look at them.

George Gershwin (American, 1898–1937) *An American in Paris:* This very "American" composer used folk sources and jazz as the bases for his semiclassical works. In addition to great songs such as "The Man I Love" and "I Got Rhythm," his popular compositions include *Rhapsody in Blue, An American in Paris,* and his opera *Porgy and Bess.*

Charles Ives (American, 1874–1964) *The Pond:* Ives managed to dream up highly original sounds that were far ahead of their time. He often used patriotic and folk songs in his music, but transformed their character into one with much dissonance and jaggedness. In *The Pond,* these qualities are present but subdued.

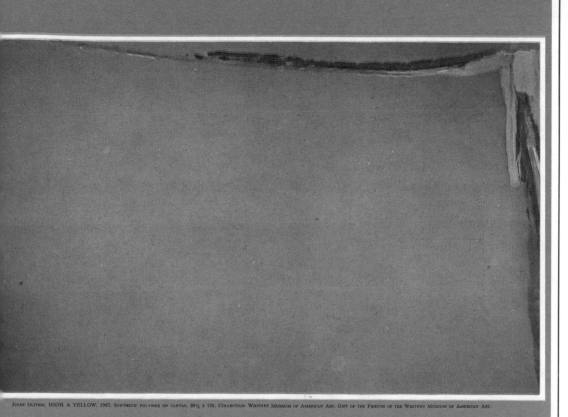

JULES OLITSKI. HIGH A YELLOW. 1967. SYNTHETIC POLYMER ON CANVAS. 89½ x 150. COLLECTION WHITNEY MUSEUM OF AMERICAN ART. GIFT OF THE FRIENDS OF THE WHITNEY MUSEUM OF AMERICAN ART.

Paintings give a feeling of movement.

Which painting seems to be more active?

Which painting seems to be more still?

Why?

Music also gives a feeling of movement. Which piece seems

to be more active? Which piece seems to be more still?

🔘 Gershwin: *An American in Paris*   🔘 Ives: *The Pond*
2   2

Both painting and music seem to have movement.

Some paintings and some music have active movement—others are still.

Each art creates a sense of movement differently, so each art gives

its own special feeling.

Beginning Experiences 37

ing across the top, the other down the side. The colors do not clash, or bang up against each other—they fade into each other. The reddish glow at the bottom left balances the lines at the top right.)

3. Write the following lists on the chalkboard.

Active	Still
fast	slow
strong beat	weak beat
short sounds	long sounds
accents	no accents
many changes	few changes

Discuss with children that music also gives a feeling of movement. Talk about the qualities in the chalkboard lists that are found in music that is active and in music that is still. Have children demonstrate the meaning of each quality by moving fast, slow; by marching to a strong beat, to a weak beat; by singing short tones, long tones; by singing a song with accents (e.g., "Ging Gong Gooli," p. 18), then singing it again, ignoring the accents; by performing different movements, quickly changing from one to the other, then performing a single arm movement over and over.

4. Play the Gershwin excerpt, then play the selection by Ives. Have children listen to both selections several times. Help draw out that (a) the Gershwin piece has qualities listed in the "active" column—fast, strong beat, short sounds, accents, many changes of musical ideas, and (b) the Ives piece has qualities listed in the "still" column—slow, weak beat, long sounds, no accents, few changes of musical ideas. In both pieces, the active or still feeling comes from a combination of such qualities.

TRY THIS

1. Have children fingerpaint or draw examples that clearly illustrate action and stillness. They should avoid *representation* in their work, since this can lead to confusion. For example, a drawing of a horse can show action; a flower can show stillness. But, depending on how it is depicted, a horse can also show stillness; a flower, action. Using only lines, shapes, and colors, as in the paintings on pp. 36 and 37, helps eliminate this problem.

2. Children can create a dance that uses active and still movements. Have some children think of a way to move that would show much energy (active). Have others think of a contrasting movement, one with little energy (still). Organize the movements into a dance; for example:

Little Energy (one or two dancers)	Much Energy (group of dancers)	Both Levels of Energy (all dancers)	Little Energy (one or two dancers)

Help children evaluate the dance: Did the dancers show the quality they intended? Was there enough contrast? Lead them to discover ways to make the dance more effective.

MODULE 1

OBJECTIVES, p. XI

TEMPO • Lesson 1

MATERIALS
Pupil's Book, p. 38

VOCABULARY
tempo, fast, moderate, slow

IDEAS FOR TEACHING

1. The picture on p. 38 shows fast action at a basketball game. Discuss the elements of the game that show fast motion—players running from one end of the court to the other, dribbling the ball, the swift toss of the ball into the net, the quick arm motions to block a play. Then help children compare the fast speed of these motions with the slow speed at which they are shown in slow-motion playback on TV.

2. Have children choose a favorite sport and dramatize a "play" (e.g., shooting a basket, serving a tennis ball, kicking a football, swinging a baseball bat). <u>Suggestion:</u> One group dramatizes the play at a fast tempo. A second group "plays it back" at a slow tempo. A third group watches the action, observing the difference in tempo between the original action and the slow-motion playback. <u>Note:</u> Give all children experience participating in each of the three groups.

3. Have children take turns leading the class in singing any familiar song at a tempo that feels right. Each leader describes his or her tempo as fast, slow, or moderate (neither fast nor slow).

TEMPO

TEACHER INFORMATION
This module, focusing on tempo, is complete in itself with a beginning, a middle, and an end. Provide for repetition and review by using the material over a period of time. It is suggested that three or four music periods may be adequate for children to build their skills with the musical quality tempo.

Choose your own tempo for "Flea!" Will it be fast? Moderate? Slow?

Will the tempo get faster? Will it get slower?

Clapping Pattern:

FLEA! ECHO CHANT
© 1978 Pachyderm Music, CAPAC

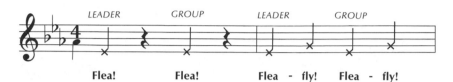
Flea! Flea! Flea - fly! Flea - fly!

Flea - fly mos-qui - to! Flea - fly mos-qui - to!

Oh, no, no, no____ more mos - qui - toes,

Itch - y, itch - y, scratch - y, scratch - y,

Oo, I got one down my back - y,

Beat that big bad bug with the bug spray. Tshsh___

MODULE 1: Tempo 39

MATERIALS
Record 2, "Flea!"; Pupil's Book, p. 39

VOCABULARY
tempo, slow, moderate, fast, getting faster, getting slower, decrescendo

IDEAS FOR TEACHING

1. As they listen to the recording, have children perform the clapping pattern on p. 39. They alternately clap hands and pat their lap throughout the chant.

2. As children perform the pattern once more, have them follow the notation for "Flea!" and join in each time the group echoes the leader. Point out: (a) The notation for the first two staffs does not represent definite pitch. The "x's" merely indicate that the voice should rise and fall while chanting. (b) Beginning with staff 3, each phrase is sung twice, first by the leader, then by the group. (c) The symbol (>) above *Tshsh* at the end of the notation stands for *decrescendo* (day-kre-shen'-doh). It indicates that the sound gets softer.

3. When children know the chant, choose someone to lead the class in performing it without the recording. The leader begins to perform the clapping pattern at a tempo of his or her choice. When others join in, the leader begins the chant for the group to echo. Suggestion: Encourage the leader to experiment with changing the tempo by (a) performing some phrases fast, others slow; (b) getting gradually faster or slower during the long phrases; or (c) beginning slow (fast) and performing each phrase faster (slower) than the one before it.

TRY THIS
Using the two-meter conducting pattern (see following), a leader conducts beats in sets of two at a fast, moderate, or slow tempo, or at a tempo that gets faster or slower. Others take turns playing a rhythm pattern on percussion instruments, following the leader's tempo. They may use a pattern made by their name:

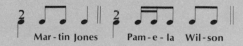
Mar - tin Jones   Pam - e - la   Wil - son

or a pattern made by the title of a song:

Mi - chael Fin - ne - gan

or the rhythm of a part of a song they know:

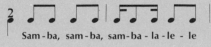
Sam - ba, sam - ba, sam - ba - la - le - le

Two-Meter Conducting Pattern:

MATERIALS
Record 2, "Dayenu"; Pupil's Book,
p. 40; tambourine

VOCABULARY
steady beat, beat getting faster,
tempo, accelerando

IDEAS FOR TEACHING

1. Play the recording and have children clap the beat. Questions: Does
the beat remain steady throughout
the song? (No) What happens to the
beat during the second section (section B)? (It gets faster.) Point out: In
the song notation (p. 40), the word
accelerando (ah-che-le-rahn'-doh)
above staff 3 means "gradually getting faster."

2. Have children take turns playing
the beat on a tambourine as others
sing with the recording. Encourage
children who can to play a rhythm
pattern to accompany the singing.
Note: Remind players that they must
always follow the tempo of the
music, playing the beat or their pattern faster as the tempo gets faster.
Suggestion: Experiment with ways to
play the tambourine—shaking it,
striking it with hand, on knee, on
elbow, etc.

TRY THIS

1. Children can dance a simple hora
with the recording of "Dayenu" (see
below for directions). Mainstreaming
Suggestion: Have nonambulatory and
motor-impaired children play the tambourine or sing with the recording.

2. Choose someone to lead the singing of "Dayenu" at his or her tempo,
using this four-meter pattern:

How does the tempo change in "Dayenu"?

Does it get faster, or slower? Faster

DAYENU

HEBREW PASSOVER SONG   ENGLISH WORDS BY ELIZABETH S. BACHMAN

Piano acc., p. 255

2. He has given us the Sabbath, given us the holy Sabbath,
   He has given us the Sabbath, *dayenu. Refrain*

3. He has given us the Torah, given us the blessed Torah,
   He has given us the Torah, *dayenu. Refrain*

40 Tempo

DANCE DIRECTIONS
Children practice a step-hop pattern with the recording:

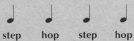

step   hop   step   hop

When they can move easily, six or eight dancers stand behind one another in a line. Each one places his or her right
hand on the left shoulder of the person in front. As they
perform the pattern (beginning with the left foot) with the
music, the child at the head of the line leads them from
place to place in the room. Suggestion: Have children form
as many lines as the area will accommodate.

TEACHER INFORMATION
The hora is one of the most popular dances of the Balkan
countries and the Middle East. It is performed in a circle,
open or closed, and in serpentine figurations. Dancers are
joined with scarves or sashes or with arms linked, or with
hands or sometimes only a single finger on each other's
shoulders. There is usually one basic step repeated over
and over, getting gradually faster. Swings, hops, bends, and
heel placements are used to vary the basic step.

How does the tempo change in "Lazy Coconut Tree"?

Does it get faster, or slower?   Slower

MATERIALS
Record 2, "Lazy Coconut Tree"; Pupil's Book, p. 41; maracas, bongos, claves

VOCABULARY
steady beat, beat getting slower, tempo, rallentando

IDEAS FOR TEACHING
1. Play the recording and have someone play the beat on claves. Questions: Does the beat remain steady throughout the song? (No) What happens to the beat during the second section (section B)? (It gets slower.)

2. Play the recording again. Have children follow the notation (p. 41) and clap or tap the beat to feel it getting slower during section B. Point out: The word *rallentando* (rah-len-tahn'-doh) above staff 4 means "gradually getting slower."

3. When children know the song, have individuals accompany the singing on maracas, bongos, or claves (see below for parts). Point out: (a) Both singers and players follow the tempo of the music, getting slower as the music gets slower. (b) The claves part has the same rhythm as the word *co-co-co-co-nut* in the song. Thinking the word over and over will help the player keep the rhythm. Suggestions: (a) Have one instrument play during section A, a different one during section B. (b) Have one child sing section A as a solo without percussion accompaniment. A group sings section B accompanied by one or more instruments.

LAZY COCONUT TREE

MUSIC BY DOUGLAS COOMBES   WORDS BY JOHN EMLYN EDWARDS

FROM TA-RA-RA-BOOM-DE-AY. PUBLISHED BY A & C BLACK LTD. REPRINTED BY PERMISSION OF DAVID HIGHAM ASSOCIATES LIMITED.

Piano acc., p. 290

1. Some folk like to go fish-ing____ far a-cross the bay,
2. I could be a rich mer-chant____ in some fine ba-zaar,

I would rath-er be dream-ing____ on the beach all day.
But I'd rath-er be hap-py____ nod-ding to a star.

(optional harmony part)*
Like the la - zy co-co-co - co-nut, co-co-co - co-nut tree,

gradually getting slower (rallentando)
Like the la - zy co-co-co - co-nut, co-co-co - co-nut tree.

*The optional harmony part for this song and for others in Book 4 (e.g., "Find the Ring," p. 72, "Remember Me," p. 92, and "Sands Get into Your Shoes," p. 96) is provided for classes that are ready for additional experiences with part singing. Each harmony part is included on the recording in at least one verse or one playing of the song.

Tempo 41

PERCUSSION PATTERNS

TEACHER INFORMATION

Calypso music originated in Trinidad, where calypso songs were sung as long ago as the 18th century. A calypso song is traditionally in two meter or in four meter, and shows strong Spanish and African influences in melody and in rhythm. True calypso songs are spontaneous. Singers make them up on the spur of the moment about almost any topic—personal opinions, local happenings, world news. The words are often witty, playful, teasing, or even sarcastic. When composers use the calypso style, as in "Lazy Coconut Tree," they try to incorporate some or all of these qualities.

TEMPO • Lesson 5

MATERIALS

Record 2, "Dry Bones"; *Call Chart 2: Tempo*; Pupil's Book, pp. 42 and 43; tambourine

VOCABULARY

fast, moderate, getting faster, getting slower

IDEAS FOR TEACHING

1. The song "Dry Bones" invites immediate participation. As children listen to the recording, have them keep the beat by tapping the palm of their hand or by tapping their lap or their desk. When the song tells about the "bones" (section B), children stand and tap the beat on their foot bone, leg bone, knee bone, etc., moving from one to the other as it is mentioned in the lyric. For the last part of the song (section C), they return to tapping as they did at the beginning. Mainstreaming Suggestion: To enable children with poor body awareness to physically feel the tempo, have classmates gently tap the appropriate "bones" for them as each is mentioned in the song. Questions: What happened to the tempo when you tapped the beat on your bones? (It got faster.) What happened to the tempo on the last phrase of the song? (It got slower.)

2. Play the recording of "Dry Bones" and have children tap the beat during section A. They stand and tap the beat on their bones for section B. For section C, they keep the beat by "walking around" in their own way (e.g., doing a "fancy walk"). Remind children that their tapping and walking must always follow the tempo of the music. ———→

DRY BONES

BLACK SPIRITUAL

Piano acc., p. 261

42 Tempo

TRY THIS

1. Have children sing the following countermelody or play it on bells during section C of "Dry Bones."

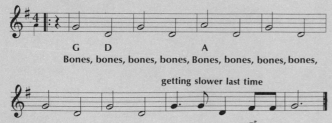

2. Have children take turns playing the beat on a tambourine during sections A and C of "Dry Bones." Help them notice the difference in the tempo of the two sections. (Section A has a moderate tempo; section C has a fast tempo until the last phrase.)

3. Encourage children to find objects in the room that imitate the sound of rattling bones. Then, as others sing and move with the recording, have a small group add a pattern of "bone" sounds to accompany section C.

The jaw bone con-nect - ed to the head bone,

Now hear the word of the Lord.

fast

Them bones, them bones gon-na walk a-round, Them bones, them bones gon-na

walk a - round, Them bones, them bones gon - na walk a - round,

getting slower last time

Now hear the word of the Lord.

CALL CHART 2: TEMPO

Here are selections from a set of pieces.

Listen for the tempo in each piece.

As each number is called, look at the chart.

It will help you hear what the beat is doing.

Satie: *Sports et Divertissements*

1. SLOW ("CHANT")

2. FAST ("FIREWORKS")

3. MODERATE ("SEE-SAW")

4. FAST ("THE HUNT")

5. MODERATE ("FISHING")

Tempo 43

3. As some children sing with the recording (notation, pp. 42 and 43), have one or two children play the beat on a tambourine during section A, have others tap their bones during section B, and still others walk around during section C. Take time to talk about the tempo of each section. Elicit from children that the beat remains steady throughout section A, then gets faster during section B; section C has a steady beat until the last phrase, when the beat gets slower.

4. Play the recording for *Call Chart 2*. Whenever a number is called on the recording, have children look at the word beside that number in the chart on p. 43. The word describes the tempo they are hearing.

5. Have groups of children move to the music in *Call Chart 2*. In addition to reflecting the tempo of each piece, encourage them to consider other aesthetic qualities in their movement—line (will the movements be long, smooth, and connected, or short, sharp, and disjointed?), pattern (will the movement consist of repeated patterns, or will it change throughout the piece?), and use of space (will the movements be large and expansive, taking up a great amount of space, or will they be small and close, taking up little space?). Note: While each piece in the Call Chart has a descriptive title, this should not limit the type of movements the children use. For example, for the piece called "The Hunt," any fast, energetic movements would be appropriate.

TEACHER INFORMATION

Call Charts are instructional materials that direct children's attention to specific qualities in music. *Call Chart 2* uses music from Erik Satie's *Sports et Divertissements* to focus on the quality of tempo.

Erik Satie (French, 1866–1925) *Sports et Divertissements:* Satie liked to poke fun at some of the overly serious composers of his time. His pieces are usually short and sometimes have silly titles such as *Three Pieces in the Shape of a Pear, Unpleasant Glances,* and *The Dreamy Fish.*

MATERIALS

Record 2, "I'm Gonna Walk"; Pupil's Book, pp. 44 and 45; maracas, bongos

VOCABULARY

beat stops and holds, fermata

IDEAS FOR TEACHING

1. Play the recording and ask children to listen for the place where the beat stops and holds. Have them follow the notation on pp. 44 and 45 as they listen. <u>Note</u>: The beat stops and holds in the second staff on p. 45, on the word *Well*. <u>Question</u>: What sign do you see in the notation when the beat stops and holds? (Children should indicate ⌒, called a *fermata*—fehr-mah'-tah.)

2. As others sing with the recording, have individuals or small groups take turns walking to the beat, being certain to stop and hold for the fermata. <u>Suggestion</u>: Have children try a "fancy walk," performing a special motion at the fermata. For example, they might walk, snapping their fingers after each step, then stop and wave their arms when the beat stops and holds. Or, they might walk, kicking their free foot after each step, stopping and bouncing (by repeatedly bending and straightening the knees) for the fermata.

3. Have children take turns playing maracas or bongos (see below for parts) to accompany "I'm Gonna Walk" as others sing. When the fermata occurs, players stop and play the instrument a different way. For example, a child playing maracas might simultaneously shake both maracas; a child playing bongos might play rapid sounds by striking →

Some music makes you want to move.

Try some "fancy stepping" with this song.

I'M GONNA WALK   WORDS AND MUSIC BY DAVID EDDLEMAN

Piano acc., p. 277

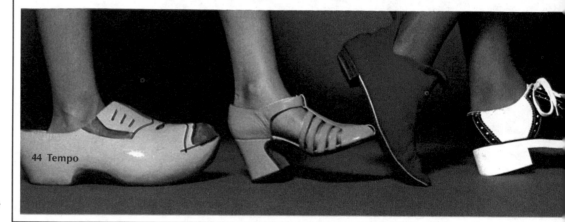

44 Tempo

PERCUSSION PATTERNS

TEACHER INFORMATION

Being aware of similarities and differences in song notation aids music reading. Help children discover the following about "I'm Gonna Walk."

 (a) The notation that follows the fermata is the same as that at the beginning of the song.

 (b) At the end of the song, the phrase *Walk with me* is repeated over and over. (<u>Note</u>: This kind of ending is called a *coda*—koh -dah.)

Some children may be able to determine that the form of the song is ABA with coda.

<u>Mainstreaming Note</u>: An adaptation for "I'm Gonna Walk" appears in *Silver Burdett Music for Special Education*.

one thing that I love ____ the best ____ Is

walk - in' all a - bout. ____ Well, ____ I'm gon - na

put, put, put on my walk - in' shoes, I'm gon - na

but-, but-, but - ton up my coat, I'm gon - na

walk right a - cross the land, there's lots o' things to see, And if you

wan - ta you can walk with me, ____ Walk with me, ____

Walk with me, ____ Walk with ____ me.

Find the place in the music where the beat stops and holds.

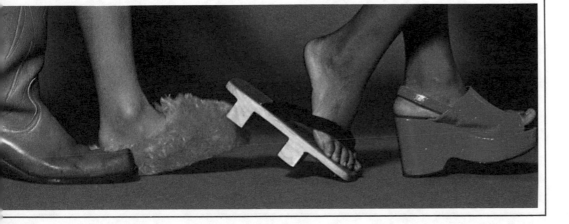

one of the drumheads with alternating left and right hands. After the fermata, players resume their part as notated. <u>Note:</u> Both at the beginning of the song and after the fermata, percussion players begin their pattern on the strong beat (on the first *put*). <u>Suggestion:</u> In addition to the non-pitched percussion sounds, children can add a pitched sound by rapidly striking the D bell over and over during the fermata. To play rapid sounds on the bell, children use two mallets, one in each hand. Keeping the mallets above the metal bar of the bell, one slightly in front of the other, they strike the bell over and over with alternating left and right mallets. Encourage them to use a wrist motion, gently "waving" the wrist up and down as they play.

4. Put it all together. As one group sings with the recording, another group moves, and a third group plays percussion instruments.

MATERIALS

Pupil's Book, p. 46; 4 cassette recorders and tapes; 4 tempo cards, 4 time-span cards, 4 number cards

VOCABULARY

tempo, time span, chance

IDEAS FOR TEACHING

1. Choose four children who each have a cassette recorder and cassette tapes of their favorite music (two or more examples).

2. Prepare three sets of four cards each (see below). One set indicates tempos; another, time spans; the third set contains cards numbered from 1 through 4.

3. Place the tempo and time-span cards face down and have each child choose one from each set by chance.

4. Give children time to listen to their cassette to find a section in the music that matches the tempo indicated on their tempo card, and to discover how much of the music can be played within the time shown on their time-span card. <u>Note:</u> It may be necessary for children to pool their resources to find music that matches the tempo on their card.

5. When children are ready, place the number cards face down and have each child choose one, again by chance.

6. Children perform their sound piece by playing the appropriate section of their cassette in the order indicated by their number card—first, second, third, or fourth.

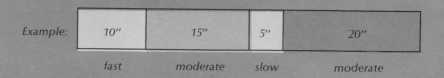

SOUND PIECE 1: Chance Music   WYNN CHECK

Select a tempo by chance.   **Select a time span by chance.**

fast   slow   moderate   5"   10"   15"   20"

Example:	10"	15"	5"	20"
	fast	*moderate*	*slow*	*moderate*

Play a section from a cassette tape in the tempo and time span you have chosen.

To perform a complete piece with others, select the order, by chance, in which you will play.

46 Tempo

SOUND PIECE CARDS

Tempo Cards

| Fast | Moderate | Slow | Moderate |

Time-Span Cards

| 5 seconds | 10 seconds | 15 seconds | 20 seconds |

Number Cards

| 1 | 2 | 3 | 4 |

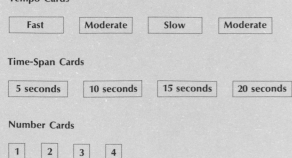

TRY THIS

1. Have children listening to the sound-piece performance try to determine the tempo of each section—fast, slow, or moderate.

2. Children in groups of four follow the directions on p. 46 to create sound pieces, using percussion instruments instead of cassette tapes. Each child makes up a pattern to play at the tempo and for the length of time indicated on the cards chosen. When the groups perform their sound pieces, a "conductor" signals when each player's time is up.

WHAT DO YOU HEAR? 2: TEMPO

Each time a number is called, decide which of the two answers is correct.

Choose the answer that best describes what is happening in the music.

Dvořák: *Slavonic Dances*, Op. 46, No. 7

1. (FAST)   SLOW
2. GETTING FASTER   (GETTING SLOWER)
3. (FAST)   SLOW
4. GETTING FASTER   (GETTING SLOWER)
5. (FAST)   SLOW

Stravinsky: *Fireworks*

1. (FAST)   SLOW
2. FASTER   (SLOWER)
3. (GETTING FASTER)   GETTING SLOWER

WHAT DO YOU HEAR? 3: TEMPO

Choose the word that best describes the tempo. Is it fast, or slow?

Do you hear the beat stop and hold? If you do, choose the fermata sign ⌒.

If you do not, choose no ⌒.

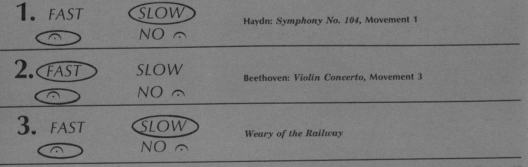

1. FAST   (SLOW)   Haydn: *Symphony No. 104*, Movement 1
   ⌒   NO ⌒

2. (FAST)   SLOW   Beethoven: *Violin Concerto*, Movement 3
   ⌒   NO ⌒

3. FAST   (SLOW)   *Weary of the Railway*
   ⌒   NO ⌒

Tempo 47

MATERIALS
Record 2, *What Do You Hear? 2: Tempo*; *What Do You Hear? 3: Tempo*; spirit masters

VOCABULARY
fast, slow, slower, getting faster, getting slower, fermata

TEACHER INFORMATION
The last part of many of the modules in this book will be a What Do You Hear? evaluation. This kind of activity requires the children to demonstrate what they have learned by responding to the instructions on the recording. It also gives the children and the teacher a concrete assessment of progress toward increased musical perception.

The What Do You Hear? evaluations can be done with a large group in a classroom situation or with a small group using earphones. Spirit masters are available so that each child can respond individually.

Sometimes it may be feasible to write the items on the chalkboard so that the group can answer the questions together. Children can take turns circling the correct answers.

Suggestions: (a) When you use *What Do You Hear? 3*, play the recording twice. The first time, children listen for the tempo of the music; the second time, for the presence or absence of fermatas. (b) Whenever a complete work is included in a What Do You Hear? evaluation (e.g., Stravinsky's *Fireworks* in *What Do You Hear? 2*), give children the opportunity to hear it again, outside of the What Do You Hear? experience.

MODULE 2

OBJECTIVES, p. XI

THINGS PEOPLE DO WITH MUSIC

MATERIALS
Record 2, *Things People Do with Music;* Pupil's Book, pp. 48 and 49

VOCABULARY
composer, performer

IDEAS FOR TEACHING

1. (Note: This picture-sound essay may be used by one child or a group. When using the materials in a group situation, discuss some of the pictures on pp. 48 and 49. Information about the musicians in the photographs is found on this page under the heading Teacher Information.) Play the recording. Then discuss any points or questions needing clarification. Note: On the recording, Hale Smith talks about *Mini-Quintet,* a composition he wrote for SILVER BURDETT MUSIC. During the first part—the rehearsal—Mr. Smith mentions the instruments that make up a woodwind quintet: flute, oboe, French horn, clarinet, bassoon. Ask children to listen for the tone color of the individual instruments as well as the tone color that results when the instruments blend together in the ensemble. Have them look at the photograph of a woodwind quintet on pp. 176 and 177.

2. Point out that usually a composer does not have a chance to work with the musicians who perform his or her music. Likewise, the performers don't usually have the composer around to help them. They must make their own decisions based on →

THINGS PEOPLE
DO WITH MUSIC

Musicians at work

Hale Smith

48 MODULE 2: Things People Do with Music

TEACHER INFORMATION
Hale Smith (American, 1925–   ) *Mini-Quintet:* This free-lance composer and arranger is also a performer and lecturer. His music for television dramas, for documentary films, and for concerts has earned him numerous awards and commissions. His works are frequently heard in public performance. Smith composes in various contemporary musical forms. His composition *Mini-Quintet* was written specifically for SILVER BURDETT MUSIC.

Doris Hays is the composer of "Did Sid?" (p. 74) and "Busy Lizzy" (p. 75). Andre Watts is a concert pianist who has appeared as soloist with the major orchestras of the United States and Europe. David McHugh has written several songs for SILVER BURDETT MUSIC. Marilyn Horne is a soprano who has sung with the major opera companies of the United States and Europe.

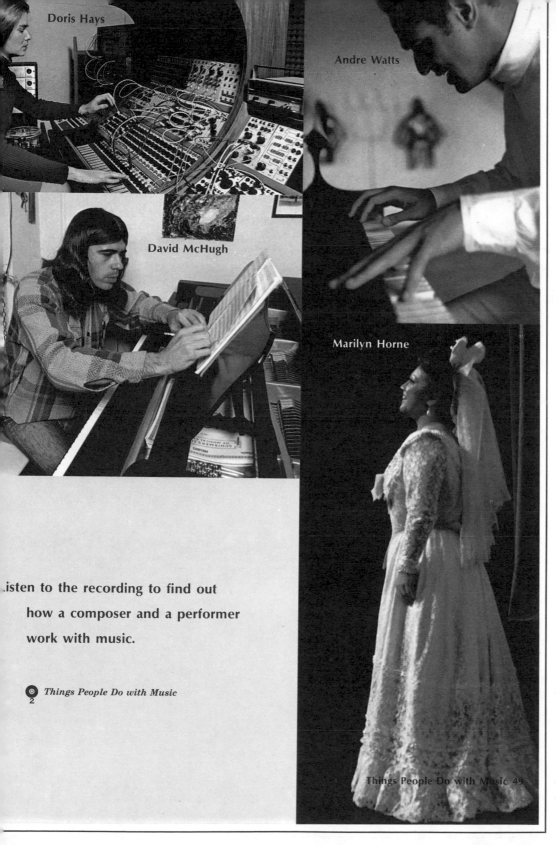

Doris Hays

Andre Watts

David McHugh

Marilyn Horne

Listen to the recording to find out how a composer and a performer work with music.

Things People Do with Music
2

Things People Do with Music 49

what they find in the score. Both composer and performers can only hope that the music will sound as the composer intended. Hale Smith and the musicians who recorded *Mini-Quintet* were lucky to have the opportunity to work together.

TRY THIS
Choose a song from Book 4 that children know. Then, without using the recording, have them make decisions about how the song should be performed; for example:

Tempo—How fast or slow seems "right"?

Dynamics—How loud or soft should it be? Should the sound get gradually louder ($<$)? Gradually softer ($>$)? Where?

Articulation—Should the tones be sung smoothly connected (legato), or short and detached (staccato)?

Tone Color—Should the singing voice be rich and full, or light and "held back"?

Rhythm—Should the beat be strong and exact, or have a less strict, "floating" quality?

When children have made their decisions, have them sing the song their way. Then play the recorded version and help children evaluate how this performance is like theirs, and how it is different. <u>Point out:</u> (a) There is no single "right" way to perform the song. (b) While a song may be performed many ways, some performance decisions are less effective than others, and some are very unmusical. <u>Note:</u> After they hear the recorded version, ask children what changes, if any, they would like to make in their interpretation of the song. Have them incorporate the changes into their performance. Help them decide whether their second performance was more musical than the first.

MODULE 3

DIRECTION

DIRECTION • Lesson 1

MATERIALS
Pupil's Book, pp. 50 and 51; bells or other keyboard instruments

VOCABULARY
direction, upward, downward, both upward and downward

IDEAS FOR TEACHING
1. Discuss the use of arrows as a way to show direction (e.g., turn left, turn right). Call attention to the arrows on p. 51 that show the direction of traffic. Then have children look at the picture on p. 50. Point out that the climber is rappelling (coming down the mountain). Have children draw an arrow that might accompany the picture to show how the climber is moving (↘).
Suggestion: Have children draw a map showing the route they take during a fire drill. Tell them to use arrows to indicate straight ahead and left and right turns.

2. Direct children's attention to the arrows in the notation on p. 51.
Questions: What do these arrows show? (The direction of the melody) Which melody moves upward? (Melody 2) Downward? (Melody 1) How does melody 3 move? (Both upward and downward) Point out: Melodies 2 and 3 contain repeated tones as well as tones that move upward and/or downward.

3. Take time to review one or more of the songs that go with the melo- →

There is direction in things we *see*.

There is direction in music we *hear*.

50 MODULE 3: Direction

TRY THIS
1. Draw four or five arrows like the following on the chalkboard:

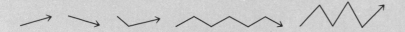

Have children take turns choosing one of them to interpret in sound by singing or playing pitches that move as the arrow indicates—upward, downward, or both upward and downward. Others identify the arrow being "performed."

Suggestions: Some children may want to "sing" their arrow, using nonsense syllables. Others may prefer to "play" their arrow, using a keyboard instrument or any other pitched sound source—for example, a set of several identical glass bottles containing varying amounts of water (the more water, the lower the sound when the bottle is tapped with a mallet; the less water, the higher the sound).

2. Pluck one of the strings of an Autoharp, guitar, or violin. While the string vibrates, turn the tuning key or peg to raise or lower the sound. Children indicate whether the sound has moved upward or downward. Suggestion: To →

dies on p. 51. <u>Note</u>: Melody 1 is the ostinato for section A of "Oh, Won't You Sit Down?" (p. 24); melody 2 is the harmony part for "Hand Me Down" (p. 14); melody 3 is the same as the last two phrases of "Pay Me My Money Down" (p. 4). <u>Suggestion</u>: If children review "Oh, Won't You Sit Down?" have a group of recorder players perform the parts on p. 29 while some children sing the song and others sing the section A ostinato.

4. Play an ear-training game. Play (or have a child play) one of the melodies on p. 51 on bells or on another keyboard instrument for children to identify the direction as upward, downward, or both upward and downward.

<u>Note:</u> Other melodies that can be used for the game include:

"When Is a Door?" (Measures 1–2), p. 9 (Except for repeated tones, the melody direction is both upward and downward.)

"Countermelody 1," p. 13 (Except for the repeated tone G, the melody direction is downward.)

Can you see direction in notation?

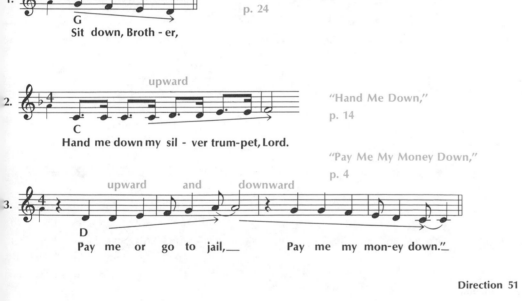

Direction 51

lessen the possibility of breaking a string, (a) when demonstrating sound moving upward, begin with the string tuned to a lower pitch than usual; (b) always turn the tuning key or peg slowly.

3. Have children take turns reading the following poem. Encourage them to read expressively, making their voice rise (upward) and fall (downward) as seems appropriate for the text.

SWIFT THINGS ARE BEAUTIFUL

Swift things are beautiful:
Swallows and deer,
And lightning that falls
Bright-veined and clear,
Rivers and meteors,
Wind in the wheat,
The strong-withered horse,
The runner's sure feet.

And slow things are beautiful:
The closing of day,
The pause of the wave
That curves downward to spray,
The ember that crumbles,
The opening flower,
And the ox that moves on
In the quiet of power.

—Elizabeth J. Coatsworth

MATERIALS
Record 2, "I Know an Old Lady"; Pupil's Book, pp. 52 and 53; bells

VOCABULARY
upward, downward, phrase

IDEAS FOR TEACHING
1. Play the recording and invite children to join in singing when they can. Note: "I Know an Old Lady" is a cumulative song. Children will be able to quickly join in on the parts that repeat.

2. Have children look at the song notation on pp. 52 and 53 to find places where the melody moves upward. Note: Although the melody moves upward in several places, most children will notice the upward melody on the words *I guess she'll die,* indicated by arrows in the music.

3. As others sing the song, have individuals take turns playing the upward melody on bells or other keyboard instruments each time the words *I guess she'll die* occur. Staff 1 at the bottom of p. 53 shows the notation for the phrase.

4. Call attention to the two staffs at the bottom of p. 53. Help children observe that the first staff shows the phrase *I guess she'll die* with tones moving in an upward direction, as they do in the song. The second staff shows a downward melody for the phrase. Using bells or other keyboard instruments, have one child play staff 1 while another child plays staff 2. They will be playing in harmony. Then as others sing the song, have pairs of children take turns playing →

When you catch on to the form of this song, join in with the recording.

I KNOW AN OLD LADY

MUSIC BY ALAN MILLS   WORDS BY ROSE BONNE

COPYRIGHT 1952 AND 1960 BY PEER INTERNATIONAL (CANADA) LTD. SOLE SELLING AGENT PEER INTERNATIONAL CORPORATION. USED BY PERMISSION.

Piano acc., p. 325

1. I know an old la - dy who swal-lowed a fly; I don't know why she swal-lowed a fly! I guess she'll die. _____ 2. I

know an old la - dy who swal-lowed a spi - der that wrig-gled and wrig-gled and tick-led in - side her; She swal-lowed the spi - der to catch the fly, But I don't know why she swal-lowed the fly. I guess she'll die! _____ I

know an old la - dy who swal-lowed a

bird! Now, how ab - surd, to
cat! Now, fan - cy that, to
dog! My, what a hog, to
goat! Just opened her throat and
cow! I don't know how she

52 Direction

TEACHER INFORMATION
Mainstreaming Suggestion: Provide cue cards to help children who are nonreaders remember the lyrics of "I Know an Old Lady." On separate cards, make simple line drawings of a fly, a spider, a bird, etc. Hold up the appropriate cards as the words occur in the song.

swal - low a bird!	3. She swal-lowed the bird	to catch	the spi - der
swal - low a cat!	4. She swal-lowed the cat	to catch	the bird,— (To 3)
swal - low a dog!	5. She swal-lowed the dog	to catch	the cat, — (To 4)
swal-lowed a goat!	6. She swal-lowed the goat	to catch	the dog,— (To 5)
swal-lowed a cow!	7. She swal-lowed the cow	to catch	the goat,— (To 6)

that wrig-gled and wrig-gled and tick-led in - side her, She swal-lowed the spi-der to

catch the fly, But I don't know why she swal-lowed the fly;

I guess she'll die!_____ I die!_____ 8. I

Know an old la - dy who swal-lowed a horse; She's dead, of course!

Here are two ways to play and sing part of the song.

Which staff shows tones that move upward? Staff 1 **Downward?** Staff 2

1.
C D E F
I guess she'll die._____

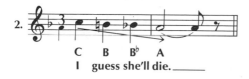

2.
C B B♭ A
I guess she'll die._____

Direction 53

staffs 1 and 2 together whenever the *I guess she'll die* phrase occurs.

5. As the class sings the song, have a small group add harmony by singing staff 2 (p. 53) on the *I guess she'll die* phrase each time.

TRY THIS

1. Write the bell melodies for phrases 1 and 2 of "I Know an Old Lady" on the chalkboard (see below). As children sing the song, have individuals play the melodies during the first two phrases of each verse on bells or other keyboard instruments. Questions: Which bell melody has only repeated tones? (The one for phrase 1) Which bell melody begins with repeated tones, then moves downward? (The one for phrase 2) Note: To help children play the rhythm correctly, the words for the phrase are included with each bell melody. Children play a tone whenever an underlined word or syllable occurs in the song.

2. Have children take turns singing the beginning of each verse as a solo. Starting with verse 3, everyone joins in when the soloist reaches the repeated section at the top of p. 53.

3. Have children write sentences about things that move upward or downward. Encourage them to place the words on paper in a way that expresses the idea of the sentence (see below for examples).

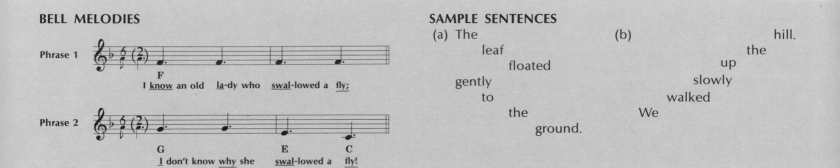

BELL MELODIES

Phrase 1
F
I <u>know</u> an old <u>la</u>-dy who <u>swal</u>-lowed a <u>fly</u>;

Phrase 2
G   E   C
<u>I</u> don't know <u>why</u> she <u>swal</u>-lowed a <u>fly</u>!

SAMPLE SENTENCES
(a) The
      leaf
          floated
      gently
          to
              the
          ground.

(b)   hill.
                              the
                          up
                      slowly
                  walked
          We

MATERIALS

Record 2, "Fisherman's Song"; Pupil's Book, p. 54; percussion instruments (bongos, maracas, claves, etc.)

VOCABULARY

calypso, both upward and downward, mostly upward

IDEAS FOR TEACHING

1. Select children to keep the beat on a percussion instrument as the recording plays. Point out: Instruments like bongos, maracas, claves, and guiro are appropriate to the calypso style of the music (see Teacher Information, p. 41).

2. Play the recording and have children sing the phrase *Round the Bay of Montserray* each time it occurs. Then repeat the activity, having them follow the notation on p. 54. Questions: What is the direction of the tones in the *Round the Bay* phrase that ends section A? (Both upward and downward) Which other *Round the Bay* phrase has tones that move in exactly the same way? (The one that ends section B) Point out: The *Round the Bay* phrase in the first staff of section B is different. Although there is a downward step at the end, the direction of the tones is mostly upward.

3. As children sing with the recording, have individuals take turns playing a percussion accompaniment. Players may create their own rhythm pattern to play over and over, or they may choose a pattern from the song; for example:

Round the Bay of Mont-ser-ray—

FISHERMAN'S SONG

CALYPSO MELODY   WORDS BY WILLIAM ATTAWAY

WORDS FROM CALYPSO SONG BOOK BY WILLIAM ATTAWAY. COPYRIGHT © 1957 BY REBUS PUBLISHING CO. COPYRIGHT ASSIGNED © 1957 TO CALYPSO MUSIC, INC. USED BY PERMISSION.

3. Fisherman's lady got a dimple knee,

Weigh up, Susianna,

She boil her porgy with rice and peas,

Round the Bay of Montserray. *Refrain*

54 Direction

TRY THIS

Give children time to practice playing the *Round the Bay* phrases on bells or other keyboard instruments. Then as the class sings, they take turns playing the phrases when they occur in the song. Note: The phrases all begin on the same tone—low C. You might have one child play the phrase at the end of each section, and another play the phrase that is different.

CLOUDS

MUSIC BY HOAGY CARMICHAEL   WORDS BY CHRISTINA ROSSETTI

Piano acc., p. 252

White sheep, white sheep, high on a wind-y hill,

When _____ the wind stops, you all stand still;

But__ when____ the wind blows, you walk a-way slow.

Oh, white sheep, white sheep, where do you go?

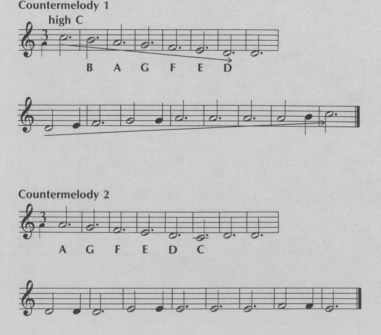

Countermelody 1
high C

B A G F E D

Countermelody 2

A G F E D C

Direction 55

MATERIALS
Record 3, "Clouds"; Pupil's Book, p. 55; bells or other keyboard instruments

VOCABULARY
direction, contour, countermelody

IDEAS FOR TEACHING

1. (Note: "Clouds" is a musical setting of a poem by Christina Rossetti.) Have children read the song lyrics on p. 55 as a poem. Encourage them to read using different vocal registers and making their voice rise (upward) and fall (downward) to express the meaning of the words. Point out: The poet uses words to create a special feeling about clouds.

2. Play the recording and have children listen to hear how a composer uses melody direction to create a setting for the words.

3. Play the recording again and ask children to trace the melody contour in the air, moving their hand from left to right for each phrase. Then have them follow the notation and sing with the recording.

4. Select children to practice countermelody 1 on bells or other keyboard instruments to play as others sing the song. Questions: Which staff of the countermelody uses tones that move mostly downward? (Staff 1) Mostly upward? (Staff 2) On which tone does the countermelody begin and end? (High C) Point out: Staff 1 uses only dotted half notes (♩.). Each one lasts as long as three quarter notes, or three beats. Staff 2 uses dotted half notes as well as half notes and quarter notes.

TRY THIS
1. Help children analyze countermelody 2 on p. 55. Then select individuals to practice it to accompany the song. Note: Countermelody 2 begins on A, a third lower than countermelody 1. In both countermelodies, the tones move in the same general direction and have the same rhythm.

2. Write countermelody 3 on the chalkboard for children who play recorder to play while others sing "Clouds." Note: Children will play the tones G, A, B. To help them play the rhythm ♩ ♩ ♩ ♩ correctly, have them think the words *White sheep, white sheep* as they occur in the song.

Countermelody 3

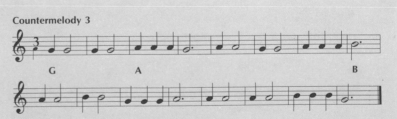

G   A   B

3. Put it all together. Choose a small ensemble to play countermelodies 1, 2, and 3 together to accompany the song. Suggestion: Add the tone color of a triangle by having a child play on the first beat of each measure, letting the sound ring for beats 2 and 3.

MATERIALS
Record 3, "Louis Moved Away";
Cowell: *Advertisement;* Pupil's Book,
pp. 56 and 57; bells or other keyboard instruments

VOCABULARY
upward, downward, contour, tied
notes

IDEAS FOR TEACHING

1. (Note: Children have sung, played,
and analyzed parts of songs that
move in an upward direction, in a
downward direction, and both upward and downward. Now they are
ready to follow the contour [shape]
of a complete melody.) Play the recording of "Louis Moved Away" and
have children follow the notation on
pp. 56 and 57. As they listen, have
them focus on the direction of the
phrases. Note: In the music, there
are many pairs of tied notes (♩♩).
Notes joined by a tie represent only
one sound: the first note is sung or
played, and the sound is held instead of repeated for the second
note. Questions: Which phrases
move mostly downward? (Phrases 1,
2, 3, 5, 6, 7) Which ones move
mostly upward? (4, 8, 9, 10)

2. Write the following bell part on
the chalkboard. When children know
the song, have them take turns playing the bell part to fill in the silence
after phrase 4. Have children compare the direction of the bell part
(upward) with that of the song
phrase that precedes it (phrase 4,
mostly upward) and the song phrase
that follows it (phrase 5, mostly
downward).

Follow the direction of the melody as you sing.

Which phrases move mostly downward?   1–3, 5–7

Mostly upward?   4, 8–10

LOUIS MOVED AWAY   MUSIC BY JIM HUNTER   WORDS BY TOM PAISLEY

Piano acc., p. 290

Lou - is___ moved___ a - way to - day;___

Lou - is___ was___ my___ friend.___

Him and___ me___ would al - ways___ play,___

He al - ways had some bread to___ spend.___   *(bell part)*

56 Direction

TRY THIS

1. Have children create a piano accompaniment for *Poem.*

POEM
I loved my friend.
He went away from me.
There's nothing more to say.
The poem ends,
Soft as it began—
I loved my friend.
                —Langston Hughes

As *Poem* is read, a child softly plays the black keys in order—from lowest to highest, or from highest to low-est—while keeping the sustaining pedal (right pedal) de-pressed. At the same time, another child plays a triangle or finger cymbals each time a period occurs in the reading (after *friend, me, say, friend*). Note: When children play the black keys in order, they are playing a pentatonic scale. Some children may be able to play a combination of black and white keys in the pattern of a whole-tone scale upward or downward on the piano as follows: ⟶

His dad - dy makes good____ pay;____

That's what they all____ say.____

And now I'll nev - er have a____ friend,____

'Cause Lou - is moved a - way.____

'Cause Lou - is moved a - way.____

'Cause Lou - is moved a - way.____

Play the last three phrases on bells or piano. They start on low A.

In which direction will you play?   Upward

Find phrases that move mostly upward or mostly downward in these songs.

"Hand Me Down," page 14

"Sourwood Mountain," page 16

"The Wise Man Built His House," page 21

Direction 57

3. As others sing, have children take turns playing the last three phrases on bells. Note: Children will need the low A, B, C♯, and D bells. If low A and B are not included in the set of bells, children may use the piano or they may play the phrases an octave higher. Silently thinking the words *'Cause Louis moved away* will help them play the rhythm correctly.

REVIEW/REINFORCEMENT
Have children determine the contour of other melodies they know; for example:
- Hand Me Down, p. 14
- Sourwood Mountain, p. 16
- The Wise Man Built His House, p. 21

TEACHER INFORMATION
Being aware of similarities and differences in song notation aids music reading. Help children observe the following about "Louis Moved Away."
(a) Only one phrase (phrase 6) moves from beginning to end without repeating tones or changing direction.
(b) Some phrases (1, 3, 4, 5, 7), have a leap or leaps that move in a different direction than the other tones.
(c) In phrase 2, the direction changes at the end.
(d) In phrases 8–10 there are repeated tones within the upward movement.
Point out: Changing direction or repeating tones within a phrase helps to give variety to music.

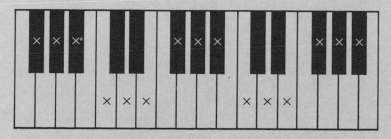

2. Play the recording of Cowell's *Advertisement.* Ask children to listen for places where the piano plays downward almost the entire length of the keyboard. Point out: In this

music, the piano plays clusters (groups of tones that are close together) rather than one tone at a time.

TEACHER INFORMATION
Henry Cowell (American, 1897–1965) *Advertisement:* This composer was an active leader in the cause of new music. His own pieces often used nontraditional techniques of piano playing—strumming the strings, pressing the keys with the forearm, and playing clusters (masses of sound) instead of chords.

MATERIALS

Record 3, "When the Saints Go Marching In"; Pupil's Book, p. 58; percussion instruments, recorders or bells

VOCABULARY

upward, downward, tied notes, dotted half notes

IDEAS FOR TEACHING

1. Play the recording and have children listen for the long sounds in the music. Then have individuals play a percussion instrument during each long sound. They may play a steady beat or a rhythm pattern of their own, or they may echo the rhythm that immediately precedes the long sound.

2. Repeat item 1 above, having some children play as others sing (notation, p. 58). <u>Point out:</u> The long sounds occur on the tied notes.

3. Direct attention to the contour of the melody. <u>Questions:</u> Do most phrases begin with tones that move upward, or downward? (Upward; phrases 1, 2, and 4 all begin upward.) Which phrase beginning has tones that move mostly downward? (Phrase 3; after a repeated tone, the melody moves downward.)

4. Some children can play the recorder part as others sing. <u>Point out:</u> The dotted half note (♩.) in staffs 2 and 3 receives three beats. <u>Note:</u> (a) The recorder part uses the tones G, A, B, and fills in some of the long sounds in the song. (b) Lyrics are included as cues to the players. (c) The part may also be played on bells.

WHEN THE SAINTS GO MARCHING IN BLACK SPIRITUAL

Piano acc., p. 323

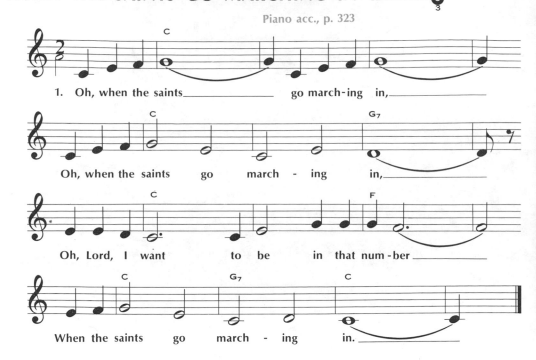

2. Oh, when the stars refuse to shine, . . .

3. Oh, when I hear that trumpet sound, . . .

Play the recorder as others sing.

Recorder or Bells

HARVEST TIME
WORDS AND MUSIC BY GRACE C. NASH

FROM MUSIC WITH CHILDREN, JUNIOR CHOIR WITH ORFF INSTRUMENTS BY MURRAY McNAIR AND GRACE C. NASH, BY SPECIAL PERMISSION OF GRACE C. NASH.

Har - vest is the sea - son to be - hold.

Har - vest with its col - ors brown and gold.

Crops are in and sum - mer work is done.

Air is crisp and snow is soon to come.

Har - vest is the sea - son to be - hold.

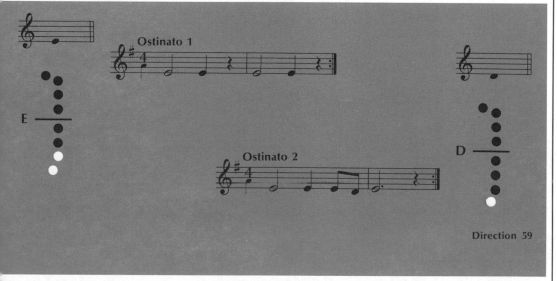

Ostinato 1

Ostinato 2

Direction 59

E

D

DIRECTION • Lesson 7

MATERIALS
Record 3, "Harvest Time"; Pupil's Book, p. 59; low drum or tom-tom, recorders or bells

VOCABULARY
accented beat, contour, ostinato

IDEAS FOR TEACHING

1. Play the recording and have children take turns playing an accompaniment on a low drum or tom-tom, using the pattern at the top of p. 59. Point out: The first beat in each measure is accented.

2. As some children continue to play a drum accompaniment, invite the class to join in singing "Harvest Time" with the recording. Question: Which phrases have the same melody shape or contour? (Phrases 1, 2, and 5; phrases 3 and 4)

3. Have a group of children choose phrase 1 or phrase 3 to sing over and over as an ostinato while others sing the song. Note: Since "Harvest Time" is a round, all the phrases fit together. Any of the phrases can be sung as an ostinato throughout the song.

4. Give children who play recorder time to practice two new tones—D and E (fingerings, p. 59). When they are ready, have them play ostinato 1 or ostinato 2 over and over as others sing "Harvest Time." Suggestion: The "Harvest Time" melody contains all the tones children have learned to play—D, E, G, A, B. Some children may be able to play the entire song. Encourage them to perform as much of the song as they can play well.

TRY THIS

1. Have children sing "Harvest Time" as a two-part round.

2. Have children combine recorders and voices to perform "Harvest Time" as a round. Recorders begin playing the entire song. Singers begin when the recorders reach the second measure.

3. Play an ear-training game. Using only D, E, G, A, and B, a recorder player plays groups of tones that move upward (D-E-G, E-G-B, etc.), or downward (B-A-G-E-D, A-G-E, etc.), or repeat (E-E-E, A-A-A, etc.). Others identify the direction of each group of tones.

TEACHER INFORMATION
Observing how the tones of a song move is an aid to music reading. Help children discover the following about "Harvest Time."
(a) Phrases 1, 2, and 5 begin with an upward leap; then, after repeated tones, they move downward, stepping upward at the end. The direction is mostly downward.
(b) While there is movement downward and upward in phrases 3 and 4, these phrases consist largely of repeated tones.

MATERIALS
Record 3, "I Love the Mountains";
Pupil's Book, p. 60; bells

VOCABULARY
ostinato, repeat sign, coda

IDEAS FOR TEACHING
1. Play the recording and have children listen for the ostinato that occurs throughout the song.

2. Have children follow the notation at the top of p. 60 and sing the ostinato with the recording. Point out: The ostinato melody ends with tones that move upward.

3. Have a small group sing the ostinato while others sing the song. Point out: The repeat sign at the end of staff 5 indicates that the song is sung again from the beginning. The coda is sung only at the very end.

4. Line up the bells F, G, A, B♭, high C, high D, and have individuals play them as follows while others sing the song. Note: Children play the bells only during measures 1 through 6 of the song. They play on the first beat of each measure, letting the sound last for four beats. Question: In which direction does the bell part move? (Upward)

F   G   A   B♭   C   D

5. Have children sing the song as a three-part round. To end, parts 1 and 2 keep repeating the last two *Boom-dee-ah-da* measures until part 3 catches up with them. Then all parts sing the coda together.

Sing this part throughout the song.

Boom, boom, boom, boom-dee-ah - da

I LOVE THE MOUNTAINS   TRADITIONAL

I   love   the   moun - tains,   I   love   the   roll - ing   hills,

I   love   the   flow - ers,   I   love   the   daf - fo - dils,

I   love   the   fire - side   When   all   the   lights   are   low,

Boom - dee - ah - da, boom-dee-ah - da, Boom-dee - ah - da, boom-dee - ah - da,

Boom-dee-ah - da, boom-dee-ah - da, Boom-dee - ah - da, boom-dee - ah - da.

CODA

Boom   did - dle - dee - dum - dum,   Boom,   boom.

TRY THIS
1. Line up the bells E, F, G, A, B♭, high C. As children sing the song, have individuals play the following bell part. Call attention to the downward movement of the tones at the beginning of the part.

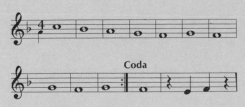

Coda

2. Have children play the following Autoharp part to accompany the song. Point out: The chord pattern between repeat signs is played over and over until the coda. Suggestion: Encourage children to experiment to find a fingering that feels right for them (one possibility: F, index finger; D min., middle finger; G min., ring finger; C₇, middle finger). If necessary, two children can perform the Autoharp part—one depressing the chord buttons while the other strums.

Coda
F   D min.   G min.   C₇   F   C₇   F

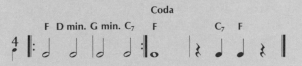

SOUND PIECE 2: Contours at the Keyboard

DAVID S. WALKER

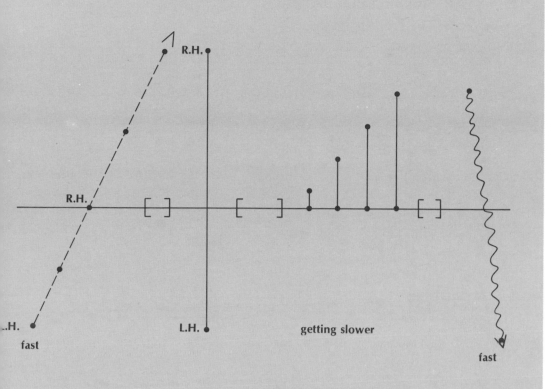

Here is the contour of the first phrase of a patriotic song.

Can you guess what it is? *"The Star-Spangled Banner"*

For the answer, turn the page.

Direction 61

DIRECTION · Lesson 9

MATERIALS
Pupil's Book, p. 61; any keyboard instrument

VOCABULARY
score, contour

IDEAS FOR TEACHING
1. Before children try to perform *Sound Piece 2,* be certain to explain each symbol in the score on p. 61 (see Sound Piece Symbols below).

2. Divide the class into small groups and give them time to work out an interpretation for the Sound Piece. Then have each group choose a member to perform the piece for the class. Have the class follow the score as each player performs. <u>Suggestions:</u> (a) In addition to tempo and direction, encourage groups to consider these musical qualities in their interpretation: *Duration*—Will the tones played together be short sounds or long sounds? How long or short will the silences be? *Dynamics*—Will all tones be loud? Soft? Will some tones be loud, others soft? (b) Encourage discussion of how successfully each group interpreted the Sound Piece. Ask questions like the following: "Did you hear what you saw in the score?" "Did the performer follow the tempo markings?" If possible, record each performance so that it can be replayed as needed during the discussion.

SOUND PIECE SYMBOLS

 The horizontal line represents any tone in the middle register of the keyboard.

 Play in an upward direction, using the chosen tone and any two tones below and above it.

[ ] Silence

 Play two tones together.

 Play from a high tone to a low one by sliding the hand (mallet) across the keys (bars).

TRY THIS
1. Children can create their own sound pieces to illustrate direction in music. Have them notate their pieces so that others can perform them. They may use the notation symbols in Sound Piece 2 or invent new ones.

2. Have children look at the contour line on p. 61, noticing the downward and upward movement, and that some dots are far apart, indicating leaps in the melody, while others are close together, indicating steps. Help children use these direction clues to discover that this is the contour of the first phrase of "The Star-Spangled Banner."

DIRECTION • Lesson 10

MATERIALS
Record 3, "The Star-Spangled Banner"; Pupil's Book, pp. 62, 61

VOCABULARY
phrase, fermata, contour

IDEAS FOR TEACHING

1. (Note: In addition to its functional use, this patriotic song is included for a musical reason. An adaptation for it appears in *Silver Burdett Music for Special Education*.) When children sing "The Star-Spangled Banner," direct their attention to the notation on p. 62. Each staff represents a phrase of the music. Questions: Which phrases have the same contour as the line on p. 61? (Phrases 1 and 3) Which phrase has the same contour as phrase 2? (4) In which phrase is there a fermata, where the beat stops and holds? (7)

2. Play an ear-training game. Sing or play any phrase of other patriotic songs children know. Have them indicate the direction of the melody by outlining its contour in the air with their hand, or by drawing a contour line on the chalkboard. Note: It is sufficient for children to show the general direction of the melody. They do not have to graph every note; for example:

Yankee Doodle

Fath'r and I went down to camp,

Contour line: ⌇

3. Share the historical material presented in Teacher Information (see below) with the class.

Follow the contour as you sing this melody.

THE STAR-SPANGLED BANNER

MUSIC BY JOHN STAFFORD SMITH   WORDS BY FRANCIS SCOTT KEY

Piano acc., p. 315

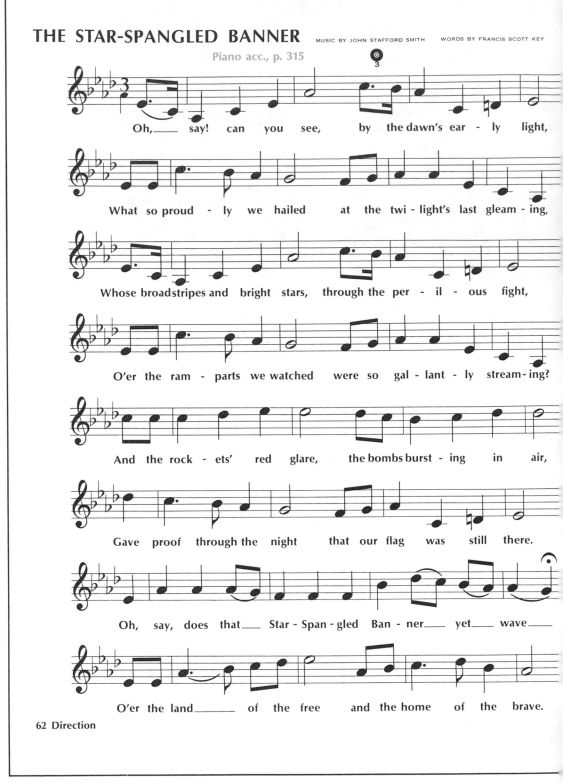

62 Direction

CALL CHART 3: DIRECTION ⊚₃

Trace the upward and downward arrows with your finger each time
you hear section A. The arrows show how the violin swoops
upward and downward.

Paganini: *Caprice No. 5 in A Minor,* Op. 1

---

1. *SECTION A (UPWARD THEN DOWNWARD)*

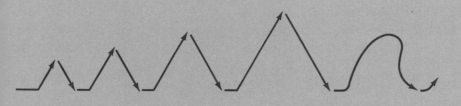

---

2. *SECTION B (BOTH UPWARD AND DOWNWARD)*

---

3. *SECTION A REPEATS.*

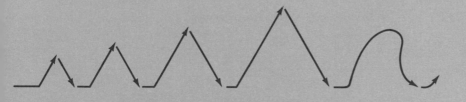

Direction 63

DIRECTION · Lesson 11

MATERIALS
Record 3, *Call Chart 3: Direction;* Pupil's Book, p. 63

VOCABULARY
upward, downward

IDEAS FOR TEACHING
1. Give children time to observe the chart on p. 63. Call attention to the symbols that show the direction of the music in each section. Point out: The arrows for section A show that the upward and downward movement changes throughout the section—e.g., in the first four sets of arrows the tones move upward to a higher pitch each time. The wavy line for section B shows that the upward and downward movement is relatively limited throughout the section.

2. Play the recording. As children listen, they use their finger to trace the symbols in the chart. When they hear the first call number, they trace the arrows for section A, tracing upward when the music moves upward, downward when the music moves downward. They trace the appropriate symbols when the remaining numbers are called. Suggestions: (a) Give children an opportunity to listen to the music before they try to trace the symbols with the recording. (b) You might draw the symbols on the chalkboard, having children take turns tracing them as the music plays. Mainstreaming Suggestion: Provide a kinesthetic aid for children with hearing, sight, or motor impairment by having classmates gently guide their finger along the symbols in the chart.

TEACHER INFORMATION
Call Charts are instructional materials that direct children's attention to specific qualities in music. *Call Chart 3* uses music from Niccolo Paganini's *Caprice No. 5 in A Minor* to focus on the quality of direction.

Niccolo Paganini (Italian, 1782–1840) *Caprice No. 5 in A Minor,* Op. 1: This violinist and composer was a child prodigy. His ability on the violin was unsurpassed: he executed passages that were considered impossible to play, playing with charm and brilliance. Paganini's astonishing violin playing introduced an age of virtuosity in instrumental performance.

DIRECTION • Lesson 12

MATERIALS
Record 3, "Go, Tell It on the Mountain"; Pupil's Book, p. 64

VOCABULARY
phrase, countermelody, fermata

IDEAS FOR TEACHING

1. Play the recording and have children listen for the direction of the melody (mostly downward) each time the words say *Go, tell it on the mountain.*

2. Invite children to sing with the recording (notation, p. 64). At first, have them omit the countermelody in section B. When they are ready, assign a small group to sing the countermelody. Point out: (a) The music of section B is performed in rhythm; it has a steady beat. In section A, the beat stops and holds at each half note and dotted half note, even though there are no fermatas (⌢) until the end of the section. Tell children that the direction "Freely" at the beginning of section A allows the singer to "stop and hold" whenever it feels right for the music.
(b) On the recording, an accompaniment is provided by men's voices singing in harmony, as well as by instruments.

3. Choose a different solo singer to perform each verse of section A; everyone sings section B. Suggestion: Try this activity without the recording so that each singer can interpret section A in his or her own way.

How does the melody move when you sing the words *Go, tell it on the mountain?* Mostly downward

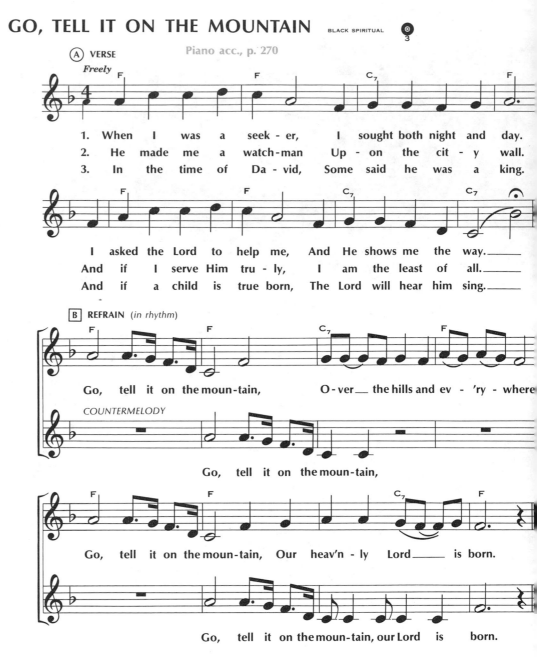

64 Direction

TRY THIS
1. Have children take turns playing an accompaniment on the Autoharp as everyone sings. Note: The chords are indicated above each staff on p. 64.

2. Have children add a rhythm accompaniment during section B by alternately stamping and clapping—stamp, clap, stamp, clap—in time with the steady beat.

TEACHER INFORMATION
As an aid to music reading, help children observe the following about "Go, Tell It on the Mountain."
(a) In section A, the first phrase (*When I was a seeker*) and third phrase (*I asked the Lord to help me*) are almost identical. Although tones are repeated within the phrases, the general direction is both upward and downward.
(b) In section B, the phrase *Go, tell it on the mountain* has tones that move upward on the word *mountain* in the melody (top staff) and repeated tones on *mountain* in the countermelody. In both melody and countermelody the phrase begins with repeated tones.

WHAT DO YOU HEAR? 4: DIRECTION

Listen to these pieces. Choose the answer that describes
the direction in which the melody is mostly moving.

---

1. UPWARD (DOWNWARD) BOTH UPWARD
AND DOWNWARD

Beethoven: **Symphony No. 1**, Movement 1

---

2. UPWARD DOWNWARD (BOTH UPWARD
AND DOWNWARD)

The Star-Spangled Banner

---

3. UPWARD (DOWNWARD) BOTH UPWARD
AND DOWNWARD

Poulenc: **Mouvement Perpétuel No. 1**

---

4. UPWARD (DOWNWARD) BOTH UPWARD
AND DOWNWARD

Cowell: **Advertisement**

---

5. (UPWARD) DOWNWARD BOTH UPWARD
AND DOWNWARD

Mussorgsky: **Pictures at an Exhibition:** "The Little
Hut on Chicken's Legs"

---

6. UPWARD DOWNWARD (BOTH UPWARD
AND DOWNWARD)

Paganini: **Caprice No. 5 in A Minor**

Were you able to hear the difference in direction?

If you can *hear* the difference, you can *feel* the difference.

Direction 65

DIRECTION • Lesson 13

MATERIALS
Record 3, *What Do You Hear? 4: Direction;* spirit master

VOCABULARY
upward, downward, both upward and downward

TEACHER INFORMATION
The last part of many of the modules in this book will be a What Do You Hear? evaluation. This kind of activity requires the children to demonstrate what they have learned by responding to the instructions on the recording. It also gives the children and the teacher a concrete assessment of progress toward increased musical perception.

The What Do You Hear? evaluations can be done with a large group in a classroom situation or with a small group using earphones. Spirit masters are available so that each child can respond individually.

Sometimes it may be feasible to write the items on the chalkboard so that the group can answer the questions together. Children can take turns circling the correct answers.

MODULE 4

OBJECTIVES, p. XI

STYLE: Classic—Expressionistic

MATERIALS
Record 3, *Crossing*; *Slowly*; Mozart: *Cassation in B♭ Major*, "Menuetto No. 1"; Schoenberg: *Five Pieces for Orchestra*, No. 1; Pupil's Book, pp. 66 and 67

VOCABULARY
style differences

IDEAS FOR TEACHING
1. Have children examine the poems on pp. 66 and 67. Call attention to the way each one looks. Question: What makes the poems look so different? Note: Each poem has its own special look. In *Crossing*, (a) each line of a stanza is indented from the line before it; (b) there is a variety of type style and size; (c) there are seven stanzas of different lengths, the longest (stanza 1) having eleven lines, the shortest (3), two lines. In *Slowly*, (a) the lines are all printed flush left; (b) the words are all printed in the same type style and size; (c) there are two stanzas, both the same length (four lines).

2. Point out that the poems not only look as if they are in different styles, they sound different, too. Play the recording of each poem. Question: What makes the poems sound so different?
Note: *Crossing* keeps changing from loud to soft, from slower to faster. The excitement builds to the very last word. *Slowly* has an even sound: the pace is slow and the dynamic →

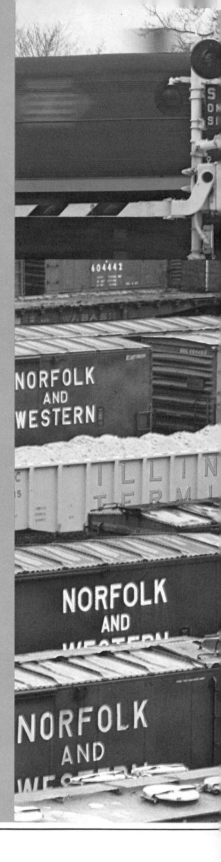

STYLE

Do the poems on these pages look as if they are in the same style, or in different styles? Different styles

CROSSING

STOP   LOOK   LISTEN
　as gate stripes swing down,
　　count the cars hauling distance
　　upgrade through town:
　　　warning whistle, bellclang,
　　　engine eating steam,
　　　engineer waving,
　　　　a fast-freight dream:
　　　　B&M boxcar,
　　　　　boxcar again,　　　　FIFTY-NINE, SIXTY,
　　　　　Frisco gondola,　　　　hoppers of coke,
EIGHT-NINE-TEN,　　　　Anaconda copper,
　Erie and Wabash,　　　hotbox smoke,
　Seaboard, U.P.,　　　EIGHTY-EIGHT,
　Pennsy tankcar,　　　red-ball freight,
TWENTY-TWO, THREE,　Rio Grande,
　Phoebe Snow, B&O,　　Nickel Plate,
THIRTY-FOUR, FIVE,　　Hiawatha,
　Santa Fe cattle　　　Lackawanna,
　shipped alive,　　　rolling fast
　　red cars, yellow cars,　　and loose,
　　orange cars, black,　　NINETY-SEVEN,
　　Youngstown steel　　coal car,
　　down to Mobile　　boxcar,
　　　on Rock Island track,　CABOOSE!

66 MODULE 4: Style　　　　　　　　*Philip Booth*

TEACHER INFORMATION
Wolfgang Amadeus Mozart (Austrian, 1756–1791) *Cassation in B♭ Major*, "Menuetto No. 1": Starting his career as a composer at age 4, Mozart created enduring masterworks in his short life of thirty-five years. His music is the height of "classic" in its balance of musical form and deep yet restrained expression. His works range from small pieces for entertainments to grand works of opera and symphony.

Arnold Schoenberg (Austrian, 1874–1951) *Five Pieces for Orchestra*, No. 1: Schoenberg experimented with new organizations of pitches. He invented a system in which the traditional functions of the twelve scale tones were no longer followed, each of the twelve now being treated as equal in importance. Such music (*atonal* or *serial* because the twelve tones were used in carefully planned series) has had an enormous influence on composers since that time, changing the course of music history in a fundamental way.

SLOWLY

Slowly the tide creeps up the sand,

Slowly the shadows cross the land.

Slowly the cart-horse pulls his mile,

Slowly the old man mounts the stile.

Slowly the hands move round the clock,

Slowly the dew dries on the dock.

Slow is the snail—but slowest of all

The green moss spreads on the old brick wall.

James Reeves

Poems can be in different styles. Music can be in different styles, too.

Listen to these pieces to discover the differences between them—

the things that tell you they are in different styles.

 Mozart: *Cassation in B♭*, Menuetto No. 1

 Schoenberg: *Five Pieces for Orchestra*, No. 1

How many things can you hear that make the style of one piece

different from that of the other?

There are different ways of planning poems and music to create

different styles. Each style has its own special way of feeling.

Listen to hear what makes

the poems different in style.

Crossing   Slowly

Style 67

---

level remains the same throughout. It is more peaceful than the energetic, driving *Crossing*.

3. Have children try reading the poems aloud, switching the styles (i.e., reading *Crossing* in a slow, quiet style, and *Slowly* in a fast, excited style). Discuss the result. Point out: Each poem seems to *want* its proper style. The poems were created to be read in a style appropriate to their images and tone of feeling; they sound strained and out of kilter when read in the wrong style.

4. Play the recording of the Mozart and Schoenberg selections. Question: Are these pieces in the same style, with the same general sound, or are they in different styles, with many things different about them? Note: The pieces represent two very different styles. The Mozart work comes from the musical style period called "Classic" (about 1750 to 1820), and exemplifies the classic sound: (a) The phrases are all the same length. (b) There is a strong pull to a tonal center. (c) The beat is steady. (d) The dynamic level is moderate throughout. The Schoenberg piece represents the music of the early twentieth century (about 1912 to 1930), when the style called "Expressionistic" was developed. It has the following characteristics: (a) The phrases are of varied lengths. (b) The music is atonal (no pull to a tonal center). (c) The beat is not steady. (d) There are sudden changes in dynamics.

REVIEW/REINFORCEMENT

Two general painting or visual styles are "representational" (i.e., having recognizable objects or people) and "nonrepresentational" (i.e., having no recognizable "picture" of anything). Examples in Book 4 that children can identify as being one style or the other include the following. Representational: *Early Sunday Morning*, pp. 156 and 157; *The Sargent Family*, p. 131; *Swimmers and Sunbathers*, pp. 82 and 83. Nonrepresentational: *Battle of Lights*, p. 36; *Dusk*, p. 83; *Tondo*, p. 239

TRY THIS

1. Spend some time on the general idea of "style" in our world and in our lives. Discussions, demonstrations, and other activities can be easily planned to illustrate style in the following dimensions of the children's experience: (a) Dress (formal, casual, old-fashioned, etc.); (b) Food (ethnic—e.g., Italian, Chinese; regional—e.g., Southern); (c) Automobiles (classic, sport, luxury, etc.). Encourage other explorations according to children's interests. Invite "show and tell" guest speakers whenever possible.

2. Have children find other poems with different "looks" and moods to read aloud in an appropriate style.

MODULE 5

OBJECTIVES, p. XI

METER • Lesson 1

MATERIALS
Pupil's Book, pp. 68 and 69, 8; percussion instruments, other sound sources

VOCABULARY
steady beat, meter in 2, meter in 3, meter in 4, strong beat

IDEAS FOR TEACHING

1. Review the hand jive on p. 8. Have children perform each motion two times (meter in 2), then three times (meter in 3). Finally, have them experience meter in 4 by performing each motion four times. Point out: Each hand-jive motion represents one beat. Changing the motions at even intervals (i.e., performing each one twice or three times or four times) separates the beats into groups or sets.

2. Have children take turns playing steady beats in sets of two, three, or four on a percussion instrument for others to identify the meter:

Meter in 2: ♩♩│♩♩│ etc.

Meter in 3: ♩♩♩│♩♩♩│ etc.

Meter in 4: ♩♩♩♩│♩♩♩♩│ etc.

Note: Remind players to stress the first beat (strong beat) of each set. Stressing the strong beat separates steady beats into groups or sets.

METER

68 MODULE 5: Meter

Meter 69

3. Play a meter game. A group of children sit in a circle. Each child has a sound source—e.g., a percussion instrument, a book to tap with a pencil, a pair of mittens to wear while clapping hands. One child, the leader, plays steady beats in sets of two, three, or four, stressing the first beat of each set. After the leader plays four sets of beats, the child to the left immediately plays one set in the same meter. Each child in turn plays one set of beats. The beat remains steady throughout the game, passing from child to child without pause. The game ends when the beat returns to the leader. <u>Suggestions:</u> (a) Play the game several times, with a different leader each time. (b) Extend the game by having the beat pass around the circle several times. Each time it is the leader's turn, he or she plays four sets of beats, either in the meter originally established, or in a different meter. If the leader changes the meter, everyone else in turn must play the new meter.

4. Call attention to the pictures on pp. 68 and 69. The ones in the top row show meter in 2; those in the bottom row show meter in 3. In each row, the "standing" child represents the strong beat. <u>Suggestion:</u> Have children follow the pictures to clap beats in two meter and in three meter. Remind them to stress each strong beat. Challenge them to change from one meter to the other without missing a beat.

5. Have children make up their own visuals to represent meter in 2, meter in 3, and meter in 4. They may use illustrations from magazines, photographs, or drawings (e.g., pictures of cars, shoes, chairs, etc., displayed in sets of two, three, or four).

REVIEW/REINFORCEMENT
Have children review the chant "I Was Born in a Frying Pan" (see Try This, Teacher's Edition p. 9).

TRY THIS
Thirteen children, each with a percussion instrument or other sound source, sit in a circle. One of them, the leader, plays four sets of beats in two, three, or four meter. Beginning with the child to the leader's left, each child in turn then plays one beat in the same meter. The meter determines whether the beat will be played with a stress or not. Each time the beat returns to the leader, he or she plays four sets of beats in a different meter. The activity is then repeated around the circle in the new meter. <u>Suggestions:</u> (a) Since it is difficult for children to maintain a steady beat when they are each playing only one sound, choose someone to keep the steady beat on a percussion instrument. (b) When children are comfortable with the game, they may vary it by moving the beats around the circle in the opposite direction each time the leader changes the meter, or by changing the tempo each time the meter changes.

METER • Lesson 2

MATERIALS
Record 3, "Sasa Aberewa"; Pupil's Book, pp. 70 and 71; kalimba or wooden xylophone

VOCABULARY
meter in 2, measure, bar line

IDEAS FOR TEACHING
1. Play the recording as children follow the notation on p. 70. Have them join in the singing when they can. Note: The four-measure chant is sung six times on the recording. Except for one tone, the melody of measures 3 and 4 is the same as that of measures 1 and 2. A phonetic pronunciation for the lyrics is provided in parentheses.

2. (a) Have children stand facing a partner. They stretch hands out in front, left palm facing up, right palm facing down. Each child's right hand is positioned above the partner's left. As they sing with the recording, children keep the beat by alternately hitting their partner's left palm with their right hand (top left picture, p. 70), and clapping (middle left picture). Question: Are the beats grouped in sets of two, or in sets of three? (In sets of two)
(b) As they sing with the recording, have children keep the beat another way. For the first beat of each set (measure), they hit their partner's left palm (top left picture, p. 70). For the second beat, they turn hands so that the right palm is facing up, the left palm down, and hit their partner's right palm (bottom left picture).

3. Have partners play the game on p. 71 as they sing "Sasa Aberewa." For measures 1 and 2, they alter- →

Are the beats in this singing game grouped in sets of two, or in sets of three? Sets of two

SASA ABEREWA SINGING GAME FROM AFRICA

FROM AFRICAN SONGS AND GAMES FOR CHILDREN COMPILED AND TRANSCRIBED BY KOJO FOSU BAIDEN AND GERALDINE SLAUGHTER. © 1970, KOJO FOSU BAIDEN AND GERALDINE SLAUGHTER.

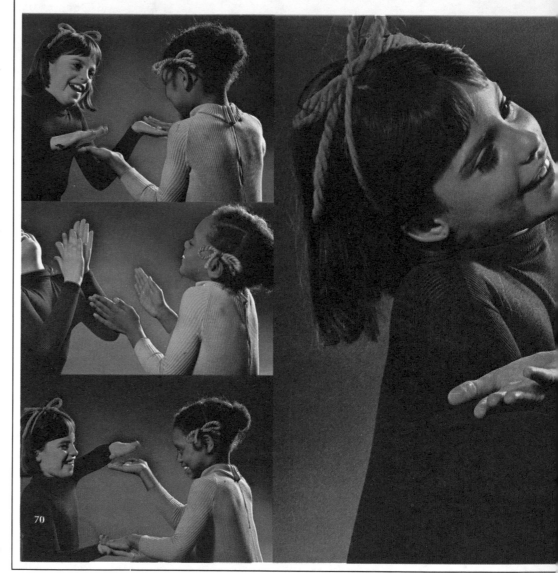

Sa   s'a bere wa   o de hyee, Sa   s'a bere wa   o de hyee
(Sah   sah bray wah   hoh dee shee, Sah   sah bray wah   hoh dee shee

70

TEACHER INFORMATION
"Sasa Aberewa" is traditionally performed by girls. Kalimba and handclapping usually accompany the chant, as they do on the recording. The kalimba is an African instrument that is also known as a sanza, mbira, or "thumb piano."

REVIEW/REINFORCEMENT
Have children play the game for "Hand Game Song" (item 4, Teacher's Edition p. 7). Call attention to the left-right motion of the stick pattern that helps them feel the beats grouped in sets of two.

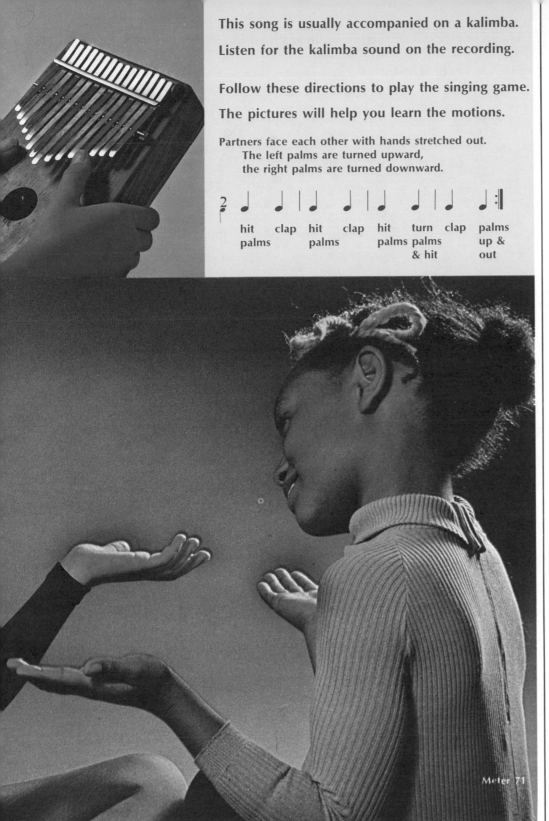

This song is usually accompanied on a kalimba.

Listen for the kalimba sound on the recording.

Follow these directions to play the singing game.

The pictures will help you learn the motions.

Partners face each other with hands stretched out.
The left palms are turned upward,
the right palms are turned downward.

| hit palms | clap | hit palms | clap | hit palms | turn palms & hit | clap | palms up & out |

Meter 71

nately hit and clap as in item 2a (Teacher's Edition p. 70); for measure 3, they hit, then turn palms and hit again as in item 2b. For measure 4, they clap on the first beat, then stretch out hands, palms facing up, on the second beat (large picture). Mainstreaming Note: Encourage children with deficient motor skills to respond to the meter in their own way—by clapping, foot tapping, etc. Point out: The quarter notes in the game directions stand for the beats in "Sasa Aberewa." Vertical lines called bar lines are used to separate the beats into sets or measures. Suggestion: When children are comfortable with the game, have them form a double circle of partners, one partner facing the center of the circle, the other with back to the center. As they sing and play the game, they move the circle clockwise or counterclockwise by performing a step-close pattern, stepping to the side with one foot on beat 1, and bringing the other foot next to it on beat 2.

4. Some children may be able to play a kalimba as others sing "Sasa Aberewa." They may play the entire melody by ear, starting on F and using the tones D, E, F, G, or they may play only the part that uses F and E:

Note: The top picture on p. 71 shows how to hold a kalimba. To play a tone, the child depresses one of the metal bars with the thumb, then slides the thumb off the front edge, causing the bar to vibrate.

TRY THIS.
Make a wooden version of a kalimba as follows (directions from Silver Burdett's *Pipeline*, Vol. 3, No. 2).

Materials: a piece of sanded board about 4" x 6"; two pieces of board about 4" x 1"; two screws; five (or more) metal or bamboo strips of different lengths (for tongues)

Directions: Bore two holes in each board (see following diagrams). Insert tongues between the two narrow pieces of board, the longest in the center, the shortest on the outsides. Tongues can be tuned by loosening the screws and lengthening or shortening the vibrating length. Note: This

instrument will not duplicate the tone color of the kalimba. However, as children make each tongue vibrate, they will learn how the kalimba sound is produced.

METER • Lesson 3

MATERIALS

Record 3, "Find the Ring"; Pupil's Book, pp. 72 and 73; 70 and 71; any percussion instrument, tambourine, recorders or bells; ring

VOCABULARY

meter signature, measure, meter in 3, meter in 2

IDEAS FOR TEACHING

1. Have children hold their left hand out in front of them. As someone plays a steady beat on a percussion instrument, children use their right hand to "touch the air" to their left three times, then touch their left hand three times, then "touch the air" to their right three times, and finally touch their left hand again three times. Have them repeat the entire pattern several times. Question: Are the motions grouped in sets of two, or in sets of three? (In sets of three)

2. Play the recording and have children keep the beat by performing the pattern of hand motions throughout the song. Question: Are the beats in this song grouped in sets of two, or in sets of three? (In sets of three) Suggestion: Take time to review the "Sasa Aberewa" clapping game (pp. 70 and 71) so that children can feel the difference between meter in 2 and meter in 3.

3. When children know the song (notation, p. 72), have one group sing with the recording while another group plays the Ring Game (see below for directions).

4. (a) Call attention to the meter signature in the song notation (³₄). →

Are the beats in this singing game grouped in sets of two, or in sets of three?

Sets of three

FIND THE RING

FOLK SONG FROM GREECE   ENGLISH WORDS BY MARIA JORDAN

Piano acc., p. 266

(optional harmony part)

1. Find the ring, the ring that keeps mov-ing,
2. Find the ring, the ring that keeps mov-ing,

Find the ring, oh, where did it go?
Find the ring of sil-ver or gold.

The se-cret ring's in some-bod-y's hand, Some-
Pass it to me, I'll pass it to you, We

bod-y you know, come guess if you can!
must-n't get caught, what-ev-er we do!

Don't say a word if you are the one, Don't

give it a-way and spoil all the fun!

Play one of these patterns on a tambourine as others sing.

72 Meter

RING GAME

Children form a circle, all facing the center where one child, the leader, stands. They hold their left hand out in front, palm up and slightly cupped. One child holds a ring hidden in his or her right hand. As the song is sung, children keep the beat by using their right hand to (a) touch the left hand of the child on their left three times; (b) touch their own left hand three times; (c) touch the left hand of the child on their right three times; (d) touch their own left hand three times. As children perform the pattern of motions over and over, they pass the ring from hand to hand, trying to conceal its whereabouts from the leader. When the music ends, the leader tries to guess who has the ring. If the guess is correct, the leader changes places with the one holding the ring. If the guess is incorrect, the leader is out of the game, and the child with the ring becomes the new leader. Note: (a) To move the ring around the circle, children pass it to the person on their left during the first set of motions in the pattern. Whoever receives the ring holds onto it during the rest of the motions. The ring is passed once for each pattern of four motions. (b) The pictures on p. 73 show the motions for the game. (c) Before each repetition of the game, the teacher secretly gives the ring to one of the players.

Play a game with "Find the Ring." Form a circle and follow these motions to pass the ring from one to the other.

| touch left 3 times | touch own left hand 3 times | touch right 3 times | touch own left hand 3 times |

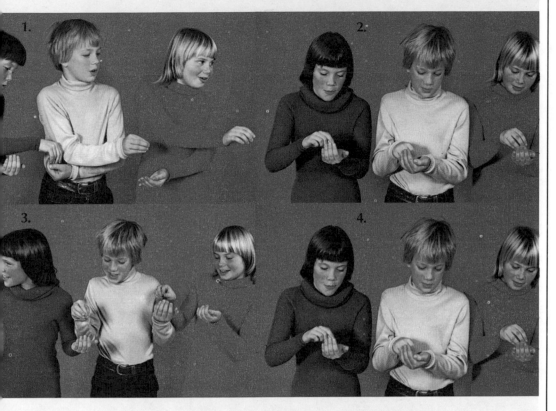

Play this part on recorder or bells as others sing and play the game.

Recorder or Bells

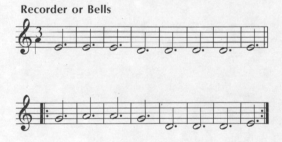

Meter 73

Point out: The number tells how many beats are in each measure (3); the note tells what kind of note receives one beat (quarter note). (b) Have children find the meter signature in the notation for "Sasa Aberewa" (p. 70). Question: What do the number and note in this meter signature show? (That there are two beats in a measure, and the quarter note receives one beat)

5. Direct attention to the rhythm patterns on p. 72. Have children take turns playing one of them on a tambourine as others sing the song. Questions: Which pattern has notes that each last for three beats? (Pattern 3) Notes that show the steady beat? (1) Long sounds followed by shorter sounds? (2)

6. Children who play recorder can play the part on p. 73 as others sing. Point out: The part uses the tones D, E, G, A and has dotted half notes (each lasting for three beats) throughout. Suggestion: When children know the part, have them play a pattern of quarter notes (♩♩♩) or of half notes and quarter notes (♩♩) in place of each dotted half note.

TRY THIS

While some children sing "Find the Ring," someone plays a rhythm accompaniment on a tambourine, others play the recorder part, and still others play the Ring Game. To complete the ensemble, someone plays chords on the Autoharp, using one long strum per measure. Note: The Autoharp part uses three chords—C, G₇, F. Players use their left index finger (left-handed players may use their right ring finger) for the C button, middle finger for G₇, and ring (index) finger for F. They follow the chord indications above the song notation, playing each chord until a different chord name occurs. Suggestion: When players are comfortable with the Autoharp part, have them experiment with other strumming patterns—i.e., short strums or a combination of long and short strums.

METER • Lesson 4

MATERIALS
Record 3, *Sound Piece 3: Did Sid?*;
Pupil's Book, p. 74

VOCABULARY
meter in 2, meter in 3, ostinato

IDEAS FOR TEACHING

1. Have children feel beats grouped in sets of three by chanting the ostinato (*Did, did, diddle; Did, did, diddle;* etc.) in part 2 of *Did Sid?* (notation, p. 74). <u>Point out</u>: The ostinato is a repeated pattern of quarter notes and eighth notes.

2. Ask children to observe the notation for part 1 to discover that the meter alternates between meter in 3 and meter in 2 throughout the part. Questions: What is the meter at the beginning of part 1? (Meter in 3) At the end of part 1? (Meter in 2) <u>Point out</u>: Each meter lasts until a new meter signature appears in the notation.

3. Have children chant part 1 with the voices on the recording. Encourage them to stress the first beat (strong beat) of each measure. <u>Note</u>: If stereo is available, use the Pick-a-Track technique to de-emphasize part 2 on the recording.

4. When children can chant each part of *Did Sid?* without missing a beat, have them put the parts together, one group chanting part 1 while another group chants part 2. <u>Point out</u>: Part 1 is silent during the first two measures of the Sound Piece. Choose a third group to listen to the performance to hear the sound of different meters occurring simultaneously. <u>Note</u>: Give each child an opportunity to participate in all three groups.

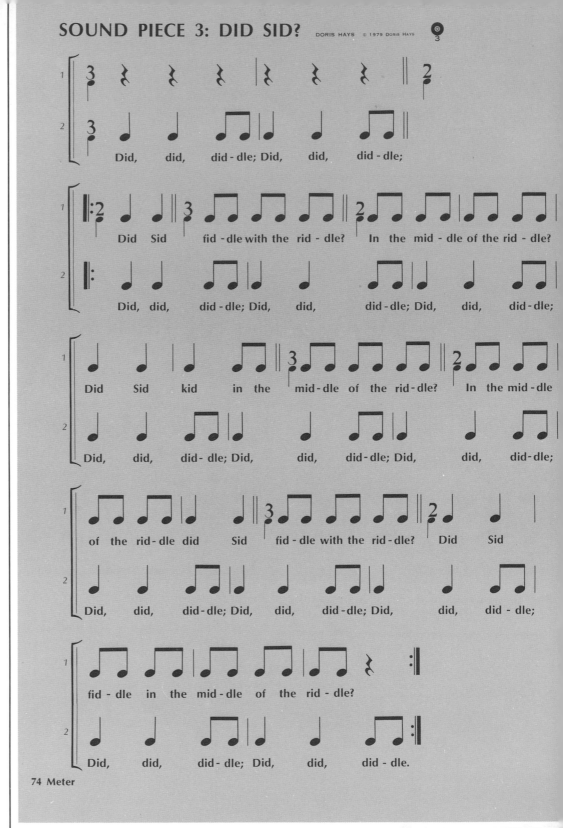

SOUND PIECE 3: DID SID? DORIS HAYS © 1979 DORIS HAYS

74 Meter

TEACHER INFORMATION
Sound pieces like this one should be developed over a period of time. The focus should be on the process involved in working up to a final performance, not on the performance itself.

The *African Rhythm Complex* on pp. 88 and 89 gives children experience with performing several different rhythms simultaneously.

SOUND PIECE 4: BUSY LIZZY

DORIS HAYS   © 1979 Doris Hays

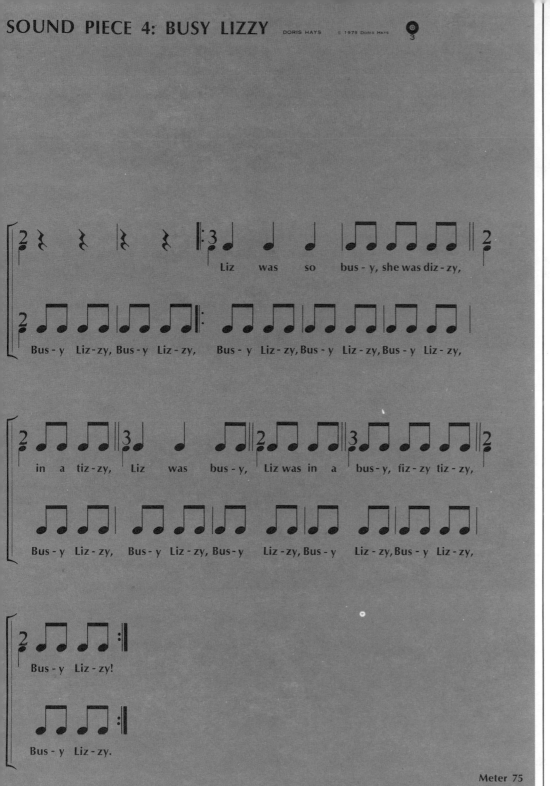

Meter 75

MATERIALS

Record 3, *Sound Piece 4: Busy Lizzy*; Pupil's Book, p. 75

VOCABULARY

meter in 2, meter in 3, ostinato

IDEAS FOR TEACHING

1. Have children look at the notation for *Busy Lizzy* on p. 75 to discover that the ostinato in part 2 (*Busy Lizzy, Busy Lizzy*, etc.) is in two meter. Then have them chant the ostinato to feel the beats grouped in sets of two. Point out: The rhythm of the ostinato is made up of repeated eighth notes.

2. Ask children to look at the notation for part 1. Help them observe that the meter alternates between meter in 2 and meter in 3 throughout the part. Point out: (a) Each meter lasts until a new meter signature occurs in the notation. (b) The beginning and ending of part 1 are in the same meter— meter in 2.

3. Have children chant part 1 with the recording. Remind them to stress the first beat (strong beat) of each measure. Note: If stereo is available, use the Pick-a-Track technique to de-emphasize part 2 on the recording.

4. When children can chant each part without missing a beat, have one group chant part 1 while another group chants part 2. Point out: Part 1 is silent for the first two measures of the Sound Piece. Choose a third group to listen to the performance to hear the sound of different meters occurring together. Note: Give every child an opportunity to participate in all three groups.

TRY THIS

1. Encourage groups of children to choose either *Sound Piece 3* (p. 74) or *Sound Piece 4* (p. 75) to practice outside of class. When they are ready, have them perform their sound piece. They may give a "live" performance or make a tape recording to play for the class.

2. Using either *Sound Piece 3* or *Sound Piece 4,* have a group of children make a tape recording of their performance of part 1, and a different tape recording of their performance of part 2. Then have them play back the two tape recordings at the same time, being certain that the voices on part 1 are silent for the first two measures. Have children notice whether or not the tapes "stayed together" during the playback. Call attention to the importance of (a) keeping a steady beat throughout the sound piece and (b) performing both parts in the same tempo.

3. Have children create nonsense sentences or simple verses that emphasize a particular vowel sound or rhyming pattern as in *Sound Piece 3* (*Did Sid?*) and *Sound Piece 4* (*Busy Lizzy*); for example:

    Matt the cat sat on that hat,
    An acrobat was Matt the cat!

METER • Lesson 6

MATERIALS

Record 3, "Mañana"; Pupil's Book, p. 76; tambourine, castanets, Autoharp

VOCABULARY

meter in 3, strong beat, accent

IDEAS FOR TEACHING

1. Play the recording and have children take turns playing steady beats in sets of three on a tambourine. Remind them to stress the first beat (strong beat) of each set.

2. As some children sing with the recording, others take turns playing the tambourine part at the top of p. 76. <u>Point out</u>: (a) Each quarter note in the part receives one beat. (b) In the second measure, the dotted quarter note lasts as long as three quarter notes, or three beats. (c) The accent (>) at the beginning of the last measure indicates that the strong beat gets an added stress. The quarter rests stand for silences that each last for one beat. <u>Note</u>: The tambourine part begins on the first strong beat of the song, on -ña of *Mañana*.

3. When children know the song, add the part for castanets at the bottom of the page. <u>Point out</u>: Each pair of eighth notes (♫) is played as two equal sounds to the beat.

4. Give children time to practice the Autoharp pattern (strumming low strings for beat 1 in each measure, high strings for beats 2 and 3) on p. 76 while depressing the G-chord button. Then have them strum in the same way as they play the G and D_7 chords indicated in the music to accompany the song.

Feel meter in 3 by playing this tambourine part with the recording.

MANANA   FOLK SONG FROM SPAIN   COLLECTED AND ADAPTED BY BEATRICE LANDECK   ENGLISH WORDS BY ROSEMARY JACQUES

Piano acc., p. 267

Now play another pattern in three meter.

76 Meter

TRY THIS

Have a group of children sing the following counter-melody or play it on bells as others sing "Mañana."

TEACHER INFORMATION

The Spanish words of "Mañana" literally say, "Tomorrow morning you passed, Jane, by my workshop, *la ran le* (no meaning). I swear to you that I feel like seeing, Jane, the tip of your foot." They are pronounced as follows.

Ma - ña - na, por la ma - ña - na pa - sas - te,
mah-nyah-nah pohr lah mah-nyah-nah pah-sahs-teh

Jua - na, por mi ta - ller, *la ran le.*
whan-nah pohr mee tah-yehr lah rahn leh

Te ju - ro que ten - go ga - na de ver - te,
teh whoo-roh keh tehn-goh gah-nah deh vehr-teh

Jua - na, la pun - ta el pie.
whah-nah lah poon-tah ehl pyeh

Feel meter in 4 by strumming this low-high pattern on the strings of the Autoharp.

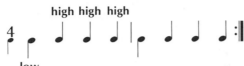

GREAT BIG SEA FOLK SONG FROM NEWFOUNDLAND

FROM OLD TIME SONGS AND POETRY OF NEWFOUNDLAND. REPRINTED BY PERMISSION OF GERALD S. DOYLE LTD.

Piano acc., p. 259

3. "Oh, mother dear, I wants a sack,"

Right fol-or-al taddle diddle I-do.

"Oh, mother dear, I wants a sack

With beads and buttons down the back,"

To me right fol-didy fol-dee.

Play these four-meter patterns on the low- and high-C bells.

Meter 77

MATERIALS
Record 3, "Mañana"; "A Great Big Sea"; Pupil's Book, pp. 76, 77; Autoharp, bells

VOCABULARY
meter in 3, meter in 4

IDEAS FOR TEACHING
1. Play the recording of "Mañana" and have children pretend to strum the Autoharp, using the three-meter pattern at the bottom of p. 76 ("strumming" low strings for beat 1, high strings for beats 2 and 3). Then play the recording of "A Great Big Sea" and have children pretend to strum the four-meter pattern at the top of p. 77 ("strumming" low strings for beat 1; high strings for beats 2, 3, and 4). Point out: (a) For meter in 4, children "play" three high strums instead of two. (b) In each meter, the low strum occurs on the strong beat.

2. As some children sing "A Great Big Sea," others take turns playing an accompaniment on the Autoharp. They use the four-meter strumming pattern to play the chords F and C₇ as indicated in the music. Note: (a) Children begin to play on the first strong beat, on the word great. (b) In the next-to-last measure, players change from the F chord to C₇ on the third beat.

3. Have children take turns playing one of the four-meter patterns at the bottom of p. 77 while others sing "A Great Big Sea." Point out: Pattern 1 uses only quarter notes, one sound per beat. In pattern 2, the last note of each measure is a half note; its sound lasts for two beats. The eighth notes in pattern 3 are played two equal sounds to the beat.

TEACHER INFORMATION
Hove, the past tense of the verb *heave*, may strike some children as an odd past-tense form. Actually, many of the oldest English verbs form their past tense just as *heave* does, by changing the middle vowel sound. Some of these verbs are among the most commonly used. Their past forms sound so familiar that children would probably never stop to think of them as "odd" or "irregular": weave/wove; ring/rang; teach/taught; bring/brought; dive/dove; hold/held. However, when a word is heard that is no longer frequently used, it may have a somewhat funny sound, as heave/hove.

In the bell patterns on p. 77, notes with stems pointing down are played with the left mallet; notes with stems pointing up, with the right.

TRY THIS
When children know "A Great Big Sea," have individuals sing the solo parts while the rest of the class sings the chorus parts. Suggestion: Choose a different child to sing the solo parts in each verse.

MATERIALS
Record 3, *Balkan Hills Schottische*;
Pupil's Book, p. 78; wood block

VOCABULARY
schottische, meter in 4

IDEAS FOR TEACHING

1. As the recording plays, have children take turns playing steady beats in sets of four on a wood block, stressing the first beat of each set. Then repeat the activity, having them make the last beat of each set a silent beat (ξ), as in the second row of notation on p. 78.

2. Direct attention to the rhythm of the basic schottische step. Point out: The movements occur in sets of four to match the meter of the music.

3. Have children practice the schottische step with the recording, alternately beginning with one foot, then the other—e.g., right-left-right-hop, left-right-left-hop. Suggestion: Children should find a space where they can move without bumping into anyone. As the recording plays, they practice schottische steps in various directions—moving sideways to the left, sideways to the right, forward, backward.

4. Have children try the step-hop variation in their book. Encourage them to work out a dance sequence that uses both the basic step and the variation.

Play beats in sets of four on a wood block.

Make the first beat of each set stronger than the others.

Now practice making the fourth beat silent.

Wood Block Pattern

Play the wood block pattern along with the recording.

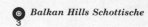
Balkan Hills Schottische

You have played the rhythm of a dance called the *schottische*.

To dance a schottische, walk forward on the first three beats of the measure and hop on the fourth beat. Begin with either foot. Make your movements match the meter of the music.

Schottische step

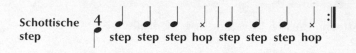
step step step hop step step step hop

Vary the schottische step this way.

step hop step hop step hop step hop

78 Meter

TRY THIS
Have children perform this version of the schottische.

Formation: Partners stand side by side in a circle, facing counterclockwise, and with inside hands joined.

Phrase 1 (8 beats): Starting with the outside foot, take two schottische steps forward.

Phrase 2 (8 beats): Starting with the outside foot, take two schottische steps backward.

Phrase 3 (8 beats): Take one schottische step sideways, away from your partner (4 beats);

take one schottische step sideways toward your partner (4 beats).

Phrase 4 (8 beats): Join both hands with your partner and step-hop (schottische-step variation) in a circle in place, ending in your original position.

Note: After phrase 4, the dance immediately begins again. Dancers may keep the same partner throughout, or they may change partners (dancers on outside of circle move forward one place) just before the dance repeats.

Play beats in sets of three on a tambourine. Make the first beat of each set stronger than the others.

Now shake the tambourine on beat 3 of each set.

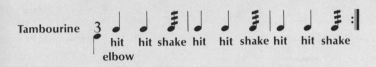

Play the tambourine pattern along with the recording.

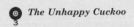 *The Unhappy Cuckoo*

You have played the rhythm of a dance called the *mazurka*.

To dance a mazurka, walk forward on the first two beats of the measure and hop on the third beat. Begin with either foot. Make your movements match the meter of the music.

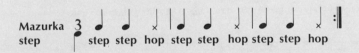

Try the mazurka step, stepping sideways to the left or to the right.

Meter 79

METER • Lesson 9

MATERIALS
Record 3, *The Unhappy Cuckoo*; Pupil's Book, p. 79; tambourine

VOCABULARY
mazurka, meter in 3

IDEAS FOR TEACHING

1. As the recording plays, have children take turns playing steady beats in sets of three on a tambourine, stressing the first beat of each set.

2. Have children practice the second tambourine pattern on p. 79 with the recording. Call attention to the shake on beat 3 each time. Suggestion: Children can experiment with other ways to strike the tambourine for beats 1 and 2—with the heel of the hand, with the knuckles, on the knee.

3. Direct attention to the notation for the basic mazurka step. Questions: Does a mazurka have the same meter as a schottische? (No. A mazurka is in three meter; a schottische, in four meter.) How are the basic mazurka and schottische steps different? (The mazurka has two steps and a hop; the schottische, three steps and a hop.)

4. Have children practice the mazurka step with the recording to discover that the movements match the meter of the music. Point out: In the schottische, a different foot begins the basic-step pattern each time. In the mazurka, the same foot, either right or left, begins each pattern. Suggestion: Have children dance mazurka steps in various directions—forward, backward, to the right or left side.

TRY THIS
When children are comfortable with the basic step, have them try this version of the mazurka with the recording.

Formation: Children find a space in the room and stand with hands on hips.

Phrase 1 (9 beats): Starting with the right foot, take two mazurka steps to the right (6 beats), then stamp three times—right, left, right (3 beats).

Phrase 2 (9 beats): Starting with the left foot, take two mazurka steps to the left (6 beats), then stamp three times—left, right, left (3 beats).

Phrase 3 (9 beats): Repeat the movements for Phrase 1.
Phrase 4 (9 beats): Repeat the movements for Phrase 2.

Suggestions: (a) Have children experiment with other formations for the mazurka. For example, they might form two circles, one inside the other. Dancers in the outside circle have backs to the center; those in the inside circle face the center. When they perform the mazurka, circles will move in opposite directions. (b) Some children can play the tambourine part as others dance to the recording.

METER • Lesson 10

MATERIALS

Record 3, *Emilia Polka;* "In Bahia Town"; Pupil's Book, p. 80; percussion instruments

VOCABULARY

polka, meter in 2

IDEAS FOR TEACHING

1. Play the polka recording, and have children keep the beat by performing sliding steps to the right. Then have them take sliding steps to the left.

2. When children can do sliding steps in both directions, have them try changing from one direction to the other without missing a beat. Point out: This is the basic step for a polka. A quick "hop" prepares the change of direction each time. When children add the hop to their movement, the rhythm becomes dotted (♩♪ instead of ♪♪—see Basic Polka Step below).

3. While some children dance, others play the polka rhythm (notation, p. 80) on percussion instruments. Questions: Does the polka have the same meter as the mazurka? As the schottische? (Each dance has its own meter: the polka, two meter; the mazurka, three; the schottische, four.)

4. Play the recording of "In Bahia Town." When children can identify section B of the music, have a small group do polka steps each time the section occurs. Invite others to sing when they can (notation, p. 80). Point out: Although section B does not use the same rhythm pattern as the basic polka step, the music and the dance can be performed together because their meter is the same—meter in 2.

Tap this polka rhythm as you listen to the recording.

○3 *Emilia Polka*

Dance the polka step throughout section B of this song.

IN BAHIA TOWN
FOLK SONG FROM BRAZIL   ENGLISH WORDS BY VERNE MUÑOZ

MELODY FROM FOLK SONGS AND DANCES OF THE AMERICAS. PUBLISHED BY THE GENERAL SECRETARIAT OF THE ORGANIZATION OF AMERICAN STATES.

Piano acc., p. 2

1. In Ba-hi-a town, So they say,
2. In Ba-hi-a town, So it seems,

They sell co-co-nuts for a pen-ny In the mar-ket place.
You can buy a sew-ing ma-chine That stitch-es like a dream.

In Ba-hi-a town, So they say,
In Ba-hi-a town, So it seems,

They sell fish that's bet-ter than an-y You will ev-er taste.
You can buy a lamp made of glass In shades of blue and green.

La la la la la la la la la, La la la la la la la,

La la la la la la la la la, La la la la la la.

80 Meter

BASIC POLKA STEP

| Step on R* | Slide L next to R | Step on R | Hop on R | Step on L | Slide R next to L | Step on L | Hop on L |

*(R—right foot; L—left foot)

TRY THIS

Perform this folk dance to the music of "In Bahia Town."

Formation: Partners face each other in two rows, keeping a distance of four or five steps between rows.

*Section A—***Phrase 1:** Walk three steps toward partner, clapping hands on each step, then snapping fingers once (4 beats). Walk three steps backward, using same hand sounds (4 beats).

Phrase 2: Walk three steps forward, clapping

→

WHAT DO YOU HEAR? 5: METER ⊙

Can you hear meter in this music?

Listen to the recording to discover whether the meter

is in 2 or in 3.

---

1. METER IN 2　　(METER IN 3)　　Stravinsky: *Suite No. 2 for Small Orchestra,* "Valse"

---

2. (METER IN 2)　　METER IN 3　　Bizet: *Carmen Suite,* "March of the Street Urchins"

---

3. (METER IN 2)　　METER IN 3　　Gershwin: *An American in Paris*

---

4. METER IN 2　　(METER IN 3)　　Dvořák: *Slavonic Dances,* Op. 46, No. 6

---

5. (METER IN 2)　　METER IN 3　　Scruggs: *String Bender*

---

6. METER IN 2　　(METER IN 3)　　Saint-Saëns: *Carnival of the Animals,*
"The Elephant"

Meter 81

MATERIALS
Record 4, *What Do You Hear? 5: Meter;* spirit master

VOCABULARY
meter in 2, meter in 3

TEACHER INFORMATION
Suggestion: Before playing the recording, remind children that movement can help them decide the meter of the music. Tell them to think of the hand-jive motions (p. 8) when they listen. Would they perform the motions in sets of two or in sets of three? Tell them to think of the way the basic polka and mazurka steps feel. Which step would fit the music? If necessary, let children move to the music in *What Do You Hear? 5* before they indicate their answers.

---

and snapping as in Phrase 1 (4 beats), then change places with partner by passing right shoulders and turning to face each other (4 beats).

Phrase 3: Repeat movements for Phrase 1.
Phrase 4: Repeat movements for Phrase 2.

Section B—Do the polka step as follows. Partners stand side by side and join inside hands. Partner on right starts with right (outside) foot; partner on left starts with left (outside) foot. Partners polka around the room, turning toward each other on the first polka step (step-slide-step-

hop), and away from each other on the next. They continue to alternately face and turn away from each other to the end of the section.

To vary section A for the second verse, children in each row turn so they are standing behind one another, and place hands on the shoulders of the one directly in front. They step to the beat while following the leader, who takes them wherever he or she chooses. This variation is called *path to the field* (*caminho da roca*). By the end of the section, children must be back in original positions, ready to do the polka step for section B.

MODULE 6

OBJECTIVES, p. XII

MODERN STYLES: Electronic—Folkloric

MATERIALS
Record 4, Piston: *The Incredible Flutist,* "Tango of the Merchant's Daughters"; Maxfield: *Night Music;* Copland: *Billy the Kid,* "Celebration"; Babbitt: *Ensembles for Synthesizer;* Pupil's Book, pp. 82–85

VOCABULARY
Styles: Electronic, Folkloric, Non-representational, Representational

IDEAS FOR TEACHING
1. Give children time to look at the paintings on pp. 82 and 83. Tell them that both paintings are examples of Modern art; both were painted by 20th-century artists. However, there are many styles of Modern art. Each of these paintings is in a different Modern style. Questions: (a) How are the paintings different in style? (By discussion and questioning, help children discover that one painting has recognizable things in it—swimmers, towels, shore, rocks, forest. When a painting is a "picture" of something you can recognize, the style is called Representational. There is nothing recognizable in the other painting. Because there are no references to anything outside the painting itself, it is in a style called Nonrepresentational.) What is the same about the two paintings? (They both use colors, shapes, lines, textures—smooth, rough—and directions—up, down, side to side, diagonal.)

2. Play the recording of the Piston ⟶

MODERN STYLES

These are two modern paintings.

What makes them different in style?

How are they alike?

82 MODULE 6: Modern Styles

TEACHER INFORMATION
Milton Avery (American, 1893–1965) *Swimmers and Sunbathers:* This landscape painter uses oils, but in a flat, spare manner that gives the impression of watercolor. While one can identify the objects as people, rocks, water, etc., the objects have been so simplified that they seem almost abstract.

William Baziotes (American, 1912–1963) *Dusk:* This artist started as a representational painter, but later his works became completely abstract, or nonrepresentational. The rich, fluid color with strange shapes overlaid creates a fascinating visual world.

Milton Babbitt (American, 1916–   ) *Ensembles for Synthesizer:* This composer is also a distinguished writer and commentator on avant-garde music. He is an influential spokesman for experimental approaches to composition. Babbitt's music depends on elaborate electronic equipment for production and alteration of sounds, and he often uses complicated mathematical formulas by which the sounds are organized. ⟶

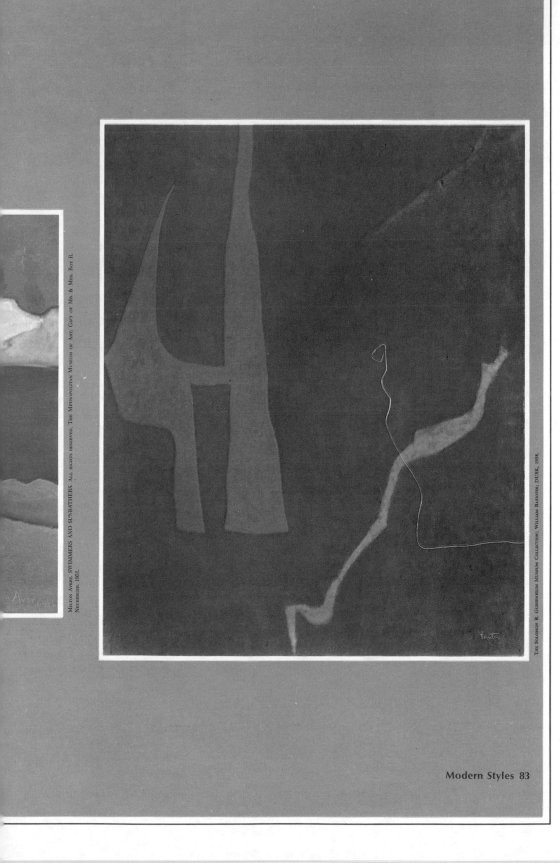

Modern Styles 83

work. As children listen, have them follow the first column of words on p. 84 to help them hear that the music is performed by an orchestra; has a singable melody with recognizable beat; has clearly defined phrases with cadences (points of rest) between phrases; has harmony as well as melody; is tonal, with an important "home" or "key" tone to which the other tones often move. Note: This music is an example of Folkloric style. Folkloric music uses traditional folk tunes and other melodies of a "folk" nature; it often has a dance-like rhythm.

3. Play the recording of the Maxfield piece, having children follow the second column of words to help them hear these qualities: the sounds are made on a synthesizer, an electronic machine that produces and changes sounds as the composer wishes; there is no beat in the music, and no singable melody; there are no phrases and no cadences; there is no harmony—although sounds overlap, they are not arranged in traditional chords; the music is atonal—there is no home tone to which the other tones move. Note: This is an example of a style of Modern music called Electronic.

4. Point out that even though the Piston and Maxfield works are in different styles, some things about them are the same, as shown in the last column of words, p. 84. Help children discuss each of the qualities listed. Play parts of each piece to illustrate as the qualities are discussed.

5. Play the recording of the Copland selection. Question: Is the style of this music Folkloric, like the Piston, or Electronic, like the Maxfield? (Folkloric)

Aaron Copland (American, 1900–   ) *Billy the Kid,* "Celebration": This famous composer, author, conductor, teacher is regarded as one of the musical giants of this century. His early music—*Appalachian Spring, Billy the Kid, A Lincoln Portrait, Rodeo*—used American folk songs and dances, giving an unmistakably national feeling.

Richard Maxfield (American, 1927–1969) *Night Music:* The sounds of this piece were made by using electronic machines in very complicated ways. From a large library of sounds so produced, the composer selected only a few

that seemed to him of high musical interest. *Night Music* was first performed as part of a dance production.

Walter Piston (American, 1894–1976) *The Incredible Flutist,* "Tango of the Merchant's Daughters": Piston's music has a virile, rhythmic quality and a fairly dissonant sound. His music for the ballet *The Incredible Flutist* is probably best known.

Then play the recording of the Babbitt and have children identify its style (Electronic). For each piece, review the qualities in the appropriate column of words on p. 84.

6. Give children time to enjoy the visual impact of the poem on p. 85. Then lead them to discover some of the following qualities: (a) The poet has used groups of single letters that spell the word *geranium* (i.e., groups of G's, of E's, R's, etc.) to create a visual representation of the flower. Each letter group represents a petal. (b) Starting with the group of G's at the top left, the letter groups in the outside circle of petals spell the word *geranium* when read in a clockwise direction. (c) The letter groups in the inside circle of petals also spell *geranium* when read in a clockwise direction. (d) The first letters of the words closest to the center of the flower spell the word *geranium*: God's Exit Resounds A capella No one Interprets Umbellar Measures. (Note: The word *umbellar* refers to an arrangement of flowers in a circle around a common center— "umbrella-like.") (e) Each of the words that are closer to the petals begins with the last letter of a word at the center: *Summer* (God's); *Times* (Exit); *Summer* (Resounds); *Answers* (A capella); *Each* (No one); *Seen* (Interprets); *Red* (Umbellar); *Silence* (Measures).

7. Have children compare *Geranium* with another modern poem, *Crossing* (p. 66). Point out: (a) *Crossing* is much more what we expect a poem to be: the words are arranged in lines that are grouped into stanzas that have meter and rhyme. (b) Although the two poems look different, they are alike in what they do: they use arrangements of words or

→

These are two modern pieces of music. As you listen, follow the words that show what makes these pieces different in style. How are these pieces alike?

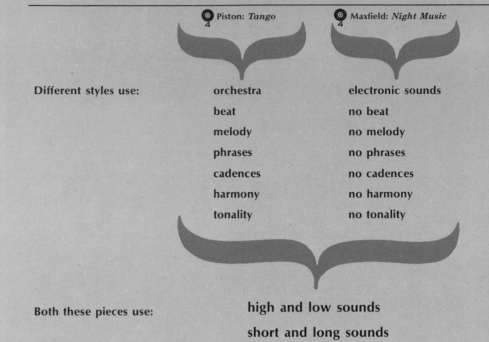

Piston: *Tango*   Maxfield: *Night Music*

Different styles use:

orchestra	electronic sounds
beat	no beat
melody	no melody
phrases	no phrases
cadences	no cadences
harmony	no harmony
tonality	no tonality

Both these pieces use:

high and low sounds

short and long sounds

repeated sounds

steps and leaps

several sounds together

upward and downward direction

Copland: *Celebration*   Babbitt: *Ensembles for Synthesizer*

Modern painting and modern music have many styles. Some things are different in different styles, but some things are the same no matter what the style.

84 Modern Styles

REVIEW/REINFORCEMENT

1. Have children listen to other examples of music in Folkloric and Electronic styles and compare them with the music in this lesson; for example:

Gershwin: *An American in Paris,* p. 37 (Folkloric)
Varèse: *Poème électronique,* p. 202 (Electronic)

2. Folk songs are closely connected to their folk origins. In the Classified Index in the back of the Teacher's Edition, folk songs are listed according to various styles—African, American Indian, Black American, songs from the British Isles, etc. Have children sing songs representing two different folk styles—e.g., Canadian and Japanese. Encourage them to compare and contrast the general sound of the songs.

GERANIUM

Mary Ellen Solt

parts of words in a manner that allows us to experience a new way of feeling or responding.

TEACHER INFORMATION

The poem *Geranium*, both in the visual arrangement of letters and words and in the meaning of the words, is *suggestive* of a flower, not a true picture of one. In the sense that the words suggest an image, *Geranium* is like any other poem. However, *Geranium* goes beyond traditional poetry by presenting its words and letters in a way that gives a visual suggestion of the flower to reinforce the mental image the words alone create. *Geranium* belongs to a style of poetry called Concrete Poetry. A concrete poem has the "look" of the image its words suggest.

TRY THIS

1. Continue the discussion of style in our world and in our lives that was begun in the previous style lesson (see Try This, Teacher's Edition p. 67).

2. Children can invent their own concrete poems, using these suggestions:
   (a) Arrange a word like *flower, fire, apple,* or *pencil* on the page to look like its meaning (see *a* below).
   (b) Scatter letters of a word so that the word is hidden (see *b*).
   (c) Arrange words in "word plays" (see *c*).

Note: Encourage experimentation. A good device for trying out ideas is to use letter cards (one letter to a small card) that can be arranged in a variety of ways. With a stack of blank cards and a marker, a child can make letter cards as needed to develop a poem idea.

SAMPLE CONCRETE POEMS

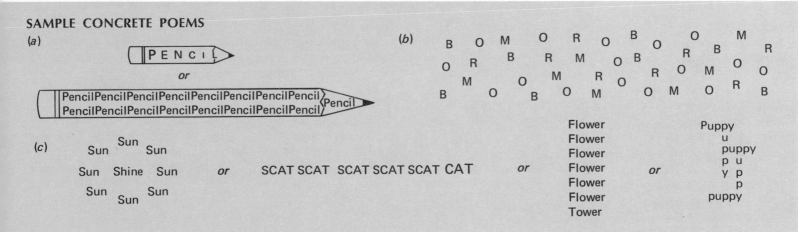

OBJECTIVES, p. XII

DYNAMICS • Lesson 1

MATERIALS
Record 4, *Tom and Joe; The Hi-Dee-Ho Man;* "Up the Street the Band Is Marching Down"; Pupil's Book, pp. 86 and 87

VOCABULARY
dynamics, soft (p), moderately loud (mf), loud (f), staccato, accents

IDEAS FOR TEACHING
1. Direct attention to the volume-control knobs pictured on p. 86. Be certain children know that the dial in the pictures would point straight down if the volume were turned off, and that they would turn the knob clockwise to make the sound louder. Questions: What does the first picture show about the volume? (That the sound is soft) Which picture shows that the sound is loud? (The last one) Help children see that the middle picture shows a level of sound between soft and loud—moderately loud. Point out: The knobs show three different dynamic levels. In music, dynamics are shown by letters—*p (piano*—pee-ahn'-oh), soft; *mf (mezzo forte*—met'-soh fohr'-tay), moderately loud; *f(forte*—fohr'-tay), loud.

2. Using the recording of a familiar song, have a child adjust the volume of the record player to soft, moderately loud, or loud. The class identifies the level and matches it as they sing. Take time to discuss the appropriateness of the dynamic level.
→

DYNAMICS

What do these pictures show about volume?

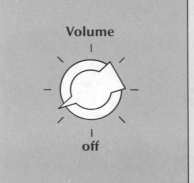 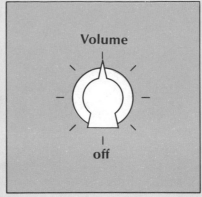 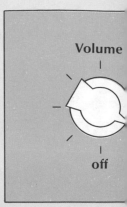

 Tom and Joe
4

TOM AND JOE

Tom loves to be heard;

Joe not at all.

Boom!

Can you hear Joe's small

voice? No? It seems to have died!

Boom!

You can hear *that,* though?

Yes? Well, *I told you so!*

I imply—I've implied;

You infer—you've inferred

that I'm *not* on Tom's side,

nor on Joe's. My one word

is: *Don't* be a Tom

who explodes like a bomb.

And oh, yes: on the other

hand, *Don't* be a Joe!

David McCord

 The Hi-Dee-Ho Man
4

86 MODULE 7: Dynamics

TRY THIS
1. Have children take turns reading *Tom and Joe,* using appropriate dynamics. Then have them plan how they would use dynamics in poems like *Crossing* (p. 66) and *Slowly* (p. 67) or in other poems they know. When children read the poems, discuss whether the dynamics suit the words. If possible, record the children's reading of the poems as an aid to the discussion.

2. Have children work in groups to make lists of words, phrases, and sentences that express loud and soft sounds.

3. Suggest "loud" and "soft" words or phrases—a dripping faucet, the screaming ambulance—for children to use as subjects for original poems. Have several children work with the same subject in order to compare how different individuals interpret a particular image.

4. Encourage children to choose selections from library or classroom books about "loud" or "soft" subjects. Ask individuals to read portions of their chosen stories or poems aloud, then discuss as a class the words that were used to convey the noisy or quiet image. ——→

Will you sing this music soft (p), moderately loud (mf), or loud (f)? Loud

P THE STREET THE BAND IS MARCHING DOWN

WORDS AND MUSIC BY LUIGI ZANINELLI

Up the street the band is march-ing down,

Hear the fi - fers shrill, See the drum-mer's skill,

Tramp, tramp, tramp, round the town, round the town;

If the trum-pets make an er - ror, See their fac - es pale with ter - ror.

Dynamics 87

3. Play the recording of *Tom and Joe,* so children can hear whether the voice always uses the same dynamics, or whether the dynamics change. (They change.)

4. Play the recording of *The Hi-Dee-Ho Man,* a chant in which a group of voices (response) echoes a solo voice (call). Question: Was each response the same dynamic level as its call? (Yes) Were the call-response sets all loud, all soft, or different dynamic levels? (Different levels) Suggestion: If stereo is available, use the Pick-a-Track technique to de-emphasize the responses on the recording and (a) have children chant each response at a different dynamic level from the call; (b) have individuals perform the responses either at the same dynamic level as the call or at a different level. The class indicates whether the dynamics for each call-response set were the same or different.

5. Have children look at the notation on p. 87. Questions: Will this song be sung loud or soft? (Loud) How do you know? (There is a letter *f* in the music, above the first staff.) What letter(s) would mean to sing soft? (p) Moderately loud? (mf)

6. Play the recording of "Up the Street the Band Is Marching Down" while children follow the notation. Invite them to sing when they can. Suggestion: Play only the first part of the recording until children know the melody. Point out: The dots—staccato (stuh-kah'toh) markings—in the second staff indicate that the eighth notes are sung short and crisply. The accents in staff 4 show that the word *terror* is stressed. Staccato notes, accents, and dynamics help to make the music expressive.

5. Have children sing "Up the Street the Band Is Marching Down" as a round. At first, try it as a two-part round. When children are ready, add the third, and then the fourth part.

MATERIALS
Record 4, *African Rhythm Complex*, Pupil's Book, pp. 88 and 89; African bells (or tin cans), rattle or maraca, high drum

VOCABULARY
polyrhythm, loud and soft dynamics

IDEAS FOR TEACHING

1. Establish a steady beat in a moderate tempo, and have children chant the first line of numbers on p. 88, clapping on each enlarged number. Have them repeat the line several times without pause. Then have them silently *think* the numbers while clapping aloud on each enlarged number. Performing the line over and over in this manner will help them feel the rhythm. Repeat the activity for each of the remaining lines. Suggestion: Have children use other natural sounds—snapping, stamping, "brushing" palms against each other—to vary the dynamic level as they perform the rhythms, sometimes loud, sometimes soft.

2. When children are ready, divide the class into groups to perform two lines, then three, and finally all four lines simultaneously. Note: When the lines are combined, children are experiencing polyrhythm (several different rhythms performed at the same time). Suggestion: When children can perform the combined rhythms easily, have them try the activity at a faster tempo. Be careful not to set a tempo that is too fast for children to perform accurately.

3. Help children discover that p. 89 shows the notation for the rhythms they have clapped. Point out: In Af-

→

AFRICAN RHYTHM COMPLEX

Say the numbers in each line below. Clap each time you say a large-size number.

1 ₂ 3 ₄ 5 6 ₇ 8 ₉ 10 ₁₁ 12

1 ₂ 3 4 ₅ ₆ 7 ₈ ₉ 10 ₁₁ 1

1 ₂ 3 4 5 6 7 8 9 10 11 12

1 2 3 4 ₅ ₆ 7 8 9 10 ₁₁ 1

Now use percussion instruments to play the rhythms you clapped.

Follow the notation on p. 89.

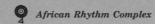

African Rhythm Complex

Here is the notation for the rhythms you clapped.

Bell 1

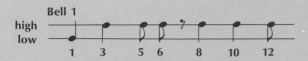

high
low

1 3 5 6 8 10 12

Bell 2

low

1 4 7 10

Rattle

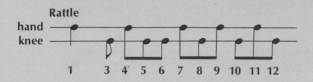

hand
knee

1 3 4 5 6 7 8 9 10 11 12

High Drum

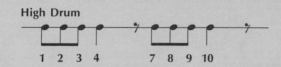

1 2 3 4 7 8 9 10

gankogui   axatse   kagan

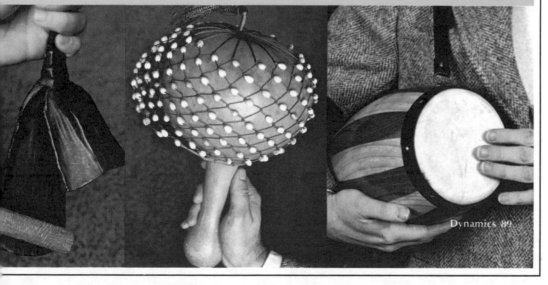

Dynamics 89

rica, the first two rhythms might be played on a gankogui (gahn-koh⁻ gwee), a metal bell that is struck with a stick. The gankogui has a large section that produces a low pitch, and a small section that produces a high pitch. The third rhythm might be played on an axatse (ahks-ah⁻tsay), a gourd rattle covered with beads. The fourth rhythm might be played on a kagan (kah⁻gahn), a small drum. These instruments are pictured on p. 89.

4. Have children follow the notation to play the rhythms. Silently counting from *one* to *twelve* will help them play accurately. If African instruments are not available, children can use large and small tin cans for the "Bell" rhythms, a maraca for the "Rattle" rhythm, and any high drum for the last rhythm. <u>Note:</u> For the "Rattle" rhythm, the instrument is hit against the hand or the knee as indicated in the notation. <u>Suggestion:</u> Have children begin by playing the rhythm for Bell 1 with the recording. If stereo equipment is available, use the Pick-a-Track technique to de-emphasize the sound of the other instruments. Have children add the other rhythms one at a time. Combine only as many of the rhythms as they can manage successfully.

5. Have children follow the notation on p. 89 as they listen to the recording. They will be seeing and hearing polyrhythm.

TEACHER INFORMATION
Polyrhythm is one of the most distinctive features of African music. It consists of the simultaneous use of highly contrasting rhythm patterns. Polyrhythm occurs in both vocal and instrumental music.

MATERIALS
Record 4, "Dundai"; Pupil's Book,
p. 90; tambourine, recorders or bells

VOCABULARY
accent, ostinato

IDEAS FOR TEACHING

1. As the recording plays, have someone keep the steady beat by playing a tambourine. Then have children take turns playing the tambourine patterns on p. 90 with the recording. One child plays during section A, another during section B. <u>Questions:</u> Which pattern has accents, or sudden loud sounds? (The one for section A) Will you play the section B pattern loud, or soft? (Soft) Why? (The *p* in the notation means "soft.")

2. When children know the song, have them sing with the recording. Choose a small group to sing ostinato 1 during section A. <u>Point out:</u> Since each note has an accent, the "dun-dai" (doon-dī) syllables should each be sung with a sharp, clear sound. Remind children to sing the ostinato softer than the melody.

3. Have children who play recorder review the fingering for low D (see p. 59) and play ostinato 2 as others sing with the recording. The recorders play only during section B. <u>Suggestion:</u> When children can play the half-note pattern in their book, have them try playing the rhythm of the words on the tone D during section B. <u>Point out:</u> Section B uses eighth notes, quarter notes, and half notes. Each quarter note lasts as long as two eighth notes. Each half note lasts as long as two quarter notes. <u>Note:</u> Bells may be used instead of recorders.

Play these patterns on a tambourine when you sing "Dundai."

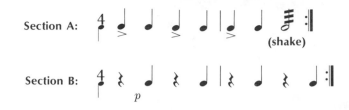

DUNDAI   HEBREW FOLK SONG   ENGLISH WORDS BY HAROLD AKS   Piano acc., p. 267

Land of Is - ra - el, O land of mine,

On you the sun and moon and stars do shine.

Dun - dai, dun - dai, dun - dai, Dun - dai - dai,

Dun - dai, dun - dai, dun - dai, Dun - dai - dai.

Sing this ostinato throughout section A.

Dun - dai, dun - dai, dun - dai, dun - dai

Play this ostinato during section B.

90 Dynamics

TRY THIS

1. As others sing with the recording, some children dance a simple hora, using the step-hop pattern described on Teacher's Edition page 40 (see Try This, item 1).

2. Have children take turns playing this phrase on bells or other keyboard instruments each time it occurs in the song:

F A C B♭ A G F E D

Encourage them to analyze the phrase before they try to play it. <u>Questions:</u> In which direction do the tones mostly move? (Downward) Does the phrase begin with steps, leaps, or repeated tones? (Leaps) How do the tones move at the end? (Downward by step)

TEACHER INFORMATION
The word *dundai* is a nonsense word. It has no meaning.

How are dynamics used in this music? Listen to the recording.

As each number is called, look at the chart. It will help you

hear the changes in dynamics.

CALL CHART 4: DYNAMICS 🎵 4

Ward: *America, the Beautiful*

1. MF   (MODERATELY LOUD)

2. P   (SOFT)

3. ＜   (GETTING LOUDER)

4. P   (SOFT)

5. ＜   (GETTING LOUDER)

6. P   (SOFT)

7. MF   (MODERATELY LOUD)

8. ＜   (GETTING LOUDER)

Play these tambourine parts during "Ging Gong Gooli." Be certain

to follow the dynamic markings.

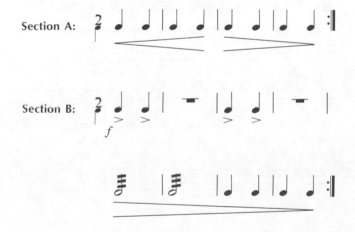

Dynamics 91

DYNAMICS • Lesson 4

MATERIALS
Record 4, *Call Chart 4: Dynamics;*
Pupil's Book, pp. 91, 18; tambourine

VOCABULARY
crescendo, decrescendo, getting
louder, getting softer, accent

IDEAS FOR TEACHING
1. Play the recording and have children follow the chart on p. 91 to help them hear how the dynamics change. Point out: Each time a number is called on the recording, children find the number in the Call Chart. Next to it are the letter(s) or symbol and word(s) that describe the dynamics they are hearing. The symbol ＜ stands for *crescendo* (kre-shen'-doh), getting louder.

2. Write the symbol ＜ on the chalkboard and have children take turns playing steady beats that get louder on a tambourine. Then change the symbol to ＞ (*decrescendo*—day-kre-shen'-doh). Question: What do you think this symbol means? (To get softer) Have children play steady beats that get softer.

3. Have children find the symbol for getting louder, then softer (＜ ＞) in the tambourine part (p. 91) for section A of "Ging Gong Gooli." Have them find the accents (＞) that indicate a sudden loudness in the part for section B. After practicing, have children take turns playing either tambourine part as others sing "Ging Gong Gooli" (p. 18). Questions: Does the part for section B begin loud or soft? (Loud, indicated by *f*) What happens at the end? (It gets softer.)

TEACHER INFORMATION
Call Charts are instructional devices that focus children's attention on a specific quality or qualities within a musical selection. A number is called at moments when the quality (e.g., soft dynamics, loud dynamics, dynamics getting louder) can be perceived in the music.

When children perform the tambourine part for section A or B of "Ging Gong Gooli," they must focus on two qualities, rhythm and dynamics: they add the dynamics indicated while playing the rhythm correctly.

DYNAMICS • Lesson 5

MATERIALS
Record 4, "Remember Me"; Pupil's Book, p. 92

VOCABULARY
dynamics, soft, loud, moderately loud

IDEAS FOR TEACHING

1. Play the recording and ask children to listen for changes in the dynamics. <u>Note:</u> There are none; the song is recorded at the same dynamic level throughout.

2. Select a child to vary the dynamics of the recording by using the record player's volume control. Have him or her follow the dynamic markings in the notation on p. 92. <u>Point out:</u> Each staff represents a phrase of the song. For phrases 1, 2, 3, 4, and 8, the dynamics are indicated by a letter(s) above the staff. For phrases 5–7, the symbol $<$ $>$ above the staff shows the dynamics. <u>Questions:</u> Which phrase will be soft throughout? (Phrase 2) Which phrases will be moderately loud throughout? (1, 3) Loud? (4, 8) Which phrases will get louder, then softer? (5–7) <u>Suggestion:</u> Over a period of time, give many children an opportunity to experience dynamics in this way.

3. When children know the song, encourage them each to plan their own dynamics for it; for example: performing the verse soft throughout, the refrain loud; or beginning each section soft and getting louder to the end. Have them take turns leading the class in singing the song their way. <u>Point out:</u> No one plan of dynamics is necessarily correct. Dynamics is one of the qualities of music that helps create a sense of feeling.

REMEMBER ME
BLACK SPIRITUAL

Piano acc., p. 328

VERSE

1. When chill-y winds blow from the North,___ I've got to go;
2. I've got a home in glo-ry land,___ out-shines the sun;

When chill-y winds blow from the North,___ I've got to go;
I've got a home in glo-ry land___ out-shines the sun;

When chill-y winds blow from the North,___ I've got to go;
I've got a home in glo-ry land___ out-shines the sun;

A-way up be-yond ___ the moon.

REFRAIN
(optional harmony part)
Do, Lord, O do, Lord, O do re-mem-ber me;

Do, Lord, O do, Lord, O do re-mem-ber me;

Do, Lord, O do, Lord, O do re-mem-ber me;

A-way up be-yond___ the moon.

92 Dynamics

TRY THIS

As others sing "Remember Me," have some children play the rhythm of the words on a percussion instrument. Singers and players follow the dynamics in the notation on p. 92, or a plan of dynamics that they have devised. <u>Note:</u> Some children may notice that both in the verse and in the refrain, the first three phrases have the same rhythm.

WHAT DO YOU HEAR? 6: DYNAMICS

Listen to these pieces. Each time a number is called,

decide which of the three answers is correct.

Choose the answer that best describes what is happening in the music.

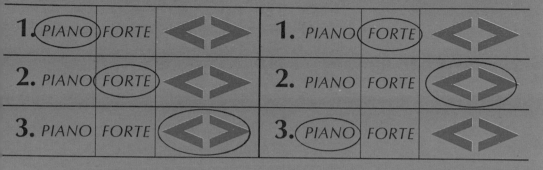

Mendelssohn: *Symphony No. 5, Mvt. 2*   Bizet: *Scènes Bohémiennes, No. 3*

WHAT DO YOU HEAR? 7: DYNAMICS

Listen to these pieces. Choose the answers that best describe the dynamics.

Is the music all soft? All loud? Soft and loud?

Do you hear accents? If you do, choose the word *accents*.

If you do not, choose the words *no accents*.

1.	ALL P	ALL F	(P AND F)	(ACCENTS) NO ACCENTS	Stockhausen: *Klavierstück*
2.	(ALL P)	ALL F	P AND F	ACCENTS (NO ACCENTS)	Ives: *The Pond*
3.	ALL P	(ALL F)	P AND F	(ACCENTS) NO ACCENTS	Olantunji: *Jin-Go-Lo-Ba*
4.	ALL P	ALL F	(P AND F)	(ACCENTS) NO ACCENTS	Alkan: *Les Diablotins*

Dynamics 93

DYNAMICS · Lesson 6

MATERIALS
Record 4, *What Do You Hear? 6: Dynamics; What Do You Hear? 7: Dynamics;* spirit masters

VOCABULARY
piano, forte, accents

TEACHER INFORMATION
For *What Do You Hear? 7*, you may wish to play the recording twice—once for children to identify the dynamic level(s), and once for them to indicate whether or not they hear accents.

TRY THIS
1. Children can make up a What Do You Hear? evaluation of their own. Have them tape-record environmental sounds that illustrate the qualities of dynamics presented in this module. Have them play their sounds for others to identify the dynamics.

2. Write the score for *Dynamic Boxes* (see Sound Piece below) on the chalkboard. Choose two players, each of whom selects a different sound source (e.g., a percussion instrument). When they perform the Sound Piece, they follow the dynamics for each box in their part. Except for the boxes containing accents, they may play one sound per box, or a series of sounds. They may play sounds that have a steady-beat rhythm, or a more complicated rhythm. A leader signals players when to begin, and when to move from one box to the next. When the piece is performed for the class, call attention to the qualities of tempo, rhythm pattern, and register, as well as dynamics. Suggestion: Have children create their own sound pieces to illustrate dynamics.

SOUND PIECE: *Dynamic Boxes* by Wynn Check

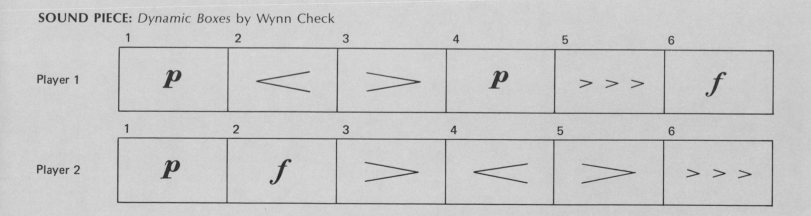

MODULE 8

OBJECTIVES, p. XII

FORM • Lesson 1

MATERIALS
Record 4, Giuliani: *Grand Sonata in A Major for Flute and Guitar,* "Scherzo"; Pupil's Book, pp. 94 and 95

VOCABULARY
form, repetition and contrast, AB, ABA, ABC

IDEAS FOR TEACHING
1. Reinforce the concept of repetition and contrast by arranging things in the room—e.g., placing two identical chairs beside a desk (chair-chair-desk or chair-desk-chair) or placing a pair of shoes beside one shoe of a different style. Arrange children wearing same and different colors or styles of sweaters, jeans, shirts, etc., to further illustrate repetition and contrast in everyday things.

2. Call attention to the photograph on p. 94. Help children recognize the contrast in shape between the large circular form and the arched forms at the bottom of the picture. Help them observe the repetition and contrast in line, shape, and color within the large circular form—for example, the repetition of shapes in each concentric circle as well as the contrast in shapes as the eye moves from the outermost circle to the innermost one.

3. Write the following Call Chart on the chalkboard. Then play the recording of Giuliani's "Scherzo." As →

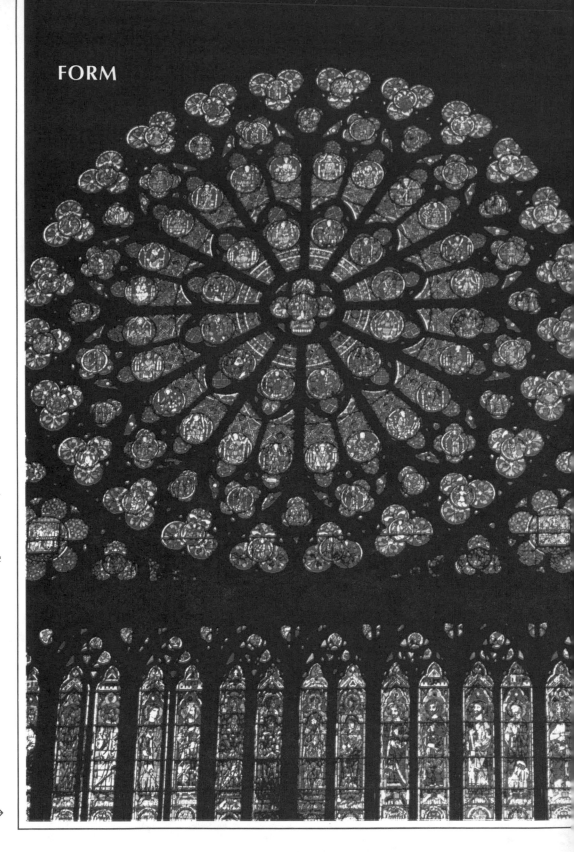

Shapes and letters can show form in music.

Which shapes and letters show the form of songs you know?

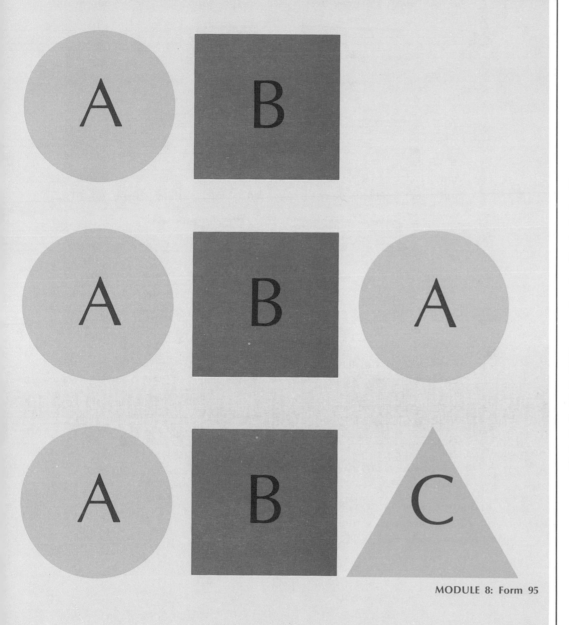

MODULE 8: Form 95

children listen, the chart will help them hear which sections of the music are the same and which are different. Note: The chart tells what is happening in the music at the point where each number is called on the recording.

1. Section A
2. Contrast of A
3. Repetition of A
4. Contrast of A
5. Repetition of A

4. Call attention to the shapes and letters on p. 95 that are used to show repetition and contrast. As children sing the following songs, or others that they know, have them point to the set of shapes and letters that identifies the form of each one.

Ⓐ Ⓑ

• Scratch, Scratch, p. 6
• Ging Gong Gooli, p. 18
• Dayenu, p. 40

Ⓐ Ⓑ Ⓐ

• Oh, Won't You Sit Down? p. 24

Ⓐ Ⓑ △

• Dry Bones, p. 42

Suggestion: If you do not use all of the songs listed above, or if you decide to use other songs, be certain to include "Dry Bones." Many songs children know illustrate the form AB or ABA. "Dry Bones" is an example of a song with three contrasting sections—A, B, C.

TEACHER INFORMATION
Page 94 of the Pupil's Book shows a photograph of a rose window. It is characteristic of windows that are still found in cathedrals in France and England built during the Middle Ages. As can be seen in the photograph, the window consists of small pieces of colored glass set in lead strips.

FORM • Lesson 2

MATERIALS
Record 4, "Sands Get into Your Shoes"; *Flop-Eared Mule;* Pupil's Book, pp. 96 and 97; bongos, maracas, cowbell, wood block, Autoharp

VOCABULARY
section A, section B, contrast

IDEAS FOR TEACHING

1. Play the recording of "Sands Get into Your Shoes." Have children show that they hear two contrasting sections in the music by listening during section A, and performing a stamp-clap pattern (see Movement Pattern a below) during section B.

2. Ask children to make up their own pattern to keep the beat during section A of the song. They may use motions that have sound—stamps, claps, knee pats, finger snaps—or motions that are silent—flipping the wrist, shrugging the shoulders, bending the knees, nodding the head—or they may make up a pattern that combines "sound" motions with silent ones (see Movement Pattern *b* below for an example). Mainstreaming Note: Encourage motor-impaired, nonambulatory, and mentally retarded children to use the full range of movements they are capable of making, no matter how limited this may be.

3. Choose two small groups, one to create a pattern of motions for section A, the other to create a different pattern for section B. As others sing the song (notation, p. 96), the groups each perform their pattern during the appropriate section.

4. Have children show the contrast →

This song has two sections, A and B. How are they different?

SANDS GET INTO YOUR SHOES
WORDS AND MUSIC BY ARTHUR CARTER

USED BY PERMISSION.
Piano acc., p. 309

1. You have -n't lived___ in the sum - mer-time___
2. The sun comes beat - ing down on your head,___

Un - til you've gone___ to the beach,___
The dust gets in - to your eyes,___

And tast - ed ice - cream: the lem - on lime,___
Your feet they hurt,___ but the thing you dread's___

Ba - na - na, wal - nut and peach.
The mos - qui - toes___ and the flies.

(optional harmony part)
And sands, and sands, and sands get in - to your o - pen shoes,

And sands, and sands, and sands get in - to your shoes.

3. You leave your things by the waterside,
   And then somehow you forget
   To move them back from the rising tide—
   Your towels and blanket get wet.
   And sands . . .

96 Form

MOVEMENT PATTERNS

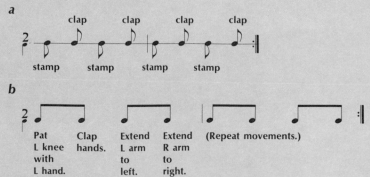

a

clap   clap   clap   clap

stamp   stamp   stamp   stamp

b

Pat   Clap   Extend   Extend   (Repeat movements.)
L knee   hands.   L arm   R arm
with   to   to
L hand.   left.   right.

Play these percussion parts during section A.

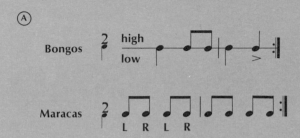

Here are parts to play during section B.

This dance music has two sections, A and B. Use movement to show the contrast between the sections.

Flop-Eared Mule
4

Form 97

between the sections of "Sands into Your Shoes" by playing the percussion parts on p. 97. <u>Point out</u>: (a) The bongos part has an accent (>) on the last beat of the pattern. (b) The wood-block part has the same rhythm as the words *sands get into your open shoes* in the song. Thinking the words over and over will help the player keep the rhythm. (c) The bongos and maracas parts begin on the first strong beat of the song, on the syllable *have* of *haven't*.

5. Give children time to practice the Autoharp part for "Sands Get into Your Shoes" from the score on p. 96. When they are ready, have them take turns accompanying the singing. <u>Note:</u> Children may play a long strum on the first beat of each measure, or they may make up their own pattern to strum.

6. Take time to discuss some of the ways in which the sections of "Sands Get into Your Shoes" contrast:
• The melody is different for each section.
• The rhythm is different for each section.
• Some phrases in section A are identical; each phrase in section B is different.

7. Play the recording of *Flop-Eared Mule* so that children may hear the contrasting sections. Then divide them into groups to create contrasting movement patterns, one for section A, one for section B. When they are ready, the groups take turns performing their movement patterns with the recording.

MATERIALS
Record 4, "Run, Run, Run"; Pupil's Book, pp. 98 and 99, 95; any percussion instrument, recorders or bells

VOCABULARY
ABA form, D. C. al Fine, Fine, syncopation

IDEAS FOR TEACHING

1. Play the recording and have children show the contrasting sections by moving in their own way during section A and playing a percussion instrument during section B. <u>Note:</u> (a) Children may play steady beats or a more complicated pattern (e.g., ♩♫♩♩) during section B. (b) Some children may remember the song from the Beginning Experiences section. Invite them to sing with the recording (notation, p. 98).

2. Children will hear that section A is repeated after section B on the recording. Have them find the place in the music that indicates this. <u>Note:</u> *D. C. al Fine* (Dah kah'-poh ahl Fee'-nay) above the last staff means "Repeat from the beginning and continue to the word *Fine* (Fee'-nay)." <u>Question:</u> How is the form of "Run, Run, Run" different from that of "Sands Get into Your Shoes"? ("Run, Run, Run" is in ABA form; "Sands Get into Your Shoes" is in AB form.)

3. Have children find the set of shapes and letters on p. 95 that shows the form of "Run, Run, Run." (Ⓐ Ⓑ Ⓐ)

4. Help children become aware of some of the qualities that make the sections of "Run, Run, Run" sound ⟶

This song has repetition and contrast. Find the place in the score that tells you section A repeats.

RUN, RUN, RUN WORDS AND MUSIC BY CHRIS DEDRICK

© 1972 ALMITRA MUSIC COMPANY, INC.

Piano acc., p. 305

Run, run, run ___ through the sun-light, Run, run, run ___ through the sno
Run, run, run, ___ don't be up-tight, Run, run, run, ___ Free-dom, go. ___
If you're glad that you can use your legs, they're free;
If you're glad that you can use your eyes to see,
If you're glad the world has trea-sures you can find,
Go and run so fast your cares are left be-hind.

D.C. al Fi

98 Form

TEACHER INFORMATION
<u>Mainstreaming Note:</u> An adaptation for "Run, Run, Run" appears in *Silver Burdett Music for Special Education.*

Play this part on recorder or bells when it comes in the song.

It uses G and A.

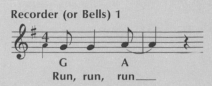

Recorder (or Bells) 1

G A
Run, run, run___

To play more of section A, you will need two new tones—high C and D.

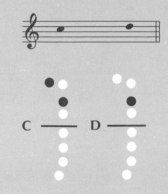

C D

Now try playing this part during section A.

Recorder (or Bells) 2

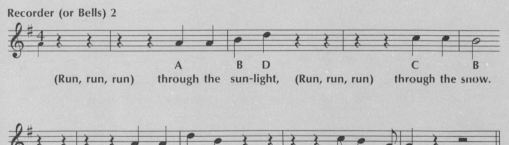

 A B D   C B
(Run, run, run) through the sun-light, (Run, run, run) through the snow.

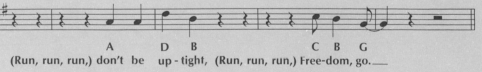

 A D B   C B G
(Run, run, run,) don't be up-tight, (Run, run, run,) Free-dom, go.___

Form 99

different. <u>Note</u>: Section A has syncopation (a special rhythmic feeling created by stressing a beat that is normally weak, as on the words *Run, run, run*—♪♩ ♪♩♩), frequent skips, and much melodic movement; section B has a steady quarter-note rhythm, many repeated tones, less melodic movement.

5. As others sing, have children who can play G and A (fingerings, p. 27) on recorder play the notation for Recorder 1 (p. 99) each time the words *Run, run, run* occur. <u>Note</u>: Bells may be used instead of recorders.

6. Give recorder players time to practice the fingerings for the new tones high C and D on p. 99, and to review the fingerings for G, A, B on p. 27. Then have them play the notation for Recorder 2. <u>Point out</u>: Recorder 2 plays the part of the section A melody that follows the words *Run, run, run* each time. <u>Suggestion</u>: Have one group play the Recorder 1 part, another, the Recorder 2 part. Children will then be playing during all of section A.

REVIEW/REINFORCEMENT
Have recorder players practice the fingerings for G, A, B (p. 27), low D and E (p. 59), and high D (p. 99). Then they can play the melody of section B as others sing "Run, Run, Run."

TRY THIS
Select children to practice the following Autoharp accompaniment for "Run, Run, Run." <u>Point out</u>: (a) Section A uses two chords (G, D₇); section B, three chords (G, D₇, C). (b) Section A has a half-note rhythm; section B, a rhythm of half notes and quarter notes. (c) The chord pattern for section A is played twice each time. <u>Note</u>: Have the Autoharp play four G chords as an introduction. The singing begins on the fourth chord:

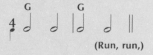

G G

(Run, run,)

MATERIALS
Record 4, "Don't Count Your Chickens"; Pupil's Book, pp. 100 and 101; bells or piano, recorders

VOCABULARY
ABA form, cluster

IDEAS FOR TEACHING
1. Have children listen to the recording to discover the two contrasting sections, A and B. Question: Which section of the song uses clapping sounds near the end? (Section A)

2. Play the recording so that children can add their own clapping sounds near the end of section A. Have them listen for the frequent repetition of the words *they hatch* throughout the section.

3. Have children look at p. 101 to discover ways to add the tone color of bells, piano, or recorders on the words *they hatch*. Then, as others sing (notation, p. 100), some children play clusters on the instrument of their choice each time *they hatch* occurs. Question: Is the form of the song AB, or ABA? (ABA) How do you know? (Section A is repeated after section B.)

4. Call attention to some of the musical qualities that make section A different from section B. Note: The sections are different in melody (A has mostly leaps and repeated tones; B moves mostly by step), rhythm (A has dotted rhythms; B uses mostly eighth notes), and harmony (A uses two chords—G, D_7; B uses three chords—G, D_7, C). ⟶

Listen to discover repetition and contrast in the sections of this song. Is the form AB, or ABA?   ABA

DON'T COUNT YOUR CHICKENS   WORDS AND MUSIC BY CARMINO RAVOSA

© 1971 Carmino Ravosa

Piano acc., p. 257

100 Form

mor-row may just bring a lot-ta sor - row. Don't you sor - row.

Don't count your chick-ens be-fore they hatch, Be-fore they hatch,

be - fore they hatch. Don't count your chick-ens be - fore they hatch,

Be - fore they hatch, (*clap clap*) they hatch!

As you sing the song, take turns adding a cluster of tones on
the words *they hatch*. To play a cluster, strike a group of
bells with the edge of a small wooden ruler. Or play a
group of piano keys with your knuckles.

Will you play a cluster of high tones, or low tones?

high cluster

low cluster

Ask two friends to help you play clusters of tones on recorders.
One recorder plays G, another plays A, the third plays
B—all at the same time.

they hatch

Form 101

REVIEW/REINFORCEMENT
Have children use tone clusters to
fill in the silences during section B
of "Scratch, Scratch" (p. 6). If a
piano is available, have them experiment with playing thin and thick
clusters, using fingers (simultaneously
playing consecutive keys), fist, heel
of hand, forearm, elbow, etc.
Suggestion: Children might notate
patterns of clusters for others to
play, using the symbols for high and
low clusters shown on p. 101.

TRY THIS
1. Encourage children to create movements that show the
contrast between sections A and B of the song; for example:
    Section A—Children strut around the room with a
        jerking motion, like chickens pecking.
    Section B—Children quickly shuffle feet, like chickens
        scurrying.

2. Have children who study violin try to play the double
stops (sounds played on two strings at once) in measures
1 and 2 of the introduction (p. 100).

3. Children can add a percussion accompaniment that
shows the contrast between sections A and B of the song.
For example, if a jaw harp (an instrument that is held in
the teeth and struck with the finger to produce sound) is
available, children might try playing it during section A, as
on the recording. They might play short sounds on sticks
during section B. Suggestion: If possible, use the Pick-a-
Track technique so children can get ideas by listening to
the recording with the instrumental track highlighted.

MATERIALS
Record 5, *Call Chart 5: Form;* Pupil's Book, p. 102

VOCABULARY
repetition, contrast

IDEAS FOR TEACHING
1. Have children read the instructions for *Call Chart 5* (p. 102).

2. Play the recording and have children listen as the numbers are called to hear whether the music is a repetition of A or a contrast.

TRY THIS
Have individuals select a familiar song in AB or ABA form to prepare as a Call Chart experience. Give them time to practice. Then have them play the recording for the class, calling a number for each section of the music. For each number, the class decides whether they are hearing section A or section B. Possible songs include:

AB Form: "Sambalele," p. 22
"Lazy Coconut Tree," p. 41
"In Bahia Town," p. 80

ABA Form: "Hand Me Down," p. 14
"Oh, Won't You Sit Down?" p. 24
"Run, Run, Run," p. 98

CALL CHART 5: FORM ⊙

Can you hear form in music? Listen to the recording to discover the form of these pieces. When number 1 is called, you are hearing section A. When you hear another number, the music will be either a repetition of section A, or a contrast. Follow the chart to help you hear what is happening in the music.

---

1.   A
2. *CONTRAST*   B   *Notebook for Anna Magdalena Bach, "Minuet"*

---

1.   A
2. *CONTRAST*   B
3. *REPETITION*   A   **Bichel:** *Happy Moments*

---

1.   A
2. *REPETITION*   A
3. *CONTRAST*   B
4. *REPETITION*   A   *Notebook for Anna Magdalena Bach, "Musette"*

---

102 Form

TEACHER INFORMATION
Call Charts are instructional devices that focus children's attention on a specific quality or qualities within a musical selection. A number is called at moments when the quality (e.g., repetition, contrast) can be perceived in the music.

Create a sound piece that has three different sections. Use the tone colors and rhythm patterns shown below.

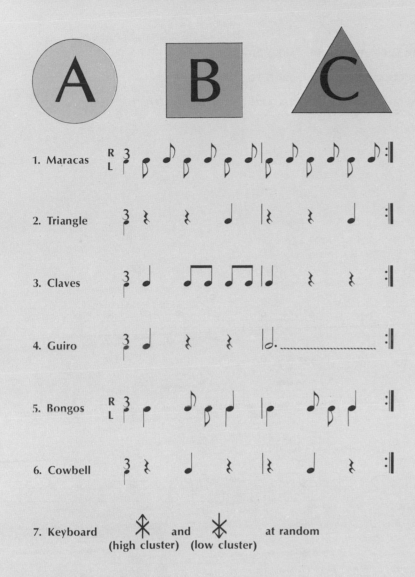

Ways to contrast sections:

1. **Different tone colors**
2. **Different rhythm patterns**
3. **Different dynamics—p, mf, f, < >**
4. **Different tempos**

Form 103

MATERIALS
Pupil's Book, pp. 42, 103; percussion instruments

VOCABULARY
ABC form, contrast

IDEAS FOR TEACHING

1. Review "Dry Bones" (p. 42) and have children analyze how the three sections are different. Note: The sections use different words; have different rhythms; have melodies sung in different registers and at different tempos.

2. Use the following ideas to help children create a sound piece that has three different sections:
(a) Direct attention to the percussion patterns on p. 103. Point out: Each pattern has its own tone color and rhythm.
(b) Help children choose contrasting percussion patterns— one for section A, another for B, a third for C; for example: Ⓐ-pattern 1, B-4, C-7 or Ⓐ-pattern 5, B-2, C-1.
(c) Encourage them to use different tempos and dynamics to further contrast the sections of the piece.
(d) Choose a leader and have children perform their piece. For each section, they repeat the pattern over and over until the leader signals a new section to begin.

3. Have small groups make up their own sound pieces in ABC form and perform them for the class. Discuss how contrast is shown in each piece. Use the information on p. 103 to aid the discussion. If possible, record the sound pieces that children create.

MATERIALS
Record 5, "Tina, Singu"; Pupil's Book,
p. 104; African instruments or substitutes for them

VOCABULARY
ABC form, contrast, repeat signs

IDEAS FOR TEACHING

1. Have children look at the notation
on p. 104 to discover that each section of "Tina, Singu" has repeat signs
(see Teacher Information below).
Then play the recording and have
children sing when each melody is
repeated. Question: What is the form
of "Tina, Singu"? (ABC form)

2. When children know the song,
divide them into three groups, one
to sing each section. Questions:
Which section has a tone that repeats many times? (Section A) Sets
of repeated tones that move upward
and downward by step? (B) Tones
that leap as well as tones that move
by step? (C)

3. Have children point out the song's
contrasting sections as follows:
(a) by performing the melody of
each section with a different tone
color (e.g., recorder for A, bells for B,
voices for C). Note: Recorders play
the tones G, A, B, high C, high D;
bells play B, high C, high D.
(b) by using different dynamics for
each section (e.g., f for A, < >
for B, < for C).
(c) by using a different tone color to
accompany each section (e.g., kagan
for A, gankogui for B, axatse for C).
Note: A high drum, high- and low-
sounding tin cans, and a maraca may
be substituted for the African instruments in the example (see Teacher's
Edition p. 89, item 4).

How many sections are in "Tina, Singu"? 3

Find the sections that begin with repeated tones. A, B

Find the section that has leaps and tones that move by step. C

TINA, SINGU FOLK SONG FROM AFRICA Piano acc., p. 268

FROM CHANSONS DE NOTRE CHALET. COURTESY OF WORLD AROUND SONGS. BURNSVILLE. N.C.

Ti - na, Sing - u, le - lu - vu - tae - o.

Wat - sha,___ Wat - sha,___ Wat - sha.___

Wat-sha,___ Wat-sha,___ Wat-sha,___ Wat-sha,___ Wat-sha.___

La, la - la - la - la - la - la, la - la - la - la - la - la -

la, la - la - la - la - la - la - la - la - la - la - la.

104 Form

TRY THIS
Divide children into two groups to sing sections B and C
of "Tina, Singu" simultaneously. They will be singing in
harmony. Note: Be certain that children are thoroughly
familiar with the melody before trying this activity.

TEACHER INFORMATION
The repeat sign (:|) at the end of section A of "Tina,
Singu" means "Repeat from the beginning of the song."
An initial repeat sign (|:) is not necessary when the first
section repeats from the beginning.

The words of "Tina, Singu" literally mean "We are the
burning fire; we burn; we burn." They are pronounced as
follows:

Ti - na, Sing - u, le - lu - vu - tae - o.
tee-nah sing-oo leh-loo-voo-tay-oh
Wat - sha, Wat - sha, Wat - sha.
waht-shah waht-shah waht-shah

CALL CHART 6: FORM 🔊
5

Repetition and contrast can be used in many ways to give music form.

Listen to the recording to discover how contrast is used to make

version 2 of this piece different from version 1.

Following the chart will help you to hear what is

going on in the music.

Kingsley: *Electronic Rondo*, Versions 1 and 2

Version 1

1.		A
2.	FIRST CONTRAST	B
3.	REPETITION	A
4.	FIRST CONTRAST	B
5.	REPETITION	A

Version 2

1.		A
2.	FIRST CONTRAST	B
3.	REPETITION	A
4.	SECOND CONTRAST	C
5.	REPETITION	A

Form 105

FORM • Lesson 8

MATERIALS
Record 5, *Call Chart 6: Form;* Pupil's Book, p. 105

VOCABULARY
repetition, contrast

IDEAS FOR TEACHING
Have children follow the chart on p. 105 as they listen to the recording. Note: Children will hear two versions of *Electronic Rondo.* In each version, a number is called at the beginning of the sections. As they listen, children find each number in their chart. The chart tells whether they are hearing section A, a repetition of A, or a contrasting section. Question: How is version 2 different from version 1? (Version 2 has two contrasting sections, B and C; version 1 has only one contrasting section, B.) Point out: In both versions, section A is repeated after each contrasting section.

TRY THIS
1. Have children make cardboard cutouts in the shape of circles, squares, and triangles. As they listen to the music, they indicate the arrangement of the sections by placing down a circle for each section A, a square for each section B, a triangle for section C.

2. Divide children into three groups—one for section A, another for B, the third for C. Give each group time to work out a movement pattern for their section. Then play the recording. Each group moves when they hear their section of the music. Note: Group C will move only during version 2 of the music.

TEACHER INFORMATION
Both versions 1 and 2 of *Electronic Rondo* are in rondo form, a form in which section A keeps returning after contrasting sections. If children are ready, introduce the term *rondo.* Otherwise, they may refer to the form of version 1 as ABABA, and to that of version 2 as ABACA.

Gershon Kingsley (American, c. 1926–   ) *Electronic Rondo:* This composer has created many works for the electronic synthesizer. He is the founder of the First Moog Quartet. Kingsley composed *Electronic Rondo* especially for SILVER BURDETT MUSIC and performed the piece on a synthesizer.

MATERIALS

Record 5, "Guava Berry Song"; Pupil's Book, pp. 106 and 107; maracas, claves, bongos, cowbell

VOCABULARY

ABC form, contrast, harmony

IDEAS FOR TEACHING

1. Play the recording of "Guava Berry Song." <u>Question</u>: Is the form of this song AB, ABA, or ABC? (ABC: the music has three different sections.)

2. Play the recording again while children follow the notation (pp. 106 and 107). Have them focus on the different ways musical qualities are treated in each section of the music; for example:

Meter: The meter is in 3 for sections A and B, in 4 for section C.

Rhythm Pattern: Section A uses mostly quarter notes; B has many eighth notes and uses dotted rhythms; C uses the same rhythm for each staff, with one change (♩ instead of ♫) in the last staff.

Tone Color: Each section uses different tone colors on the recording: section A—voices, guitar, maracas; B—voices singing in harmony, flute; C—voices, trumpet, steel drum. <u>Note:</u> Although other tone colors are present in each section, the ones mentioned are among the most obvious.

Texture: Each section creates harmony in a different way: section A—guitar plays chords; B—voices sing in two parts with flute countermelody; C—voices sing in unison while trumpet and steel drum play countermelodies.

3. As the class sings with the record- →

GUAVA BERRY SONG

CHRISTMAS SONG FROM THE VIRGIN ISLANDS   ENGLISH WORDS BY JOAN GILBERT VAN POZNAK

FROM UNICEF BOOK OF CHILDREN'S SONGS, COMPILED AND WITH PHOTOGRAPHS BY WILLIAM I. KAUFMAN, COPYRIGHT 1970 BY WILLIAM I. KAUFMAN, PUBLISHED BY STACKPOLE BOOKS.

Piano acc., p. 284

Come let us be joy-ful, and min-gle our song,

And hail the sweet joys which this day brings a-long.

We join our glad voic-es in one hymn of praise

To ___ Him ___ who has kept us, and ___ length-ened our days.

A mer-ry Christ-mas to you all, A mer-ry Christ-mas to you all,

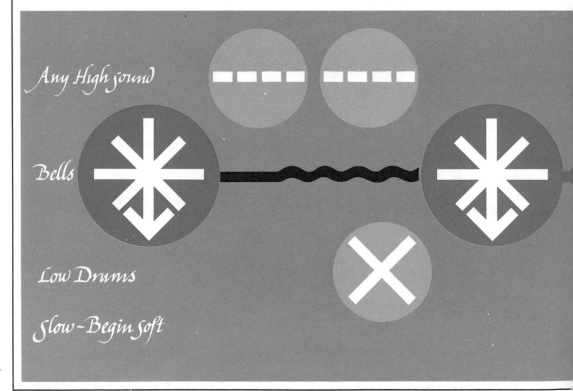

Any High sound

Bells

Low Drums

Slow—Begin soft

TEACHER INFORMATION

<u>Mainstreaming Note</u>: An adaptation for "Guava Berry Song" appears in *Silver Burdett Music for Special Education.*

A mer-ry Christ-mas, A mer-ry Christ-mas, A mer-ry Christ-mas to you all!

Good morn - in', good morn - in', We wish you a mer - ry Christ - mas,

Good morn - in', good morn - in', We wish you a mer - ry Christ - mas,

Good morn - in', good morn - in', We've come for the gua - va ber - ry,

Good morn - in', good morn - in', Oh put it on the ta - ble.

ing, have individuals play percussion instruments to accompany each section (see below for parts). <u>Note:</u> Each percussion part begins on the first strong beat of the section: in section A, on the word *let*; in B, on the first syllable of *Christmas*; in C, on the first syllable of *mornin'*. <u>Suggestion:</u> When children are ready, have a small group sing the harmony (lower notes with stems pointing down) during section B. <u>Point out:</u> Except for two measures (the last and the third from last), the harmony has the same contour as the melody, but it is sung an interval of a third lower.

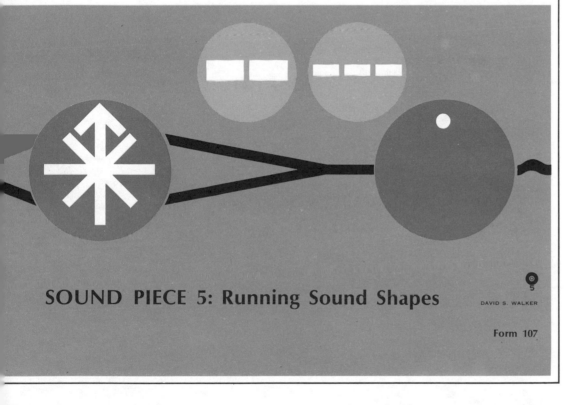

SOUND PIECE 5: Running Sound Shapes

DAVID S. WALKER

Form 107

PERCUSSION PARTS

Section A Maracas

Section B Claves

Section C { Bongos / Cowbell

TEACHER INFORMATION

The symbols at the bottom of pp. 106 and 107 represent the beginning of *Sound Piece 5,* which continues to p. 111 of the Pupil's Book. Instructions for performing the Sound Piece begin on p. 108.

MATERIALS

Record 5, *Sound Piece 5: Running Sound Shapes;* Pupil's Book, pp. 106–111; bells, low drum, any high-pitched instrument

VOCABULARY

AB form, legend, cluster

IDEAS FOR TEACHING

1. Have children look at the notation for *Sound Piece 5* at the bottom of pp. 106–111 to discover the form (AB). Questions: How many sections does the piece have? (Two) How do you know? (The notation uses circles for section A, pp. 106–109, and squares for section B, pp. 110 and 111.)

2. Have children read the legend on pp. 108 and 109 to discover what the symbols in the Sound Piece mean. Give them time to find the symbols in the notation, looking first at the bell part, then the top part, and finally the drum part. Note: The top part is written for any high-pitched instrument—e.g., finger cymbals or triangle.

3. Play the recording as children follow the notation. Then divide the class into groups of three to work out their own interpretation for the Sound Piece. Give each group an opportunity to perform for the class. Take time to discuss the ways in which the various interpretations differ. Point out: There is no single right way to perform the Sound Piece. The recording shows one interpretation. Children should use their own musical ideas to interpret the Sound Piece their way. Note: The nature of the Sound Piece leaves →

The music at the bottom of pages 106–111 in your book is written using the shapes ● and ■.

This is to show that the piece has two sections.

Where does section B begin?   On p. 110

Here is what the symbols in *Sound Piece 5* stand for.

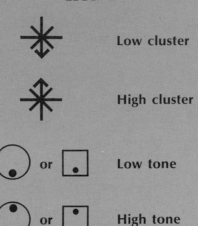

LEGEND

✳	Low cluster
✳	High cluster
◉ or ▪	Low tone
◉ or ▫	High tone

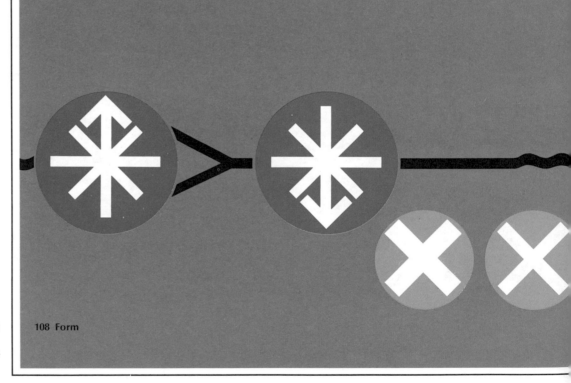

108 Form

▬ ▬ ▬ I	Continue to play.
◄	Continue to play, getting louder.
►	Continue to play, getting softer.
∿∿∿	Let the tone ring.
▬ or ✕	Play loud.
— or ✕	Play soft.

Now practice section A. While you play the bells, have one friend play the drum part, another the top part.

Another time, try section B. When your ensemble is ready to play *Sound Piece 5,* perform for the class.

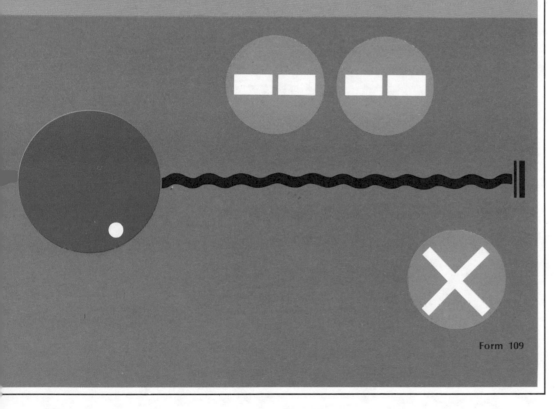

Form 109

room for individual interpretation; for example: bell players may use the same high bell each time a high sound is called for, or they may use a different high bell each time; they may play thick clusters of tones (having many sounds) or thin clusters (having few sounds). For the top part, players may use all long sounds, all short sounds, or sounds of different lengths. Suggestion: Have children try playing the bell part on a different instrument—for example, piano or Autoharp.

TRY THIS
1. When children have learned to play *Sound Piece 5,* have them perform it changing the form from AB (○ □) to ABA (○ □ ○) by repeating the A section after B.

2. Encourage children to make up a third section (C or △) for the Sound Piece. Have them notate it using triangles and the symbols shown in the legend on pp. 108 and 109.

REVIEW/REINFORCEMENT
Take time to review some of the sound pieces already presented in Book 4:
Sound Piece 1: Chance Music, p. 46
Sound Piece 2: Contours at the Keyboard, p. 61
Sound Piece 3: Did Sid? p. 74
Sound Piece 4: Busy Lizzy, p. 75

TEACHER INFORMATION
Throughout Book 4, sound pieces are used to reinforce children's understanding of musical qualities, to give them an opportunity to use what they know, and to stimulate musical creativity. Children should always be encouraged to approach the sound pieces with imagination and inventiveness.

Give children an opportunity to reexperience the sound pieces from time to time. If a period of time elapses before a sound piece is reviewed, children will bring increased musical awareness and understanding to their interpretation.

MATERIALS
Record 5, *What Do You Hear? 8: Form*; spirit master

VOCABULARY
repetition, contrast

IDEAS FOR TEACHING
Suggestion: Play the recording of *What Do You Hear? 8* two times. The first time, children listen to each piece to hear the overall structure of the work. The second time, they indicate whether they hear repetition or contrast when each number is called.

Children are now ready to take Test 1 for Book 4. Additional information about Silver Burdett Music Competency Tests is found in the introduction of this book.

WHAT DO YOU HEAR? 8: FORM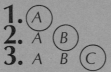

Can you hear repetition and contrast in these pieces? When number "one" is called, you will hear the musical ideas in section A. As the other numbers are called, decide whether the music is a repetition of A, a first contrast of A (B), or a second contrast of A (C).

1. (A)
2. A (B)

Purcell: Fanfare

1. (A)
2. A (B)
3. A B (C)

Guava Berry Song

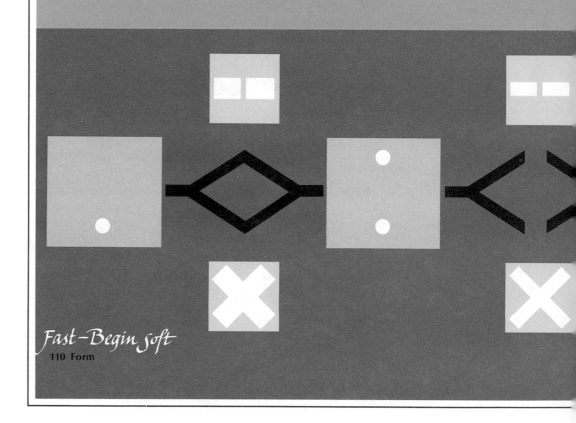

Fast–Begin soft
110 Form

TEACHER INFORMATION
Besides providing a tool for evaluation, the What Do You Hear? activities expose children to music in a wide variety of styles, written for a wide variety of performance media—vocal works as well as instrumental ones, solos as well as works for small ensembles and orchestra, works for conventional instruments as well as for electronic synthesizer. In *What Do You Hear? 8*, children hear a work from the 17th century (Purcell: *Fanfare*), a contemporary piece for recorders (Britten: *Scherzo*), and an electronic work composed especially for SILVER BURDETT MUSIC (Kingsley: *Electronic Rondo*).

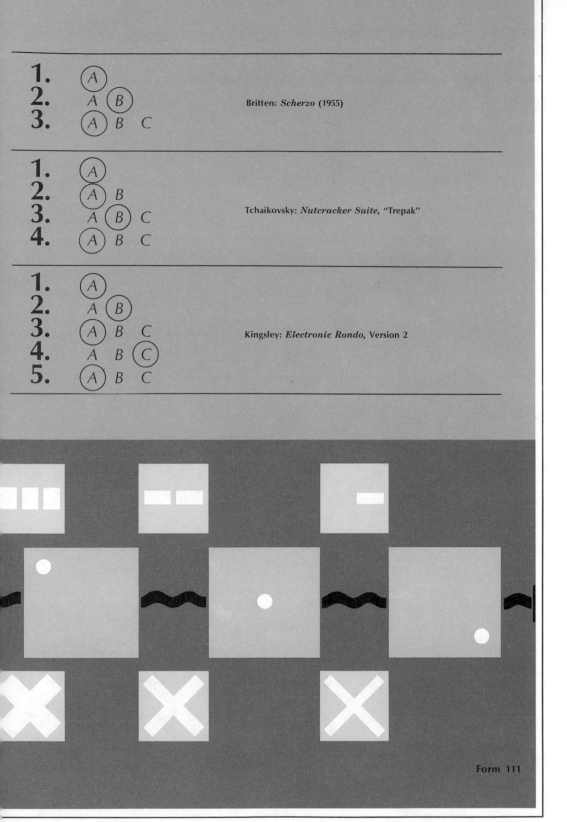

1. (A)

2. A (B)

3. (A) B C

Britten: *Scherzo* (1955)

1. (A)

2. (A) B

3. A (B) C

4. (A) B C

Tchaikovsky: *Nutcracker Suite,* "Trepak"

1. (A)

2. A (B)

3. (A) B C

4. A B (C)

5. (A) B C

Kingsley: *Electronic Rondo,* Version 2

Form 111

MODULE 9

OBJECTIVES, p. XII

STYLE

MATERIALS
Record 5, *Combining Sounds; What Do You Hear? 9: Style* (Marcello: *Sonata in F for Flute and Continuo,* Movement 4; Caplet: *Petite Valse*); Marcello: *Sonata in F for Flute and Continuo,* Movement 2; Pupil's Book, pp. 112–115; spirit master

VOCABULARY
style, parts, whole

IDEAS FOR TEACHING
1. Direct children's attention to the illustrations on p. 112 that show pieces or parts of a picture at the top, and the pieces assembled to form the whole picture at the bottom. Discuss the idea of a "whole" being the result of putting parts together; for example:
- To make a whole book, covers, pages, illustrations, text, etc., are put together;
- To make a whole shoe, heel, sole, leather, laces, etc., are put together;
- To make a whole car, wheels, body, engine, seats, etc., are put together.

2. Call attention to the numbers and colors on p. 113. Help children observe that the numbers 11, 9, 8, and 2 are "parts" that when added together make up the "whole," 30; and that the colors yellow and blue are "parts" that when put together make up the "whole," green. <u>Point out</u>: If the order of the numbers (parts) is reversed—2+8+9+11—or changed in any other way—e.g., ⟶

STYLE

Everything is made of parts.

Put the parts together and you get a "whole."

112 MODULE 9: Style

What do these numbers and colors add up to?

$$11 + 9 + 8 + 2 = 30$$

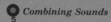

When you add the numbers, the answer is 30.

When yellow and blue are combined, the result is green.

On the recording *Combining Sounds,* you will hear the following sounds combined in two ways.

1. *LOW, SOFT SOUNDS*

2. *HIGH, LOUD SOUNDS*

3. *LONG AND SHORT SOUNDS*

4. *SOUNDS MOVING IN BOTH UPWARD AND DOWNWARD DIRECTIONS*

Do the combined sounds result in the same general sound each time?

Combining Sounds

When certain numbers or colors are combined, the result is always the same.

When certain qualities of sounds are used, the combinations of sounds may result in the same style, or in different styles.

Style 113

8+11+2+9—the result of adding them together (the whole) would still be 30. Likewise, no matter in what order the colors (parts) are put together—yellow added to blue or blue added to yellow—the result (the whole) will always be green.

3. Play the recording *Combining Sounds.* Most children will hear that the result of the first combination of sounds is different from that of the second. Some children may describe the first combination as strange, or spooky. However, steer children's comments toward the *qualities* of the sounds themselves so they are heard more perceptively. Help children describe the sound, *not* the sound effect.
In the first example, the sounds are thick, active, full, with some sounds repeated. There is no melody, beat, or harmony. The style is Electronic.
In the second example, the sounds are thinner and moderately active, with some sounds repeated. The music has a singable melody, a strong beat, and harmony. The style is Folkloric.

4. Play the recording of the Marcello work (Movement 4), having children follow the *What Do You Hear?* chart on p. 114 to help them perceive the musical qualities listed there as they listen. Help children hear the following in the music:
Tone Color—flute and piano
Texture—melody with harmony
Form—repetition and contrast
Direction—both upward and down-
   ward
Duration—both long and short
Dynamics—both soft and loud
Phrases—both short and long
<u>Note:</u> Children will not be able to perceive all the qualities at one hear-
→

ing. Play the recording more than once so that they can focus on two or three of the qualities at a time.

5. Play the recording of the Caplet piece, having children follow the chart on p. 115. Help them discover that this music has exactly the same qualities as the Marcello work (see Item 4). Question: The piece by Marcello and the one by Caplet both use many of the same musical qualities. Are the qualities put together in the same way in both pieces so that they both have the same general sound or style? (No. The qualities are put together differently in each piece. Each piece has a different general sound. Each piece is in a different style.) Point out: In music, composers use the same qualities. However, there are many different ways that the qualities can be put together. When two composers put the same musical qualities together in the same way, the music that results is in the same style. When two composers put the same musical qualities together in different ways, the music that results is in different styles.

6. Play the recording of the Marcello work (Movement 2). Question: Is this music in the same style as the first piece you heard (Marcello, Movement 4), or is it in the style of the second piece (Caplet)? (Help children discover that the style is the same as the first piece. The two pieces are different movements of the same work: Marcello's *Sonata in F for Flute and Continuo*. They both have the same general sound. They are both in the same style.)

TRY THIS
Children can compose pieces in vari- →

WHAT DO YOU HEAR? 9: STYLE ⊚ 5

1. Listen to this piece.

It uses many musical qualities—tone color, texture, etc.

Decide what you hear for each quality listed below.

Marcello: *Sonata in F*, Movement 4

TONE COLOR	TRUMPET SAXOPHONE	(FLUTE PIANO)
TEXTURE	(MELODY WITH HARMONY)	MELODY ALONE
FORM	NO REPETITION AND CONTRAST	(REPETITION AND CONTRAST)
DIRECTION	UPWARD DOWNWARD	(BOTH UPWARD AND DOWNWARD)
DURATION	LONG SHORT	(BOTH LONG AND SHORT)
DYNAMICS	SOFT LOUD	(BOTH SOFT AND LOUD)
PHRASES	SHORT LONG	(BOTH SHORT AND LONG)

114 Style

TEACHER INFORMATION
Benedetto Marcello (Italian, 1686–1739) *Sonata in F for Flute and Continuo*, Movements 2 and 4: This composer and poet was known as a satirist who poked fun at some of the overblown arias (elaborate songs) in the operas of his day.

André Caplet (French, 1878–1925) *Petite Valse:* This composer was active in France as a choral and operatic conductor. He also conducted opera in the United States with the Boston Opera Company and in London at Covent Garden (one of the great musical theaters of the world).

Although most of Caplet's music is scored for voices with instrumental accompaniment, *Petite Valse* is scored for instruments only—flute and piano.

2. Now listen to another piece.

It uses the same musical qualities as the first piece.

What do you hear for each quality in this music?

Caplet: *Petite Valse*

TONE COLOR	*TRUMPET* *SAXOPHONE*	*(FLUTE* *PIANO)*
TEXTURE	*(MELODY WITH* *HARMONY)*	*MELODY* *ALONE*
FORM	*NO REPETITION* *AND CONTRAST*	*(REPETITION AND* *CONTRAST)*
DIRECTION	*UPWARD* *DOWNWARD*	*(BOTH UPWARD* *AND DOWNWARD)*
DURATION	*LONG* *SHORT*	*(BOTH LONG* *AND SHORT)*
DYNAMICS	*SOFT* *LOUD*	*(BOTH SOFT* *AND LOUD)*
PHRASES	*SHORT* *LONG*	*(BOTH SHORT* *AND LONG)*

Style 115

ous styles, using a familiar folk song as a basis.

(a) Have children sing "Hear the Rooster" (p. 10).

(b) Call attention to the pattern of short sounds followed by a long sound used in each phrase of part III:

(c) Using that rhythm pattern for each phrase, have children create compositions that have four phrases as follows:

- A composition for mouth sounds—children use sounds like popping, tongue-clucking, hissing, buzzing for the short sounds, a sound like *aah, oooh, eeeh, ooow* for the long sounds. Encourage them to use different short and long sounds for each phrase.

- A composition for classroom instruments—Children use instruments like sticks, wood block, drum for the short sounds, instruments like piano, recorder, Autoharp, bell for the long sounds. Have them experiment with different combinations of instruments for each phrase. For example, sticks and wood block together might play the short sounds, a tambourine shake might be used for the long sounds. Or, a drum might play the short sounds; piano and Autoharp together might play the long sounds.

- A composition for piano—children might play the black keys for phrase 1, the white keys for phrase 2, both black and white keys for phrase 3, high and low tone clusters for phrase 4. Encourage other explorations of the keyboard.

MODULE 10

OBJECTIVES, p. XII

REGISTER—RANGE • Lesson 1

MATERIALS
Record 5, *Shoo-Be-de-doop;* Pupil's
Book, pp. 116 and 117

VOCABULARY
high register, middle register, low
register

IDEAS FOR TEACHING
1. Direct children's attention to the
photographs on pp. 116 and 117.
Help them observe the position of
the figures. Point out: (a) The boy is
shown in three placements—low
(lying on the floor), middle (hanging
from the balance beam), high (walking on the balance beam). (b) In the
photograph of the birds, one bird is
placed low in the picture, another
near the middle, the third, high in
the picture.

2. Play the recording and have children identify the tone colors that are
producing high sounds, low sounds,
and sounds in the middle (neither
high nor low). Point out: In music,
highness or lowness of sound is
called register. Note: Most children
will immediately recognize that the
women's voices are singing in high
and middle registers, while the men's
voices are singing in a low register.
Play the recording as many times as
necessary for them to focus on the
registers used in the instrumental
accompaniment. Children should discover that the piano is playing in a
high register, the electric bass in a
low register. Although they may not
→

REGISTER—RANGE

Shoo-Be-de-doop

116 MODULE 10: Register—Range

be able to identify the saxophone by name, children should hear that the instrument is playing in a middle register.

TRY THIS
Have children create a bulletin-board display that shows low, middle, and high. They might use, for example, pictures of a flag about to be raised (low), flying at half mast (middle), fully raised (high), or pictures of a basketball player dribbling the ball (low), passing it to another player (middle), tossing it into the basket (high).

Register—Range 117

REVIEW/REINFORCEMENT
Give children an opportunity to focus on register in some of the songs and bell experiences introduced in previous modules; for example:
Playing low and high bells to accompany "Here I Go," "When Is a Door?" and "Sandy McNab," Teacher's Edition p. 9
Playing low and high bells to accompany "Hear the Rooster," Teacher's Edition p. 10
Singing the low harmony part for "Hand Me Down," p. 14
Playing the high and low bell parts in *African Rhythm Complex*, p. 89

Playing high and low tone clusters to accompany "Don't Count Your Chickens," p. 100
Playing high and low tone clusters in *Sound Piece 5*, p. 106

REGISTER—RANGE • Lesson 2

MATERIALS
Record 5, "Island Hopping"; Pupil's Book, pp. 118 and 119; bells or other keyboard instruments

VOCABULARY
register, interval, triplet

IDEAS FOR TEACHING
1. Play the recording while children follow the notation on p. 118. Invite them to sing the echo (small notes) each time it occurs in section A. Note: The echo is written in octaves. During early experiences with the song, have children sing the echo in a low register (bottom notes). When they are familiar with the song, they can choose which register they will sing—low, or high (top notes). Question: Throughout the echo, what is the distance or interval from each low note to the high note above it? (An octave) Note: Remind children to determine the interval by calling the low note *one*, then counting each line and space above it, ending with the high note (eight).

2. Divide the class into three groups—one to sing the song, another to sing the echo in a low register, the third to sing the echo in a high register. Mainstreaming Note: Have children with limited voice range sing the echo in a low register.

3. Call attention to the bell part on p. 119. Help children observe that this is the notation for the echo in "Island Hopping." Have them take turns playing the echo (on bells or other keyboard instrument) in either a high register (top notes) or a low register (bottom notes). Point out: In the first measure, the group of eighth ⟶

ISLAND HOPPING
FOLK SONG FROM GREECE ENGLISH WORDS BY MARIA JORDAN

Piano acc., p. 280

1. Bags are packed and all is rea - dy, can't wait ___ to start; (can't wait ___ to start;) Boat is board-ing at the jet - ty, soon we'll ___ de - part. (soon we'll ___ de - part.)

B G (optional harmony part)
Is - land hop - ping we ___ are ___ go - ing,
Sea is calm, a soft ___ wind's ___ blow - ing,
We can feel ex - cite - ment ___ grow - ing
in ev - 'ry heart, ___ *Ahs-toh kah-loh,* ___ In ev - 'ry ___ heart.

118 Register—Range

TEACHER INFORMATION
Hydra, Spetsai, and Poros are three islands very close to the city of Piraeus, a Greek seaport. On weekends, many Greeks board a ferryboat in Piraeus and journey to the islands for a short holiday. The first stop on the excursion is Aegina, an island located an hour's ride away. After that, the ferryboat continues on to Poros, Hydra, and finally to Spetsai.

In the song "Island Hopping," the words *ahstoh kahloh* are a phonetic respelling of a Greek goodby wish that means "Go in safety; have a good trip." The names of the islands are pronounced as follows:
Hydra—ee'-thrah
Spetsai—spe'-tsay
Poros—bo'-rohs
In pronouncing *Hydra* and *Poros,* the *r* is slightly rolled.

Parents with their sons and daughters planned for this day;

Now the boat glides 'cross the waters, we're on our way.

Grecian islands lie before us—

Hydra, Spetsai, lovely Poros

Beckon us as, in a chorus, "Come," they all say, *Ahstoh kahloh,*

"Come," they all say.

[Pl]ay the echo in section A in a high register, or in a low register.

Bells

E   C♯   B   A   D

[A]rrange the high bells like this.

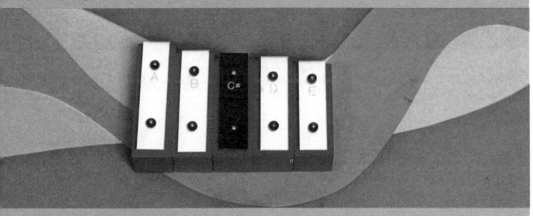

[A]rrange the low bells like this.

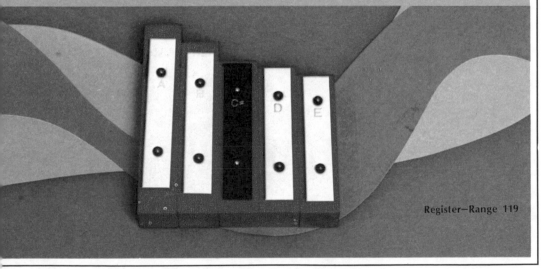

Register—Range 119

notes with a "3" above (below) them is called a triplet. The triplet is played as three equal sounds to the beat. <u>Suggestion</u>: If children use bells to play the echo, have them line up the low or high bells as shown on p. 119. This will help them see and feel the intervals (steps and leaps) they are playing as well as hear them.

TRY THIS

1. As others sing "Island Hopping," have individuals play the echo on the piano, using a high, middle, or low register. <u>Point out</u>: The beginning tone (E) is the white key to the right of any set of two black keys. Children can play the echo starting on any E on the piano keyboard.

2. Have individuals practice the Autoharp part for "Island Hopping" (see below). Then have them take turns accompanying the singing. <u>Point out</u>: (a) In the pattern, notes with stems down indicate strums on the low strings; notes with stems up, strums on the high strings. (b) The chord pattern for section A is played two times. (c) At the beginning of section B, the accents indicate that the strums should be played with an added stress. <u>Suggestions</u>: (a) Write the Autoharp part on the chalkboard or on an index card so that children can practice on their own. (b) The Autoharp part for section A uses two chords—D, A_7; the part for section B uses three chords—D, G, A_7. It is not necessary for one child to accompany the entire song. Let each child play the section with which he or she can be successful.

AUTOHARP STRUMMING PATTERN

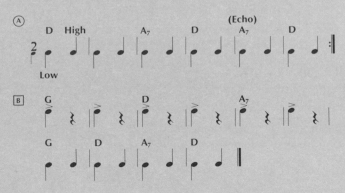

REGISTER—RANGE • Lesson 3

MATERIALS
Record 5, "Rally Song"; Pupil's Book, pp. 120 and 121; any string instrument, Autoharp, recorders or bells

VOCABULARY
register, range

IDEAS FOR TEACHING
1. Choose a child to pluck the lowest-sounding string, then the highest-sounding one on any string instrument (e.g., Autoharp, guitar) for others to hear the difference. Then have children play a game as follows. <u>Game:</u> A leader plays a pattern of four tones, using only the highest- and lowest-sounding strings of the instrument—e.g., high-low-low-high or low-low-high-low. The leader then chooses someone to play the same pattern on the instrument. If it is played correctly, the player becomes the new leader. If not, the original leader gets another turn. <u>Note:</u> Since this is an aural experience, children should not watch as the leader plays.

2. Play the recording and have children pretend to strum the Autoharp pattern on p. 120 as an accompaniment. They use a motion away from them to "strum" the low strings, a motion toward them to "strum" the high strings. <u>Note:</u> The pattern of two strums per measure matches the steady beat of the song.

3. Play the recording and have children take turns playing the low-high Autoharp pattern to accompany "Rally Song." Invite others to sing when they can (notation, p. 120). <u>Suggestions:</u> (a) Provide finger and thumb picks to make the Autoharp pattern easier to strum. (b) Children can vary the accompaniment by →

To accompany "Rally Song," press the D min. chord button on the Autoharp. Use the following strumming pattern, or make up one of your own.

RALLY SONG   ROUND FROM THE BALKANS   5

FROM THE 1960 REVISED VERSION OF THE DITTY BAG BY JANET TOBITT. USED BY PERMISSION.

Mi ha - bi lu - lu be-shem-bel. Mi ha-bi lu - lu be-shem-bel.

Mi ha - bi lu - lu be-shem-bel. Mi ha - bi lu - lu be-shem-bel.

Another time, play an Autoharp accompaniment using only the strings in the middle register.

You have played in the low, middle, and high registers of the Autoharp.

120 Register—Range

TRY THIS
1. One child chooses a percussion instrument with a high sound (e.g., finger cymbals); another, an instrument with a low sound (e.g., low drum). The two children play the rhythm of "Rally Song," first each instrument alone, then both instruments together. When they are ready, they play the rhythm as a round. The second player begins when the first one reaches measure 5. <u>Note:</u> Thinking the words as they play will help children keep the rhythm. Call attention to the sound of the high and low registers when played alone and when played in combination.

2. Play an ear-training game. One child plays pattern 1, 2, or 3 (p. 121) for others to identify. Whoever identifies the pattern correctly then chooses a pattern to play and the game continues.

TEACHER INFORMATION
The Arabic words of "Rally Song" literally mean "My sweetheart to my heart." They are pronounced as follows:

Mi ha - bi lu - lu be - shem - bel.
mee hay-bee loo-loo beh-shehm-behl

Take turns accompanying "Rally Song" by playing one of these patterns on recorder or bells.

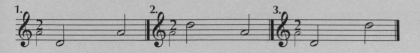

Which pattern has the widest range? Pattern 3

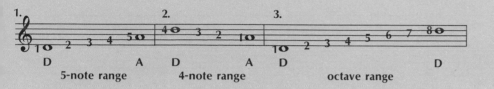

Look at the score of "Rally Song" on p. 120. Does it have a 4-note range? A 5-note range? An octave range? Octave range

"RALLY SONG" COUNTERMELODY

Recorder or Bells

Register—Range 121

strumming only the strings in the middle register of the Autoharp or by strumming in all three registers— sometimes low, sometimes high, sometimes in the middle. (c) Have children sing the song in unison until they are ready to sing it as a round.

4. Give children who play recorder time to review the fingerings for D (p. 59), A (p. 27), and high D (p. 99). Then have them choose pattern 1, 2, or 3 on p. 121 to play as an ostinato as others sing "Rally Song." <u>Note:</u> The patterns can also be played on bells.

5. (<u>Note:</u> While register refers to highness and lowness of sounds, *range* refers to the spread of the pitches in a melody, from lowest to highest.) Have children examine the range of the patterns on p. 121. <u>Point out:</u> Range is determined by calling the lowest note *one*, then counting each line and space above it, ending with the highest note. Pattern 1 has a 5-note range; pattern 2, a 4-note range; pattern 3, an 8-note or octave range. <u>Note:</u> Some children may notice that range is "counted" in the same way that intervals are "counted." Have children find the lowest note (D) and the highest note (high D) in "Rally Song" and "count" the range (an octave).

6. Ask children to determine the range of the pitches in "Rally Song Countermelody" on p. 121 (an octave—D to high D). Then have children who play recorder practice the countermelody to play while others sing the song. <u>Note:</u> When "Rally Song" is sung as a round, the countermelody can be played as a round as well. Part II begins when part I reaches measure 5.

REGISTER—RANGE • Lesson 4

MATERIALS
Record 5, "Hold On"; Pupil's Book,
p. 122

VOCABULARY
range, octave, AB form, contrast

IDEAS FOR TEACHING

1. Ask children to find the lowest
note (D) and the highest note (high
D) in "Hold On," p. 122. Questions:
Which section of the song has an
octave range? (Section B) What is
the range of section A? (5 notes, D
to A) What is the range of the entire
song? (An octave, D to high D)

2. When children know the song,
divide them into two groups. As one
group sings section A with the recording, the other group listens and
follows the notation. The groups re-
verse activities for section B. <u>Note:</u>
Activities like this focus children's
attention on the score to help them
see what they hear.

3. Direct children's attention to the
notation to discover the form of
"Hold On" (AB). Then help them
observe some of the qualities that
make section B a contrast of section
A; for example:
• The melody has a different range
  for each section.
• The rhythm is different for each
  section.
• In section A, phrases 1–3 begin
  with an upward melody (except for
  verse 2). In section B, the first
  phrase begins upward, the second
  downward.
• In section A, the melody is almost
  the same for phrases 1–3. Each
  phrase of section B has a different
  melody.

HOLD ON
<small>AMERICAN FOLK SONG</small>

Piano acc., p. 286   Orff-instrument acc., p. 338

3. Keep on plowin' and don't you tire,
    Ev'ry row goes higher and higher.
    Keep your hand on that plow,
    Hold on, hold on, hold on. *Refrain*

4. If that plow stays in your hand,
    Head you straight for the promised land
    Keep your hand on that plow,
    Hold on, hold on, hold on. *Refrain*

122 Register—Range

TRY THIS
Select individuals to practice the Autoharp part for "Hold
On." Encourage them to develop their own strumming
pattern, sometimes using the high strings, sometimes the
middle strings, and sometimes the low strings. When they
are ready, they accompany as the class sings the song.
<u>Note:</u> The Autoharp chords change less frequently in sec-
tion A than in section B. Some children may be able to
play only section A. Others may be able to accompany the
entire song. Invite them to play as much as they can manage successfully.

OLD BLUE

SOUTHERN MOUNTAIN SONG   Piano acc., p. 298

(A) VERSE
1. I had an old dog,____ And his name was Blue,____
And I bet-cha five dol-lars he's a good dog, too.

(B) REFRAIN
Come on, Blue,____ you good dog,____ you;
Come on, Blue,____ you good dog,____ you.____

2. I grabbed my axe and I tooted my horn,
   Gonna git me a 'possum in the new-ground corn. *Refrain*

3. Chased that ol' 'possum up a 'simmon tree,
   Blue looked at the 'possum, 'possum looked at me. *Refrain*

4. Blue grinned at me, I grinned at him,
   I shook out the 'possum, Blue took him in. *Refrain*

5. Baked that 'possum all good and brown,
   And I laid them sweet potatoes 'round and 'round. *Refrain*

6. Well, old Blue died, and he died so hard,
   That he shook the ground in my back yard. *Refrain*

7. I dug his grave with a silver spade,
   I let him down with a golden chain. *Refrain*

8. When I get to heaven, first thing I'll do,
   Grab me a horn and blow for old Blue. *Refrain*

Stravinsky: *Greeting Prelude*

Register—Range 123

REGISTER—RANGE • Lesson 5

MATERIALS
Record 6, "Old Blue"; Stravinsky: *Greeting Prelude*; Pupil's Book, p. 123; Autoharp, bells

VOCABULARY
low register, high register, score

IDEAS FOR TEACHING
1. Play the recording of "Old Blue" and invite children to join in on the refrain (section B) when they can. When they know the song, divide the class into two groups, one to sing the verse (section A), the other to sing the refrain (song notation, p. 123).

2. Select children to practice the Autoharp chords from the score on p. 123. Then have them play steady beats to accompany the singing. Suggestion: Encourage players to create rhythm patterns to strum on the high strings or on the low strings during the long sounds (on the words *Blue* and *you*) in section B.

3. Select children to take turns playing bells during the long sounds in section B. They play a rhythm pattern on the high- or low-G bell when the word *Blue* is sung, on the high- or low-F bell when *you* is sung. Suggestion: Have children indicate whether each player used a high register or a low register.

4. Play the recording of *Greeting Prelude* so children can hear how a modern composer has given a new sound to a familiar song ("Happy Birthday to You") by having some melody notes played in a low register, others in a high register.

TRY THIS
Have children make up echos to sing in a high register or a low register during the long sounds in section B of "Old Blue"; for example:

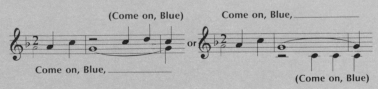

(Come on, Blue)   Come on, Blue,____
or
Come on, Blue,____   (Come on, Blue)

TEACHER INFORMATION
Igor Stravinsky (Russian born, 1882–1971) *Greeting Prelude:* Stravinsky was one of the greatest composers of the 20th century. His music was once thought to be so "far out" as to be an affront to the ear. But by the end of his life his acceptance as a mainstream composer was total. Stravinsky's music has a distinctive sound: it is lean, lively, moderately dissonant, and rhythmically complex.

Mainstreaming Note: An adaptation for "Old Blue" appears in *Silver Burdett Music for Special Education.*

MATERIALS
Record 6, *Zither Music;* Pupil's Book, pp. 124 and 125; any melody instrument

VOCABULARY
register, event, legend, ostinato

IDEAS FOR TEACHING
(Note: *Sound Piece* 6 may be performed by individual children, each creating their own organization and interpretation, or the class may decide as a group how it will be played. Possible sound sources include bells, Orff instruments, voices, piano, high and low strings of a guitar or Autoharp.)

1. Have children observe the boxes on p. 124 as you explain the legend (see below). Then give them time to practice the event in each box. Note: The boxes give information about register and tempo. Help children make decisions about other musical qualities. For example, in boxes 1 and 2, will the sound for the large dot be louder than for the smaller dots? Longer? In boxes 3 and 4, will all the sounds be loud? Soft? Will they begin soft and get louder (crescendo)? Begin loud and get softer? (decrescendo)? Will players use the same high and low sounds for box 6 that they use for box 5? How long will the silence last for box 7?

2. When children can play the events in the order given, have them determine their own order. They may repeat or omit events as they choose. <u>Suggestion:</u> Copy each event onto an index card. Make three complete sets of cards. Children can then determine an order for the events as fol- →

SOUND PIECE 6: Music Boxes JOYCE BOGUSKY-REIMER © 1980 JOYCE BOGUSKY-REIMER

Choose an instrument that makes both high and low sounds.

Then practice the events in the boxes below.

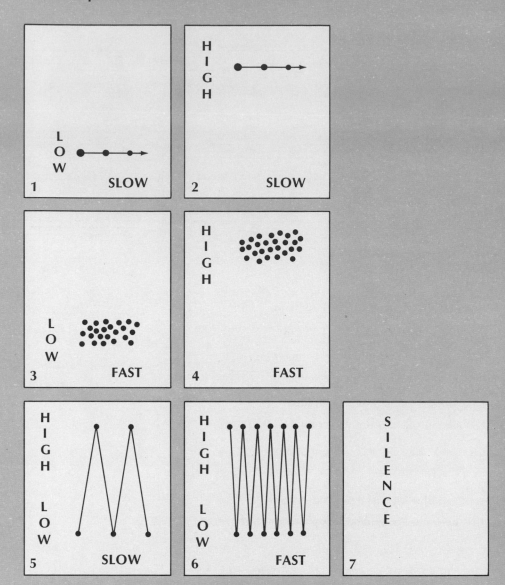

Now play the boxes in an order that gives the piece form.

You may start with any box, repeat some boxes, or omit some boxes.

124 Register—Range

LEGEND
Boxes 1 and 2: Play repeated tones.

Boxes 3 and 4: Choose several high or low tones and play them singly or in clusters, repeating tones as desired. <u>Note:</u> The number of sounds played need not match the number of dots in the boxes.

Boxes 5 and 6: Choose one high tone and one low tone. Play them, alternating the two tones as shown in the boxes.

On the recording, an African performer of the Kpelle tribe plays the triangular framed zither. Listen for the different registers in the music—low, middle, high.

🎧 *Zither Music*
6

Register—Range 125

lows: (a) by chance—combining the twenty-one cards, or as many as they wish to use, into one stack, shuffling them, and arranging them in rows on a table top or desk; (b) by organizing the events into a musical form like AB or ABA; for example:

(A) 1, 2 [B] 5, 6

(A) 5, 2, 6 [B] 3, 4 (A) 5, 2, 6

When children are ready, they perform for the class. If possible, tape-record several performances of the Sound Piece. Lead children to discuss what is the same about the performances (e.g., the same musical materials or events are used), and what is different (e.g., tone color, organization of events, interpretation of each event, etc.).

3. Play the recording of *Zither Music,* calling attention to the use of register. <u>Point out</u>: The music is made up of repeated melodies played in low, middle, and high registers. In the low register, there is an ostinato that moves back and forth between two tones. In the middle register, there is a five-note ostinato that uses mostly repeated tones and leaps. Both these ostinatos eventually change, then return to their original form. In the high register, there is a series of melodies, each one repeating several times before moving on to the next. Play the recording more than once so that children can focus on what is happening in each register. <u>Note:</u> *Zither Music* is played on an African instrument, the triangular framed zither, by a member of the Kpelle tribe. The instrument is pictured on p. 125.

TRY THIS

1. Children can use nontraditional sounds to perform *Sound Piece 6*—high and low sounds made on objects that are in the room or that they bring from home. Suspended flower pots offer one such possibility. They produce a sound when struck with a pencil or dowel.

Use a cord to suspend clean, unglazed, earthenware flower pots from a pole. A number of different-size pots will provide a range of pitches. Even pots of the same size can differ in pitch by as much as two scale tones. Place pots with low sounds toward the left end of the pole, those with high sounds toward the right end.

2. Encourage children to create their own sound pieces using low, middle, and high registers. Have them notate their pieces, using symbols from *Sound Piece 6,* or symbols that they create. When they are ready, they take turns performing their sound pieces for the class.

REGISTER—RANGE • Lesson 7

MATERIALS
Record 6, "Song of the Angel"; Pupil's Book, p. 126

VOCABULARY
wide range

IDEAS FOR TEACHING

1. As children listen to the recording, have them follow the notation on p. 126 to discover the lowest note (low C) and the highest note (high D) in the song.

2. Have children determine the range for "Song of the Angel" by counting the lines and spaces from low C to high D. Help them conclude that the song has a wide range—9 notes.

3. When children know the song, choose small groups to sing some of the verses; for example:
Verse 1—All sing.
Verse 2—One small group sings.
Verse 3—Another small group sings.
Verse 4—All sing.

Find the lowest note and the highest note in this song.

What is the range? 9 notes, C to high D

SONG OF THE ANGEL MENNONITE MELODY Piano acc., p. 312

© 1966 BY LAWSON-GOULD MUSIC PUBLISHERS, INC. USED BY PERMISSION

1. Fear not, fear not, good shep-herds all,

Let faith your fear de-stroy;

For lo, this night I bring to you

Good ti-dings of great joy,

Good ti-dings of great joy.

2. Awake your ears and hark to me,
To hear the glorious Word:
For unto you is born this day
A Saviour, Christ the Lord,
A Saviour, Christ the Lord.

3. You'll find the Babe in Bethlehem,
Born of the Mary maid;
All wrapped in swaddling clothes is He,
And in a manger laid,
And in a manger laid.

4. So join us now with one accord
To sing this wondrous birth:
Give praise to God, our heav'nly King,
And peace to men on earth,
And peace to men on earth.

126 Register—Range

TRY THIS
1. Call attention to the use of direction in some of the phrases of "Song of the Angel." Note: Each staff represents a phrase of the song. Questions: Which phrase begins with tones that move downward and ends with tones that move upward? (Phrase 4) Which phrase has tones that move downward from high D to F? (5)

2. Have children plan what dynamics they will use for each verse of the song. Remind them that they can sing soft, moderately loud, loud, getting louder, or getting softer. Encourage them to use the words as a clue to choosing appropriate dynamics.

Do these songs have a wide range, or a narrow range?   Wide

THE SEASONS OF THE YEAR

WORDS AND MUSIC BY PETER CROSSLEY-HOLLAND

I
Rain and sun and frost and snow;

II
Spring and Sum - mer, Au - tumn, Win - ter,

III
Round and round the sea - sons go.

Ostinato—Recorder or Bells

G A B A

FOR HEALTH AND STRENGTH   OLD ENGLISH ROUND

I F   II   III
For health and strength and dai - ly food We praise Thy name, O Lord.

Register—Range 127

MATERIALS
Record 6, "The Seasons of the Year"; "For Health and Strength"; Pupil's Book, p. 127; recorders or bells

VOCABULARY
register, wide range, narrow range, ostinato

IDEAS FOR TEACHING
1. Play the recording of "The Seasons of the Year" so that children can hear that the first phrase uses high notes, the third, low notes, and the second, notes in a middle register. Then have children look at the notation (p. 127) to discover the lowest and highest notes (D, high D). Question: What is the range of the song? (An octave)

2. Divide the class into three groups, one for each phrase of "The Seasons of the Year." Each group sings its phrase when it occurs on the recording. Repeat the activity, switching parts so that each group learns all three phrases. Then have children sing the entire song as a round.

3. Choose someone to play the recorder (bell) ostinato as others sing "The Seasons of the Year." Question: Does the ostinato have a wide range, like the song, or a narrow range? (A narrow, 3-note range—G to B)

4. When children know "For Health and Strength" (p. 127), have them sing it as a two-part, then a three-part round. Question: Does this song have as wide a range as "The Seasons of the Year," or is the range narrower? (Both songs have the same wide range, an octave: "The Seasons of the Year"—D to high D; "For Health and Strength"—C to high C.)

TRY THIS
Children can play "For Health and Strength" on piano or other keyboard instruments. Note: The melody leaps from C to high C, then, except for repeated tones, steps downward to E, then back up to F. Point out: The beginning tone C is the white key to the left of a set of two black keys. The ending tone F is the white key to the left of a set of three black keys. Children may begin the melody on any C except the highest one on the instrument (the melody uses the beginning C and the C an octave above). Let children discover by ear that they must play B♭ instead of B to make the melody sound right. Suggestion: When they can play the melody easily, have two or three children play it as a round.

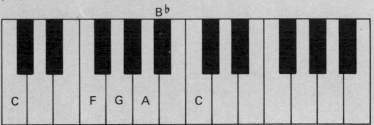

MATERIALS

Record 6, Bruckner: *Two Little Pieces,*
No. 1; Pupil's Book, p. 128, piano

VOCABULARY

treble, bass, melody, accompaniment,
score, octave sign, duet

IDEAS FOR TEACHING

1. Play the recording and have children listen for the high part and the low part in the music. <u>Note:</u> The music is a piano duet for two players at one piano. The high part (treble) plays the melody. The low part (bass) plays an accompaniment. <u>Suggestion:</u> If stereo is available, use the Pick-a-Track technique to allow children to hear each part of the duet highlighted.

2. Have children follow the score on p. 128 as they listen to the recording. <u>Question:</u> Does the notation show the high part or the low part of the duet? (High part) <u>Point out:</u> In the first pair of staffs, the notes for both hands are identical. However, the octave sign (*8va* followed by a broken line) above the top staff tells the player to play the notes for the right hand an octave higher than written. When the broken line ends, the notes are played as written.

3. Have children who study piano prepare the treble part to play for the class. <u>Point out:</u> In section A each time, both left and right hands play the same notes an octave apart. In section B, the right hand plays alone. <u>Note:</u> When children perform the piece, the teacher or an advanced piano student can play the bass part. It is notated on Teacher's Edition p. 330.

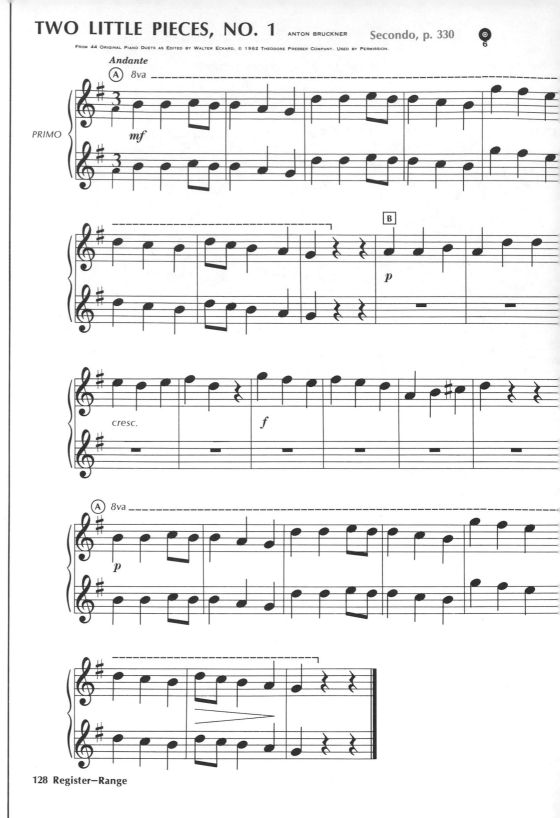

TWO LITTLE PIECES, NO. 1   ANTON BRUCKNER   Secondo, p. 330

FROM 44 ORIGINAL PIANO DUETS AS EDITED BY WALTER ECKARD. © 1962 THEODORE PRESSER COMPANY. USED BY PERMISSION.

128 Register—Range

TRY THIS

Some children may be seeing a piano score for the first time. Help them observe the following.

- A pianist reads from two staffs at the same time.
- The staffs are joined in pairs at the left side by a straight line and a brace. Within the music, bar lines go from the top of one staff to the bottom of the other.
- The notes on the top staff are usually played with the right hand; those on the bottom staff, with the left hand.
- When piano music is written for one player, the melody is usually notated on the top staff; the accompaniment, on the bottom staff.

TEACHER INFORMATION

Anton Bruckner (Austrian, 1824–1896)   *Two Little Pieces,* No. 1: This composer was also a teacher and organist. Bruckner wrote many important orchestral works. His music is characterized by lively rhythms and skillful use of tone color.

WHAT DO YOU HEAR? 10: REGISTER

Listen to this piece. Each time a number is called, choose

the answer (or answers) that best describes the register.

Haydn: *Chorale St. Antonie*

1.	(HIGH REGISTER)	MIDDLE REGISTER	LOW REGISTER
2.	HIGH REGISTER	MIDDLE REGISTER	(LOW REGISTER)
3.	HIGH REGISTER	(MIDDLE REGISTER)	LOW REGISTER
4.	(HIGH REGISTER)	(MIDDLE REGISTER)	(LOW REGISTER)

WHAT DO YOU HEAR? 11: RANGE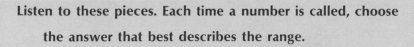

Listen to these pieces. Each time a number is called, choose

the answer that best describes the range.

1.	NARROW RANGE	(WIDE RANGE)	Webern: *Variations for Orchestra*
2.	(NARROW RANGE)	WIDE RANGE	Gregorian Chant
3.	NARROW RANGE	(WIDE RANGE)	Tchaikovsky: *The Sleeping Beauty*
4.	(NARROW RANGE)	WIDE RANGE	Ai a la o Pele

Register—Range 129

REGISTER—RANGE • Lesson 10

MATERIALS
Record 6, *What Do You Hear? 10: Register; What Do You Hear? 11: Range;* spirit masters

VOCABULARY
high register, middle register, low register, wide range, narrow range

TEACHER INFORMATION
The listening examples in *What Do You Hear? 10* and *What Do You Hear? 11* offer a sampling of several musical styles: Medieval—*Gregorian Chant;* Classical—Haydn: *Chorale St. Antonie;* Romantic—Tchaikovsky: *The Sleeping Beauty;* Contemporary—Webern: *Variations for Orchestra.* Give children an opportunity to listen to the music again, outside of the What Do You Hear? experience.

MODULE 11

THE ARTS: REPETITION WITH VARIETY AND CONTRAST

OBJECTIVES, p. XII

THE ARTS: Repetition with Variety and Contrast

MATERIALS
Record 6, Eddleman: *For Health and Strength* (*Ground with Variations*); *Rally Song* (*Ground*); Pupil's Book, pp. 130–133; bells (or recorder), Autoharp, tambourine

VOCABULARY
repetition, variety, contrast, ground, low register, high register

IDEAS FOR TEACHING
1. Direct children's attention to the photograph on p. 130. Questions: What is repeated in the photograph? (The subject—vase with flower; the vases are all identical.) What is varied in the photograph? (The type of flower in each vase)

2. Point out that repetition and variety also occur in sound. Divide the class into two groups and have them do the following:
(a) Both groups pat a quarter-note rhythm pattern over and over on their lap (see Rhythm Pattern *a* below).
(b) While group 1 continues to pat pattern *a*, group 2 claps a pattern of eighth notes, two equal sounds to the beat (see pattern *b*).
(c) While group 1 continues to pat pattern *a*, group 2 claps a pattern of triplets, three equal sounds to the beat (see pattern c).
(d) While group 1 continues to pat pattern *a*, group 2 claps a pattern →

Follow the rhythm patterns below as you listen to the recording.
They will help you hear what is going on in the upper parts
of the music.

 Eddleman: *For Health and Strength* (*Ground with Variations*)

1. Ground (melody) alone

130 MODULE 11: The Arts—Repetition with Variety and Contrast

RHYTHM PATTERNS

TEACHER INFORMATION
Mainstreaming suggestion: Repeat the activity in item 2 of the lesson from time to time. At first, assign slower-reacting children to group 1. Then, in subsequent experiences with the exercise, have a child from group 2 (who can clap the patterns accurately) sit near the slower-reacting children to provide a model for them to imitate. Finally, as each one becomes ready, assign these children to group 2.

of sixteenth notes, four equal sounds to the beat (see pattern *d*). <u>Point out</u>: In this pat-clap exercise, both groups perform patterns that show repetition—the same rhythm over and over. However, the children in group 2 also experience variety in that they change from one repeated pattern to another.

3. Play the recording of *For Health and Strength* (*Ground with Variations*). <u>Point out</u>: In this piece there are two parts—a low one and a high one. <u>Questions</u>: Which part, high or low, is repeated over and over? (Low) Which part changes, or is varied? (High)

4. Have children follow the rhythm patterns on p. 130 as they listen to *For Health and Strength* (*Ground with Variations*) once more. <u>Note</u>: Children should hear that the melody is played as a ground (i.e., repeated over and over in a low register) with different things added each time in the upper part (played in a high register). Help children discover that in the upper parts of *For Health and Strength* (*Ground with Variations*) the beat is divided into two sounds (♫), then three sounds (♫♪), then four sounds (♬). Some children may notice that this matches the rhythm patterns that group 2 performed in the pat-clap exercise (see item 2).

5. Give children time to look at the painting on p. 131. <u>Questions</u>: What do you see in the painting that repeats? (The pattern in the rug, in the wallpaper, and in the chair fabric; the bird cages on either side of the draped window; the shapes in the bird cages; the two identical chairs along the wall) What do you see

Can you see repetition as well as variety and contrast in these paintings?

THE SARGENT FAMILY, UNKNOWN ARTIST. GIFT OF EDGAR WILLIAM AND BERNICE CHRYSLER GARBISCH, NATIONAL GALLERY OF ART, WASHINGTON, D.C.

The Arts—Repetition with Variety and Contrast 131

TEACHER INFORMATION
David Eddleman (American, 1936–   ) *For Health and Strength* (*Ground with Variations*): Among other larger works, this versatile composer has created many pieces for children that use modern styles in attractive ways. He wrote the music for "End of Summer," a song that appears in Book 4 on page 237.

Unknown Artist *The Sargent Family:* This American painting of a comfortable family has the awkwardness of a posed snapshot. Yet there is a kind of elegance in the artist's balancing of all the figures against the carefully arranged background.

The Arts: Repetition with Variety and Contrast · 131

that is not repeated—that provides variety or contrast? (The different poses of the people; the large chair that is different from the matching ones; the dog as opposed to the human figures; the contrast between the design of the wallpaper, the scene outside the window, and the design of the rug)

6. Have children review "Rally Song" (p. 120), singing it in unison and as a round. Then play the recording of *Rally Song* (Ground) so children can recognize that this is the melody of the song they have just sung. <u>Note</u>: On the recording, a cello and string bass play the melody six times in a low register.

7. Assign groups of children to practice the accompaniment parts on p. 133—bells (or recorder), Autoharp, round, tambourine. When they are ready, have them add the parts in this order as others sing with the recording *Rally Song* (Ground):

First time—Ground only.
Second time—Add bells only.
Third time—Add Autoharp only.
Fourth and fifth times—Add round only.
Sixth time—Add tambourine only.

Then have children try the arrangement given on p. 132. <u>Note</u>: When the round is added to the ground, part I sings the entire song two times; part II sings the song once through, then begins again, ending with the fourth measure. Two playings of the ground are needed to accommodate the round. <u>Suggestion</u>: Encourage children to create their own arrangement for adding the accompaniment parts to the ground on the recording. Help them recognize that in each arrangement, the recording provides repetition by playing

Use the melody of "Rally Song" as a ground. Add variety and contrast by performing one of the parts on p. 133. Use the recording of the ground while you practice your part.

Rally Song (Ground)

When you and your classmates are ready, follow this arrangement as the ground repeats on the recording.

1. *ground alone*

2. *ground, bells, and Autoharp*

3.
4. } *ground, round, and tambourine*

5.
6. } *ground, bells, Autoharp, round, and tambourine*

Ground ("Rally Song") FROM THE 1960 REVISED VERSION OF THE DITTY BAG BY JANET TOBITT. USED BY PERMISSION.

132 The Arts—Repetition with Variety and Contrast

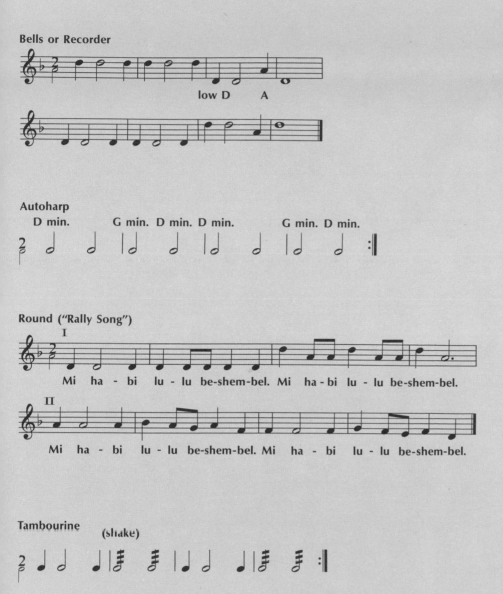

Bells or Recorder

low D   A

Autoharp

D min.   G min.   D min.   D min.   G min.   D min.

Round ("Rally Song")

I

Mi ha - bi lu - lu be-shem-bel. Mi ha - bi lu - lu be-shem-bel.

II

Mi ha - bi lu - lu be-shem-bel. Mi ha - bi lu - lu be-shem-bel.

Tambourine   (shake)

The Arts—Repetition with Variety and Contrast 133

the melody over and over (ground); the accompaniment parts provide variety.

TRY THIS
Have children take a "discovery walk"—around the classroom, through the school building, around the school grounds, around the neighborhood—to find things that show repetition or variety and contrast. Children can keep a log of their observations to share with the class. Suggestion: Have children make a bulletin-board display showing their repetition-contrast discoveries. Each child can participate by writing a description of the most unusual or interesting thing he or she has found. Children might use photographs or drawings to illustrate their discoveries.

REVIEW/REINFORCEMENT
1. Encourage children to look for repetition and contrast in other works of art in their book; for example:
Battle of Lights, p. 36
Swimmers and Sunbathers, p. 82

2. Take time to review other musical experiences children have had with repetition and contrast; for example:
Call Chart 5: Form, p. 102
Call Chart 6: Form, p. 105
What Do You Hear? 7: Form, p. 110

MODULE 12

OBJECTIVES, p. XIII

RHYTHM PATTERNS 1 • Lesson 1

MATERIALS
Pupil's Book, pp. 134 and 135

VOCABULARY
pattern, long and short sounds

IDEAS FOR TEACHING

1. Have children look at the photographs on pp. 134 and 135. Discuss how the repetition and contrast of colors, lines, and shapes create patterns in the leaves, corn, I beams (I-shaped beams used in construction), palm branch, and wallpaper sample. Ask children to find other examples of pattern in magazine illustrations or photographs. Mainstreaming Suggestion: Provide materials in a variety of knitted and woven textures to give children a tactile experience with pattern.

2. Help children observe that just as colors, lines, and shapes create patterns in things that they see, so long and short sounds create patterns in things that they hear. Call attention to recurring rhythm patterns in songs children know (see below for examples).

3. Play some of the listening selections in Book 4 so children can hear patterns of long and short sounds; for example:
Gershwin: *An American in Paris,*
      p. 37
Maxfield: *Night Music,* p. 84
Giuliani: *Grand Sonata in A Major*
      for Flute and Guitar, $\longrightarrow$

RHYTHM PATTERNS 1

RHYTHM PATTERNS

"Sourwood Mountain," p. 16

Hey   de-ing dang did-dle al - ly day.

"The Wise Man Built His House," p. 21

Oh, the wise man built   his house up-on the rock,

"Run, Run, Run," p. 98

Run, run, run___

Rhythm Patterns 1 135

"Scherzo," Teacher's Edition
p. 94
Note: Play only as much of each
piece as necessary for children to
hear that the music is made up of
long and short sounds.

TRY THIS
1. Increase children's awareness of
pattern by having them find patterns
in clothing, in the classroom decor,
in game boards they use, and in the
photographs in *Silver Burdett Music,
Book 4* (e.g., pp. 94 and 131).

2. Have children use materials such
as scraps of paper, aluminum foil,
fabric, and yarn to create a collage
that shows pattern.

RHYTHM PATTERNS 1 • Lesson 2

MATERIALS
Record 6, "Old Texas"; *Call Chart 7: Rhythm Patterns*; Tchaikovsky: *Capriccio Italien*; Pupil's Book, pp. 136 and 137; Autoharp

VOCABULARY
long sounds, short sounds, rhythm pattern, score, crescendo

IDEAS FOR TEACHING
1. Play the recording of "Old Texas" as children follow the notation on p. 136. Point out: (a) "Old Texas" is written for two parts. (b) Part 2 has the same melody as part 1, beginning one measure later. (c) Throughout the song, whenever one part has a long sound to sing (♩ ♪, ♩, or ♪♩.), the other part has short sounds.

2. Have children choose part 1 or part 2 of "Old Texas" to sing with the recording.

3. Play the recording of "Old Texas" and have children focus on the guitar accompaniment. Help them hear that a different strumming pattern is used for each verse.

4. Have children make up their own pattern of long and short strums on the Autoharp as an accompaniment for "Old Texas." Note: Players will use the chords F and C₇, playing each chord until the other chord name appears in the score.

5. Play the recording *Call Chart 7: Rhythm Patterns* while children follow the chart on p. 137. Note: As each number is called, they find the word next to that number in the chart. The word *long* or *short* describes the →

Follow the voice parts as you listen to the recording of "Old Texas." Notice that one part sings short sounds while the other sings long ones.

As others sing the long sounds in the melody, take turns strumming a rhythm pattern on the Autoharp. The score will tell you when to play the F chord and when to play the C₇ chord.

OLD TEXAS OKLAHOMA COWBOY SONG

Piano acc., p. 299

1. I'm goin' to leave_____ old_ Tex - as now,

1. I'm goin' to leave_____ old_ Tex - as now,

They've got no use_____ for the long-horn cow.

___ They've got no use_____ for the long-horn cow.

2. They've plowed and fenced my cattle range,
   And the people there are all so strange.

3. I'll take my horse, I'll take my rope,
   And hit the trail upon a lope.

4. Say *adios* to the Alamo
   And turn my head toward Mexico.

136 Rhythm Patterns 1

TEACHER INFORMATION
Mainstreaming Note: An adaptation for "Old Texas" appears in *Silver Burdett Music for Special Education*.

CALL CHART 7: RHYTHM PATTERNS ⊙

Listen to this piece. Each time a number is called, decide whether
you are hearing long sounds, or short sounds. Look at the chart to
check your answers.

Schumann: *Fantasiestücke*, Op. 12, No. 6, "Fable"

1. LONG

2. SHORT

3. LONG

4. SHORT

5. SHORT

6. LONG

7. LONG

There are many ways to combine long and short sounds and long
and short silences to make rhythm patterns.

Can you hear long and short sounds played at the same time in
this music? Strings play the long sounds. Brass instruments
play the short sounds.

⊙ Tchaikovsky: *Capriccio Italien*

Rhythm Patterns 1 137

kinds of sounds they are hearing.
Suggestion: Play the recording again
so children can focus on other qualities in the music—direction, tempo,
dynamics.

6. Have children read the text that
follows *Call Chart 7*. Then play the
Tchaikovsky work so they can hear
the combination of the long sounds
in the strings with the short sounds
in the brass. Note: Throughout the
excerpt, the brasses mostly "answer"
the strings, playing repeated tones
while the strings play a long sound.
Encourage children to make as many
observations as they can about the
music; for example: (1) the strings
play a melody that has direction
upward and downward, while the
brasses play repeated tones each
time; (2) in the string part the tones
are mostly played smooth and connected (legato), while in the brass
part the tones are played short and
crisp (staccato); (3) in both parts
there are crescendos from soft to
loud dynamics.

TEACHER INFORMATION
Robert Schumann (German, 1810–1856) *Fantasiestücke*,
Op. 12, No. 6, "Fable": This composer wanted to be a pianist, but turned to composition after a practicing device
injured his hand. The very personal and literary nature of
Schumann's piano pieces and song cycles distinguish him
as a Romantic composer. His compositions also include
works for small ensembles and for orchestra.

Peter Ilyitch Tchaikovsky (Russian, 1840–1893) *Capriccio
Italien*: The music of this composer (including the music
for the ballets *The Nutcracker*, *Swan Lake*, and *The Sleeping Beauty*) is among the most popular ever written. Capti-
vating melodies, lively rhythms, and colorful use of instruments help account for the music's appeal.

MATERIALS
Record 6, *Tabla Solo* (Alla Rakha);
Pupil's Book, p. 138; bongos

VOCABULARY
tabla, pattern

IDEAS FOR TEACHING
<u>Note</u>: In this lesson, children play
drum rhythms as they might be performed in India. Bongos are used in
place of the Indian tabla. As many
bongos as possible should be provided for children's use.

1. Direct attention to the first tabla
diagram on p. 138. As children chant
the drum syllable *Dhe,* they strike
the low bongo just above the middle
of the drumhead. Then they chant
Na while striking near the edge of
the high bongo drumhead. Finally,
they strike *Dhe* and *Na* at the same
time, chanting the syllable *Dha.*

2. Have children look at the second
tabla diagram. Once again they
chant *Dhe,* striking the low bongo
just above the middle. Then they
chant *Tin* while striking the high
bongo near the middle. Finally, they
strike *Dhe* and *Tin* at the same time,
chanting *Dhin.*

3. Direct children's attention to the
pattern of drum syllables near the
bottom of p. 138. Give them time to
practice chanting the syllables while
thinking how they will perform each
one. Then they play the bongos
while chanting. Have them play
slowly until they are comfortable
with the pattern.

4. Play the recording. Children will
hear the drummer recite the syllables
for a pattern that he then plays on
tabla.

Tabla are among the most popular drums of India.

1. Dhe + Na = Dha   2. Dhe + Tin = Dhin

Indian Drum Syllables

> **Dhe** (pronounced *dhuh*)—left-hand (low) drum struck just above the middle
>
> **Na** (pronounced *nah*)—right-hand (high) drum struck near the edge
>
> **Tin**—right-hand drum struck near the middle
>
> **Dha** (pronounced *dhah*)—*Dhe* and *Na* performed at the same time
>
> **Dhin**—*Dhe* and *Tin* performed at the same time

Chant the syllables while playing this pattern on low and high drums.

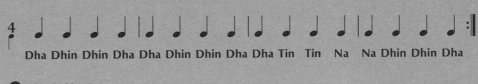

Dha Dhin Dhin Dha Dha Dhin Dhin Dha Dha Tin Tin Na Na Dhin Dhin Dha

🔘 *Alla Rakha*
6

138 Rhythm Patterns 1

TRY THIS
Have children create their own pattern of Indian drum syllables, using some or all of the syllables listed on p. 138.
Have them take turns playing their pattern for the class.
They may use a steady-beat rhythm like the quarter-note
rhythm in their book, or they may play a combination of
long and short sounds.

TEACHER INFORMATION
Tabla are high and low drums that are played mostly by
men in northern India. They are used to accompany vocal
as well as instrumental music (e.g., music played on a
sitar).

JOY TO THE WORLD

WORDS AND MUSIC BY HOYT AXTON   Piano acc., p. 260

COPYRIGHT © 1970 BY LADY JANE MUSIC. USED BY PERMISSION.

1. Jer-e-mi-ah was a bull-frog, Was a good___ friend of mine. Nev-er un-der-stood a sin-gle word he said,___ but we al-ways had a might-y fine time.___ Yes, we al-ways had a might-y fine time.

Sing-ing joy to the world. All___ the boys and girls___ now. Joy to the fish-es in the deep blue sea.___ Joy to___ you and me.___

2. If I were the king of the world, tell you what I'd do,
Throw away the fears and the tears and the jeers,
And have a good time with you.
Yes, I'd have a good time with you. *Refrain.*

Countermelody

Sing-ing joy to the world, Joy to the world;

Joy, joy, joy, joy, Joy to___ you and me.___

Rhythm Patterns 1 139

RHYTHM PATTERNS 1 • Lesson 4

MATERIALS
Record 6, "Joy to the World"; Pupil's Book, p. 139; Autoharp, drum, maracas

VOCABULARY
dotted half note, whole note, tied notes, long sounds, short sounds

IDEAS FOR TEACHING
1. Play the recording so children can hear the two sections of "Joy to the World"—A and B.

2. Play the recording again and have children join in singing section B (notation, p. 139) each time it occurs. Point out: There are several long sounds in section B. These are shown in the notation by dotted half notes (♩.) on the words *joy* and *now,* by a whole note (𝅝) on the word *world,* and by tied notes (♩♪ or ♪♩) on the words *all, sea,* and *me.*

3. As children sing the entire song with the recording, have individuals play an accompaniment during section B (see below for parts). Point out: (a) The Autoharp plays long sounds (half notes), using two long strums per measure. (Note: The chord names in the score indicate which buttons to press.) (b) The drum pattern (quarter notes) matches the steady beat. (c) The maracas play short sounds (eighth notes), two equal sounds per beat.

ACCOMPANIMENT PARTS FOR SECTION B

Autoharp

Drum

Maracas

TRY THIS
1. As the class sings the song, have a small group sing the countermelody on p. 139. Point out: The countermelody uses both long and short sounds. Note: To give singers security, have someone play the countermelody along with them on bells, xylophone, or piano.

2. Combine the countermelody with one or more of the parts in item 3 above to accompany section B of "Joy to the World." Encourage children to listen carefully as they sing and play so that the accompaniment parts do not drown out the melody.

RHYTHM PATTERNS 1 • Lesson 5

MATERIALS
Record 6, "Naughty Little Flea"; *A-E-I-O-U*; Pupil's Book, p. 140; percussion instruments (maracas, bongos, claves)

VOCABULARY
rhythm pattern

IDEAS FOR TEACHING
1. Play the recording of "Naughty Little Flea" and ask children to listen for the section that has the longest silences in the melody (section A).

2. Play the recording of "Naughty Little Flea" and have children take turns performing a pattern of long and short sounds during each silence in section A. They perform their pattern (a) using natural sounds—clapping hands, snapping fingers, patting lap; (b) using percussion instruments that are appropriate to the style of the music—maracas, bongos, claves. Note: Some children may use a rhythm from the song; others will create a pattern of their own. Invite the class to sing when they can (notation, p. 140).

3. Play the recording and have children clap the rhythm each time the vowels are chanted in *A-E-I-O-U*:

Note: The rhythm remains the same even when the order of the vowels changes. When children are familiar with the chant, have them take turns performing their own rhythm pattern whenever the voices are silent on the recording.

Fill in the silences in the melody with a pattern of long and short sounds.

NAUGHTY LITTLE FLEA

WORDS AND MUSIC BY NORMAN THOMAS

Piano acc., p. 322

TRANSCRIBED FROM THE RECORDING BY MIRIAM MAKEBA AND HARRY BELAFONTE

© 1957 PINEBROOK MUSIC CORP. c/o H/B WEBMAN & COMPANY. USED BY PERMISSION.

Where did the naught-y lit-tle flea go?
Won't some-bod-y tell me? Where did the naught-y lit-tle flea go? Won't some-bod-y tell me?

1. There was a naught-y lit-tle flea; He climbed up on the dog-gie's knee; He climbed some here, he climbed some there; He was climb-ing ev-'ry-where. Tell me,

2. He climbed some here,
    he climbed some there;
He was climbing everywhere.
And now at last he's found a nest
Where he can get some food and rest.
Tell me, . . .

3. He bit him here,
    he bit him there;
He bit him almost everywhere.
When he was done he wanted more;
He never tasted such a dog before.
Tell me, . . .

Listen for the rhythm pattern when the vowels are chanted in *A-E-I-O-U*.

A-E-I-O-U

140 Rhythm Patterns 1

TRY THIS
1. Have children create a pattern of long and short sounds to strum on the Autoharp as an accompaniment for "Naughty Little Flea"; for example:

Note: Children play low strings (strumming away from the body) for notes with stems pointing down, high strings (strumming toward the body) for notes with stems pointing up.

2. Have children take turns playing the following percussion patterns during section B of "Naughty Little Flea." Note: The wood block part matches the rhythm of the words *There was a naughty little flea.*

WHAT DO YOU HEAR? 12: RHYTHM PATTERNS

Listen to these pieces. Do you hear mostly short sounds, mostly

long sounds, or short and long sounds together? Each time

a number is called, decide which of the three answers is

correct. Choose the answer that best describes what is

happening in the music.

1. **(MOSTLY SHORT)**   MOSTLY LONG   SHORT AND LONG TOGETHER   Stockhausen: *Klavierstück*

2. MOSTLY SHORT   **(MOSTLY LONG)**   SHORT AND LONG TOGETHER   Mendelssohn: *Nocturne*

3. MOSTLY SHORT   MOSTLY LONG   **(SHORT AND LONG TOGETHER)**   Tchaikovsky: *Capriccio Italien*

4. MOSTLY SHORT   MOSTLY LONG   **(SHORT AND LONG TOGETHER)**   Vivaldi: *The Four Seasons*, "Winter"

5. **(MOSTLY SHORT)**   MOSTLY LONG   SHORT AND LONG TOGETHER   *Goin' down the Road Feeling Bad*

Rhythm Patterns 1 141

RHYTHM PATTERNS 1 • Lesson 6

MATERIALS
Record 6, *What Do You Hear? 12: Rhythm Patterns*; spirit master

VOCABULARY
short sounds, long sounds, short and long together

TEACHER INFORMATION
In this module, children have experienced long and short sounds through singing, listening, and playing percussion instruments. This *What Do You Hear?* evaluation gives them an opportunity to demonstrate how well they hear long and short sounds. <u>Note</u>: The examples in *What Do You Hear? 12* represent several different periods of music composition. The Vivaldi work is from the Baroque period; the Mendelssohn and Tchaikovsky works are from the Romantic period; the Stockhausen and *Goin' down the Road Feeling Bad* represent two different styles from the Contemporary or Modern period.

MODULE 13

OBJECTIVES, p. XIII

RHYTHM PATTERNS 2 • Lesson 1

MATERIALS

Record 6, "The Mosquito"; Mozart: *Variations on "Ah, vous dirai-je, Maman?"*; *Din Don*; Pupil's Book, pp. 142 and 143; percussion instruments (maracas, bongos, claves); wood block, finger cymbals, recorders or bells

VOCABULARY

triplet, fermata

IDEAS FOR TEACHING

<u>Note</u>: Through singing, listening, and playing instruments, children have experienced rhythm patterns that have the beat divided into two equal sounds [♫]. In each phrase of "The Mosquito," they will encounter this rhythm along with the triplet, the beat divided into three equal sounds [♪♪♪]. The triplet was introduced in "Island Hopping," p. 118.

1. As they listen to the recording of "The Mosquito," have children follow the notation on p. 142. Help them observe that the rhythm of the first phrase (*I went to the Sierra Blanca*) is repeated throughout the song.

2. When children know "The Mosquito," ask them to sing with the recording. Have them take turns playing the rhythm of the melody on an appropriate percussion instrument (e.g., maracas, bongos, claves). <u>Note</u>: Thinking the words will help children play the rhythm accurately.

→

RHYTHM PATTERNS 2

Notice the triplet ♪♪♪ in each phrase as you sing this song.

How many triplets can you find?

THE MOSQUITO

FOLK SONG FROM COLOMBIA   ENGLISH WORDS BY MARGARET MARKS

Piano acc., p. 294

1. I went to the Sie-rra Blan-ca   To hunt with my dog, Pe-rri-to,

When sud-den-ly I en-count-ered   a great o-ver-grown mos-qui-to.

I dropped to my knees and fired,___   And star-tled by that ex-plo-sion,

The an-i-mal lost his bal-ance   And tum-bled in-to the o-cean.

2. So huge was this big mosquito,
A tidal wave swelled the water,
His head lay in Cádiz harbor,
His feet lay across Gibraltar.
And then the ordeal was over,
The bug ceased to make a motion,
I called for a crane and derrick,
You've never seen such commotion.

3. They made from his hide ten thousand
High boots of the finest leather,
And just from the bits left over,
A hundred or so umbrellas;
And even now, ten years later,
Though nothing could seem absurder,
The whole of the Spanish Army
Is eating mosquito-burger!

Can you hear triplets in this piece for piano?

🎯 Mozart: *Variations on "Ah, vous dirai-je, Maman?"*
6

142 MODULE 13: Rhythm Patterns 2

TRY THIS

Children can add an accompaniment for "The Mosquito" by plucking the A and (either high or low) E strings of a guitar. The following diagram shows which strings to pluck. The notation shows the order and rhythm for playing the tones. <u>Note</u>: Children begin playing on the first strong beat of the song, on the word *went*.

Play entire pattern *four times*.

OPTIONAL PARTS FOR ORFF INSTRUMENTS OR BELLS (*Din*

(Alto Gl. = Alto Glockenspiel; Alto Met. = Alto Metallophone; Bass Xyl. = Bass Xylophone)

ind the triplets in this music.

IN, DON   FOLK MELODY FROM SPAIN

MUSICAL SETTING FROM THE BABY'S SONG BOOK © 1971 ELIZABETH POSTON. USED BY PERMISSION OF THOMAS Y. CROWELL AND THE BODLEY HEAD.

Percussion Parts

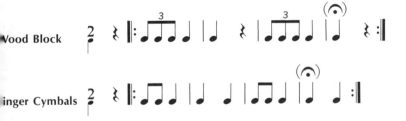

Wood Block

inger Cymbals

Rhythm Patterns 2 143

3. Play the recording of the Mozart work so children can hear triplets in an instrumental (piano) composition. <u>Note</u>: The recording includes the theme and variations 3 and 4. Triplets occur throughout the two variations—in the treble (high register) in variation 3, in the bass (low register) in variation 4. Children will recognize that the theme is similar to the melody they know as "Twinkle, Twinkle, Little Star."

4. Play the recording of *Din Don* while children follow the notation on p. 143. Question: Where do you see triplets in this music? (On staffs 3 and 4) Then have children who can play G, A, B on recorder (fingerings, p. 27) play along with the recording. Give them time to practice first. <u>Point out</u>: (a) The notation is exactly the same for staffs 1, 2, and 5. (b) Except for the fermata (⌢), staff 4 is an exact repetition of staff 3. <u>Note</u>: *Din Don* may also be played on bells or other melody instruments.

5. While some children play the melody of *Din Don,* have others take turns playing the percussion parts on p. 143. <u>Point out</u>: The wood block part uses triplets; the part for finger cymbals does not. <u>Note</u>: Percussion players have a rest (𝄾) for the first note of the *Din Don* melody; they begin playing on the second melody note. Remind them to observe the fermata when it occurs in the music.

6. Children can accompany *Din Don* on Orff instruments (notation of parts begins at the bottom of Teacher's Edition p. 142).

MATERIALS
Record 7, "Kookaburra"; Pupil's Book, p. 144; percussion instruments

VOCABULARY
sixteenth notes, pattern, ostinato, phrase

IDEAS FOR TEACHING

1. Have children follow the notation on p. 144 as they listen to the recording. Note: Play only the part of the recording that is sung in unison. Then ask children to tap the rhythm of the melody as they listen again. Question: Where did you tap the shortest sounds, four in a row? (On the word *kookaburra* each time, and on *merry, merry*) Point out: The notes that have the shortest sounds are sixteenth notes. Four sixteenth notes last as long as one quarter note.

2. As the class sings "Kookaburra," have children take turns playing the rhythm of the words on a percussion instrument. Suggestion: When children know the song, they can sing and play the rhythm as a two-part round: part 2 begins when part 1 reaches the fifth measure. When they are ready, have children perform "Kookaburra" in four parts as written.

3. Call attention to the rhythm patterns at the bottom of the page. Note: Each pattern shows the rhythm for a phrase of the song—pattern 1, phrase 1 or 2; pattern 2, phrase 3; pattern 3, phrase 4. Have children take turns playing one of the patterns as an ostinato throughout the song as others sing. Thinking the words of the phrase will help the player keep the rhythm.

Tap the rhythm of the melody. On which words do you tap the shortest sounds?

KOOKABURRA
WORDS AND MUSIC BY MARION SINCLAIR
FROM THE DITTY BAG, COMPILED BY JANET E. TOBITT. USED WITH PERMISSION. Orff-instrument acc., p. 345

Choose one of these rhythm patterns to play on a percussion instrument throughout "Kookaburra."

144 Rhythm Patterns 2

TEACHER INFORMATION
Some children may notice that there are two sixteenth notes at the end of measures 1 and 3 in "Kookaburra." Point out: Two sixteenth notes last as long as one eighth note.

The kookaburra is a bird found in Australia. Like the kingfisher, it has a large crested head and a short tail. Its call sounds like loud laughter. The gum tree mentioned in the song is a eucalyptus tree.

TRY THIS
1. Have children take turns playing an Autoharp accompaniment as others sing "Kookaburra." The score will tell them which chords to use (C, F) and when to change from one chord to the other. Children may play a steady-beat rhythm, or a rhythm pattern that they create.

2. Have children play these ostinatos on bells as others sing "Kookaburra." Each ostinato may be played separately, or all three may be played at the same time.

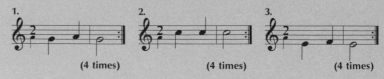

SOUND PIECE 7: Intersections

DAVID S. WALKER

Each vertical column in the score stands for one beat.

Follow the red, green, or purple line to see where the beat is divided. Is the beat divided into two, three, or four sounds?

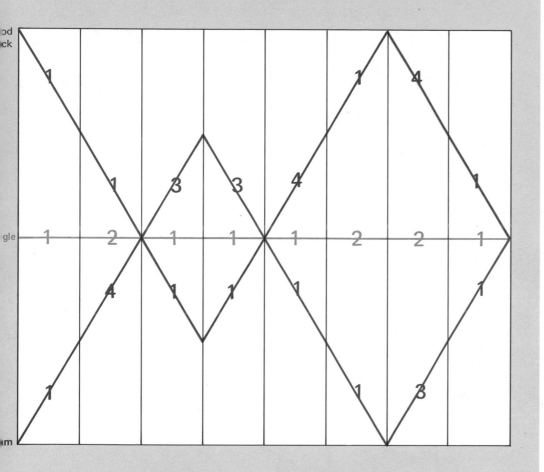

Choose one of the parts to play. Team up with two others to perform your version of *Sound Piece 7*.

MATERIALS
Pupil's Book, p. 145; wood block, triangle, drum

VOCABULARY
beat divided into two sounds, three sounds, four sounds

IDEAS FOR TEACHING
<u>Note</u>: (a) *Sound Piece 7* may be performed by three children or by three groups of children. (b) Wood block follows the red line throughout; triangle, the green line; drum, the purple line. (c) In the score, each vertical column represents a beat. As the red, green, and purple lines pass through each column, they have a number on them. The number tells how many sounds to play for that beat: *1* means one sound ($\quarternote$); *2* means two equal sounds ($\eighthnote\eighthnote$); *3*, three equal sounds ($\triplet$); *4*, four equal sounds ($\sixteenths$).

1. Have children look at the score on p. 145 to discover places where the beat is divided. <u>Questions</u>: Which part has some beats divided into two sounds? (Triangle) Into three sounds? (Wood block) Into four sounds? (Drum)

2. Give players time to practice. Then have them play the parts separately and in combinations of two parts, or all three parts together.

3. Encourage children to consider other qualities when performing *Sound Piece 7*: how fast or slow the tempo should be, when to play loud dynamics, when to play soft dynamics, etc.

TRY THIS
1. Have players extend the Sound Piece as follows:
   (a) Repeat the Sound Piece several times without interruption.
   (b) Play each part separately, then in various combinations of two parts together, and finally all three parts together.
   (c) Play the Sound Piece as a round. (<u>Note</u>: One player begins. The other players each enter when the preceding player reaches beat 2.)

2. Have children substitute other instruments for the ones in the score. Pitched instruments—e.g., recorder, bells—might be used as well as percussion instruments. <u>Note</u>: If more than one pitched instrument plays at a time, they should play the same tone—for example, G.

3. Have children write each part of the Sound Piece in traditional notation, using $\quarternote , \eighthnote\eighthnote , \triplet , \sixteenths$

4. Encourage children to create their own sound pieces using steady beats and beats divided into two, three, and four sounds. Have them each make a score of their sound piece so that others can play it. They may use notes, numbers, or other symbols to represent the sounds.

MATERIALS
Record 7, "Ta-ra-ra Boom-de-ay";
Pupil's Book, p. 146; percussion instruments, recorders or bells

VOCABULARY
rhythm pattern, dotted rhythm

IDEAS FOR TEACHING
1. Play the recording so children can hear that the words *Ta-ra-ra boom-de-ay* are repeated throughout the song with the same rhythm pattern each time. Invite them to join in tapping the rhythm when they can. Call attention to the feeling of the dotted rhythm on *boom-de-ay* as contrasted with the eighth-note rhythm of *Ta-ra-ra*. <u>Point out</u>: The use of dotted rhythms adds a special feeling to a rhythm pattern.

2. Choose one or two children to play the repeated rhythm on a percussion instrument (e.g., tambourine) as others sing "Ta-ra-ra Boom-de-ay" (notation, p. 146) with the recording.

3. Help children observe that the dotted-eighth-and-sixteenth-note rhythm (♪♬) receives one beat; that it has the same sound as four sixteenth notes with the first three tied (♫♬).

4. Have recorder players practice the fingering for F♯ (p. 146), then play the recorder part as others sing the song. <u>Point out</u>: (a) The recorders are silent during the *ta-ra-ra's;* they play each time *boom-de-ay* is sung. (b) The recorder part matches the rhythm of *boom-de-ay* in the song. Thinking *boom-de-ay* will help children play the rhythm correctly. <u>Note</u>: Bells may be used instead of recorders.

TA-RA-RA BOOM-DE-AY
WORDS AND MUSIC BY HENRY SAYERS
Piano acc., p. 330

Ta - ra - ra boom - de - ay,   Ta - ra - ra boom - de - ay,

Ta - ra - ra boom - de - ay,   Ta - ra - ra boom - de - ay,

Ta - ra - ra boom - de - ay,   Ta - ra - ra boom - de - ay,

Ta - ra - ra boom - de - ay,   Ta - ra - ra boom - de - ay.____

Practice this new tone on recorder.
Then play the part that follows
as others sing the song.
Be sure to play dotted rhythms.

F♯

Recorder or Bells

F♯   G

146 Rhythm Patterns 2

TRY THIS
Have children play the rhythm throughout "Ta-ra-ra Boom-de-ay," using objects in the room to provide unusual tone colors—e.g., tapping chalk on the chalkboard, tapping a ruler on a metal object. Children may wish to use two different tone colors, one for the *Ta-ra-ra* rhythm, the other for the *boom-de-ay* rhythm.

TEACHER INFORMATION
The pupil's page shows the German fingering for the tone F♯. Another way to play F♯ is to use the baroque fingering, which is like the German fingering but leaves the bottom hole uncovered. The baroque fingering for F♯ is shown in the Recorder Fingering Chart on page 250 of the pupil's book.

, RED ROBIN
WORDS AND MUSIC BY HARRY WOODS

COPYRIGHT © 1921 BY BOURNE CO. COPYRIGHT RENEWED. THIS ARRANGEMENT COPYRIGHT © 1981 BY BOURNE CO. ALL RIGHTS RESERVED. USED BY
PERMISSION OF BOURNE CO. AND EMI MUSIC PUBLISHING LIMITED.

Piano acc., p. 302

When the red, red rob - in comes bob, bob, bob-bin' a - long, a -

long, There'll be no more sob - bin' when he starts throb-bin' his old sweet

song. "Wake up, wake up, you sleep - y head! Get up, get up, get out_ of bed;

Cheer up, cheer up, the sun_ is red; Live, love, laugh and be hap - py!"

What if I've been blue, now I'm walk - in' through fields of flowers;

Rain may glis - ten but still I'll lis - ten for hours and hours.

I'm just a kid a - gain, do - in' what I did a - gain, Sing - ing a

song, When the red, red rob - in comes bob, bob, bob - bin' a - long._____

147

MATERIALS
Record 7, "Red, Red Robin"; Pupil's Book, p. 147; percussion instruments

VOCABULARY
dotted rhythm

IDEAS FOR TEACHING
1. As they listen to the recording, have children follow the notation on p. 147 to find other phrases that end like phrase 1, with a long-short-long pattern: *-long, along* (phrase 2, *old sweet song*; phrase 7, *fields of flowers*; phrase 8, *hours and hours*). Then play the recording again and have them tap the dotted rhythm written in small notes above the staff during each of the long sounds in those phrases. Point out: The small notes have the same rhythm as the words *When the red* at the beginning of the song. Thinking *When the red* the way it occurs in the song will help children tap the dotted rhythm correctly. Note: Some children may recognize the dotted rhythm as the same one that occurs on each *boom-de-ay* in "Ta-ra-ra Boom-de-ay" (p. 146).

2. Have individuals play the small notes on a percussion instrument as others sing "Red, Red Robin" with the recording.

TRY THIS
One child can play the rhythm of the melody of "Red, Red Robin" on a percussion instrument. Another child can play the small notes above the staff on a different-sounding instrument.

RHYTHM PATTERNS 2 • Lesson 6

MATERIALS
Record 7, "Let the Sun Shine Down on Me"; Pupil's Book, pp. 148, 92

VOCABULARY
rhythm pattern, short sound, long sound, syncopation

IDEAS FOR TEACHING

1. Have children look at the rhythm patterns on p. 148. Questions: What is the same about the patterns? (They both use eighth notes and ties.) What is different? (The ties are in different places.)

2. Establish a steady beat and have children chant each pattern. Remind them that for the tied notes, they chant on the first note, then hold the sound for the second note. Note: Children should discover that the patterns sound different: pattern 1 begins with a long sound; pattern 2, with a short sound. Point out: In music, when there is a short sound on a strong beat, followed by a long sound that begins on a weak beat (or on a weak part of the beat), the rhythm has a special feeling called syncopation. The rhythm of pattern 2 is syncopated.

3. Have children sing "Remember Me" (p. 92) to hear and feel the syncopation on the words *Do, Lord, O do, Lord* each time.

4. Play the recording of "Let the Sun Shine Down on Me" as children follow the notation (p. 148). Ask them to find the places that are syncopated (the words *down on* in the phrases *Let the sun shine down on me*). Have children join in the singing when they can.

Here is part of a song you know written two ways.

How are the patterns alike? How are they different?

Find the syncopation in this song.

148 Rhythm Patterns 2

TRY THIS

1. When children sing "Let the Sun Shine Down on Me," have individuals play an Autoharp accompaniment. Players may strum a steady-beat pattern (♩ ♩ | ♩ ♩ etc.) or a syncopated pattern (♩♩♩|♩♩♩ etc.). Note: Autoharp chords are marked in the score. For measures with two chords, players using syncopated strumming should change chords on the last strum of the pattern.

2. Have children try to find other places in "Remember Me" (p. 92) where the rhythm is syncopated (on the words *I've got to* [verse] each time; on the words *-way up beyond the* in the last phrase of each section).

REVIEW/REINFORCEMENT
Have children follow the notation as they sing these familiar songs to find places where the rhythm is syncopated.
• Hear the Rooster, p. 10 (on the words *crowing, it's* in part I; on *wake, get* in part II)
• In Bahia Town, p. 80 (at the beginning of measures 1, 3, 5, 7 of section B)
• Run, Run, Run, p. 98 (on the words *Run, run, run* each time, and on *Freedom, go* at the end of section A)

TINGA LAYO

CALYPSO FROM THE WEST INDIES ENGLISH VERSION BY MARGARET MARKS

Piano acc., p. 331

(A) REFRAIN

Tin - ga Lay - o! Run, lit - tle don - key, run!
¡Ven, mi bu - rri - to, ven!

Tin - ga Lay - o! Run, lit - tle don - key, run! run!
¡Ven, mi bu - rri - to, ven! ven!

[1.-3.] [Last time only]

(B) VERSE

1. My don - key yes, my don - key no,
1. Bu - rri - to sí, bu - rri - to no.

My don - key stop when I tell him to go!
¡Bu - rri - to co - me con te - ne - dor!

D.C.

2. My donkey hee, my donkey haw,
   My donkey sit on the kitchen floor! *Refrain*

3. My donkey kick, my donkey balk,
   My donkey eat with a silver fork! *Refrain*

Play one of these patterns throughout the song.

Which one uses syncopation? 3

1. (steady beat)

2. Tin - ga Lay - o! Tin - ga

3. Run, lit - tle don - key, run!

Rhythm Patterns 2 149

RHYTHM PATTERNS 2 • Lesson 7

MATERIALS
Record 7, "Tinga Layo"; Pupil's Book, p. 149; percussion instruments (bongos, maracas, claves)

VOCABULARY
syncopation, syncopated pattern, rhythm pattern

IDEAS FOR TEACHING
1. Play the recording and have children follow the notation on p. 149 to hear and see where there is syncopation in section A (in measures 3 and 7, on the words *Run, little*).

2. When children are ready, have them perform "Tinga Layo" with the recording as follows. During section A, they sing while individuals take turns playing the rhythm of *Run, little donkey, run!* on an appropriate percussion instrument (e.g., bongos, maracas, claves) each time it occurs. During section B, everyone sings and claps the rhythm of the melody. Question: Where did you clap a syncopated pattern in section B? (On the words *stop when I*, second to last measure)

3. Direct attention to the rhythm patterns on p. 149. Have children take turns playing one of them on a percussion instrument throughout the song as others sing. Suggestions: (a) Thinking the words *Tinga Layo* and *Run, little donkey, run!* will help children keep the rhythm for patterns 2 and 3. (b) Children can perform two or all three of the patterns simultaneously to accompany the singing. Combine only as many of the patterns as children can manage successfully.

TRY THIS
1. Tell children that "Tinga Layo" comes from the West Indies, where the donkey is thought of as a member of the family. Encourage them to make up additional verses for the song that tell about other things the donkey might do; for example:

My donkey laugh, My donkey bray,
My donkey wake me to come and play!

2. Children can accompany "Tinga Layo" on the Autoharp, using the chords C, G₇, and F. Give them time to practice first. They may strum a steady-beat pattern or create a rhythm pattern of their own. Some children may be able to strum the syncopated rhythm on the phrase *Run, little donkey, run!* each time it occurs.

TEACHER INFORMATION
The Spanish words of "Tinga Layo" are pronounced as follows.

. . . ¡Ven, mi bu - rri - to, ven!
. . . *vehn mee boo-ree-toh vehn*

Bu - rri - to sí, bu - rri - to no
boo-ree-toh see boo-ree-toh noh

¡Bu - rri - to co - me con te - ne - dor!
boo-ree-toh koh-meh kohn teh-neh-thohr

MATERIALS

Record 7, "See, Can't You Jump for Joy"; Pupil's Book, p. 150; percussion instruments, bells

VOCABULARY

syncopation, ostinato

IDEAS FOR TEACHING

Note: Syncopation gives rhythm a special feeling by using weak beats where strong beats are usually felt, and strong beats where weak ones usually occur. Since syncopated patterns can be written in many ways, stress the way syncopation *feels* rather than the way it is notated.

1. Have children perform the stamp-clap pattern at the bottom of p. 150 with the recording. Note: The pattern matches the steady beat of the song. Keeping the beat will help children hear the syncopation on the *See, can't you* part of every phrase that says *See, can't you jump for joy.* Some children may also hear the syncopation on *for joy* each time.

2. When children know the song (notation, p. 150), have individuals play the rhythm of the melody on a percussion instrument while others keep the steady beat by performing the stamp-clap pattern. Note: The steady beat might also be played on a percussion instrument that has a contrasting sound.

3. While children sing the song, have someone play an ostinato on the bells (see below). Note: (a) Children may recognize that the ostinato melody matches the first phrase of the song. Have a small group sing the ostinato, using the words *My Lord calls me.* (b) Some children can play the ostinato on recorder.

Feel the syncopation every time you sing the phrase *See, can't you jump for joy.*

SEE, CAN'T YOU JUMP FOR JOY
BLACK-AMERICAN RING SHOUT

Orff-instrument acc., p. 346   Piano acc., p. 324

Do a stamp-clap pattern as you sing the song.

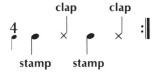

BELL OSTINATO

TRY THIS

Some children may be able to play the Autoharp to accompany "See, Can't You Jump for Joy," using the chords G, C, A₇, D. Give them time to experiment to find a comfortable fingering for the chord buttons and a strumming pattern that feels right.

Listen to this song. In which section can you feel syncopation? B

Does the melody of each section sound as it looks in the notation? Yes

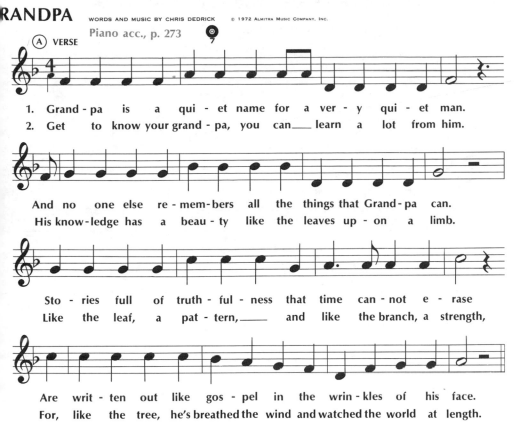

RANDPA   WORDS AND MUSIC BY CHRIS DEDRICK   © 1972 ALMITRA MUSIC COMPANY, INC.

Piano acc., p. 273

A VERSE

1. Grand - pa is a qui - et name for a ver - y qui - et man.
2. Get to know your grand - pa, you can___ learn a lot from him.

And no one else re - mem - bers all the things that Grand - pa can.
His know - ledge has a beau - ty like the leaves up - on a limb.

Sto - ries full of truth - ful - ness that time can - not e - rase
Like the leaf, a pat - tern,___ and like the branch, a strength,

Are writ - ten out like gos - pel in the wrin - kles of his face.
For, like the tree, he's breathed the wind and watched the world at length.

B REFRAIN*

Grand - pa, Grand - pa - pa,___   Grand - pa - pa - pa,___

Grand - pa - pa - pa - pa._____

Repeat refrain last time.

Sometimes you can sit with him and never say a word.

You start to think of silence as a sound that can be heard,

And, hearing it, you're led into a diff'rent place to live

Where nothing scares or hurts you, and there's nothing to forgive.

Rhythm Patterns 2 151

RHYTHM PATTERNS 2 • Lesson 9

MATERIALS
Record 7, "Grandpa"; Pupil's Book, p. 151

VOCABULARY
syncopation, contrast, interlude, key

IDEAS FOR TEACHING
1. As children follow the notation on p. 151, play the recording so they can determine which section of the song uses syncopation (section B).

2. When they are ready, have children sing section B each time it occurs on the recording. Point out: Section B looks different from section A. It has syncopated patterns (e.g., ♪ ♩ ♪♩ |), and rests at the beginning of several measures. These things help to make section B contrast with section A. Note: The refrain (section B) is sung twice after verse 3.

3. Select individuals or small groups to sing the verses (section A); everyone sings the refrain (section B). Suggestion: Direct children's attention to the instrumental interlude before verse 3 on the recording. Help them discover that the music changes to a different pitch level (key) during the interlude. Question: Is verse 3 sung higher or lower than verses 1 and 2? (Higher, by one step)

TRY THIS
To emphasize the contrast between the lack of syncopation in section A and its use in section B, have children play the rhythm of the song on percussion instruments. They use one tone color (e.g., sticks) for section A, a different tone color (e.g., tambourine) for section B. Note: Children might use contrasting natural sounds like clapping and patting lap or snapping fingers and tapping instead of percussion instruments.

MATERIALS
Record 7, *What Do You Hear? 13: Rhythm Patterns;* spirit master

VOCABULARY
syncopation

TEACHER INFORMATION
Suggest that children quietly tap the steady beat as they listen to each piece of music. This will help them hear and feel when syncopation occurs.

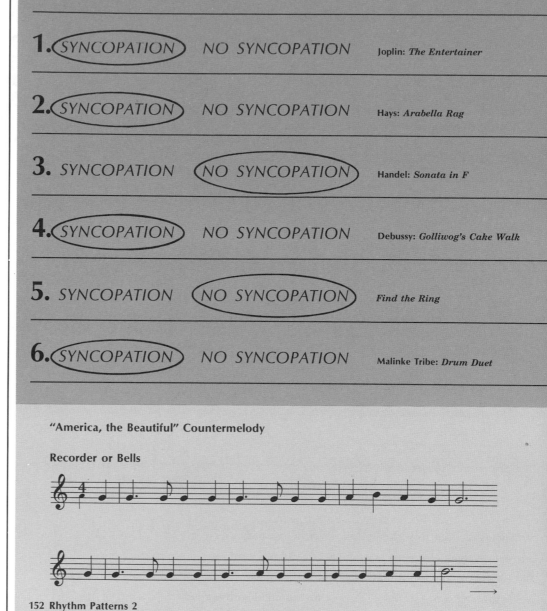

WHAT DO YOU HEAR? 13: RHYTHM PATTERNS

Listen to these pieces. Do you hear syncopation, or no syncopation? Each time a number is called, decide which of the two answers is correct. Choose the answer that best describes what is happening in the music.

1. (SYNCOPATION)   NO SYNCOPATION   Joplin: *The Entertainer*

2. (SYNCOPATION)   NO SYNCOPATION   Hays: *Arabella Rag*

3. SYNCOPATION   (NO SYNCOPATION)   Handel: *Sonata in F*

4. (SYNCOPATION)   NO SYNCOPATION   Debussy: *Golliwog's Cake Walk*

5. SYNCOPATION   (NO SYNCOPATION)   *Find the Ring*

6. (SYNCOPATION)   NO SYNCOPATION   Malinke Tribe: *Drum Duet*

"America, the Beautiful" Countermelody

Recorder or Bells

152 Rhythm Patterns 2

Notice that each phrase of "America, the Beautiful" uses the same rhythm pattern.

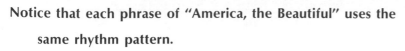

AMERICA, THE BEAUTIFUL
MUSIC BY SAMUEL A. WARD   WORDS BY KATHARINE LEE BATES

Piano acc., p. 252

O beau - ti - ful   for   spa - cious skies, For   am - ber waves of   grain,
O beau - ti - ful   for   pa - triot dream That sees   be - yond the   years

For   pur - ple moun - tain maj - es - ties   A - bove the fruit - ed   plain!
Thine al - a - bas - ter cit - ies gleam, Un-dimmed by   hu - man   tears!

A - mer - i - ca!   A - mer - i - ca!   God shed His grace on   thee

And crown   thy good with broth - er - hood From sea   to   shin - ing   sea!

Rhythm Patterns 2 153

RHYTHM PATTERNS 2 • Lesson 11

MATERIALS
Record 7, "America, the Beautiful"; Pupil's Book, pp. 152 and 153; recorders or bells

VOCABULARY
dotted rhythms, countermelody

IDEAS FOR TEACHING
Note: Dotted rhythms give music a special feeling, just as syncopation does.

1. Have children sing "America, the Beautiful" (p. 153) with the recording. Help them observe that all four phrases of the song have the same rhythm. Note: Each staff of notation represents a phrase of the music.

2. Draw children's attention to the instrumental accompaniment on the recording. Questions: Does the accompaniment for verse 1 have the same general rhythm as the melody, or a different rhythm? (The same general rhythm) In verse 2, which instruments play a rhythm that is very different from that of the melody? (Trumpets) Note: If stereo is available, use the Pick-a-Track technique to highlight the instrumental accompaniment.

3. Have children look at the notation for the countermelody at the bottom of pp. 152 and 153 to discover that its rhythm matches that of the melody of "America, the Beautiful."

4. Have children who can play G, A, B, high C on recorder play the countermelody as others sing the song. Note: Recorder fingerings for G, A, B are found on p. 27; the fingering for high C is on p. 99. The countermelody can also be played on bells.

TEACHER INFORMATION
The story of how "America, the Beautiful" came to be written can be told over and over again. Briefly, it was inspired by the view that a schoolteacher got from a vantage point on top of Pikes Peak in Colorado. As Katharine Lee Bates looked out over the verdant panorama and saw a vast land of liberty and abundance, she felt the thrill of being an American. From this experience came the poem, which another American, Samuel Ward, set to music.

Only the first and fourth stanzas of the poem are included in the Pupil's Book, but children heard the entire poem performed by the Mormon Tabernacle Choir and The Philadelphia Orchestra when they studied *Call Chart 4* on p. 91. Give them an opportunity to hear the poem again.

RHYTHM PATTERNS 2 • Lesson 12

MATERIALS
Record 7, "Clementine"; Pupil's Book, p. 154; sticks, tambourine, Autoharp

VOCABULARY
dotted rhythms, triplets

IDEAS FOR TEACHING
1. As children sing "Clementine" with the recording (p. 154), have them clap the rhythm of the words. Help them observe that the rhythm is the same for each staff of the notation.

2. Call attention to the percussion parts notated on p. 154. Question: Which part uses the same rhythm pattern as each staff of "Clementine"? (The part for sticks)

3. Give children time to practice the percussion parts for "Clementine." Then have them play the parts as others sing the song. Point out: (a) Dotted rhythms occur in the parts for sticks and Autoharp. (b) The triplets in the tambourine part are played three equal sounds to the beat. Suggestion: Have children play each part alone to accompany the song. When they are ready, have them play in combinations of two parts (e.g., sticks and Autoharp, tambourine and Autoharp), and finally all three parts together. Call attention to the sound of different rhythm patterns played simultaneously.

CLEMENTINE
AMERICAN FOLK SONG

Piano acc., p. 253

1. In a cav-ern, in a can-yon, Ex-ca-vat-ing for a mine,
2. Light she was, and like a fair-y, And her shoes were num-ber nine,
3. Drove she duck-lings to the wa-ter Ev-'ry morn-ing just at nine,

Dwelt a min-er, for-ty-nin-er, And his daugh-ter, Clem-en-tine.
Her-ring box-es with-out top-ses, San-dals were for Clem-en-tine.
Hit her foot a-gainst a splin-ter, Fell in-to the foam-ing brine

REFRAIN
(optional harmony part)
Oh, my dar-ling, oh, my dar-ling, Oh, my dar-ling Clem-en-tine,

You are lost and gone for-ev-er, Dread-ful sor-ry, Clem-en-tine.

Play these rhythm patterns to accompany "Clementine."

Sticks (Play four times.)

Tambourine (Play four times.)

Autoharp

154 Rhythm Patterns 2

TRY THIS
When children accompany "Clementine," encourage them to create their own strumming pattern for the Autoharp part. For example, for measures 1 through 8 they might use short strums to play sounds that move upward (on the low strings, then the middle, then the high strings) or that move downward (on the high strings, then the middle, then the low strings), or they might alternate, playing upward sounds for one measure, downward sounds for the next.

WHAT DO YOU HEAR? 14: RHYTHM PATTERNS

Listen to these pieces. Each time a number is called, decide which pattern you are hearing.

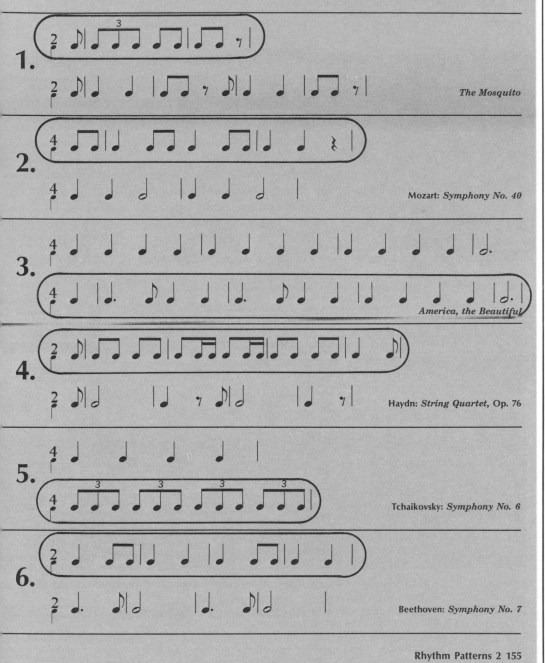

1. *The Mosquito*

2. Mozart: *Symphony No. 40*

3. *America, the Beautiful*

4. Haydn: *String Quartet, Op. 76*

5. Tchaikovsky: *Symphony No. 6*

6. Beethoven: *Symphony No. 7*

Rhythm Patterns 2 155

RHYTHM PATTERNS 2 • Lesson 13

MATERIALS
Record 7, *What Do You Hear? 14: Rhythm Patterns*; spirit master

VOCABULARY
rhythm pattern

TEACHER INFORMATION
The What Do You Hear? evaluations in this module each focus on a different aspect of rhythm pattern. In *What Do You Hear? 14,* children demonstrate their ability to see what they hear by choosing the notation that matches the sounds on the recording. In each excerpt, the pattern occurs several times. To help children decide their answer, suggest that they follow one line of notation, then the other, alternating throughout each recorded excerpt.

MODULE 14

OBJECTIVES, p. XIII

THE ARTS: Pattern

MATERIALS
Record 6, "The Mosquito"; Record 7, Chopin: *Prelude in A Minor;* Pupil's Book, pp. 156–159, 142

VOCABULARY
pattern, line, direction, horizontal, vertical, diagonal, melody contour

IDEAS FOR TEACHING
Note: Have children work with a partner for items 1 through 3 of this lesson. One partner's book should be open to the painting on pp. 156 and 157; the other's to the diagrams on p. 158. In this way, all children will be able to see the painting and the diagrams simultaneously.

1. Provide time for children to look at the painting on pp. 156 and 157. Discuss some of the things they respond to, calling attention to the use of light and shadow and to the repetition of colors—blues, reds, yellows, greens, blacks.

2. Have children look at the drawings on p. 158. Question: What do the drawings show about the painting on pp. 156 and 157?
Note: The drawings show that the painting includes many patterns of repeated shapes and lines. Each drawing shows a different shape pattern or line pattern as follows: Drawing 1—a pattern of horizontal lines (roof line, line running across the middle of the building, shadows on the street); Drawing 2—a pattern of

→

156 MODULE 14: The Arts—Pattern

TEACHER INFORMATION
Edward Hopper (American, 1882–1967) *Early Sunday Morning:* This artist specialized in carefully constructed, realistic paintings of city scenes. As a young man, Hopper spent a good deal of time in Paris, the main result of which was a fascination with the play of light on buildings. His works explore the effects of morning, afternoon, and evening lights.

The Arts—Pattern 157

vertical rectangles arranged from side to side (windows on the second floor); Drawing 3—larger rectangles arranged from side to side (shop windows); Drawing 4—a pattern of rectangles and broken lines (roof supports, tops of the windows, sills at the bottom of the windows). Children may discover patterns made by other objects in the painting—window shades, curtains, awnings, decorations under the roof line, doors to the shops. Help them observe that each pattern shows repeated shapes or lines, that the patterns all work together to give the painting its special look.

3. Ask children to look at the painting once more. Question: As your eyes travel around the painting, which directions seem to be most important—side to side (horizontal), up and down (vertical), or from corner to corner (diagonal)? Note: All three directions are important in the painting; all three directions work together. The strong horizontals and verticals are given added interest, tension, and force by the strong diagonal cutting across the painting from lower left to upper right (from the street line through the fire hydrant, through the barber pole, to the color block). Suggestion: Use the diagrams on p. 158 to emphasize the use of direction in the painting. Have children show the directions by "tracing" each diagramed pattern in the air with their finger.

4. Have children look at the rhythm pattern notated on p. 159. Tell them that it is repeated over and over in a song they know. Have children clap the pattern over and over to help them determine that it is the rhythm of "The Mosquito." Then play the

$\longrightarrow$

recording and have them clap the repeated rhythm pattern as they sing the song (notation, p. 142).

5. Direct children's attention to the contour lines on p. 159. The lines show the contour of the melody in the song "The Mosquito." Help children observe that the pattern of upward and downward movement (contour) is similar for the first three lines, different for the fourth line. Have them trace the contour lines as they listen to the recording.

6. Play the recording of the Chopin prelude. <u>Point out:</u> (a) The music is made up of a melody (upper part) with an accompaniment (lower part). (b) The prelude begins with the accompaniment alone; the melody comes in later. By listening and discussing, help children discover that the accompaniment is made up of a pattern of even sounds moving up and down. The melody is made up of a long pattern of longer and shorter sounds, with the entire pattern repeated several times.

7. Take time to discuss the following ideas:
(a) In painting, patterns are *seen* in an "all at once" way. In music, patterns are *heard* one after the other as the music goes along.
(b) In painting, lines are drawn and are also suggested by the way shapes are placed. In music, there is no real line, but an impression of line is heard by the way melody notes are connected.
(c) In painting, the eye sees the direction of patterns and lines. In music, the ear hears the direction of tones moving upward and downward. ⟶

What do these drawings show?

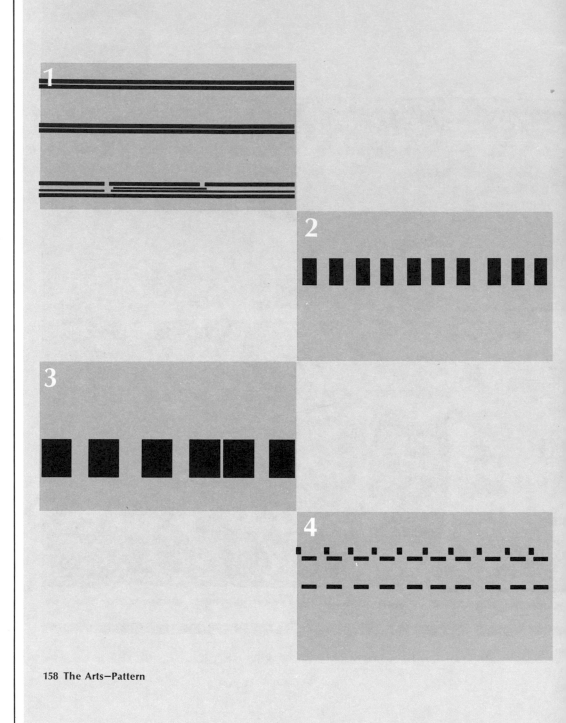

158 The Arts—Pattern

TEACHER INFORMATION
Frédéric Chopin (Polish, 1810–1849) *Prelude in A Minor:* Chopin composed a great deal of music, practically all of it for a single instrument—the piano. Chopin's piano music fully exploits the potential of the instrument, and it is frequently performed in recital. The beautiful melodies and fascinating harmonies of Chopin's music typify the romanticism of the 19th century.

This rhythm pattern is from a song that you know.

Can you name the song?   "The Mosquito"

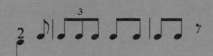

What do these lines show?   The melody contour of "The Mosquito"

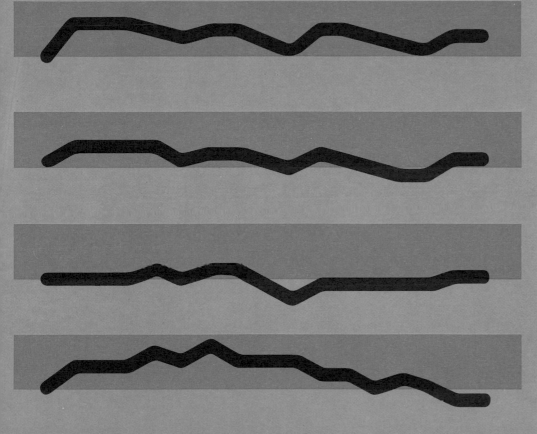

A painting can have pattern, line, direction. Can a piece of music have pattern, line, and direction also? Yes

 Chopin: *Prelude in A Minor*

The Arts—Pattern 159

REVIEW/REINFORCEMENT
1. Help children discover repeated patterns in other paintings and photographs in their book; for example:
    Photograph—rose window, p. 94
    Painting—*The Sargent Family*, p. 131
    Photographs—leaves, corn, I beams, etc., pp. 134 and 135

2. Help children hear repeated patterns in other songs they know; for example:
• Scratch, Scratch, p. 6
• Dayenu, p. 40

TRY THIS
1. Have children draw "pattern pictures" that emphasize repeated shapes or lines, or both shapes and lines. Note: Some children may prefer to use cutouts instead of drawing. If they fold a piece of paper in quarters before they cut out a shape, they will have four identical shapes to arrange on a background. Encourage them to arrange the repeated shapes in interesting ways.

2. Have children create movements that repeat—hand movements, arm movements, head movements, foot movements. Then have them put several movements together in a "pattern dance." The dance might have three sections, each using a different combination of movement patterns. Mainstreaming Suggestion: Have children with auditory or visual impairment work with a partner—one who has strong motor skills. Encourage them to use the full range of movements that they are capable of making.

MODULE 15

OBJECTIVES, p. XIII

TONE COLOR · Lesson 1

MATERIALS
Record 7, *Swing Low, Sweet Chariot;*
Pupil's Book, p. 160

VOCABULARY
tone color, register, solo, chorus

IDEAS FOR TEACHING

1. Play the recording and ask children to listen for the contrast between men's and women's voices. Question: Do you hear a man's voice or a woman's voice on the solo parts? (Man's voice) What voices do you hear on the chorus parts? (Both men's and women's voices) Point out: Each voice has its own special quality of sound, called tone color.

2. Play the recording again and have children listen for the harmony produced by the men's and women's voices sounding together. Point out: On the recording, harmony is produced by the voices alone, without instrumental accompaniment.

3. Have children add the tone color of their voices by singing the chorus parts along with the recording.

4. Give children time to look at the picture of a chorus on p. 160. Point out: In a chorus, singers are usually grouped according to the tone color and register of their voice—high women's voices (sopranos), low women's voices (altos), high men's voices (tenors), low men's voices (basses).

TONE COLOR VOICES

In the recording of *Swing Low, Sweet Chariot,* you hear both women's and men's voices.

 Swing Low, Sweet Chariot

160 MODULE 15: Tone Color

TEACHER INFORMATION
This would be an appropriate time to show the sound/color filmstrip *The Newark Boys Chorus.*

TRY THIS
1. To help make children aware of the many different vocal tone colors they hear every day, have them tape-record several familiar voices—the principal's, the secretary's, the school nurse's, teachers', etc. Provide time for them to play their recording for others to try to identify each voice from its tone color.

2. Review other songs that have solo and chorus parts; for example:
• Hand Me Down, p. 14
• Sourwood Mountain, p. 16
• Oh, Won't You Sit Down? p. 24
Let children help decide how to perform each one—e.g., teacher sings solo parts, class sings chorus parts; one child sings solo parts, a group of children sings chorus parts.

LL HID TRADITIONAL · **Piano acc., p. 250**

All hid, All hid, All hid,— All hid,

Five, ten, fif - teen, twen - ty, all hid;

Five, ten, fif - teen, twen - ty, all hid, All hid.

Five, ten, fif - teen, twen - ty,

Twen - ty - five, thir - ty, thir - ty - five, for - ty,

For - ty - five, fif - ty, fif - ty - five, six - ty,

Six - ty - five, seven - ty, seven - ty - five, eight - y,

Eight - y - five, nine - ty, nine - ty - five, hun - dred.

D.C. al Fine

Tone Color 161

TONE COLOR · Lesson 2

MATERIALS
Record 7, "All Hid"; Pupil's Book,
p. 161

VOCABULARY
tone color, solo, chorus

IDEAS FOR TEACHING
1. Play the recording of "All Hid" so
children can hear the contrast in
vocal tone color. Questions: What
voice sings the solo parts? (Man's
voice) The chorus parts? (Children's
voices) Point out: The man's voice
and children's voices are heard together at the end of section A, and
throughout section B.

2. Ask children to follow the notation on p. 161 as they listen to the
recording. Invite them to join in on
the parts labeled *Chorus* and *All.*

3. Have individuals take turns singing the solo parts in "All Hid." The
rest of the class sings the chorus
parts, and everyone sings the parts
marked *All.*

TRY THIS

1. Have children listen to the recording of "All Hid" to
discover some of the instrumental tone colors used (trumpet, guitar, electric bass, wood block).

2. As others sing "All Hid," have individuals take turns
playing the rhythm of the words on a wood block during
section B.

3. Have children take turns playing the following ostinato
on piano or on another keyboard instrument as others sing
"All Hid." They may play in a high register or in a low register.

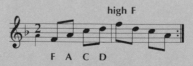

high F

F A C D

MATERIALS

Record 7, *Sound Piece 8: Windy Winter Rain;* Pupil's Book, pp. 162 and 163

VOCABULARY

tone color, score, legend

IDEAS FOR TEACHING

1. Have several children take turns reading aloud the poem on p. 162. Call attention to the way each child uses his or her voice. Suggestion: Encourage the class to describe each voice in terms of register (Does the voice pitch rise to high sounds? Fall to low sounds?), duration (Does the reader stretch out some words? Make other words short and clipped?), dynamics (Is the voice loud? Soft?), and tempo (Is the reading fast? Slow? Moderate?).

2. Direct children's attention to the musical setting of *Windy Winter Rain . . . (Sound Piece 8)* on p. 163. Point out: The score is written in contemporary notation. In it, the words of the poem are combined with symbols. Some of the symbols—e.g., for quarter and eighth notes ($\quarternote$, $\eighthnote$); to indicate dynamics ($<$ $>$)—are familiar to the children. Symbols that are unfamiliar are explained in the legend on p. 162.

3. Have children follow the score on p. 163 as they listen to the recording to hear the various vocal tone colors used in the Sound Piece.

4. Some children may be able to perform *Sound Piece 8.* Divide them into two groups, one to perform the parts marked *1* in the score; the other, the parts marked *2.* After the

$\longrightarrow$

Use the tone color of your natural speaking voice when you read this poem.

Windy winter rain . . .
My silly big umbrella
Tries walking backward.

Shisei-Jo

Now look at the notation for the Sound Piece on p. 163. Notice that the score uses symbols to stand for different voice sounds. The legend below tells what the symbols mean.

LEGEND

Œ   **Blow.**

φ   **Whistle.**

↓   **Whisper.**

∞   **Make the sound continue.**

⊓⊓⊓   **Make unvoiced lip and mouth sounds without breathing out.**

162 Tone Color

SOUND PIECE 8: Windy Winter Rain ALLEN BRINGS

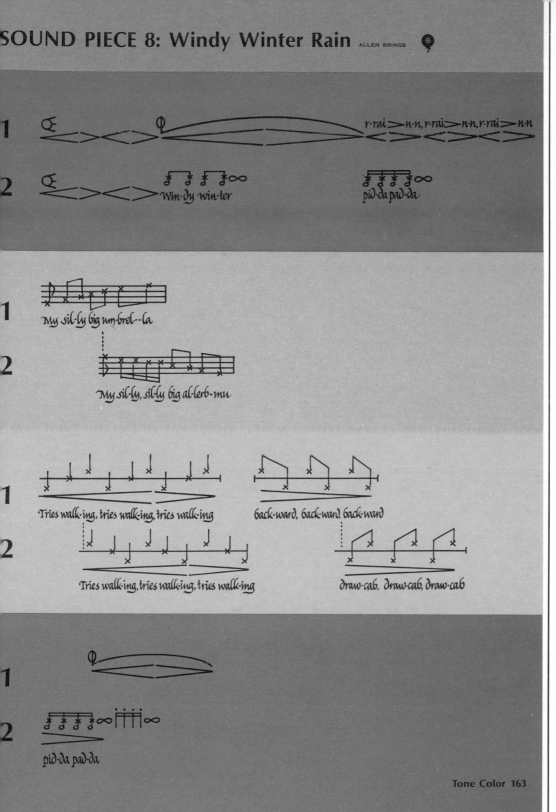

Tone Color 163

groups have practiced, let them perform for the class. <u>Suggestion</u>: Discuss how the children's performance is different from that on the recording. <u>Note</u>: The composer has left many decisions for interpreting the score up to the performers—e.g., how fast or slow each event should be; how long the blowing, whistling, and whispering sounds should last. For this reason, each performance of the Sound Piece will be different. <u>Point out</u>: Because of the way they are notated, many contemporary works sound different each time they are performed.

TRY THIS

1. Children can create a sound piece of their own that uses a variety of vocal tone colors. To begin, they choose a short, familiar poem or write a poem of their own (see Try This, item 2). Then they decide what voice sound and dynamics to use for each line. They notate their sound piece using a different symbol for each voice sound. <u>Note</u>: Remind children to include a legend that explains what each symbol stands for. This will enable others to perform the sound piece.

2. Explain that the poem "Windy Winter Rain" is an example of haiku, a form of Japanese poetry that has three unrhymed lines, with five syllables in the first line, seven in the second line, and five in the third. Have children try writing a haiku poem about rain in a different season. They might use one of the following as a first line: "Chilly autumn rain," "Misty April rain," "Teeming summer rain." <u>Note</u>: Some children may wish to use their poem for the activity in Try This, item 1.

MATERIALS
Record 7, "Don Gato"; Pupil's Book, pp. 164 and 165; percussion instruments

VOCABULARY
tone color, ballad, legend

IDEAS FOR TEACHING

1. Choose six children and assign each one a verse of "Don Gato" (pp. 164 and 165) to read aloud. Help the class discover that the verses tell a story. Suggestions: (a) Encourage children to read expressively. Give them time to look over their verse before reading aloud to decide how they will use their voice in terms of dynamics, tempo, and register.
(b) Discuss with the class whether the dynamics, tempo, and register were appropriate for each verse.

2. Play the recording of "Don Gato" for children to hear the ballad sung with instrumental accompaniment. Call attention to the instrumental effects after the first two phrases of some of the verses. Make a list of the instruments that produce the effects:
• Verse 1—guitar
• Verse 2—flute
• Verse 3—xylophone (and wood block)
• Verse 5—flute
Suggestion: Help children recognize the tone color of the castanets throughout the accompaniment for verse 3, of the tambourine throughout verse 4, and of the drum and castanets in the accompaniment for verse 6.

3. Have children make up a sound effect for each of the symbols on →

Read the lyrics to learn the story of Don Gato. Then sing the song.

A song that tells a story is called a ballad.

DON GATO FOLK SONG FROM MEXICO ENGLISH WORDS BY MARGARET MARKS

Piano acc., p. 256

1. Oh, Se - ñor Don Ga - to was a cat,_____
2. "I a - dore you!" wrote the la - dy cat,_____

On a high, red roof Don Ga - to sat._____
Who was fluff - y, white, and nice and fat._____

He went there to read a let - ter, meow, meow, meow,
There was not a sweet - er kit - ty,

Where the read - ing light was bet - ter, meow, meow, meow,
In the coun - try or the cit - y,

'Twas a love note for Don Ga - to!_____
And she said she'd wed Don Ga - to!_____

164 Tone Color

3. Oh, Don Gato jumped so happily
   He fell off the roof and broke his knee,
   Broke his ribs and all his whiskers, . . .
   And his little solar plexus, . . .
   "¡Ay carramba!" cried Don Gato!

4. Then the doctors all came on the run
   Just to see if something could be done,
   And they held a consultation, . . .
   About how to save their patient, . . .
   How to save Señor Don Gato!

5. But in spite of everything they tried
   Poor Señor Don Gato up and died,
   Oh, it wasn't very merry, . . .
   Going to the cemetery, . . .
   For the ending of Don Gato!

6. When the funeral passed the market square
   Such a smell of fish was in the air,
   Though his burial was slated, . . .
   He became re-animated! . . .
   He came back to life, Don Gato!

Decide on a sound effect for each of these symbols. Add the sound effects when you sing "Don Gato."

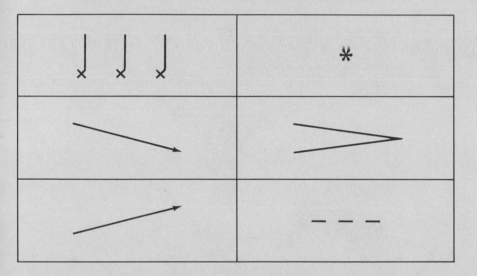

Tone Color 165

p. 165. Write a legend on the chalkboard that identifies the sound children have chosen for each symbol (see below for a sample legend). Then, as they sing "Don Gato," have children add one of the sound effects after phrases 1 and 2 of each verse. Suggestions: (a) As children become more comfortable with this activity, encourage them to choose sounds that are appropriate to the action described in the lyrics. In verse 3, for example, children may wish to use one sound effect after phrase 1 to indicate jumping sounds (e.g., a series of short, upward glissandos on a xylophone) and a different one after phrase 2 to indicate Don Gato's fall and breaking bones (e.g., a cymbal crash and tambourine shake). (b) Have children make up their own symbols to notate their sound effects.

SAMPLE LEGEND

↓ ↓ ↓ "Meowing" sounds
＼ A downward strum on the Autoharp with no chord buttons depressed
／ An upward glissando (i.e., quickly sliding the mallet across the bars) on the xylophone
* A loud drum beat or cymbal crash
＞ A long, spoken "oo" sound, beginning loud and getting softer
- - - Short sounds played on a wood block

TONE COLOR • Lesson 5

MATERIALS
Record 7, McKenzie: *Three Dances,* "Samba"; Pupil's Book, p. 166; percussion instruments

VOCABULARY
tone color, percussion instruments

IDEAS FOR TEACHING
1. Have children look at the photograph on p. 166. Ask them to identify each instrument (bongos, triangle, wood block, timpani, guiro).

2. Play the recording so children can hear how a composer has used the tone colors of these instruments to make an interesting composition. Have children point to each instrument in the photograph as it is introduced in the music. <u>Note:</u> The instruments enter in this order: bongos, triangle, wood block, timpani, guiro.

3. Play the recording so children can discover how the instruments are used singly and in combination. <u>Note:</u> The piece begins with bongos alone. Soon triangle and wood block join the bongos and all three tone colors are heard in combination. Near the end of this event, the timpani are added for a combination of four tone colors. Then bongos, triangle, and wood block drop out and timpani are heard alone. For the final event, guiro and bongos are used along with timpani.

4. Have children choose a familiar song and decide on a percussion instrument that is appropriate for it. As others sing, have individuals take turns playing a percussion accompaniment, using a rhythm pattern from the song, or one that they create.

PERCUSSION INSTRUMENTS
Listen to an ensemble of percussion instruments in this recording.

 McKenzie: *Samba*

You have played percussion instruments to accompany many songs that you know. Decide on a song, then choose a percussion instrument to play while the class sings along.

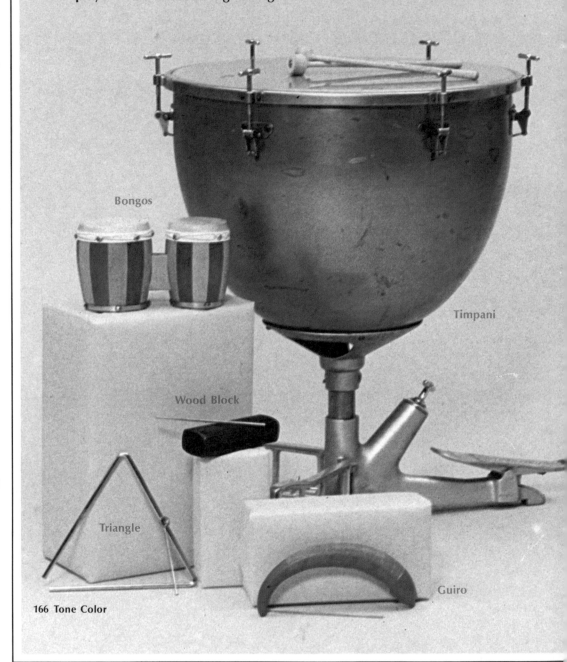

Bongos

Timpani

Wood Block

Triangle

Guiro

166 Tone Color

TRY THIS
Have groups of children create their own piece for percussion instruments. Get them started by offering the following suggestions:
- Limit the number of instruments to four or five.
- Think of the various ways each instrument can be played (e.g., a tambourine can be struck, shaken, scraped with fingernails). Decide which tone colors sound most interesting and include them.
- Use a variety of rhythm patterns.
- Use the instruments alone and in various combinations.

Give the groups an opportunity to perform for one another.

TEACHER INFORMATION
Some children will have had previous experience hearing the tone color of a variety of instruments—traditional, ethnic, electronic. They also may be aware of how instrumental sounds are produced—by blowing, bowing, striking, scraping, shaking, strumming. As far as possible, the lessons on pp. 166–177 include opportunities for children's performance in conjunction with the recorded sounds of instrumental ensembles. The lessons need not be presented in order. This allows children, depending on individual interest, to choose the lessons they want to pursue. Allow time for them to work independently, as well as in the group.

Think of a way to accompany this song on percussion instruments.

Which tone colors will you use?

SHE'LL BE COMIN' ROUND THE MOUNTAIN SOUTHERN MOUNTAIN SONG

Piano acc., p. 312

1. She'll be com - in' round the moun - tain when she comes,_____
2. She'll be driv - in' six white hor - ses when she comes,_____

She'll be com - in' round the moun - tain when she comes,_____
She'll be driv - in' six white hor - ses when she comes,_____

She'll be com - in' round the moun - tain,
She'll be driv - in' six white hor - ses,

She'll be com - in' round the moun - tain,
She'll be driv - in' six white hor - ses,

She'll be com - in' round the moun - tain when she comes._____
She'll be driv - in' six white hor - ses when she comes._____

3. Oh, we'll kill the old red rooster when she comes, . . .

4. Oh, we'll all have chicken and dumplings when she comes, . . .

5. Oh, we'll all go out to meet her when she comes, . . .

Follow the chord names in the music to play an accompaniment on

the Autoharp. You will use the chords G, D₇, C.

Tone Color 167

TONE COLOR • Lesson 6

MATERIALS
Record 7, "She'll Be Comin' Round the Mountain"; Pupil's Book, p. 167; percussion instruments, Autoharp

VOCABULARY
tone color, rhythm pattern, strong beat

IDEAS FOR TEACHING

1. Play the recording and have children listen for the long sounds in the song. Help them discover that they occur on the word *comes* each time.

2. As others sing with the recording (notation, p. 167), have individuals take turns adding the tone color of a percussion instrument by playing a rhythm pattern during each long sound. Suggestions: (a) Have a different child play for each verse. (b) Have each player use a different-sounding instrument. (c) Encourage players to each make up a different pattern to play.

3. Ask children to think of other ways to use percussion tone colors to accompany the song. Possible suggestions include the following:
• Play the steady beat.
• Play only the first beat (strong beat) of each measure.
• Play the rhythm of the words.
• Make up a rhythm pattern to play throughout the song.

4. Choose individuals to accompany the song on the Autoharp. Give them time to experiment to find a strumming pattern that feels right. Note: Repeat this activity from time to time so that each child has the experience of playing the Autoharp to accompany the class singing.

TEACHER INFORMATION
Mainstreaming Suggestion: When accompanying the song on percussion instruments, (a) have children who are neurologically impaired or mentally retarded play only the first beat (strong beat) of each measure until they are ready to play the steady beat; (b) focus the attention of children with speech impairment on the inflections and rhythms of speech by having them play and say the words rhythmically.

TONE COLOR · Lesson 7

MATERIALS
Record 7, "Hotsia!"; Pupil's Book, pp. 168 and 169, 89; cowbell, high drum, rattle

VOCABULARY
tone color, polyrhythm

IDEAS FOR TEACHING

1. Play the recording and have children join in singing the word *hotsia* each time it occurs. Note: The word *hotsia* begins each phrase of the song. It is always sung on the same tones.

2. In "Hotsia!" each phrase is twelve beats long. As children listen to the recording, have them follow the notation on pp. 168 and 169 and tap the steady beat. Point out: (a) The numbers above the first staff show the beats in the first phrase. (b) In the first phrase, most sounds last for one beat (♪); two of the sounds last for two beats (♩). (c) Each phrase of "Hotsia!" follows the same pattern of long and short sounds.

3. Have children read the instructions at the top of p. 168. Then have them try clapping the rhythm of each percussion part. Remind them to clap only the beats shown with large-size numbers. (Mainstreaming Suggestion: Have children with limited motor abilities clap with a partner in "pat-a-cake" fashion to experience the feel of each percussion rhythm.) When they are ready, have individuals play each rhythm on the appropriate percussion instrument as others sing "Hotsia!" Suggestion: At first, use only one percussion part at a time to accompany the chant. When children are comfortable with →

Play these percussion parts to accompany "Hotsia!"

In each part, silently say the numbers in time with the steady beat.

Play the instrument whenever you say a large-size number.

Cowbell

1 2 3 4 5 6 7 8 9 10 11 12

High Drum

1 2 3 4 5 6 7 8 9 10 11 12

Rattle

1 2 3 4 5 6 7 8 9 10 11 12

HOTSIA!

VENDA CHILDREN'S SONG   ENGLISH WORDS BY RICHARD MORRIS

THIS IS A FREE TRANSLATION OF A VERY SIMPLE CHILDREN'S SONG. ORIGINALLY PUBLISHED AS "HOTSIA" IN J. A. R. BLACKING, VENDA CHILDREN'S SONGS (JOHANNESBURG, WITWATERSRAND UNIVERSITY PRESS, 1967), P. 108, AND REPRODUCED HERE WITH THE PERMISSION OF THE WITWATERSRAND UNIVERSITY PRESS AND OF THE AUTHOR.

Ho - tsi - a! The bul - bul scratched my eye,____

Ho - tsi - a! It hurts so, I could cry.____

Ho - tsi - a! How can you laugh that way?____

168 Tone Color

Ho - tsi - a! You're not my friend to - day.____

Ho - tsi - a! Oh, did - n't we have fun? ____

Ho - tsi - a! How those ba - boons did run____

Ho - tsi - a! From old Ne - khum - be's gar - den,

Ho - tsi - a! When we all yelled and chased them

Ho - tsi - a! Back up in - to the moun - tains.

The word *hotsia* means "sneeze." In Africa, this sound is supposed

to frighten away birds, baboons, and other pests that eat

the crops.

Tone Color 169

the rhythm, try combining two parts, and finally all three as an accompaniment. Call attention to the sound that results when the parts are played together. Some children may recall that the sound of different rhythms played together is called polyrhythm. <u>Point out:</u> In Africa, the rhythms on p. 168 might be played on the instruments gankogui, axatse, and kagan. These are pictured in the Pupil's Book on p. 89.

REVIEW/ REINFORCEMENT
Have children perform the African Rhythm Complex on pp. 88 and 89. At first have them perform one line at a time, then various combinations of two lines together (e.g., lines 1 and 2, 2 and 4, 1 and 3), of three lines together, and finally the entire complex as written.

MATERIALS
Record 8, "Skip to My Lou"; "Billy Boy"; "Polly Wolly Doodle"; "Ain't Gonna Rain"; Pupil's Book, pp. 170 and 171; Autoharp, variety of picks

VOCABULARY
tone color, Autoharp, strum, pluck

IDEAS FOR TEACHING
<u>Note:</u> Children have had many opportunities to play the Autoharp to accompany the class singing. Some children have probably become quite adept at playing Autoharp accompaniments consisting of three or more chords. The songs on pp. 170 and 171 are intended to give each child a satisfying experience with the Autoharp. The songs are largely familiar ones. Each one can be accompanied on the Autoharp using only two different chords. The familiarity of the songs and the simplicity of their chord patterns will enable children to be as inventive as their imagination permits in exploring the possibilities of the Autoharp as an accompanying instrument. <u>Mainstreaming Note:</u> Children who have difficulty with other music activities are sometimes able to strum the Autoharp strings if someone else depresses the chord buttons.

1. Have children take turns accompanying the class singing by playing the strumming pattern provided with each song on pp. 170 and 171. <u>Note:</u> The underlined word in the first verse indicates when the Autoharp part begins.

2. When children are comfortable with the pattern of chord changes, have them try a strumming pattern →

AUTOHARP

SKIP TO MY LOU   AMERICAN GAME SONG   Piano acc., p. 313

1. <u>Flies</u> in the buttermilk, shoo, fly, shoo!
   Flies in the buttermilk, shoo, fly, shoo!
   Flies in the buttermilk, shoo, fly, shoo!
   Skip to my Lou, my darling.

2. Little red wagon painted blue,

3. Lost my partner, what'll I do?

4. I'll get another, better than you!

BILLY BOY   FOLK SONG FROM ENGLAND   Piano acc., p. 269

1. Oh, <u>where</u> have you been, Billy Boy, Billy Boy?
   Oh, where have you been, charming Billy?
   I have been to seek a wife,
   She's the joy of my life,
   She's a young thing and cannot leave her mother.

2. Did she bid you to come in, Billy Boy, Billy Boy?
   Did she bid you to come in, charming Billy?
   Yes, she bid me to come in,
   There's a dimple in her chin,
   She's a young thing and cannot leave her mother.

3. Did she give you a chair, Billy Boy, Billy Boy?
   Yes, she gave me a chair,
   But there was no bottom there . . .

4. Can she make a cherry pie, Billy Boy, Billy Boy?
   She can make a cherry pie,
   Quick as a cat can wink her eye . . .

5. Can she cook and can she spin, Billy Boy, Billy Boy?
   She can cook and she can spin,
   She can do most anything . . .

6. How old is she, Billy Boy, Billy Boy?
   Three times six and four times seven,
   Twenty-eight and eleven . . .

POLLY WOLLY DOODLE   AMERICAN FOLK SONG   Piano acc., p. 320

1. Oh, I <u>went</u> down South for to see my Sal,
   Singing Polly Wolly Doodle all the day;
   My Sal, she is a spunky gal,
   Singing Polly Wolly Doodle all the day.

Refrain
   Fare thee well, fare thee well,
   Fare thee well my fairy fay,
   For I'm goin' to Louisiana, for to see my Susyanna,
   Singing Polly Wolly Doodle all the day.

2. Oh, my Sal, she is a maiden fair,
   Singing Polly Wolly Doodle all the day;
   With curly eyes and laughing hair,
   Singing Polly Wolly Doodle all the day.

3. The partridge is a pretty bird,
   It has a speckled breast,
   It steals away the farmer's grain,
   And totes it to its nest!

4. The raccoon's tail is ringed around,
   The 'possum's tail is bare,
   The rabbit's got no tail at all,
   Just a little bitty bunch of hair!

5. The June-bug he has golden wings,
   The lightning bug totes a flame,
   The caterpillar's got no wings at all,
   But he gets there just the same!

8   Piano acc., p. 329

AIN'T GONNA RAIN   AMERICAN FOLK SONG

1. The <u>wood</u>chuck, he's a-choppin' wood,
   The 'possum, he's a-haulin'.
   My poor old dog fell off a log
   And killed himself a-bawlin'.

Refrain
   It ain't gonna rain, it ain't gonna rain,
   It ain't gonna rain no more.
   Come on down, ev'rybody sing.
   It ain't gonna rain no more.

2. Just bake them biscuits good and brown,
   It ain't gonna rain no more.
   Swing your ladies round and round,
   It ain't gonna rain no more.

3. I'll tune the fiddle, you get the bow,
   It ain't gonna rain no more.
   The weatherman just told me so,
   It ain't gonna rain no more.

4. Oh, what did the blackbird say to the crow?
   "It ain't gonna rain no more.
   It ain't gonna hail, it ain't gonna snow,
   It ain't gonna rain no more."

Tone Color 171

of their own. Encourage them to experiment with a wide variety of strums; for example:

- long strums upward from lowest (longest) string to highest (shortest), and downward from highest string to lowest
- short strums on the high, middle, and low strings
- combinations of long and short strums
- strums played on the section of the strings to the right of the chord buttons

3. Have children experiment with different kinds of "picks"—plastic ones, metal ones, felt ones, rubber ones (e.g., a small rubber doorstop), fingertips (brushed gently over the strings), fingertips while wearing leather gloves or a cloth oven mitt—to hear how they affect the tone color of the Autoharp.

4. Have children explore possibilities other than strumming as a means of producing sounds on the Autoharp: (a) plucking individual strings—e.g., plucking an F string or a C string instead of strumming the chord F or C₇ (Note: Marking the strings in some way, perhaps with colored chalk, will help players find them easily); (b) lightly tapping the strings with the open hand, the forearm, or an object like a ruler while depressing the appropriate chord button.

5. When children have fully explored the Autoharp, have them sing the songs on pp. 170 and 171 with the recording, paying close attention to the accompaniments. Note: For the first verse of each song, the accompaniment matches the one notated in the Pupil's Book. For the rest of the verses, children will hear a variety of strumming patterns.

TRY THIS
Have children create Autoharp accompaniments for other two-chord songs in Book 4, for example, "The Wise Man Built His House," p. 21, or "Old Blue," p. 123. Some children may need the challenge of working with a three-chord song like "Find the Ring," p. 72, or "Run, Run, Run," p. 98.

TEACHER INFORMATION
Mainstreaming Note: An adaptation for "Polly Wolly Doo-dle" appears in *Silver Burdett Music for Special Education.*

TONE COLOR • Lesson 9

MATERIALS
Record 8, *In Dulci Jubilo;* Pupil's
Book, pp. 172 and 173; recorders

VOCABULARY
consort, soprano, tenor, alto, bass,
ensemble, tone color

IDEAS FOR TEACHING
1. Have children look at the photograph of a recorder consort on
p. 172. Help them observe that four
different kinds of recorders are pictured—soprano, alto, tenor, bass.
Point out: The four recorders differ
in size and in the sounds they produce: the smaller the instrument, the
higher the sounds; the larger the instrument, the lower the sounds.
Questions: Which recorder will produce the highest sounds? (Soprano)
The lowest sounds? (Bass)

2. Play the recording for children to
hear the soprano, alto, tenor, and
bass recorders sounding together as
an ensemble (consort). Question:
Which recorder is playing the melody? (Soprano) Point out: While it is
possible to distinguish the sound of
the individual instruments in the
consort, it is the sound of the instruments blending together that is most
important. The four recorders playing
together create a tone color that is
different from that of any of the instruments sounding alone.

3. Direct attention to the fingering
chart for high E on p. 173. Have children who play recorder learn the fingering for the new tone and review
the fingerings for the tones G, A, B
(fingering charts, p. 27); low E
(p. 59); high C and D (p. 99); and F#
(p. 146). Then give them time to
⟶

RECORDERS

Soprano Alto Tenor Bass

172 Tone Color

REVIEW/REINFORCEMENT
For another experience with the tone color of a recorder
consort, have children listen to Widmann's *Margaretha*
(see Teacher's Edition p. 26, item 2).

Listen to a soprano recorder as it plays in a consort, or group. The soprano recorder plays in a higher register than the alto, tenor, and bass recorders.

🔘 *In Dulci Jubilo*

The soprano recorder part you heard is notated below. Practice the part so you can play along with the recording. You will need a new tone, high E.

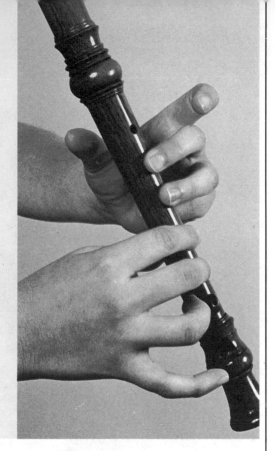

practice the melody of *In Dulci Jubilo* from the notation on p. 173. When they are ready, have children play the melody with the recording. Suggestion: If stereo is available, use the Pick-a-Track technique. In this way, children can practice the melody with the soprano recorder emphasized, or they can become part of the consort by adding their soprano recorder sound to the highlighted sound of the other three recorders.

IN DULCI JUBILO   GERMAN MELODY

Tone Color 173

TRY THIS
Invite older children who play recorder to perform for the class. Ask them to prepare something that the class knows, as well as a recorder piece of their choice. Suggestion: As a thank-you, recorder players in the class might play *In Dulci Jubilo* with the recording.

TEACHER INFORMATION
The melody of *In Dulci Jubilo* dates from the 14th century. Many composers since that time have written arrangements of it for voices and/or instruments. The arrangement on the recording was written by Hans Leo Hassler in 1608.

TONE COLOR • Lesson 10

MATERIALS
Record 8, M. Franck: *Intrada II;* "America," Versions 1 and 2; Pupil's Book, pp. 174 and 175; trumpet

VOCABULARY
brass instruments, wind instruments, trumpet, trombone, ensemble

IDEAS FOR TEACHING
Note: Like the sound of recorders, the sound of brass instruments is produced by blowing. For this reason, recorders and brass instruments are sometimes referred to as wind instruments.

1. Direct attention to the photograph of a brass ensemble on p. 174. Point out: The ensemble is composed of two trumpets and two trombones. Question: Which of the instruments make the highest sounds? (The trumpets) Which make the lowest sounds? (The trombones)

2. Play the recording of *Intrada II* so children can hear the sound of a brass ensemble. Ask them to listen for changes in the dynamics as the instruments play sometimes loud, sometimes soft.

3. Have children follow the notation on p. 175 to sing "America" with the recording (Version 1). Point out: The accompaniment is provided by a brass ensemble like the one pictured on p. 174. Suggestion: Play version 2 of the recording so children can hear the brass ensemble without voices (the voices might also be de-emphasized by using the Pick-a-Track technique with Version 1). Help children hear the following: (a) One trumpet is playing the melody. (b) The other ⟶

BRASS INSTRUMENTS

You have heard the tone color of recorders playing in an ensemble. The tone colors of brass instruments can be combined in an ensemble also. Listen to this music for brass ensemble.

⊚ M. Franck: *Intrada II*
8

Trombones

Trumpets

174 Tone Color

TEACHER INFORMATION
Melchior Franck (German, 1573–1639) *Intrada II:* This composer was music director for the magnificent court at Coburg, a center for the arts and learning in the early 17th century. He was a strong individualist and a prolific composer who wrote in all forms for voices and instruments.

Lessons 10 through 12 (pp. 174–179) deal with the tone color of brass, woodwind, and string instruments. Any point during these lessons would be an appropriate time to show the sound/color filmstrip *A Youth Orchestra.*

AMERICA

TRADITIONAL MELODY   WORDS BY SAMUEL FRANCIS SMITH

Piano acc., p. 251

My coun - try! 'tis of thee, Sweet land of lib - er - ty,
Our fa - thers' God, to Thee, Au - thor of lib - er - ty,

Of thee I sing; Land where my fa - thers died,
To Thee we sing; Long may our land be bright

Land of the Pil - grim's pride, From ev - 'ry __ moun - tain - side
With free - dom's ho - ly light; Pro - tect __ us __ by Thy might,

Let __ free - dom ring!
Great __ God, our King!

**If you play trumpet, practice the part below. Then play along with
the brass ensemble on the recording as others sing "America."**

Trumpet

Tone Color 175

---

trumpet is playing a harmony part.
(c) The trombones are also playing
harmony parts, one higher than the
other. <u>Note:</u> Be certain that children
understand that the two trumpets are
identical; they are only playing different parts. The same is true of the
trombones.

4. Some children may be studying
trumpet. Give them time to practice
the melody of "America" from the
trumpet notation on p. 175. When
they are ready, have them play the
melody with the recording (Ver-
sion 2). <u>Suggestion:</u> If stereo is available, use the Pick-a-Track technique.
In this way, children can practice
with the recorded trumpet melody
emphasized, or they can become
part of the ensemble by adding their
trumpet sound to the highlighted
harmony parts.

5. As others sing "America," have
one or two children play the trumpet
melody with the recording (Ver-
sion 2). <u>Suggestion:</u> If no one in the
class plays trumpet, invite an older
trumpet student or the instrumental
teacher to play the trumpet melody.

TRY THIS

Invite older children who play brass instruments to perform for the class. Give the class an opportunity to hear as
many different brass tone colors as possible—trumpet,
trombone, French horn, tuba, etc. Encourage performers to
explain to the class what things besides blowing are involved in playing each instrument—depressing valves,
moving a slide, etc.

TEACHER INFORMATION

Some children may notice that the trumpet part for "America" (p. 175) has a different key signature—one sharp (key
of G)—from that of the song notation—one flat (key of F).
They may be interested to know that the trumpet is a
transposing instrument. When the trumpet plays music that
is written in the key of G, the sound that comes from the
instrument is in the key of F.

MATERIALS

Record 8, Ibert: *Trois pièces brèves*, No. 3; "America," Version 2; Pupil's Book, pp. 176 and 177, 175; clarinet, flute

VOCABULARY

tone color, woodwind quintet, flute, oboe, clarinet, bassoon, French horn

IDEAS FOR TEACHING

Note: The brass instruments make up one family of instruments. The woodwind instruments are another family. In both families, players produce sounds on the instruments by blowing.

1. Direct children's attention to the photograph of a woodwind quintet on pp. 176 and 177. Point out: (a) A quintet is an ensemble of five instruments. (b) A woodwind quintet usually is made up of four woodwind instruments (flute, oboe, clarinet, bassoon) and one brass instrument (French horn), as shown in the photograph.

2. Ask children to identify the instrument in the photograph that plays in the highest register (flute) and the one that plays in the lowest register (bassoon).

3. Play the recording of the Ibert piece so children can hear the sound of a woodwind quintet. Point out: While it is possible to distinguish the sound of the individual instruments in the quintet, it is the sound of the instruments blending together that is most important. The five instruments playing together create a tone color that is different from that of any of the instruments sounding alone. →

WOODWIND QUINTET

Flute

Listen to the tone color of a woodwind quintet.

The picture shows the instruments

that make up the ensemble.

🔘 Ibert: *Trois pièces brèves*, No. 3
8

If you play the clarinet or flute,

practice the parts for "America"

to play for the class.

AMERICA TRADITIONAL

Clarinet

176 Tone Color

TEACHER INFORMATION

Jacques Ibert (French, 1890–1962) *Trois pièces brèves*, No 3: The music of this composer has a charming, colorful quality. There is an element of humor in his lighter works, as in his popular orchestral *Divertissements*.

Oboe

French Horn

Clarinet

Bassoon

4. Some children may be taking clarinet or flute lessons. Give them time to practice the clarinet and/or flute parts for "America" on pp. 176 and 177. <u>Point out:</u> The clarinet plays the melody of "America"; the flute plays a countermelody. <u>Suggestion:</u> When players are ready, have them play their part with the recording of "America" (Version 2). They will be adding their woodwind sound(s) to that of the recorded brass ensemble.

5. Combine as many of the instrumental parts (pp. 175–177) as possible to accompany the singing of "America" (notation, p. 175). Have children perform both with the recording and without it. <u>Suggestion:</u> If possible, tape-record the children's performance, then play it back for them. Take time to discuss the sound; for example: Do the instruments blend together, or does one instrument sound more important than the rest? Do the instruments provide a good accompaniment for the voices, or do they drown out the singing?

Countermelody

Flute

Tone Color 177

TRY THIS
Invite older children who play woodwind instruments to perform for the class. Give the class an opportunity to hear as many different woodwind tone colors as possible. Encourage performers to explain to the class what things besides blowing are involved in playing each instrument—e.g., using the proper fingering for each tone, using a satisfactory reed (for clarinet, oboe, bassoon, etc.), perhaps even learning to make reeds.

TEACHER INFORMATION
Some children may notice that the key signature for the clarinet part (p. 176)—one sharp (key of G)—is different from that for the flute part (p. 175)—one flat (key of F). They may be interested to know that, like the trumpet, the clarinet is a transposing instrument. When the clarinet plays music that is written in the key of G, the sound that comes from the instrument is in the key of F.

TONE COLOR • Lesson 12

MATERIALS

Record 8, Mozart: *String Quartet in D Minor* (K 173), Movement 4; "The Frog in the Well"; Pupil's Book, pp. 178 and 179; Autoharp, violin

VOCABULARY

tone color, string quartet, violin, viola, cello

IDEAS FOR TEACHING

<u>Note:</u> Many children have had experience playing "string" instruments like the Autoharp and guitar. These are folk instruments. In this lesson, children are introduced to orchestral string instruments—members of the string family. To produce a sound on these instruments, players make the strings vibrate either by drawing a bow across them or by plucking them.

1. Direct attention to the photograph on p. 178. <u>Point out:</u> (a) A string quartet is made up of four instruments—two violins, viola, cello. (b) The two violins are identical. They differ only in the parts they play. (c) The violins, viola, and cello differ in size and in the sounds they produce: the smaller the instrument, the higher the sounds; the larger the instrument, the lower the sounds. <u>Questions:</u> Which instrument produces the highest sounds? (Violin) The lowest sounds? (Cello)

2. Play the recording of the Mozart quartet so children can hear the sound of a string quartet. <u>Note:</u> On the recording, the instruments enter one after the other—cello, then viola, then second violin, and finally first violin. As each instrument joins in, its tone color is more prominent ⟶

STRING INSTRUMENTS

Violins

Cello

Mozart: *String Quartet in D Minor*

THE FROG IN THE WELL

FOLK SONG FROM THE SOUTHERN APPALACHIANS

Piano acc., p. 332

1. There was a frog lived in the spring,
2. The frog went swim - ming 'cross the lake,

Sing song Kit - ty can't you ki - mey O;

He was so fat he could not swim,
He got swallowed by a big, black snake,

178 Tone Color

TEACHER INFORMATION

Biographical information about Wolfgang Amadeus Mozart appears on Teacher's Edition p. 66 (see Teacher Information).

Sing song Kit - ty can't you ki - mey O.

Kee - mey O ma ki - mey O ma dir - ey O ma wear,

Me hi, me ho, me in come Sal - ly Sin - gle,

Some time Pen-ny Win-kle, In stepped nip cat, Hit him with a brick bat,

Sing song Kit - ty can't you ki - mey O.

If you play violin, add its tone color to section A of "The Frog in the Well." Choose one of the parts below to play. Will you bow the strings, or pluck them?

Section A

Section A

Tone Color 179

than that of the instruments already playing. This allows children to hear the tone color of each instrument as well as that of the blended quartet sound.

3. Play the recording of "The Frog in the Well" so children can identify the two sections, A and B. Then have them clap the rhythm of the words during section B (song notation, pp. 178 and 179). Question: Which phrases of section B use dotted rhythms? (1 and 2) Point out: The dotted rhythms help to make section B a contrast to section A.

4. When children know the song, select individuals to sing the verses in section A. Everyone sings section B.

5. Ask violin students in the class to learn one of the violin parts on p. 179. Have them play the part during section A as others sing with the recording. Note: Be certain that the violin and the recording are in tune. If they are not, adjust the violin tuning, or have children sing and play without the recording.

6. Have children accompany "The Frog in the Well" on the Autoharp. The letter names in the score will tell them which chords to play and when to change from one chord to another. Players may use a strumming pattern that matches the steady beat, or a pattern that they create.

7. Put it all together. Have children perform "The Frog in the Well" as follows.
Section A: Individuals sing verses, accompanied by Autoharp and either or both violin parts.
Section B: All sing with Autoharp accompaniment.

TRY THIS
Invite older children who play string instruments to perform for the class. Encourage them to explain what is involved in playing string instruments—e.g., learning to tune the instrument; using the correct fingering for each tone; always "listening" so that the sound is in tune; learning different types of bowings; using tremolo.

MATERIALS
Record 8, Clarke (Purcell): *Trumpet Tune,* Versions 1 and 2; Record 2, *Call Chart 2: Tempo;* Pupil's Book, pp. 180 and 181

VOCABULARY
tone color, keyboard instruments, piano, harpsichord, pipe organ, dynamics

IDEAS FOR TEACHING
1. Have children look at the pictures on pp. 180 and 181. Help them observe that each instrument is played from a keyboard. Point out: (a) A piano has one row of keys. When piano keys are depressed, hammers strike the strings inside the instrument to produce the sound. (b) A harpsichord has one or two rows of keys (manuals), one above the other. When harpsichord keys are depressed, quills (plectra) pluck the strings to produce the sound. (c) A pipe organ has from one to five manuals. When the keys are depressed, air is forced through the pipes, which are like whistles, to produce sounds.

2. Play both versions of *Trumpet Tune* so children can hear that the tone colors are different—Version 1 is played on a harpsichord, Version 2 on a pipe organ. Suggestion: Play the recordings again so children can focus on the dynamics. Point out: The harpsichord has a limited dynamic range: there is not much difference between its loud sounds and its soft sounds. The organ has a wider dynamic range. Both instruments use "stops" to achieve dynamic contrast. These are knobs, buttons, or tabs that the player pulls →

KEYBOARD INSTRUMENTS

Listen to two keyboard instruments
  playing the same piece.
Neither instrument is the piano.
Are the tone colors of the two
  instruments the same, or different?

Different

Clarke (Purcell): *Trumpet Tune*

Harpsichord

Piano

180 Tone Color

Pipe Organ

Tone Color 181

or pushes while playing. Each stop controls a different set of strings or pipes. Depending upon the combination of stops the player chooses, the dynamics will be loud or soft.

3. Ask a piano student in the class to tell how loud sounds and soft sounds are played on a piano (by striking the keys with heavy pressure for loud sounds, with light pressure for soft sounds). Then play the recording for Call Chart 2 (p. 43) so children can hear loud and soft piano sounds in pieces from Erik Satie's *Sports et Divertissements*. Suggestion: If a piano is available, have children take turns playing loud clusters and soft clusters so that they can feel the difference between playing loud and soft dynamics on a piano.

TRY THIS
Discover whether there is a pipe organ anywhere in the community. If possible, organize a field trip and arrange to have an organist (perhaps an organ student from a local college) demonstrate the instrument for the children.

MATERIALS
Record 8, *Electronic Old Blue;* Pupil's Book, p. 182

VOCABULARY
tone color, electronic instruments, amplified guitar, synthesizer

IDEAS FOR TEACHING
<u>Note:</u> Modern composers have created a variety of new tone colors in the following ways:
- by using traditional instruments in new ways
- by inventing or using new instruments
- by building electronic machines that produce sounds
- by using tape recorders to change sounds

1. Call attention to the photographs on p. 182. <u>Point out:</u> One picture shows a composer working at an electronic instrument called a synthesizer. The other shows a performer playing a traditional guitar that is amplified electronically.

2. Play the recording so children can hear a familiar song played first on amplified guitar (two times), then on synthesizer (two times). <u>Note:</u> Many children will identify the sound of amplified guitar as that used to back up many popular singing groups. Some children may have heard the sound of a synthesizer on radio or TV. <u>Suggestion:</u> Have children sing some of the verses of "Old Blue" (p. 123) with the recording.

ELECTRONIC INSTRUMENTS

Composers have always been fascinated by new possibilities for sounds. They are always looking for new ways to produce sounds and new ways to put sounds together.

 Electronic Old Blue

182 Tone Color

Synthesizer

Amplified Guitar

TRY THIS
Give children time to experiment with one way to create new tone colors. Have them tape-record several different sounds—e.g., the sound of their singing voice, the sound of water dripping into a metal container, the sound of crumpling paper, the sound of footsteps. Then play the tape back as follows: at the same speed, at a faster speed, and at a slower speed. Take time to talk about the new tone colors children hear. Encourage them to compare the tone color of each new sound with that of the sound originally recorded.

WHAT DO YOU HEAR? 15: TONE COLOR

Can you hear tone color in music?

Listen to these pieces. Each time a number is called, decide which answer is correct.

Listen. Then choose your answer.

1. PERCUSSION
VOICES
KEYBOARD
(RECORDERS)
BRASS
STRINGS
WOODWINDS

Five Villancicos, No. 4

2. PERCUSSION
(VOICES)
KEYBOARD
RECORDERS
BRASS
STRINGS
WOODWINDS

For the Beauty of the Earth

3. PERCUSSION
VOICES
KEYBOARD
RECORDERS
BRASS
(STRINGS)
WOODWINDS

Webern: *Five Movements for String Quartet, Op. 5, No. 3*

4. PERCUSSION
VOICES
(KEYBOARD)
RECORDERS
BRASS
STRINGS
WOODWINDS

Joplin: *The Entertainer*

5. (PERCUSSION)
VOICES
KEYBOARD
RECORDERS
BRASS
STRINGS
WOODWINDS

McKenzie: *Three Dances, "Samba"*

6. PERCUSSION
VOICES
(KEYBOARD)
RECORDERS
BRASS
STRINGS
WOODWINDS

Bach: *Fugue in G Minor*

7. PERCUSSION
VOICES
KEYBOARD
RECORDERS
(BRASS)
STRINGS
WOODWINDS

Locke: *Courante*

8. PERCUSSION
VOICES
KEYBOARD
RECORDERS
BRASS
STRINGS
(WOODWINDS)

Pierne: *Pastorale*

Tone Color 183

TONE COLOR • Lesson 15

MATERIALS
Record 8, *What Do You Hear? 15: Tone Color;* spirit master

VOCABULARY
tone color, percussion, keyboard, brass, strings, woodwinds

TEACHER INFORMATION
Give children an opportunity to listen to the music again, outside of the What Do You Hear? experience. Suggestions: (a) Ask children to identify the keyboard instrument used for Number 4 (Joplin: *The Entertainer*—piano) and for Number 6 (Bach: *Fugue in G Minor*—organ) from the tone color on the recording. (b) Have children compare the tone color of Number 8 (woodwinds) with that of the woodwind quintet, which includes the brass instrument French horn, in Ibert's *Trois pièces brèves,* No. 3 (p. 176).

MATERIALS

Record 8, "Hurry, Good Shepherds"; Pupil's Book, pp. 184 and 185; percussion instruments, Autoharp

VOCABULARY

tone color, score

IDEAS FOR TEACHING

1. Have children follow the notation on pp. 184 and 185 as they listen to the recording of "Hurry, Good Shepherds." <u>Point out:</u> The song is made up of four short melodies, each lasting for two staffs of the notation.

2. When children know the song, choose four small groups, one for each of the melodies. Have each group plan a percussion accompaniment for their melody, then play it as the class sings the song. Encourage children to choose appropriate tone colors for their accompaniment—e.g., maracas, bongos, claves.

3. Give children time to practice an Autoharp accompaniment. The letter names in the score will tell them which chords to play. <u>Note:</u> The second melody (staffs 3 and 4) uses the chords F, C₇, B♭. The other melodies use only F and C₇. Have players strum a steady-beat pattern, two strums per measure. <u>Suggestion:</u> Choose four players, one for each melody of the song.

4. Call attention to the harmony part for the second melody. <u>Point out:</u> The harmony part has the same contour as the melody, but is sung an interval of a third lower. If children are ready, assign a small group to sing the harmony part as others perform the melody with the recording.

Boys and girls in Puerto Rico play percussion instruments to accompany Christmas carols. Use maracas, bongos, and claves and create your own percussion parts. Then play along with the recording.

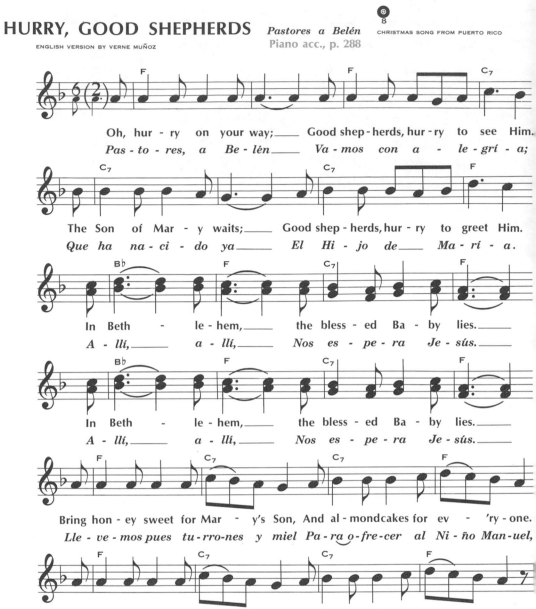

HURRY, GOOD SHEPHERDS *Pastores a Belén* CHRISTMAS SONG FROM PUERTO RICO

ENGLISH VERSION BY VERNE MUÑOZ Piano acc., p. 288

184 Tone Color

TEACHER INFORMATION

The Spanish verse of "Hurry, Good Shepherds" is pronounced as follows.

Pas-to-res, a Be-lén
pahs-toh-rehs ah beh-lehn

Va-mos con a-le-grí-a;
vah-mohs kohn ah-leh-gree-ah

Que ha na-ci-do ya
keh ah nah-see-thoh yah

El Hi-jo de Ma-rí-a.
ehl ee-hoh deh mah-ree-yah

A-llí, a-llí, Nos es-pe-ra Je-sús.
ah-yee ah-yee nohs ehs-peh-rah heh-soos

Lle-ve-mos pues tu-rro-nes y miel
yeh-veh-mohs pwehs too-roh-nehs ee myehl

Pa-ra o-fre-cer al Ni-ño Man-uel.
pah-rah oh-freh-sehr ahl nee-nyoh mahn-wehl

Va-mos, va-mos, va-mos a ver,
vah-mohs vah-mohs vah-mohs ah vehr

Va-mos a ver al re-cién na-ci-do,
vah-mohs ah vehr ahl reh-syehn nah-see-thoh

Va-mos a ver al Ni-ño Man-uel.
vah-mohs ah vehr ahl nee-nyoh mahn-wehl

Hur - ry, hur - ry, do not de - lay, Greet___ the Ba - by born___ this day,___
Va - mos, va - mos, va - mos a ver, Va - mos a ver al re - cién na - ci - do,

Greet___ the Ba - by born___ this day.
Va - mos a ver al Ni - ño Man - uel.

Play these percussion parts to accompany "Purim Song."

Grager

Tambourine   Grager   Tambourine   Grager

Grager

PURIM SONG

HASIDIC FOLK MELODY   ENGLISH WORDS BY ELIZABETH S. BACHMAN

Piano acc., p. 292

Come a - long, come a - long, Sing a mer - ry Pu - rim song.

Cel - e - brate, cel - e - brate, Joy - ous hol - i - day.

Come, twirl the gra - ger round and round; Let's fill the room with hap - py sound;

Now pass the ha - man - tash - en round; Joy - ous hol - i - day.

Tone Color 185

TONE COLOR • Lesson 17

MATERIALS
Record 8, "Purim Song"; Pupil's Book, p. 185; grager (or substitute sound), tambourine

VOCABULARY
tone color, meter in 2

IDEAS FOR TEACHING

1. Play the recording of "Purim Song" so that children can hear the two sections, A and B.

2. When children know the song, have them take turns playing the percussion parts on p. 185 as others sing. Note: (a) A grager is a rattle or noisemaker. If one is not available, have children use a percussion instrument that makes a scraping sound—e.g., a guiro. (b) Two players are needed for the section B part—one for the tambourine, the other for the grager. Suggest that the tambourine player keep the steady beat in some way—e.g., by quietly tapping a foot. This will help him or her play the rhythm correctly.

3. Have children feel the meter of the song (meter in 2) by performing one of the following movement patterns during each measure.

(a) Stepping sideways with the right foot for beat 1; then stepping, placing the left foot behind the right for beat 2.

(b) Stepping sideways with the left foot for beat 1; then stepping, placing the right foot behind the left for beat 2.

(c) Stepping forward (beat 1), then hopping (beat 2), alternating feet from measure to measure.

TRY THIS
Combine movements a, b, and c in item 3 above into a dance.

Formation: Children stand side by side in a line, with hands joined or placed on each other's shoulders.

1st time—Ⓐ Children move the line sideways to the right, using movement pattern a.

Ⓑ Stepping on the right foot, they turn to face the right, then "follow the leader," moving forward in a step-hop pattern (c).

2nd time—Ⓐ Children move the line sideways to the left, using movement pattern b.

Ⓑ Stepping on the left foot, they turn to face the left, then "follow the leader," moving forward in a step-hop pattern (c).

Children continue to alternate directions for each repetition of the dance. The leader for section B is alternately the child at the right end of the line, then the child at the left end. Mainstreaming Suggestion: Have nonambulatory children sing or play a percussion accompaniment.

TEACHER INFORMATION
Hamantashen are three-cornered cakes made especially for the Purim celebration.

STYLE: Jazz

MATERIALS

Record 8, Lewis/Gillespie: *Two Bass Hit*; Kern: *Yesterdays*; Selden: *The Magic Bus Ate My Doughnut*; Call Chart 8: *Jazz*; Pupil's Book, pp. 186 and 187

VOCABULARY

style, jazz, improvisation, big band, combo

IDEAS FOR TEACHING

1. Ask children if they know what jazz music sounds like. Discuss their comments. <u>Note</u>: Do not be surprised if styles such as popular, rock, and country are included in the discussion. Jazz has influenced all popular styles of music, as well as some folk styles, so it is often difficult to consider jazz as a style in itself.

2. Call attention to the qualities listed on p. 186. Explain the following: (a) A big band usually has ten or more players. This gives it a big, rich, full sound. (b) A small combo (short for *combination*) usually has about four or five players. Its sound is leaner, clearer, more "open" than that of the big band. (c) Improvisation means making up music on the spot—during the performance. Discuss the other qualities to be certain that children can distinguish each one.

3. Play *Two Bass Hit* and have children identify which qualities on p. 186 they hear. <u>Note</u>: The music is loud and fast. It is performed by a →

STYLE: JAZZ

Here are some musical qualities that are used in the style called *Jazz*.

LOUD	SOFT
FAST	SLOW
BIG BAND	SMALL COMBO
	IMPROVISATION

Listen to these jazz pieces. For each one, decide which qualities you hear.

⊚ Lewis and Gillespie: *Two Bass Hit*

⊚ Kern: *Yesterdays*

⊚ Selden: *The Magic Bus Ate My Doughnut*

186 MODULE 16: Style—Jazz

TRY THIS

Give children an experience with improvisation. Have them choose a song that has silences in the melody—e.g., "Scratch, Scratch," p. 6 or "Naughty Little Flea," p. 140. As the class sings, have individuals play a percussion instrument during the silences. Encourage them to play a different rhythm pattern for each silence, making up patterns as they go along.

CALL CHART 8: JAZZ 🔘

**Listen to the recording. As each number is called, look at the chart.
It will help you to hear what is going on in the music.**

Olson and Staton: *All I Recall is You*

1. SOFT, MODERATE TEMPO, PIANO IMPROVISES

2. BIG BAND ENTERS, GETS LOUDER

3. BASS INSTRUMENT IMPROVISES—BAND ACCOMPANIES

4. SAXOPHONE IMPROVISES, GETS SOFTER

5. DRUM IMPROVISES

6. BIG BAND ENTERS, GETS LOUDER

7. GETS SOFTER, THEN LOUDER

8. ENDS SOFT

Style—Jazz 187

small combo consisting of drums, piano, string bass, saxophone, and trumpet. The saxophone performs most of the improvisation.

4. Play *Yesterdays* and have children discuss its qualities. <u>Note:</u> The music is soft and slow, played by a small combo consisting of piano, drums, string bass, and vibraphone (a set of metal bars—like a large set of bells—that has tubes hanging underneath to amplify the sound; turning discs give the sound a vibrating quality called *vibrato*). The vibraphone performs improvisation.

5. Have children listen to *The Magic Bus Ate My Doughnut* to hear its musical qualities—loud, fast music played by a big band consisting of brass, woodwinds, and percussion, with the saxophone performing improvisation.

6. (<u>Note:</u> Since this lesson involves so much listening, you may wish to save this experience for another time.) When children are ready, play the recording for *Call Chart 8* while they follow the chart on p. 187. As each number is called, children look beside that number in the chart to find a description of what they are hearing. <u>Note:</u> Whenever necessary, stop the recording and replay a section to further help focus children's listening. <u>Suggestion:</u> The Call Chart gives information about the dynamics, tempo, and tone color of the music. Encourage children to discuss other musical qualities they hear— e.g., register (high sounds, low sounds), range (wide, narrow), duration (long sounds, short sounds).

REVIEW/REINFORCEMENT

1. Review the following selections so that children can hear several examples of jazz influences in music.
• Gershwin: *An American in Paris*, p. 37
• Joplin: *Bethena*, p. 8 (Teacher's Edition)
• McKenzie: *Three Dances*, "Samba," p. 166

2. Encourage children to bring in recordings from their own or their parents' collections that illustrate jazz. Ask each child to describe the qualities of the piece he or she has brought in. Play the recording and have the class discuss other musical qualities they hear.

MODULE 17

OBJECTIVES, p. XIV

MELODY • Lesson 1

MATERIALS
Record 8, "Evening"; Pupil's Book, pp. 188 and 189; bells

VOCABULARY
register, direction, intervals, steps, leaps, repeated tones, ostinato

IDEAS FOR TEACHING

1. Have children look at the pictures on p. 188. Help them observe that the photograph of the city skyline invites the eye to focus on low things and high things; that the photograph of the geese leads the eye to follow the direction in which the geese are moving; and that the final photograph draws the eye to recognize repetition in the many identical sailboats that are shown. In all three photographs, the eye sees intervals: some buildings, some geese, some sailboats are closer together than others. <u>Point out:</u> Qualities that are present in the photographs—register (high and low), direction, intervals—are also present in music: melodies use high and low tones, tones moving upward and downward, repeated tones, tones that are close together or far apart. In photography we see these qualities; in music we hear them. Each art uses the qualities in its own way.

2. Call attention to the bell parts notated on p. 189. <u>Point out:</u> Each bell part shows a different way that melody tones move. Help children review the following: ⟶

MELODY

188 MODULE 17: Melody

Play these bell patterns to accompany "Evening." Which one has tones that leap?

Tones that repeat? Tones that move by step?

D E F G A   low D high D   A

EVENING

FOLK MELODY FROM HUNGARY   ENGLISH WORDS BY ROSEMARY JACQUES   Piano acc., p. 287

Voic - es fill the eve - ning air with their hap - py sing - ing,

Joy and laugh - ter ev - 'ry-where through the land are ring - ing.

Cast - ing all their cares a - way, Danc - ers whirl till

break of day. Hear the mu - sic play.

Voic - es fill the eve - ning air with their hap - py sing - ing,

Joy and laugh-ter ev - 'ry-where through the land are ring - ing.

Melody 189

- Tones can move by step in an upward or downward direction (bell pattern 1)
- Tones can leap from low to high and from high to low (pattern 2)
- A tone can be repeated over and over (pattern 3)

Mainstreaming Suggestion: To provide a kinesthetic aid for children with hearing, sight, and motor impairments, write each bell part on a card and outline the melody contour by gluing on sand, sparkles, or another textured material.

3. Have children follow the notation for "Evening" as they listen to the recording. Questions: Which measure is sung loud? (The last measure of staff 4) Why? (The dynamic marking *f* above the measure means "loud.")

4. Have children take turns playing one of the bell parts to accompany the recording. Note: Each bell pattern can be played over and over as an ostinato. Some children may notice that bell pattern 1 has the same melody as the beginning tones of the song.

5. When children know the song, have them sing it with the recording. Suggestion: Help children observe how the tones move in "Evening." Questions: Does the melody use mostly tones that step, tones that leap, or tones that repeat? (Tones that move upward and downward by step) Which measures have two leaps in a row—one upward, one downward? (Measures 1, 3, 10, 12: A-D-A) Which measures end with repeated tones? (2, 4, 11, 13) Which one begins with repeated tones? (9)

TRY THIS

Have children sing "Evening" as a round—in two parts, then in three, and finally in four parts. Note: The parts enter two beats after one another.

MATERIALS
Record 8, "Rookoombine"; Pupil's Book, pp. 190 and 191; bells, drum, claves, maraca, Autoharp, recorders (bells)

VOCABULARY
contour, phrase, steps, leaps, repeated tones, score

IDEAS FOR TEACHING

1. As children listen to the recording, have them follow the notation for "Rookoombine" on p. 190. Ask them to pay particular attention to the melody contour—the way the tones move. Question: Which phrases of the song use repeated tones? (Phrases 3 and 4, on the word *Rookoombine* each time)

2. Play the recording again. Invite children to join in singing section B when they can. Question: How is the melody on the word *Rookoombine* different from that on the words *Santa Fe*? (The tones on *Rookoombine* repeat; those on *Santa Fe* move upward by small leaps.)

3. As the class sings with the recording, have two children play bells during section B. One child plays the rhythm pattern of the word *Rookoombine* on the F bell each time it is sung. The other plays the rhythm of the words *Santa Fe* on the bells C-E-G. Question: Which bell pattern uses syncopation? (The one for the word *Rookoombine*) Note: Some children may be able to play the entire section B melody. They will need the bells C, D, E, F, G.

4. Call attention to the bell part on p. 190. Question: How do the tones →

A melody can have tones that move upward or downward by step, tones that leap, and tones that repeat. The way the tones move gives the melody a shape, or contour.

Look at the contour of each phrase in this song. Which phrases have repeated tones? 3, 4

ROOKOOMBINE FOLK SONG FROM JAMAICA

MELODY AND WORDS OF FIRST VERSE FROM FOLK SONGS OF JAMAICA, EDITED AND ARRANGED BY TOM MURRAY. COPYRIGHT 1952 BY THE OXFORD UNIVERSITY PRESS, LONDON; WORDS OF SECOND VERSE FROM FOLK SONGS OF THE CARIBBEAN BY JIM MORSE. COPYRIGHT © 1958 BY BANTAM BOOKS. USED BY PERMISSION.

Piano acc., p. 303

1. Train top a bridge jus - a run like a breeze,
2. Went King - ston town just to have me look a - roun',

An' a gal un - der - neath it a wash her che - mise.
But in - stead look a - roun', oh, me spent ev - 'ry poun'.

Oh, Roo - koom - bine ee - na San - ta Fe,

Roo - koom - bine ee - na San - ta Fe, Oh, Roo - koom - bine.

Here is a bell part to play during section A of "Rookoombine."

Bells

C   B♭   A   G

190 Melody

TEACHER INFORMATION
Mainstreaming Note: An adaptation for "Rookoombine" appears in *Silver Burdett Music for Special Education.*

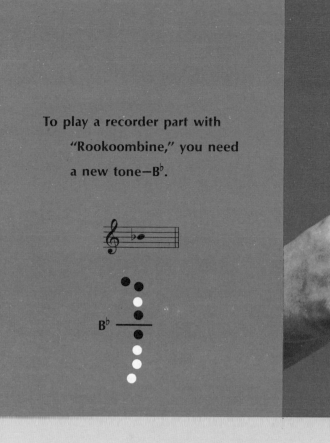

To play a recorder part with "Rookoombine," you need a new tone—B♭.

B♭

Now play this recorder part. Will you play any tones that leap? No

Recorder or Bells

C   B♭   A   G

A   B♭

Melody 191

in this bell part move? (Sets of repeated tones move downward by step.) Have individuals play the bell part during section A as others sing the song.

5. Have children play percussion instruments to accompany "Rookoombine" (see below for parts). Note: (a) The drum plays the same pattern throughout the entire song. (b) The claves play the rhythm of the words *run like a breeze* during section A. Thinking the words as they occur in the song will help children play the rhythm correctly. (c) The maraca plays during section B. Children use one maraca, hitting it against the palm of their hand for the quarter notes, shaking it for the half notes.

6. Children can accompany "Rookoombine" on the Autoharp, using the chords F, C₇, B♭. The chord names in the score will tell them when to change from one chord to another. Players may strum a pattern of steady beats, or a rhythm pattern that they create.

7. Give children who play recorder time to learn the fingering for B♭, and to practice the recorder part on p. 191. When they are ready, have them play the part while others sing "Rookoombine." Note: The recorder part can also be played on bells. Suggestion: Take time to analyze the recorder melody with the class. Help them observe that the part for section A has sets of repeated tones that move downward from C to G, while the part for section B has sets of repeated tones that keep moving upward and downward between A and B♭.

PERCUSSION PARTS

Drum R / L etc.

Claves etc.

Drum R / L etc.

Maraca hit hit shake etc.

TRY THIS
Put it all together. Have children combine some of the parts in items 3 through 7 of the lesson to accompany the singing of "Rookoombine." Have them use only as many of the parts as they can manage successfully. Encourage players to listen to one another so that no single accompaniment part sounds more important than the rest, and so that the accompaniment does not drown out the melody.

MATERIALS
Record 9, "Amazing Grace"; Pupil's
Book, pp. 192 and 193

VOCABULARY
contour, steps, leaps, repeated tones,
dulcimer, solo

IDEAS FOR TEACHING

1. Call attention to the photograph
on p. 193 of Jean Ritchie, a well-
known singer and collector of folk
songs. Ask if anyone can name the
instrument she is playing (dulcimer).
Help children observe that she is
using a quill to strum the strings.

2. Play the recording of "Amazing
Grace." <u>Note:</u> Children will hear Jean
Ritchie singing the first verse as a
solo without accompaniment. The
dulcimer accompanies the remaining
verses, with children singing verses 2
and 3, and Jean Ritchie and children
performing verse 4 together. <u>Point
out:</u> When Jean Ritchie sings alone,
she uses an authentic style of folk
singing: she "decorates" the melody
by singing extra notes that are not
printed in the music. <u>Suggestion:</u> If
stereo is available, use the Pick-a-
Track technique to highlight the accompaniment so that children can
focus on the tone color of the
dulcimer.

3. Play the recording again. Have
children listen during verse 1, then
observe the contour of the melody
in the notation (p. 192) during the
remaining verses. Invite them to sing
when they are ready. <u>Question:</u> Do
the tones in "Amazing Grace" move
mostly by leap, or by step, or do
they mostly repeat? (They move
upward and downward mostly by
leap.) ——→

**Do the tones in this melody move mostly by leap, by step, or
do they repeat? Follow the notation as you listen to the recording.**

AMAGING GRACE EARLY AMERICAN MELODY   WORDS BY JOHN NEWTON
Piano acc., p. 250

1. A - maz - ing___ grace how sweet the sound

That saved a___ wretch like me!___

I once___ was___ lost, but now___ am___ found,

Was blind, but___ now I see.

2. 'Twas grace that taught my heart to fear,
And grace my fears relieved;
How precious did that grace appear
The hour I first believed!

3. Through many dangers, toils, and snares,
I have already come;
'Tis grace has brought me safe thus far,
And grace will lead me home.

4. The Lord has promised good to me,
His word my hope secures;
He will my shield and portion be
As long as life endures.

192 Melody

TEACHER INFORMATION
The American mountain dulcimer is a homemade instrument that looks like an elongated violin. It is held across
the knees, with the neck at the player's left. The tone is
produced by brushing a sharpened turkey quill or a
wooden pick back and forth across the strings (unlike the
European dulcimer, which is played with mallets).

Listen for tones that step,

leap, and repeat in

the dulcimer part

on the recording.

Listen for the many

repeated sounds in

the accompaniment

for verse 4.

TRY THIS

Children can play a harmony part that uses repeated tones (a drone) to accompany "Amazing Grace" on the Autoharp. Players simultaneously pluck the lowest (longest) F and C strings, using the rhythm pattern below, or a pattern that they create. <u>Suggestions</u>: (a) Mark the lowest F and C strings with chalk so that children can find them easily. (b) Have children experiment with ways to pluck the strings—using fingers, using various kinds of picks (plastic, felt, metal, etc.)—to find the tone color that seems most appropriate.

MELODY • Lesson 4

MATERIALS
Pupil's Book, p. 194, keyboard diagram; piano or bells

VOCABULARY
interval, octave, prime, unison

IDEAS FOR TEACHING
(See Teacher Information below.)

1. Select a child to play the melody of "Chopsticks" on piano or bells as the class follows the notation (p. 194). Questions: Which measures use only <u>repeated</u> tones? (1–3, 5–7) Which staffs begin with tones that move downward by step? (4, 5) Where is there a large leap from the end of one staff to the beginning of the next? (From low E to high E, staff 4 to 5) <u>Point out:</u> The distance from one tone to another is an interval. Tell children that they can measure intervals by calling the first note *one*, then counting the lines and spaces above or below it until they reach the second note. Help them measure the intervals for the downward steps in staff 4 (seconds); for the leap from low E to high E (octave). Tell them that when tones are repeated, the distance from one tone to the next (interval) is called a prime or unison.

2. Have children play "Chopsticks" the traditional way, as notated at the bottom of p. 194. <u>Note:</u> Some children will already know how to play "Chopsticks" this way. Others can learn by practicing on the keyboard diagram in the front of their book. They should use the index finger of both hands, right starting on G, left on F. <u>Suggestion:</u> Have the children use two books when they practice—one open to the notation, the other to the keyboard diagram.

Find the steps, leaps, and repeated tones in "Chopsticks."

CHOPSTICKS TRADITIONAL

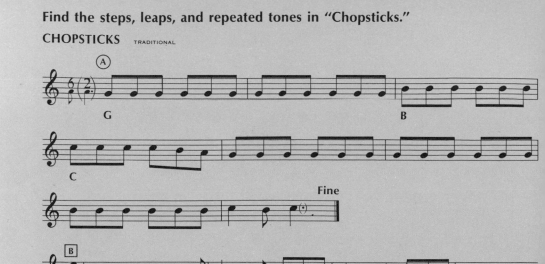

Play "Chopsticks" as follows on piano or bells.

The keyboard will help you find where to begin.

194 Melody

TEACHER INFORMATION
Children have already had experience measuring harmonic intervals—the distance from one tone to another when both are sounded together. In this lesson, they learn to measure melodic intervals—the distance from one tone to another when they are sounded separately, one after the other. The process is the same for both kinds of intervals. However, with harmonic intervals, children count from the lower note to the higher note; with melodic intervals, they count from the first note to the second.

TRY THIS
If a piano is available, have children play a duet. While one child plays "Chopsticks," another child plays the following over and over as an accompaniment. <u>Note:</u> Autoharp may be used for the accompaniment, playing the chords G_7 and C as shown above the staff. Players may use two strums per measure, or a pattern that they create.

What is your birth date? Which month?
Which day? Which year? Write it down by using
numbers. Look at the line of numbers you have
written. Do you see any number twice in a row
(repeat)? Do you see two numbers side by side
that show a large interval? A small interval?

Play your number pattern on a melody instrument.
Decide which tone will be number 1 and play
upward and downward by step or by leap,
or repeat a tone as the numbers tell you.

Do you have a zero in your number line?
Play it as a percussion sound, or make it silent.

You can vary the pattern. Change the tempo.
Change the dynamics. Change the rhythm.
Change the starting note. Play the pattern backward.

Think of a way to write down your melody.

Melody 195

MATERIALS
Pupil's Book, p. 195; bells or other
keyboard instrument

VOCABULARY
interval, leap, step, repeat

TEACHER INFORMATION
For more experience with melodic intervals, have children write a birth-
date melody (p. 195) as follows:

1. Children write their birth date in
numbers, leaving a space after each
digit. June 12, 1970, for example,
would be written:

6   1   2   1   9   7   0

2. They look at the numbers to find
whether any of them occur twice or
more in a row (repeats); whether
two numbers side by side represent a
large interval—i.e., a large leap from
a high (low) number to a low (high)
one; whether two numbers side by
side represent a small interval—i.e., a
small leap, or a step from one number to the next higher or lower one
(see Birth-Date Intervals below).

3. Children change the number 1 to
any tone name, A through G. Then
they change the other numbers in
relation to 1. For example, if they
change 1 to C, a number 2 would
become D, a number 3 would be E,
etc. The tones for the sample birth
date would be:

6   1   2   1   9   7   0
A   C   D   C high D B

4. Children play their birth-date melody on bells or other keyboard instrument. For a number zero, they
may use a percussion sound, or a silence (rest).

BIRTH-DATE INTERVALS

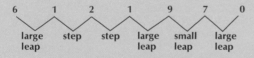

6   1   2   1   9   7   0
large step step large small large
leap   leap   leap   leap

TRY THIS
Have children play their birth-date melody in some of the
following ways:
- At various tempos—fast, slow, moderate, getting faster,
  getting slower
- With various dynamics—loud, soft, moderately loud;
  with accents, without accents
- In various rhythm patterns—using rhythms that are syncopated, rhythms that are not syncopated, dotted
  rhythms
- Starting on a different tone, changing the other tones in
  relation to it

Note: These are individual, rather than group, experiences.
Encourage children to work on their own at home or in
free time at school. Give them an opportunity to perform
their melodies for one another.

MATERIALS
Record 9, "Namane Kare"; Pupil's Book, pp. 196 and 197

VOCABULARY
contour, tambura, drone

IDEAS FOR TEACHING

1. Direct children's attention to the photographs on p. 197. Point out: One photograph shows a woman playing an instrument called a tambura (tahm-boo'-rah). The other photograph shows a close-up view of the instrument. Note: The tambura is used in India to accompany singing. It has four strings, tuned to the pitches G, high C, high C, low C. When the tambura is played, the strings are plucked in order from G to low C, usually in a flexible rhythmic style. The effect this produces is one of continuous sound, called a drone.

2. Play the recording so children can hear the tone color of the tambura accompanying the singing.

3. Play the recording again as children follow the notation on p. 196. Question: Each staff of notation represents one phrase. Which two phrases have identical melodies? (Phrases 1 and 3) Point out: The melody of phrases 1 and 3 has a contour that begins high, then moves mostly downward, with some upward movement near the end. Question: How is the contour of phrase 2 different? (Phrase 2 begins low, then moves generally upward, with downward movement at the end. There are repeated tones near the middle of the phrase.) ⟶

Play a drone accompaniment for "Namane Kare."

Pluck the C and G strings of an Autoharp

at the same time, over and over.

NAMANE KARE FOLK SONG FROM INDIA

USED BY PERMISSION OF WILLIAM M. ANDERSON.

Na - ma - ne ka - re cha - tu - re shi - ri gu - ru cha - ra - na,
(Nah-mah-nuh kah-ruh chah-too-ruh shee-ree goo-roo chah-rah-nah,

Ta - ne ma - ne ni - re - ma - le ka - re bha - ve ta - ra - na.
Tah-nuh mah-nuh nee-ruh-mah-luh kah-ruh bhah-vuh tah-rah-nah.

Na - ma - ne ka - re cha - tu - re shi - ri gu - ru cha - ra - na.
Nah-mah-nuh kah-ruh chah-too-ruh shee-ree goo-roo chah-rah-nah.)

196 Melody

TEACHER INFORMATION
The words of "Namane Kare" literally mean "Respect your teachers and keep a clean body and mind."

Singing in India is often accompanied by a drone played on a tambura.

low G
high C
high C
ow C

Melody 197

4. When children are ready, have them sing with the recording. <u>Point out:</u> This melody from India has a different kind of sound or character from the melodies children are used to singing, for example, "Polly Wolly Doodle." Help children conclude that both "Namane Kare" and "Polly Wolly Doodle" use the same qualities—tones that step, leap, and repeat—but they each put the qualities together in different ways. This helps to give each of the melodies a distinctive kind of sound.

TRY THIS

1. Have children provide their own drone accompaniment for "Namane Kare." On the Autoharp, mark the lowest C string and the G above it with chalk so that they are easy to find. Then have individuals take turns plucking the strings simultaneously throughout the song. Encourage them to vary the rhythm pattern as they play the strings over and over. <u>Suggestion:</u> If a piano is available, have individuals provide a drone accompaniment by playing the following pattern of tones over and over. Encourage them to play in a relaxed manner, changing the rhythm as they

choose. To make the drone sound continuous, have them keep the sustaining (right) pedal depressed.

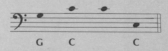

G   C   C

2. If children are ready, take time to talk about intervals. <u>Point out:</u> When children sing or play two tones, one after the other, they are performing melody. When they sing or play two tones at the same time, they are performing harmony. In both melody and harmony, the distance from one tone to the other is called an interval.

MATERIALS
Record 9, Beethoven: *Symphony No. 9 in D Minor,* Movement 4; Pupil's Book, p. 198

VOCABULARY
contour, phrase, theme

IDEAS FOR TEACHING
<u>Note</u>: From time to time, children need to stop and pull together what they have learned. This lesson gives them an opportunity to use what they know about music.

1. Play the recording and have children identify the tone color they hear (low strings).

2. Play the recording again as children follow the notation on p. 198. Help them observe that the melody has four phrases. <u>Questions</u>: Which phrases have identical, or almost identical, contours? (1, 2, 4) How do the tones in those phrases move? (By step, with some tones repeated) What makes the contour of phrase 3 different from the rest? (Some tones move by leap.)

3. Talk about other qualities in the music, playing the recording as necessary to reinforce the discussion:
- *Dynamics*—mostly soft, getting louder near the end of phrase 3, softer at the beginning of phrase 4
- *Rhythm pattern*—Phrases 1, 2, 4 have steady quarter notes, with a dotted pattern at the end; phrase 3 includes a repeated pattern of quarter and eighth notes.
- *Register*—low
- *Tempo*—moderate; does not get faster or slower
- *Meter*—meter in 4

Listen to the recording. Then follow the notation to play the theme on a melody instrument. Notice how the tones in the melody move.

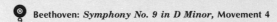
Beethoven: *Symphony No. 9 in D Minor,* Movement 4

Theme

198 Melody

TRY THIS
Children can play the theme on classroom instruments— <u>recorder</u>, <u>bells</u>, <u>piano</u>. Those who take instrumental lessons might try playing it on trumpet, clarinet, <u>flute</u>, or <u>violin</u>. Give children time to practice. When they are ready, have them perform individually or as an ensemble. Encourage ensemble players to use a tempo that is comfortable for everyone. (<u>Note</u>: Only the instruments underlined can be combined in an ensemble.)

WHAT DO YOU HEAR? 16: MELODY

Here are the melodies of some songs that you know.

Part of each melody is missing on the recording.

Listen and decide whether the missing part moves mostly

by step, by leap, or whether the tones repeat.

Listen. Then choose your answer.

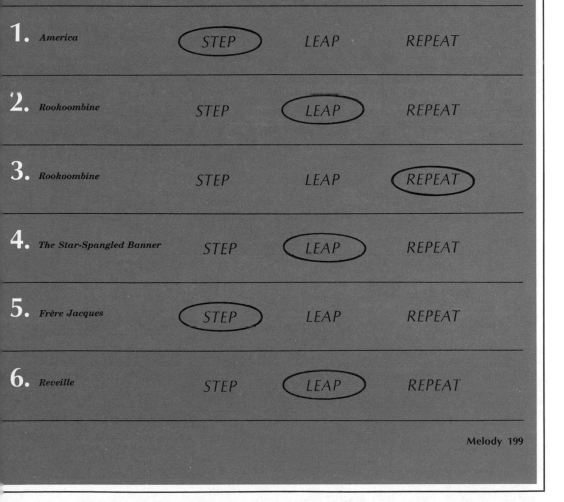

1. *America* — (STEP)   LEAP   REPEAT

2. *Rookoombine* — STEP   (LEAP)   REPEAT

3. *Rookoombine* — STEP   LEAP   (REPEAT)

4. *The Star-Spangled Banner* — STEP   (LEAP)   REPEAT

5. *Frère Jacques* — (STEP)   LEAP   REPEAT

6. *Reveille* — STEP   (LEAP)   REPEAT

Melody 199

MELODY • Lesson 8

MATERIALS
Record 9, *What Do You Hear? 16: Melody*; spirit master

VOCABULARY
steps, leaps, repeated tones

TEACHER INFORMATION
Suggest to children that they silently sing each melody with the recording. This will help them decide how the tones move in the part that is omitted.

MODULE 18

THE ARTS: Contemporary Forming Process

MATERIALS
Record 9, Varèse: *Poème électron-ique; Sound Piece 9: Theme and Tape Recorder "Alteration";* Pupil's Book, pp. 200–205

VOCABULARY
high and low sounds, upward and downward direction, fast and slow tempo, loud and soft tones, tone color, thin and thick density, wide and narrow range

IDEAS FOR TEACHING
1. Give children time to look at the print on p. 200, comparing the top and bottom rows of drawings. Help them observe the following: (a) The top row shows "static" representa-tions of (from left to right) a figure running; a distortion of the running figure; a cola bottle; a distortion of the cola bottle; an outline of the continent of Africa. Point out: Each representation is separate and dis-tinct; there is no movement from one to another. (b) The bottom row shows the running figure *becoming* Africa by moving through the stages shown separately in the top row. Encourage children to describe how the artist shows movement in the bottom row of drawings (by dupli-cating each representation several times, making the duplications over-lap). Point out: In recent years, com-puters have opened up many ave-nues for artists to explore. The subjects of the print on p. 200—the →

THE ARTS: CONTEMPORARY FORMING PROCESS

A computer helped the artist create this picture.

Look at the top line of drawings from left to right. It shows several things in a row.

Look at the bottom line of drawings from left to right. It shows how an artist can give a feeling of movement from one thing to another.

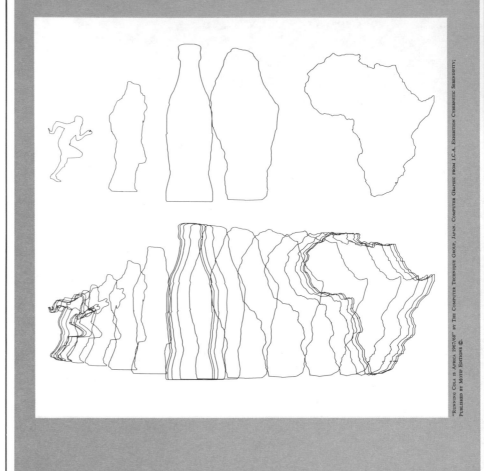

"RUNNING COLA IS AFRICA 1967/68" BY THE COMPUTER TECHNIQUE GROUP, JAPAN. COMPUTER GRAPHIC FROM I.C.A. EXHIBITION CYBERNETIC SERENDIPITY; PUBLISHED BY MOTIF EDITIONS ©.

200 MODULE 18: The Arts—Contemporary Forming Process

TRY THIS
1. Tell children that the title of the graphic on p. 200 is *Running Cola is Africa.* Ask whether the title is appropri-ate. Discuss children's answers.

2. Explain that sometimes writers have their poems and stories typeset by computer in a shape that identifies the basic theme. Some children may wish to try this technique with their own poems or short stories. They might use a typewriter if one is available, or letter them freehand on art paper. Get them started by showing them the following example.

```
           A
          big
         pine
        t r e e
      is used
   s o m e t i m e s
  f o r  f u r n i t u r e
a f t e r  i t  i s  c u t
        for
      lumber.
```

A computer helped create this work also. The artist wanted to suggest movement from one thing to another. Look at the work from left to right. Try to feel it moving along.

"MATRIX MULTIPLICATION" BY FRIEDER NAKE. COURTESY BRUCKMAN-VERLAG, MUNICH.

running figure, the cola bottle, Africa—have little in common. But the artist, using imagination, and with the help of a computer, has organized the lines and images to create an interesting graphic.

2. Have children look at the computer graphic on p. 201. Through discussion, lead them to recognize the following: (a) The graphic can be seen as a painting, but it can also be seen as a movement of color changes from left to right, which is how it would be viewed if shown as a movie or on a TV screen. (b) A computer was used to help achieve the "rippling color" effect. Point out: The computer is a tool for the artist in the same way that a brush is a tool for the painter or a chisel for the sculptor. The artist uses imagination; he or she does the creating. A computer does not have imagination; it can only do what the artist makes it do.

3. Have children follow the chart on p. 202 as they listen to the Varèse excerpt on the recording. The chart lists the musical qualities that are present in the work. Note: *Density* may be an unfamiliar term for some children. Tell them that when one or two sounds occur at the same time, they are hearing thin density. When many sounds occur at one time, they are hearing thick density.

4. Discuss what children heard in the Varèse work. Note: (a) Children should recognize that the composer used electronic machines to create the sounds. Help them become aware of movement in the piece, of the experience of sounds moving from one to another. Play the excerpt as necessary to point out these →

and other musical qualities listed in the chart. (b) If comments such as "It was scary" are given, ask, "But what did the sounds do? What happened in the music that made you respond as you did?" Help children to grasp the idea that the composer "made something happen with sound"—that he "formed" sounds so we could hear and feel them.

5. Have children read the first two paragraphs on p. 203. Then play the recording of *Sound Piece 9* as they follow the score on pp. 204 and 205. <u>Point out:</u> To create *Sound Piece 9*, the composer recorded a piano melody on a tape recorder. Then she hooked a second tape recorder into the first one. As the first tape recorder played back the piano melody, the composer changed it by manipulating the dials on the machine, the tape reels, and even the tape itself. At the same time, she used the second tape recorder to record the new sounds she was creating. <u>Note:</u> For more information, see Explanation of the Score and Sound Piece Labels, Teacher's Edition p. 204.

6. Play the recording of *Sound Piece 9* and have some children show through body movement what the sound is doing. After the performance, help children analyze the sounds they responded to, describing them in musical terms—high and low sounds, sounds moving upward and downward, sounds at fast and slow tempos, loud and soft sounds, sounds having various tone colors, sounds with thin and thick density, sounds with wide and narrow ranges.

7. Have children use the suggestions on p. 203 to create a sound piece of

⟶

Music moves from moment to moment with sounds and silences.

You can feel and hear these as they move along from a beginning to an end. Listen for the sounds and silences in this music.

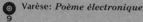 Varèse: *Poème électronique*

This chart will help you describe what you heard.

HIGH AND LOW SOUNDS	*LOUD AND SOFT SOUNDS*
UPWARD AND DOWNWARD DIRECTION	*DIFFERENT TONE COLORS*
PAUSES	*THIN AND THICK DENSITY*
FAST AND SLOW MOVEMENT	*WIDE AND NARROW RANGE*

202 The Arts—Contemporary Forming Process

TEACHER INFORMATION
A recording of Bogusky-Reimer's *Sound Piece 9: Theme and Tape Recorder "Alteration"* is used in *Silver Burdett Music*, Book 3, where it is identified by the alternative title *Speed of the Beat*.

Edgard Varèse (French, 1885–1965) *Poème électronique:* Varèse became an important leader in the contemporary experimental music movement. In this movement, melody and harmony were abandoned; music was conceived of as any sounds at all that were used in organized ways. Varèse composed for large groups of percussion instruments and for the newly available electronic instruments of his time. *Poème électronique* was conceived in partnership with the famous architect Le Corbusier for presentation at the Brussels World's Fair of 1958.

their own. Encourage them to be as creative as their imagination allows. Have them make a score of their composition, using symbols and words to describe the sounds.

Sounds and silences can be "formed" to do something as they move along from a beginning to an end.

Follow the score on pages 204 and 205 as you listen to *Sound Piece 9*. This piece was composed using a piano melody and a tape recorder.

After you have listened, try creating your own sound piece on a stereo tape recorder. Use voices or instruments or both. The chart below will help you organize your ideas.

	10"	10"	10"	10"
Channel I	sound	silence	sound	silence

Now go back to the beginning of your 40-second piece. This time, fill in the silences by recording new material on Channel II. Follow the chart below, or think of something else to do.

Channel I	sound	silence	sound	silence

Channel II		Play at a different speed.		Slow down the feed reel.

The Arts—Contemporary Forming Process 203

EXPLANATION OF THE SCORE

On the recording, *Sound Piece 9* begins with the original piano melody, the theme. The score shows this in standard notation. When the alteration begins, the score guides children's listening as follows:

- The notes outside the boxes outline the original piano melody. They show what part of the theme is being varied at each point in the Sound Piece.
- The notes and symbols in the boxes picture the new sounds children are hearing. Each one of the sixteen boxes (events) in the Sound Piece is identified by a numbered arrow. The numbers indicate the order of the events.
- The labels *Speed Change, Sound with Sound,* etc., tell how the composer created the sound for each event (see Sound Piece Labels below for a description of each one).

<u>Note:</u> Some children may notice that the part of the Sound Piece scored on p. 204 uses only the first staff of the original theme, playing it through two times. The part of the Sound Piece on p. 205 repeats material from measures 1–4 of the second staff (original theme) over and over, using measures 5–8 only at the very end.

<u>Suggestion:</u> Give children time to examine the score before they listen to the Sound Piece. Help them find the places in the alteration where they will hear speed changes, where they will hear sound with sound, etc. The more familiar children are with the printed score, the easier it will be for them to follow along with the recording, and the more alert they will be to what is happening to the sound.

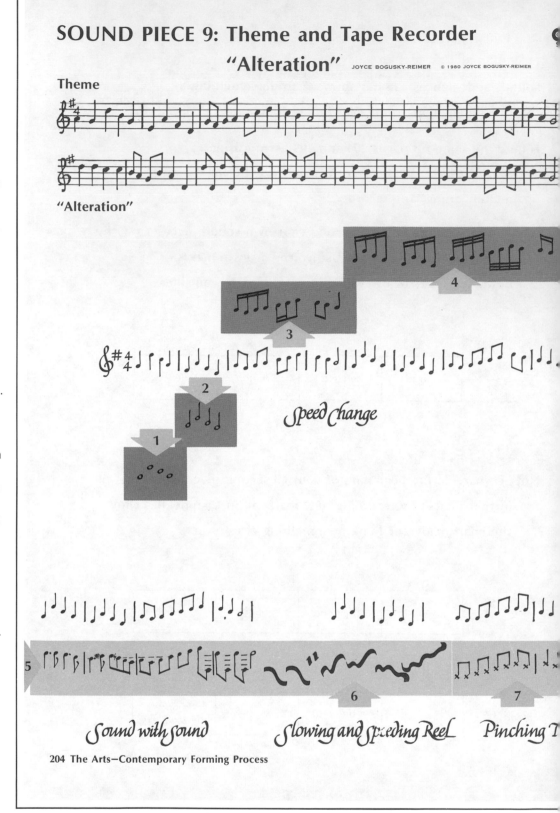

SOUND PIECE 9: Theme and Tape Recorder "Alteration"

JOYCE BOGUSKY-REIMER   © 1980 JOYCE BOGUSKY-REIMER

Theme

"Alteration"

Speed Change

Sound with Sound   *Slowing and Speeding Reel*   Pinching T

204 The Arts—Contemporary Forming Process

SOUND PIECE LABELS

Speed Change: The composer taped the original sounds at one speed and played them back at different speeds. When the sounds were played back at a faster speed, the original sounds became faster and higher. When the sounds were played back at a slower speed, the original sounds became slower and lower.

Sound with Sound: The composer used a stereo tape recorder to create this effect. A stereo tape recorder has two channels. The original piano melody was taped on channel 1. A countermelody was taped on channel 2.

Slowing and Speeding the Reel: The composer actually held the tape reel back (slowing the reel) or pushed it around faster (speeding the reel). Both of these actions altered the original sound.

Pinching Tape: The composer pinched the tape with her fingers as it went from one reel to the other.

Children are now ready to take Test 2 for Book 4. Additional information about <u>Silver Burdett Music Competency Tests</u> is found in the introduction of this book.

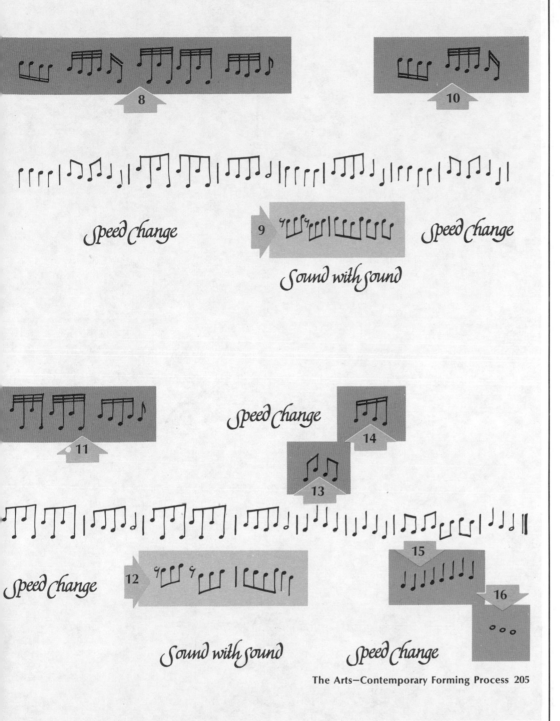

TEACHER INFORMATION

Joyce Bogusky-Reimer (American, 1944–   ) *Sound Piece 9: Theme and Tape Recorder "Alteration"*: This composer and music educator uses the tape recorder and the electronic sound synthesizer as her basic instruments for composing. *Sound Piece 9: Theme and Tape Recorder "Alteration"* was composed especially for SILVER BURDETT MUSIC.

MODULE 19

OBJECTIVES, p. XIV

METER • Lesson 1

MATERIALS
Record 1, Joplin: *Bethena;* Scruggs: *String Bender;* Record 9, "Muje Mukesin"; Desmond: *Take Five;* Pupil's Book, pp. 106, 206 and 207; tom-tom, other appropriate percussion instruments

VOCABULARY
meter in 3, meter in 2, meter in 5

IDEAS FOR TEACHING
1. Take time to review meter in 3 and meter in 2 by having children perform a hand jive with the recordings of Joplin's *Bethena* and Scruggs's *String Bender* (see Teacher's Edition p. 8). Then have them experience music that changes from one meter (meter in 3) to another (meter in 4) by singing "Guava Berry Song" (p. 106).

2. Direct children's attention to the photographs on p. 206. Help them observe that the top row represents beats grouped into sets of three and that the middle row represents beats grouped into sets of two. <u>Note:</u> In the photographs, each child represents a beat. The children standing represent strong beats; the others, weak beats. The vertical lines represent bar lines. They group the beats in each row into measures.

3. Have children look at the bottom row of photographs. <u>Question:</u> How is this row different from the other two? (It represents a measure of →

METER

TEACHER INFORMATION
The words of "Muje Mukesin" mean, "I am wearing worn-out moccasins."

TRY THIS
Play the recording of "Muje Mukesin" and have children perform the following pattern throughout.

pat clap clap pat clap pat clap clap pat clap
lap

Then have children perform this pattern throughout *Take Five:*

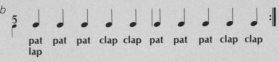

pat pat pat clap clap pat pat pat clap clap
lap

→

n some American Indian music you can hear and feel that the sets of beats keep changing from 3 to 2. To help you hear this, listen to the tom-tom accompaniment on the recording.

MUJE MUKESIN   OJIBWAY INDIAN TUNE

Mu - je muk - e - sin, aw - yaw - yon, Mu - je muk - e - sin, aw - yaw - yon,

Mu - je muk - e - sin, aw - yaw - yon, Mu - je muk - e - sin, aw - yaw - yon.

Play this pattern to accompany the song. Be certain to stress the first beat—the strong beat—of each measure.

Sometimes sets of three beats and two beats are grouped together in the same measure. When this happens, the music has a meter in 5. Listen to this music. Try to feel the beats grouped in sets of five. Listen for the strong beat at the beginning of each set.

 Desmond: *Take Five*

MODULE 19: Meter 207

---

three beats followed by a measure of two beats.)

4. Play the recording of "Muje Mukesin" so children can hear music with beats alternating between sets of three and sets of two. To help them feel the beat groupings change from one to the other, have them keep the beat in some way—e.g., by lightly clapping, or by patting their lap. Some children can play the steady beats on a tom-tom. <u>Note:</u> The tom-tom pattern on p. 207 matches the steady beat. Following the notation will help children keep the pattern of three beats followed by two beats. Remind them that the first beat of each measure is a strong beat.

5. When children know the song (notation, p. 207) and can play the beats on a tom-tom, have them add the tone color of other appropriate instruments (e.g., rattles, ankle bells, notched sticks) to accompany their singing. <u>Suggestions:</u> (a) One instrument might play only on the strong beats. (b) One instrument might play only during measures having three beats; another, only during measures having two beats.

6. Ask children to read the last paragraph on p. 207. Then play the recording of *Take Five*. Have children tap or clap the steady beat in time with the music, following the five-meter notation in their book. <u>Note:</u> The string bass and piano parts will help children hear the groupings of five beats in the music.

Finally, have children try using the motions from pattern *b* during "Muje Mukesin" and the motions from pattern *a* during *Take Five*.

Discuss whether each pattern feels the same for both works. (<u>Note:</u> The same pattern feels different for each work.) Help children conclude that there is a difference in feeling between meter in 3-2 and meter in 5.

METER • Lesson 2

MATERIALS
Record 9, "Hineh mah tov"; Pupil's Book, p. 208; tambourine, drum, wood block

VOCABULARY
dotted quarter note

IDEAS FOR TEACHING

1. Tell children to pretend they are holding a tambourine in each hand. Then, as the recording plays, have them keep the steady beat (two beats per measure) by alternately shaking one "tambourine," then the other, throughout the song.

2. Direct attention to the tambourine pattern on p. 208. It shows the steady beats in "Hineh mah tov." <u>Point out:</u> Each beat is written as a dotted quarter note (♩.).

3. Have children take turns playing the tambourine pattern to accompany the recording. Invite the class to sing when they can (notation, p. 208). <u>Suggestion:</u> If two small tambourines are available, have players shake them as in item 1 above.

4. Call attention to the drum and wood block parts. <u>Point out:</u> In the drum part, each beat is divided into three equal sounds. In the wood block part, some beats are divided into two sounds—one long, one short. Then have children take turns playing one of the parts to accompany the song.

5. Have children look at the rhythm patterns at the bottom of the page. Ask them to find each pattern in a measure of "Hineh mah tov." (Pattern 1—measures 2, 4, 5, 8; 2—1; 3—3, 7; 4—6)

Play these patterns to accompany "Hineh mah tov."

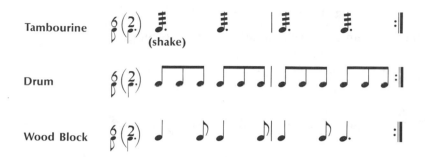

HINEH MAH TOV
HEBREW FOLK SONG

Piano acc., p. 271
Orff-instrument acc., p. 348

Hi-neh mah tov u-ma na - im, She-vet a-chim gam ya-chad.

Hi - neh mah____ tov, She-vet a-chim gam ya-chad.

Can you find these patterns in "Hineh mah tov"?

208 Meter

TRY THIS
1. Have one child play the rhythm of the first staff of "Hineh mah tov" on a drum while at the same time another child plays the rhythm of the second staff on a wood block. <u>Questions:</u> In which measures do the instruments play contrasting rhythm patterns? (In the first two measures) In which measures do they play the same rhythm patterns? (In the last two measures)

2. When children know the melody, have them sing "Hineh mah tov" as a two-part round.

3. If children are ready, call attention to the meter signature of "Hineh mah tov" (6/8). <u>Point out:</u> Music written in a meter of six often has the feeling of two beats per measure (2/♩.).

TEACHER INFORMATION
The words of "Hineh mah tov" literally mean, "Here it is good and pleasant for brethren to sit together." They are pronounced as follows:

Hi-neh mah tov u-ma na-im,
hee-nay mah tohv oo-mah nah-yeem

She-vet a-chim gam ya-chad.
sheh-vet ahkh-heem gahm yah-hkhahd

Find the part of "Paddy Works on the Railway" that uses this rhythm pattern.

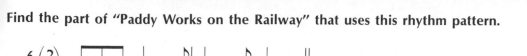

PADDY WORKS ON THE RAILWAY
IRISH-AMERICAN RAILROAD SONG

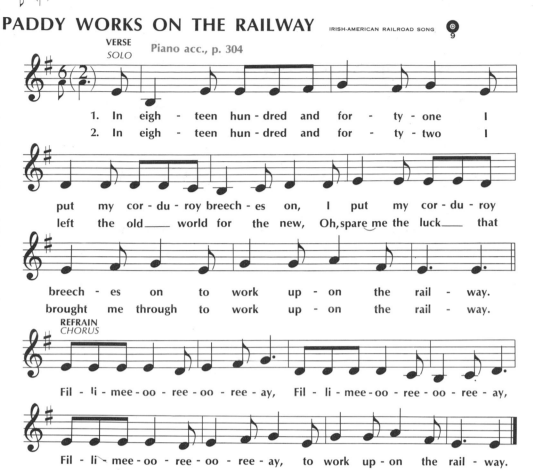

VERSE
SOLO
Piano acc., p. 304

1. In eigh - teen hun - dred and for - ty - one I
2. In eigh - teen hun - dred and for - ty - two I

put my cor - du - roy breech - es on, I put my cor - du - roy
left the old___ world for the new, Oh, spare me the luck___ that

breech - es on to work up - on the rail - way.
brought me through to work up - on the rail - way.

REFRAIN
CHORUS

Fil - li - mee - oo - ree - oo - ree - ay, Fil - li - mee - oo - ree - oo - ree - ay,

Fil - li - mee - oo - ree - oo - ree - ay, to work up - on the rail - way.

3. It's "Pat, do this," and "Pat, do that," without a stocking or cravat,

And nothing but an old straw hat, while working on the railway. *Refrain*

Sing this countermelody during the refrain.

Countermelody

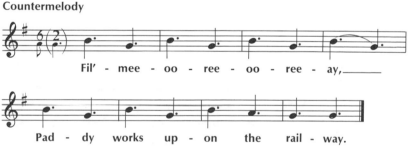

Fil' - mee - oo - ree - oo - ree - ay,___

Pad - dy works up - on the rail - way.

Meter 209

METER • Lesson 3

MATERIALS
Record 9, "Paddy Works on the Railway"; Pupil's Book, p. 209; percussion instruments

VOCABULARY
meter

IDEAS FOR TEACHING

1. Have children look at the rhythm pattern on p. 209. Help them observe the following: (a) The pattern is written in a meter of six, with a feeling of two beats per measure. (b) The pattern uses a combination of one long sound to a beat (♩.), two sounds to a beat—one long, one short (♩ ♪), and three equal sounds to a beat (♫♪).

2. Have children find the pattern in the notation for "Paddy Works on the Railway." Note: The pattern occurs in the refrain, on the nonsense syllables *Fil-li-mee-oo-ree-oo-ree-ay* each time. Have children try chanting the syllables in rhythm.

3. Play the recording as children follow the notation. Have individuals play the "Fil-li-mee-oo-ree-oo-ree-ay" rhythm on a percussion instrument each time it occurs. Invite children to join in the singing when they can.

4. As some children sing with the recording, have others use natural sounds (clapping, patting, etc.) to perform a rhythm pattern throughout the refrain. They may use pattern a or b (see Rhythm Patterns below), or a pattern they create.

5. If children are ready, have a small group sing the countermelody during the refrain.

RHYTHM PATTERNS

a

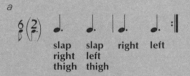

slap slap right left
right left
thigh thigh

b

pat clap clap pat clap clap
lap

TRY THIS
Have children take turns playing the following pattern of tones on the open strings of a guitar as the class sings "Paddy Works on the Railway." The diagram below shows which strings to pluck. Note: (a) Children should keep playing each tone until a new letter name appears in the pattern. (b) They begin playing on the first strong beat of the song (on the syllable *eigh-* of *eighteen*).

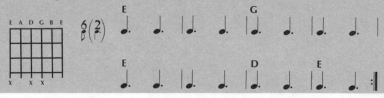

MATERIALS

Record 9, "Me and My Brother, Oliver Lee"; Handel: *Sonata in F,* Op. 1, No. 11, "Allegro Finale"; Pupil's Book, pp. 210 and 211; drum, tambourine

VOCABULARY

meter, tone color, leaps, steps, tempo

IDEAS FOR TEACHING

1. Have children look at the notation for "Me and My Brother, Oliver Lee" on pp. 210 and 211. Point out: This song has the same meter ($\frac{6}{8}$) as "Hineh mah tov" (p. 208), with a feeling of two beats per measure. Question: Are the beats mostly divided into patterns of three equal sounds, or into patterns of two sounds—one long, one short? (Into patterns of three equal sounds)

2. Direct children's attention to the drum part on p. 211. Help them observe that it uses a pattern of three equal sounds per beat. Then play the recording of "Me and My Brother, Oliver Lee" and have children take turns playing the drum part as an accompaniment. Note: Children should play notes with stems down with the left hand, notes with stems up with the right hand.

3. Have children look at the notation for the tambourine part. Question: How is this pattern different from the drum pattern? (In the tambourine part, each divided beat begins with silence instead of sound.)

4. When children know the song, have individuals take turns playing the drum part or the tambourine part to accompany the class singing.

Notice how the beats in this song are divided.

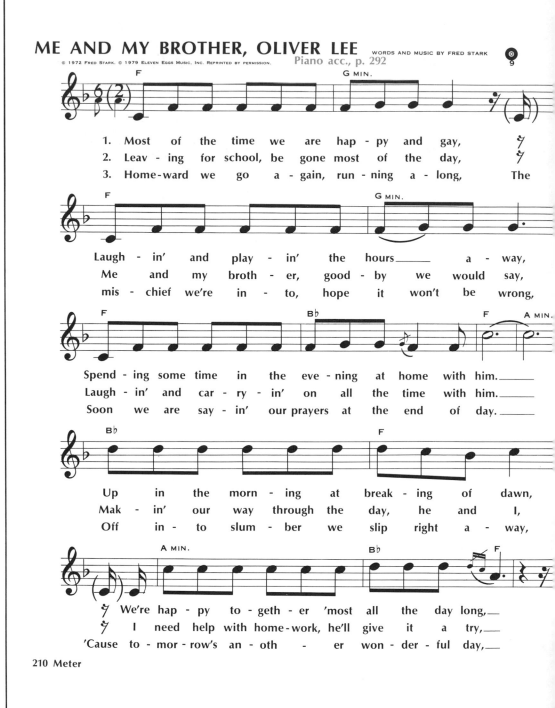

ME AND MY BROTHER, OLIVER LEE   WORDS AND MUSIC BY FRED STARK
© 1972 FRED STARK. © 1979 ELEVEN EGGS MUSIC, INC. REPRINTED BY PERMISSION.   Piano acc., p. 292

1. Most of the time we are hap - py and gay,
2. Leav - ing for school, be gone most of the day,
3. Home - ward we go a - gain, run - ning a - long, The

Laugh - in' and play - in' the hours_____ a - way,
Me and my broth - er, good - by we would say,
mis - chief we're in - to, hope it won't be wrong,

Spend - ing some time in the eve - ning at home with him._____
Laugh - in' and car - ry - in' on all the time with him._____
Soon we are say - in' our prayers at the end of day. _____

Up in the morn - ing at break - ing of dawn,
Mak - in' our way through the day, he and I,
Off in - to slum - ber we slip right a - way,

We're hap - py to - geth - er 'most all the day long,__
I need help with home - work, he'll give it a try,__
'Cause to - mor - row's an - oth - er won - der - ful day,__

210 Meter

Me and my broth - er, Ol - i - ver Lee,
Me and my broth - er, Ol - i - ver Lee,
With me and my broth - er, Ol - i - ver Lee,

Me and my broth - er, old Ol - i - ver Lee.
Me and my broth - er, old Ol - i - ver Lee.
Me and my broth - er, old Ol - i - ver,

Me and my broth - er, old Ol - i - ver Lee.

Me and my broth - er, old Ol - i - ver Lee.

Me and my broth - er, old Ol - i - ver Lee.

5. Play the recording of Handel's *Sonata in F.* Have children listen for some of these qualities in the music:
- meter in six, with the feeling of two beats per measure
- the beat divided into three equal sounds
- the beat divided into two sounds—one long, one short
- contrasting tone colors—recorder playing the melody; cello and harpsichord playing an accompaniment
- melody made up largely of tones that leap and tones that move by step
- fast tempo

<u>Note:</u> (a) Most children will be able to focus on the recorder part to hear the beat divided into three sounds at the beginning and throughout much of the movement. They will have more difficulty focusing on the accompanying instruments, cello and harpsichord. The cello part has beats divided into two sounds—one long, one short—near the end of the movement. Help children hear these long-short sounds by calling attention to them when they occur.

(b) Give children many opportunities to listen to the recording. <u>Point out:</u> Many qualities—meter, tone color, melody, rhythm pattern, etc.—work together to give music its expressiveness.

Play these parts to accompany "Me and My Brother, Oliver Lee."

As you play, feel the steady beat divided into threes.

Drum

Tambourine

Listen for the steady beat divided into threes in this music.

Handel: *Sonata in F*

Meter 211

TRY THIS
Have children follow the notation on pp. 210 and 211 as they listen to the recording of "Me and My Brother, Oliver Lee." Help them discover that in the third verse, the soloist does not follow the music exactly—e.g., at the end of staff 3 he sings *end of the day* and adds the word *yeah;* he also sings extra notes on the word *day;* in staff 4, he changes a melody note on *slumber we;* in staff 5, he changes the rhythm on the word *another.* <u>Point out:</u> When the singer changes the music in this way, he is adding his own individual style to the music. <u>Suggestion:</u> Have children compare this contemporary style with the folk-singing style

Jean Ritchie uses when she sings the first verse of "Amazing Grace" (p. 192).

TEACHER INFORMATION
George Frideric Handel (German born, 1685–1759) *Sonata in F,* Op. 1, No. 11, "Allegro Finale": Alongside J. S. Bach, Handel was the "other" great composer of the Baroque period. He spent much of his life in England and became best known for his operas. Today his oratorios (large dramatic works for orchestra with solo voices and chorus) and instrumental pieces are better known.

MATERIALS

Record 9, "Silent Night"; Pupil's Book, p. 212; Autoharp

VOCABULARY

meter

IDEAS FOR TEACHING

1. Have children follow the notation on p. 212 to sing "Silent Night" with the recording. Point out: (a) The song is in a meter of six, with a feeling of two beats per measure. (b) Some beats are divided into two sounds—one long, one short (♩. ♪). (c) When beats are divided into three sounds, the rhythm is dotted, creating a pattern of longer and shorter sounds (♩.♫).

2. Children can play the chords C, G₇, F on the Autoharp to accompany "Silent Night." The chord names above the staff tell when to change from one chord to another. At first, have children play two strums per measure in time with the steady beat. When they are comfortable with the pattern of chord changes, have them try the strumming pattern in their book. Suggestion: Encourage children to experiment with different kinds of strums—e.g., for the dotted quarter notes (♩.), they might play long strums from lowest string to highest; for the patterns of three eighth notes (♫♪), they might play short strums, one on the low strings followed by two on the high strings. Give children time to find the kinds of strums that feel right for the music. Note: For the tied notes in the last measure (♩. ♩.), children should play one long strum, making the sound last for two beats.

SILENT NIGHT

MUSIC BY FRANZ GRUBER   WORDS BY JOSEPH MOHR

Piano acc., p. 311

1. Si - lent night, ho - ly night, All is calm,
2. Si - lent night, ho - ly night, Shep - herds quake

all is bright Round yon Vir - gin Moth - er and Child.
at the sight, Glo - ries stream from heav - en a - far,

Ho - ly In - fant so ten - der and mild, Sleep in heav - en - ly
Heav'n - ly hosts sing "Al - le - lu - ia, Christ the Sav - ior is

peace, Sleep in heav - en - ly peace.
born! Christ the Sav - ior is born!"

Play the Autoharp to accompany "Silent Night." Use this strumming pattern, or create one of your own.

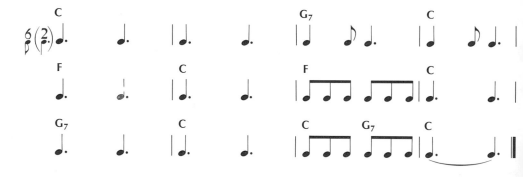

212 Meter

TRY THIS

1. When children practice the Autoharp part for "Silent Night," have them experiment with different kinds of picks (plastic, metal, felt, etc.) to find a tone color that is appropriate to the song.

2. Some children may wish to create their own strumming pattern for "Silent Night." Encourage experimentation.

TEACHER INFORMATION

"Silent Night," a carol that is sung in many languages, has an interesting history. Franz Gruber was the schoolmaster and church organist in the village of Oberndorf, Austria. On the afternoon of Christmas Eve in 1818, he went to the church and found that the organ had broken down. He knew that there would be no time to fix it before the Christmas service. Gruber suggested to the vicar of the church, Joseph Mohr, that a new song might help the situation and Mohr wrote the words of "Silent Night" immediately. Gruber set the words to music, and the song was sung that night with the accompaniment of a guitar.

WHAT DO YOU HEAR? 17: METER

Can you hear meter in this music? Each time a number is called, decide whether the meter is in 2, 3, or 5. Listen. Then choose your answer.

	METER IN	METER IN	METER IN	
1.	2	(3)	5	Telemann: *Suite in A Minor for Flute and String Orchestra*
2.	2	(3)	5	Britten: *Matinées Musicales*
3.	2	3	(5)	Desmond: *Take Five*
4.	(2)	3	5	Gould: *American Salute*
5.	2	(3)	5	*The Star-Spangled Banner*
6.	(2)	3	5	Tchaikovsky: *Capriccio Italien*
7.	(2)	3	5	Haydn: *String Quartet*, Op. 76

Meter 213

METER • Lesson 6

MATERIALS
Record 9, *What Do You Hear? 17: Meter;* spirit master

VOCABULARY
meter in 2, meter in 3, meter in 5

TEACHER INFORMATION
Suggestion: As each example plays, have children move in some quiet way—e.g., tap the palm of one hand with the fingers of the other hand—to feel the steady beats. Remind them that in music, the first beat of each measure is a strong beat. Listening for the strong beats will help them group the beats into sets of two, three, or five.

MODULE 20

OBJECTIVES, p. XIV

PHRASES • Lesson 1

MATERIALS
Record 9, "He mele o ke kahuli";
Pupil's Book, pp. 214 and 215

VOCABULARY
phrase, phrase marking

IDEAS FOR TEACHING
Note: Children have had many experiences with reading and writing sentences. They know that sentences can be long or short. When they write compositions, they put sentences together in an order that expresses their ideas. Music uses "sentences," too, called phrases. Phrases can be long or short. When composers write melodies, they put phrases together to express musical ideas.

1. Play the recording and have children listen for the phrases in "He mele o ke kahuli." Question: How many phrases are in the song? (Four)

2. Play the recording again and have children show the length of each phrase by moving their arm in the air with a curved motion (⌒).
Question: Do the phrases all have the same length, or do some phrases feel long, others short? (They all have the same length.)

3. Have children look at the notation on p. 215. Point out: The curved lines above the staffs are phrase markings. They show the phrases in "He mele o ke kahuli." Have children trace the phrase marking as each →

PHRASES

DANCE DIRECTIONS
(Note: (a) The dance for "He mele o ke kahuli" tells about tree shells that once were snails. The snails moved into the trees when cattle were brought to the Islands. Ever since, the tree shells have called upon the redbreasted plover [kolea] to bring them dew from the pink fern [akolea] for food. (b) The dance movements are pictured on pp. 214 and 215. In the directions, numbers in parentheses indicate the picture for each movement. (c) To fit the recording, children perform the dance three times, doing the "vamp" motions after phrase 4 the first two times, the "ending" motions the last time.)

Starting Position: Dancers kneel, sitting low on their heels, with toes pointing back.
Introduction: Place right hand on hip. Extend left hand forward, palm up, and put fingers and thumb together to form a "shell." (1)
Phrase 1: Keeping right hand on hip, turn "shell" inward, outward, inward, outward (4 beats). (2) Repeat with right hand as "shell," left hand on hip (4 beats).
Phrase 2: As though picking flowers for a lei, move both arms toward the floor with a waving motion (3), then bring hands to chest to show the length of the lei (4 beats). ⟶

As you listen to the recording
of this Hawaiian chant,
move your arms to show
the length of each phrase.

phrase is sung on the recording. Invite them to sing along when they can.

4. Have children look at the photographs on pp. 214 and 215. They show hand and arm movements that "picture" the meaning of the Hawaiian words of the song. Each phrase uses different movements. Select a group of girls to learn the movements and then perform them as a dance as others sing with the recording (directions begin at the bottom of Teacher's Edition p. 214).

REVIEW/REINFORCEMENT
Review other dances children know—for example, the dances for "Sourwood Mountain" (see Square Dance, Teacher's Edition pp. 16 and 17) and "In Bahia Town" (see Try This, Teacher's Edition pp. 80 and 81). Encourage children to feel the phrases as they move, to determine whether they are all the same length, or whether some are long, others short.

HE MELE O KE KAHULI   FOLK SONG FROM HAWAII

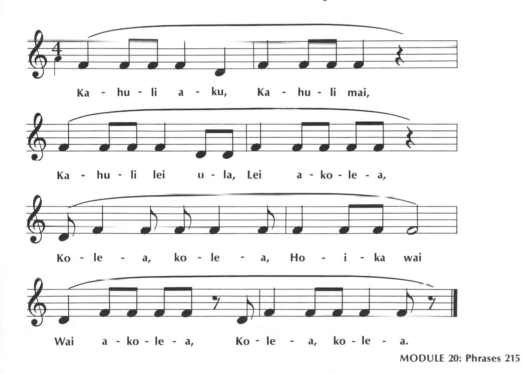

Ka - hu - li a - ku, Ka - hu - li mai,

Ka - hu - li lei u - la, Lei a - ko - le - a,

Ko - le - a, ko - le - a, Ho - i - ka wai

Wai a - ko - le - a, Ko - le - a, ko - le - a.

MODULE 20: Phrases 215

Repeat, but on the last beat, pretend to place the lei around the neck (4 beats). (4—p. 215)
Phrase 3: In two waving motions, move right hand high and diagonally backward while, at the same time, moving left hand low and diagonally forward to symbolize the wings of the "bird" (2 beats). (5) Switch hands, making left hand high and right hand low (2 beats).
Wave both arms to left (2 beats), then to right (2 beats).
Phrase 4: Wave both arms to left, cupping hands so that fingers and thumbs are pointing up to symbolize "flower buds" (4 beats). (6) Repeat to right side (4 beats).

Vamp Between Verses: Wave both arms left—left hand extended, right hand held at chest (2 beats).
Repeat to right side (2 beats).
Repeat both "vamp" motions (4 beats).
Ending: Perform a hula bow by extending arms outward at shoulder level, waving, then slowly bringing arms to center front, bowing head. (7)

Mainstreaming Note: Nonambulatory children may perform the dance while seated.

MATERIALS

Record 9, "Harvesting Tea"; Pupil's Book, p. 216; wood block, recorders or bells

VOCABULARY

phrase, countermelody, cadence

IDEAS FOR TEACHING

1. Play the recording as children follow the notation on p. 216. Questions: How many phrases are in the song? (Four) Do the phrases have the same length, or different lengths? (The same length) Which phrases have the same melody? (1 and 3) The same rhythm? (1, 2, 3) Point out: Phrase 4 has almost the same rhythm pattern as the other phrases; it uses a dotted half note instead of three quarter notes at the end.

2. When children know the song, have individuals play the rhythm on a wood block to accompany the singing. Note: Thinking the words will help children play the rhythm correctly.

3. Have children who play recorder practice the countermelody on p. 216. It uses the tones G, A, B, low D and E, high D. When they are ready, have them play as the class sings the song. Note: The countermelody can also be played on bells.

4. Direct attention to the ending of each phrase of "Harvesting Tea," called a cadence. Point out: Some of the phrases end with an "unfinished" sound (weak cadence); one phrase ends with a "finished" sound (strong cadence). Have children sing each phrase in turn to discover that phrases 1–3 end in weak cadences; phrase 4, in a strong cadence.

When you move to the Hawaiian chant "He mele o ke kahuli,"

you can feel that each phrase is the same length.

Can you discover what is the same about each phrase in this song?

HARVESTING TEA

FOLK SONG FROM JAPAN   ENGLISH WORDS BY RAYMOND MATTHEWS

Piano acc., p. 283

Play this countermelody as others sing "Harvesting Tea."

Recorder or Bells

216 Phrases

TRY THIS

1. Have some children play the melody of "Harvesting Tea" on recorder (or bells) while others play the countermelody. Note: Both melody and countermelody use the same tones.

2. Help children analyze the recorder countermelody to discover the following: The countermelody has four phrases; the phrases are all the same length; phrases 1 and 3 have the same melody; all phrases have the same rhythm pattern.

3. Put it all together. As the class sings the song, have one child play the rhythm on a wood block while others play the melody and countermelody on recorder or bells.

Sing the chorus parts when they come in this song. Will you sing long phrases, or short phrases? *Short phrases*

NE, JANE AMERICAN FOLK SONG

REPRINTED FROM SING OUT! THE FOLK SONG MAGAZINE, 505 EIGHTH AVE., NEW YORK, N.Y. 10018. USED WITH PERMISSION.

1. Hey, hey,____ Jane, Jane, My Lord-y, Lord, Jane, Jane,

I'm ____ a-gon-na buy, Jane, Jane, Three mock-ing birds, Jane, Jane,

One ____ a-for to whis-tle, Jane, Jane, One____ a-for to sing, Jane, Jane,

One____ a-for to do, Jane, Jane, Most an-y lit-tle thing, Jane, Jane.

Hey, hey, Jane, Jane,
My Lordy, Lord, Jane, Jane,
I'm a-gonna buy, Jane, Jane,
Three hunting dogs, Jane, Jane,
One a-for to run, Jane, Jane,
One a-for to shout, Jane, Jane,
One to talk to, Jane, Jane,
When I go out, Jane, Jane.

3. Hey, hey, . . .
My Lordy, Lord, . . .
I'm a-gonna buy, . . .
Three muley cows, . . .
One a-for to milk, . . .
One to plough my corn, . . .
One a-for to pray, . . .
On Christmas morn, . . .

4. Hey, hey, . . .
My Lordy, Lord, . . .
I'm a-gonna buy, . . .
Three little blue birds, . . .
One a-for to weep, . . .
One a-for to mourn, . . .
One a-for to grieve, . . .
When I am gone, . . .

Phrases 217

PHRASES • Lesson 3

MATERIALS
Record 9, "Jane, Jane"; Pupil's Book, p. 217

VOCABULARY
phrase, strong cadence, weak cadence

IDEAS FOR TEACHING

1. Play the recording and have children follow the notation on p. 217 to sing the chorus part each time it occurs. <u>Note:</u> The chorus part uses only two tones and remains the same throughout the song. Children will be able to join in singing the chorus parts immediately.

2. When children know the song, choose individuals to take turns singing the solo parts of "Jane, Jane" while the class sings the chorus parts. Question: Which part—solo or chorus—uses shorter phrases? (Chorus)

3. Help children find the solo phrases that end in strong cadences. As the recording plays, have them try to identify the solo phrases that have a "finished" sound (the fourth solo phrase—*Three mocking birds;* the last solo phrase—*Most any little thing*). <u>Point out:</u> An easy way to decide whether a phrase ending (cadence) is weak or strong is to ask, "Could the song end with this phrase?" If the answer is *yes,* the phrase ends in a strong cadence; if the answer is *no,* it ends in a weak cadence.

MATERIALS
Record 9, "Three White Gulls"; Pupil's Book, p. 218

VOCABULARY
phrase, phrase marking, sequence

IDEAS FOR TEACHING

1. Play the recording as children follow the notation on p. 218. Tell them
that the phrase markings in the score
will help them hear the short and
long phrases.

2. When children know the song,
call attention to the notation for the
short phrases in staff 4. Questions:
How are the phrases the same?
(They all have the same melody contour—repeated tones followed by an
upward step and tones that step
downward—and, except for the last
note, the same rhythm pattern.) How
are the phrases different? (The tones
in the second phrase are an interval
of a second lower than the tones in
the first phrase; the tones in the
third phrase are an interval of a second lower than those in the second
phrase.) Point out: When a phrase
of a melody is repeated at a higher
or lower pitch level, the repetition is
called a sequence. In staff 4, phrases
2 and 3 are sequences.

3. Ask children to find another example of sequence in the song notation (in staff 6, phrases 2 and 3 are
sequences).

Which phrases are long? 1, 2, 3, 7

Which phrases are short? 4, 5, 6, 8, 9, 10

THREE WHITE GULLS

FOLK SONG FROM ITALY   ENGLISH WORDS BY MARGUERITE WILKINSON

ORIGINAL TITLE "THE THREE DOVES" BY MARGUERITE WILKINSON FROM BOTSFORD COLLECTION OF FOLK SONGS—VOLUME 3. COPYRIGHT © 1921, 1922 G. SCHIRMER, INC. USED BY PERMISSION

Piano acc., p. 297

218 **Phrases**

TRY THIS
Have children take turns playing the Autoharp to accompany the class singing. Note: "Three White Gulls" uses
the chords C, G₇, F. The chord names in the score tell
when to change from one chord to another. Suggestions:
(a) Encourage players always to look ahead in the score.
While they play one phrase, they should look to see which
chords are needed for the next phrase. In this way, their
accompaniment will flow smoothly from one phrase to the
next. (b) Give children time to experiment to find a strumming pattern that is appropriate to the song.

Find the phrases in this song that are sequences. 4, 5, 6

NINE RED HORSEMEN
FOLK MELODY FROM MEXICO   WORDS BY ELEANOR FARJEON   Piano acc., p. 272

FROM ELEANOR FARJEON'S POEMS FOR CHILDREN. ORIGINALLY PUBLISHED IN SING FOR YOUR SUPPER BY ELEANOR FARJEON, COPYRIGHT, 1938, BY ELEANOR FARJEON, RENEWED 1966 BY GERVASE FARJEON. BY PERMISSION OF J.B. LIPPINCOTT, PUBLISHERS; AND HAROLD OBER ASSOCIATES, INCORPORATED.

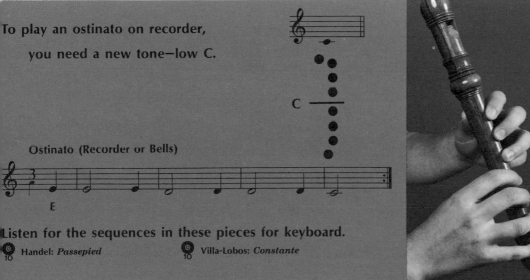

Ⓐ

1. I ___ saw nine red horse-men ride___ o - ver the plain,
2. Their___ hair streamed be - hind them, their___ eyes were a - shine;
3. Their___ spurs clinked and jin - gled, their___ laugh-ter was gay,

And ___ each gripped his horse___ by its long flow - ing mane.
They___ all rode as one man al - though they were nine.
And ___ in the red sun - set they___ gal - loped a - way.

Ⓑ

Ho hil - lo, hil - lo, hil - lo ho!   Ho hil - lo, hil - lo, hil - lo ho!

Ho hil - lo, hil - lo, hil - lo ho!   Ho hil - lo, hil - lo, hil - lo ho!

To play an ostinato on recorder,
you need a new tone—low C.

C

Ostinato (Recorder or Bells)

E

Listen for the sequences in these pieces for keyboard.

Handel: *Passepied*   Villa-Lobos: *Constante*

PHRASES • Lesson 6

MATERIALS
Record 10, "Oh, What a Beautiful City"; Pupil's Book, pp. 220 and 221; Autoharp, percussion instruments (optional)

VOCABULARY
phrase, phrase marking, strong cadence, weak cadence

IDEAS FOR TEACHING
1. Play the recording and have children follow the phrase markings on pp. 220 and 221 as they listen. Help them observe that in section A, there are four phrases—the first three equal in length, the last phrase longer. In section B, there are five phrases—the first four equal in length, the last phrase longer.

2. When children know the song, have them sing with the recording. Ask them to pay attention to the ending (cadence) of each phrase as they sing Remind them that phrases ending in a strong cadence have a "finished" sound; those ending in a weak cadence sound incomplete. Questions: Which phrases in section A end in a strong cadence? (They all do.) Which phrases in section B end in a weak cadence? (Phrases 1 and 3)

3. Have children take turns playing the Autoharp to accompany the class singing. Note: Players will use two chords, F and C$_7$. The chord names in the score tell when to change from one chord to the other. Suggestion: Children might strum a pattern of half notes (using two long strums per measure) during section A. Although the same strumming pattern can be continued throughout

→

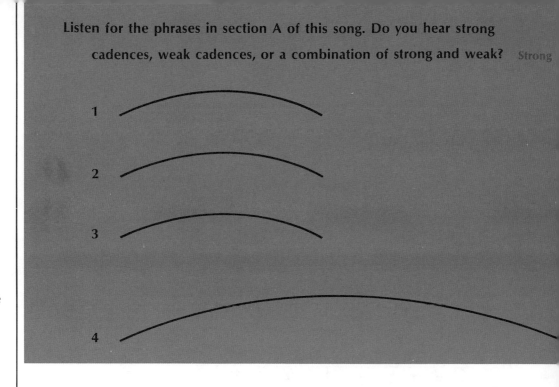

Listen for the phrases in section A of this song. Do you hear strong cadences, weak cadences, or a combination of strong and weak? Strong

1
2
3
4

OH, WHAT A BEAUTIFUL CITY
BLACK SPIRITUAL

(A) REFRAIN   Piano acc., p. 296   Orff-instrument acc., p. 340

Oh, what a beau - ti - ful cit - y, ____

Oh, what a beau - ti - ful cit - y, ____

Oh, what a beau - ti - ful cit - y, ____

Twelve gates - a to the cit - y, ____ Hal - le - lu - jah!

220 Phrases

TRY THIS
1. For item 4 of the lesson, divide the class into nine couples or small groups, one for each phrase of the song. Each couple (group) decides on a rhythm accompaniment for its phrase. Then as everyone sings, the couple (group) performs its accompaniment at the appropriate time.

2. From time to time have children make a diagram like the ones on pp. 220 and 221 to show the phrases in a song they know. Have them use short phrase markings for short phrases, longer ones for long phrases. Ask them to identify which phrases end in a weak cadence and which end in a

strong cadence. Mainstreaming Suggestion: Provide tactile reinforcement for children with visual or neurological impairment and for those who are mentally retarded by gluing sand, sparkles, or another textured material to the phrase markings in their diagram.

Listen for the combination of weak and strong cadences in section B.

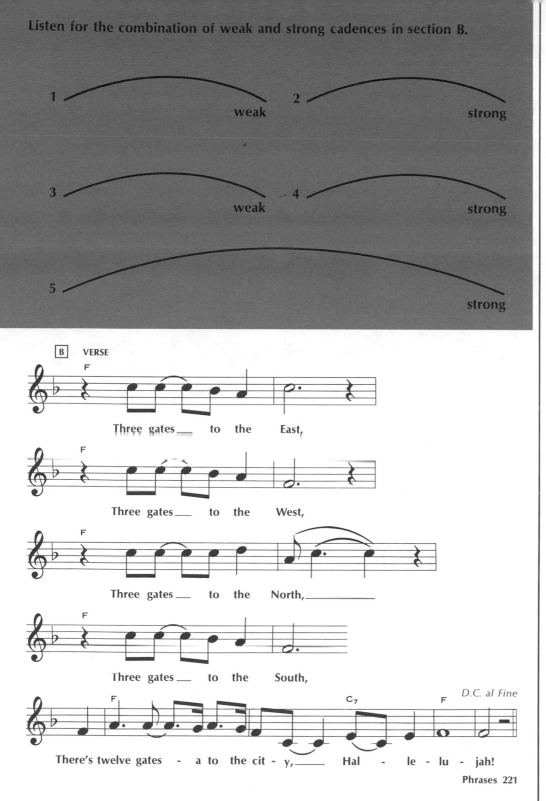

1 weak
2 strong
3 weak
4 strong
5 strong

B VERSE

Three gates___ to the East,

Three gates___ to the West,

Three gates___ to the North,_____

Three gates___ to the South,

There's twelve gates - a to the cit - y,___ Hal - le - lu - jah!

Phrases 221

the song, encourage children to use a different pattern during section B. Some children may wish to use a fancy strum in section B (e.g., playing short upward and downward strums in a syncopated rhythm such as ♪♩♪♩♪|♩♩♩ ‒ ‖) during the long sounds at the end of phrases 1–4.

4. Have children make up a rhythm accompaniment for "Oh, What a Beautiful City." They may use percussion instruments or natural sounds (clapping, snapping, stamping, etc.) or a combination of both. Encourage them to use one pattern of sound during section A, a different pattern during section B. Get them started by offering ideas such as the following:

- Perform a clapping pattern that uses sound and silence (see Rhythm Patterns, a, below).
- Alternate stamping and clapping (see Rhythm Patterns, b).
- Alternately strike and shake a tambourine (see c).
- Improvise a rhythm pattern during the long sounds in section B.

RHYTHM PATTERNS

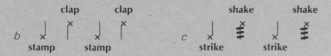

a clap clap

(Note: To keep the pattern steady, have children make a silent motion—e.g., separate the hands—for each rest.)

b clap clap stamp stamp c shake shake strike strike

PHRASES • Lesson 7

MATERIALS

Pupil's Book, pp. 222 and 223; Auto-harp, bells or other keyboard instrument, triangle, guiro, ruler or similar object (optional)

VOCABULARY

phrase, event, glissando, tremolo

IDEAS FOR TEACHING

<u>Note:</u> Each of the phrases on p. 222 contains several musical events. When each phrase is performed, the events should follow one another without pause.

Some of the events are pictured on p. 223—making all Autoharp strings sound, playing tremolo on bells and triangle, scraping notches on a guiro. Notice that to produce tremolo on the bells, children should use two mallets, one in each hand. When playing tremolo on bells or triangle, they should use a flexible wrist motion.

1. Give children time to look at the Autoharp phrase on p. 222 to discover the musical events that occur in it. <u>Point out:</u> Children can produce the sounds by using their hand to strike the low or high strings, by using their thumb and index finger to pluck one string, and by lightly dropping their forearm across the strings to make them all sound. <u>Note:</u> (a) Some children may prefer to use an object like a ruler to produce the sounds. Whatever they use, caution them always to treat the Autoharp strings gently. (b) It is not necessary for children to depress any chord buttons when playing the sounds for this phrase. $\longrightarrow$

Choose one of the phrases below. Play each event on the instrument named.

"Play" the phrase again, silently.

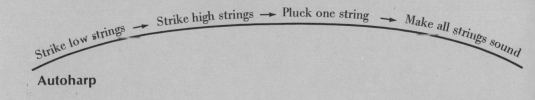

Autoharp

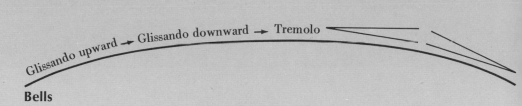

Bells

Glissando upward—Pull mallet across bells from lowest to highest.

Glissando downward—Pull mallet across bells from highest to lowest.

Tremolo—Play any two bells together, striking them

rapidly over and over.

Triangle

Tremolo—With beater inside triangle, use a circular

motion to strike the three sides over and over.

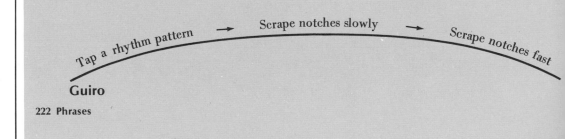

Guiro

222 **Phrases**

2. Direct attention to the bell part. (a) Have children read the definitions for *glissando* (glis-sahn'-doh) and *tremolo* (trem'-uh-loh) that are given with the phrase. Ask someone to demonstrate both techniques for the class. (b) Call attention to the symbols that follow the word *tremolo* in the phrase. Question: What should happen to the sound during the tremolo? (It should get louder, then softer.)

3. Have children look at the triangle part. (a) Help them observe that this phrase also uses tremolo, but that it is produced differently than the bell tremolo. Let individuals take turns trying to play a tremolo that gets louder, then softer. (b) Have children experiment to discover how to stop the sound of the triangle after striking it. (Taking hold of the instrument stops the vibration, thus stopping the sound.)

4. Discuss types of rhythm patterns that children might play on the guiro—patterns of long sounds, of short sounds; patterns that combine long and short sounds, with or without syncopation.

5. Have children each choose one of the phrases to practice two ways— (a) playing it aloud by producing the sounds on the appropriate instrument; (b) playing the phrase silently by going through the motions of producing the sounds. Note: Tell children that they may choose their own tempo, playing their phrase fast, slow, getting faster, or getting slower.

6. Have children extend their phrase into a composition by repeating it over and over—sometimes aloud, sometimes silently, sometimes fast, sometimes slow, etc. Give them an opportunity to perform for the class.

Phrases 223

TRY THIS
Assign each of four children to practice a different phrase on p. 222. Then have them put the phrases together for a composition. They may use the order of the phrases in their book, or they may rearrange the order, repeating phrases as they choose. Have them perform their composition for the class. If possible, tape-record the performance so that children can discuss it, replaying the tape as needed.

MODULE 21

OBJECTIVES, p. XIV

STYLE: Polynesian

MATERIALS
Record 10, *Ai a la o Pele; Tahitian Chant;* Record 9, "He mele o ke kahuli"; Pupil's Book, pp. 224–227, 215; gourd or ipu (or substitute)

VOCABULARY
Polynesian style, chant, ipu

IDEAS FOR TEACHING
1. Give children time to read the text and study the map on pp. 224 and 225. Suggestion: You might have children each choose one of the islands and find out three interesting things about it. Have them share their discoveries with the class.

2. Play the recording of *Ai a la o Pele,* an example of Polynesian music from Hawaii. Have children identify some of the musical qualities they hear. Note: The following qualities are present in the music:
- drum playing accented rhythms
- tone color of a woman's voice
- melody that has a narrow range
- many melody phrases that end with a long sound
- much repetition of melody phrases
- rhythm patterns repeated over and over on the drum
- short silences in the drum part near the middle of the song

Some children may notice the tone color of a woman's speaking voice before the singer begins, and at various times throughout the song. If children listen carefully, they will hear that the woman is a "prompter." →

STYLE: POLYNESIAN

Because people moved from island to island, the music of Polynesia spread from tribe to tribe. Look at the map to see the names of some of the islands. The people there sing and dance the stories and legends they love so well.

224 MODULE 21: Style—Polynesian

TEACHER INFORMATION
The map on pp. 224 and 225 shows the principal islands of the Polynesian group.

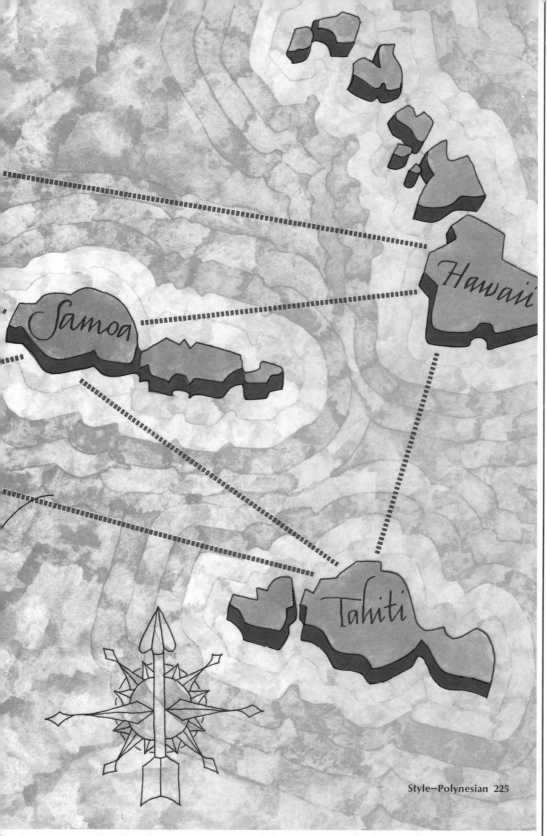

Style—Polynesian 225

She is cuing the singer by calling out the beginning words of the next phrase the singer will perform.

3. Play the recording of *Tahitian Chant,* an example of Polynesian music from Tahiti. Have children name some of the musical qualities they hear in this music. <u>Note:</u> There are three sections in the music, as follows:

Section 1—Combination singing and speaking performed as call and response.

Section 2—Begins with smoother melody, sung in "round" fashion: one group begins singing, another group sings the same melody, beginning one beat later. The two parts coming so close together in the round produce the effect of reverberation or echo. The round is followed by combination singing and speaking performed as call and response.

Section 3—Spoken chant with drum accompaniment; more rhythmic sound; accents.

Children should be able to hear some of the following qualities in the music:

- tone color of men's voices singing and speaking in a chantlike way
- call and response in the first two sections
- echo effect in the second section
- melody that has a narrow range
- phrases that end with a long sound
- steady beat in the final section
- simple rhythm in the drum accompaniment

4. Review the song "He mele o ke kahuli" on p. 215. As the girls perform the dance with the recording (see Teacher's Edition pp. 214 and 215 for directions), have the boys →

take turns playing the rhythm pattern on p. 226 as an accompaniment.
Note: If a gourd or ipu is not available, substitute a large, empty plastic bottle (e.g., the kind in which distilled water is sold).

TRY THIS

1. Have children locate the Polynesian Islands on other maps—on maps in geography texts, on wall maps, on a globe—to see them in relation to other areas of the world.

2. As part of a social studies unit dealing with the life and customs of the Polynesian people, suggest that interested children find some Polynesian folk tales in the library. They might share these with the class.

3. Children can play a rhythm accompaniment for *Ai a la o Pele* and *Tahitian Chant*. Have them choose pattern *a* or pattern *b* (see Rhythm Patterns below) for each song and play it on gourds, drums, or sticks.
Note: (a) For *Tahitian Chant,* children play only during the final section—when the drum is heard on the recording. (b) Some children may wish to use both patterns for each song, playing one pattern several times, then switching to the other pattern, alternating in this way throughout the piece.

Listen to these chants. The first is from Hawaii. The second is from Tahiti.

🔘 *Ai a la o Pele*

🔘 *Tahitian Chant*

You will find another Polynesian song on page 215 in your book. Play this rhythm pattern on a gourd or ipu as an accompaniment.

hit with heel of hand   hit with finger tips   heel   tip   tip

Polynesian music uses chant, rhythm, and movement to create a style of its own.

RHYTHM PATTERNS

Ai a la o Pele

Tahitian Chant

Style—Polynesian 227

The pictures on pp. 226 and 227 reflect the Polynesian characteristic of using things as they exist in nature. In the photograph on p. 226, the women are playing rhythm patterns on ipus, gourds that have been hollowed out. Ipus make a drumlike sound when struck or tapped. Note that the women are wearing costumes made from leaves and grass.

In the photograph on p. 227, the man is blowing into a conch, or large seashell. This produces a hollow, piercing sound. Good players can get a wide variety of sounds from this simple, natural instrument. Note that while the man's shirt is modern, it reflects the natural environment of colorful flowers. The man is not embarrassed to have a flower tucked behind his ear. It reflects local custom and is a well-accepted style. <u>Suggestion:</u> If children have a gourd or conch-like instrument at home, encourage them to bring it to school and demonstrate it for the class.

MODULE 22

OBJECTIVES, p. XV

TONALITY—ATONALITY • Lesson 1

MATERIALS
Record 10, *Reveille;* Pupil's Book, pp. 228 and 229; bells, trumpet or bugle (optional)

VOCABULARY
focus, no focus, tonal center, tonal, atonal

IDEAS FOR TEACHING
<u>Note:</u> In this module, children will learn that tones within an octave can be arranged to form scales. The primary emphasis will be on the *general sound* of each tonal organization.

1. Direct children's attention to the photographs on p. 228. Discuss the difference between them. <u>Note:</u> In one picture, everyone is reaching for the same apple. The apple is the center of interest. In the other picture, everyone has an apple. There is no focus on one particular person, object, or activity; there is no center of interest. <u>Suggestion:</u> Have children find <u>other pictures</u> that show a center of interest or no center of interest—in their textbooks, in magazines, in posters and art work displayed in the school.

2. Tell children that in music, many works have a center of interest, or focus. Some works have no center of interest, no focus.

3. Play the recording and ask children to raise their hand when they →

TONALITY—ATONALITY

228 MODULE 22: Tonality—Atonality

Listen to the bugle call *Reveille.* Try to hear how the music focuses on one important tone.

 Reveille

Now play *Reveille* on the bells D, G, B. As you play, feel the pull toward the tonal center, G.

REVEILLE

When you played *Reveille,* you used three different tones.

Now play a melody that uses twelve different tones.

Take the bells from C to B out of the box

and arrange them as follows:

A# A B C# D C D# F E F# G# G

Play the bells from left to right. Use any rhythm you choose.

Is there a pull toward a tonal center in this melody?

Is there a focus on one important tone?

Tonality—Atonality 229

think the bugle call is coming to an end. Question: How did you know the music was ending? Note: Through discussion, lead children to recognize that the music has a strong pull toward a tonal center— the final tone, G. Suggestion: Play the recording again and help children feel the pull toward G by having someone play the G bell on the final note.

4. Have children follow the notation on p. 229 to play *Reveille.* Someone may be able to play it on trumpet or bugle. Others can play it on the bells D, G, B. Have them line up the bells as shown in their book. Suggestion: Encourage children to sing the melody silently as they play. This will help them keep the rhythm. Point out: Music that has a strong pull to a tonal center is called tonal music.

5. Have children play a melody that has no tonal center. Ask them to line up the bells C, C#, D, D#, E, F, F#, G, G#, A, A#, B in the order of the row of letter names in their book. Then have them play the bells from left to right, using any rhythm they choose. Suggestion: Place the player where the class cannot see the bells, and ask children to raise their hand when they hear the melody coming to an end. Children will not be able to tell that the melody is ending from the sound alone. If anyone raises a hand, ask how he or she knew the melody was ending. Point out: It is difficult to tell when the melody is ending because it has no pull to a tonal center. Music that does not have a tonal center is called atonal music.

REVIEW/REINFORCEMENT
From time to time, give children an opportunity to review some of the songs they have learned. When they sing, call attention to the pull toward a tonal center at the end of the melody. Point out: Most of the songs they sing are tonal.

TONALITY—ATONALITY • Lesson 2

MATERIALS
Record 10, Purcell: *Fanfare;* Stravinsky: *Fanfare for Two Trumpets;* Record 6, "Joy to the World"; Record 5, "Hold On"; Pupil's Book, pp. 230 and 231, 139, 122; bells

VOCABULARY
tonal, atonal, tonal center, tonality, major scale, minor scale

IDEAS FOR TEACHING
1. Have children read the text on p. 230. Then play the recording of the Purcell and Stravinsky fanfares. <u>Note:</u> Remind children that tonal music has a strong pull to a tonal center; atonal music does not have this strong pull. <u>Questions:</u> Which fanfare is tonal? (The one by Purcell) Which one is atonal? (The one by Stravinsky)

2. Have children sing two songs they know—"Joy to the World" (p. 139) and "Hold On" (p. 122). Help them compare the songs as follows:
(a) By singing and listening to the recording, help children hear that both melodies have a strong pull toward a tonal center; they are both tonal.
(b) Have children look at the notation on p. 231. Lead them to recognize that the first two staffs show the ending of "Joy to the World" while the other staffs show the ending of "Hold On." <u>Point out:</u> Both songs have the same tonal center; they both end on D.
(c) Have children listen to the recording of the songs to discover that even though they both have the same tonal center, each song has a different general sound. →

Bugle calls and fanfares are often used to announce important events.

The first fanfare you will hear was used for many important ceremonies in England several hundred years ago.

The second one was used to open the New York State Theater at The Lincoln Center for the Performing Arts in New York City.

Which is tonal? Which is atonal?

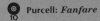 Purcell: *Fanfare*   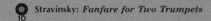 Stravinsky: *Fanfare for Two Trumpets*

TEACHER INFORMATION
The photograph on p. 230 shows the facade of the New York State Theater at Lincoln Center.

Here are the endings of two songs you know. They each have a pull toward a tonal center. Do they end on the same tone, or on different tones? Same

1.
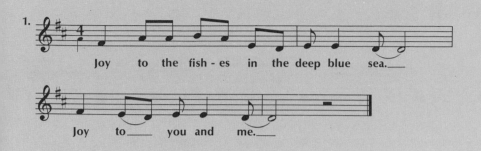

Joy to the fish- es in the deep blue sea.___

Joy to___ you and me.___

2.
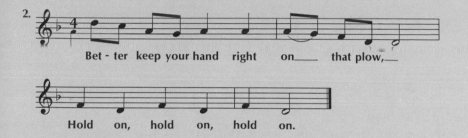

Bet - ter keep your hand right on___ that plow,___

Hold on, hold on, hold on.

Both songs are tonal. Both songs end on D. Yet each song has a different general sound or tonality.

"Joy to the World" has a major tonality.

"Hold On" has a minor tonality.

Each song uses a different arrangement of tones, or scale.

Play these major and minor scales on bells.

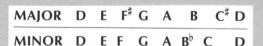

MAJOR	D E F♯ G A B C♯ D
MINOR	D E F G A B♭ C D

Tonality—Atonality 231

Point out: In music, melodies are based on arrangements of tones called scales. There are many kinds of scales. "Joy to the World" and "Hold On" sound different because each is based on a different kind of scale.

3. Have children line up the bells for the D major scale as shown next to the word *major* on p. 231. Ask someone to play the bells in order from left to right (upward) and from right to left (downward). Then have children sing or hum the beginning of "Joy to the World" to hear that the melody uses the tones of the major scale; it has a major tonality.

4. Have children line up the bells for the D minor scale as shown next to the word *minor*. After playing the scale, have children sing or hum the beginning of "Hold On" to hear that the melody uses the tones of the minor scale; it has a minor tonality.

5. Have children sing some of the following songs to determine whether the melody is based on a major scale or a minor scale. Note: All the "major" songs listed are in the key of D major; all the "minor" songs are in D minor. If necessary, play the D major and D minor scales to help children identify the tonality for each song.
Major
• Dayenu, p. 40
• Ging Gong Gooli, p. 18
• In Bahia Town, p. 80
• Louis Moved Away, p. 56

Minor
• Don Gato, p. 164
• Dundai, p. 90
• Evening, p. 189
• Rally Song, p. 120

TRY THIS
Play the following chord progressions on the Autoharp and have children identify the tonality of each one as major or minor.

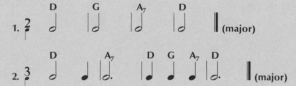

Tonality—Atonality · Lesson 2 · 231

MATERIALS
Record 10, "Chanukah Song"; Pupil's Book, p. 232; tambourine

VOCABULARY
tonal, atonal, major tonality, minor tonality, syncopation

IDEAS FOR TEACHING

1. Play the recording as children follow the notation on p. 232. Have them find the phrase in "Chanukah Song" that uses syncopation (the phrase that begins section B—*But hush now* and *come now*).

2. When children know the song, have individuals take turns playing a tambourine accompaniment as others sing. Players may use a rhythm pattern from the song, or a pattern that they create. Note: (a) If children play a pattern from the song, have them think the words of the pattern over and over as they play. This will help them keep the rhythm. (b) See Rhythm Patterns (below) for song patterns children might use.

3. Have a group of children dance a simple hora as others sing and play the tambourine with the recording (see Try This, Teacher's Edition p. 185, for directions).

4. Direct children's attention to the melody of "Chanukah Song." Questions: Does the song have a melody that is tonal, or atonal? (Tonal) Is the tonality major or minor? (Minor) Note: If children have difficulty identifying the tonality as minor, have them play the D major and D minor scales (diagrams, p. 231) to find the one that matches the general sound of "Chanukah Song."

As you sing "Chanukah Song," decide whether the tonality is major or minor.

CHANUKAH SONG
HASIDIC FOLK SONG   ENGLISH WORDS BY ALICE FIRGAU

232 Tonality—Atonality

RHYTHM PATTERNS

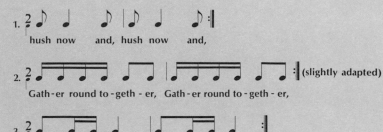

TRY THIS
Some children may be able to sing the harmony part as others sing the melody of "Chanukah Song." Point out: (a) Except for the first measure, the harmony follows the contour of the melody, but is sung an interval of a third lower. (b) Voices sing in unison at the beginning of section B.

WHAT DO YOU HEAR? 18: TONALITY—ATONALITY 🔴

Listen to the recording. Each time a number is called, choose the

word that describes the tonality. Is the music tonal, or atonal?

Listen. Then choose your answer.

---

1. (TONAL) ATONAL Prokofiev: *Classical Symphony*, "Gavotte"

---

2. TONAL (ATONAL) Webern: *Five Movements for String Quartet*

---

3. TONAL (ATONAL) Stravinsky: *Fanfare for Two Trumpets*

---

4. (TONAL) ATONAL Beethoven: *Symphony No. 9*

---

5. (TONAL) ATONAL Purcell: *Fanfare*

---

6. (TONAL) ATONAL Mozart: *Symphony No. 40*

Tonality—Atonality 233

TONALITY—ATONALITY • Lesson 4

MATERIALS
Record 10, *What Do You Hear? 18: Tonality—Atonality*; spirit master

VOCABULARY
tonal, atonal

TEACHER INFORMATION
Suggestion: Provide a challenge for children who are ready. Make the recording available so that they can listen to *What Do You Hear? 18* again, on their own, and try to identify whether each tonal excerpt is major or minor.
Answers: 1. major
          4. major
          5. major
          6. minor

MATERIALS

Record 8, "The Frog in the Well";
Record 9, "Harvesting Tea"; Record
10, "An Iroquois Lullaby"; Pupil's
Book, pp. 234, 178, 216; bells, recorders (or bells)

VOCABULARY

tonality, major, pentatonic

IDEAS FOR TEACHING

1. Have children look at the two
scale arrangements on p. 234.
Questions: How are the scales alike?
(They begin and end on G.) How are
they different? (One scale has seven
different tones, the other has only
five.)

2. Have children arrange the bells in
the order of the G major scale, and
play them upward and downward to
hear the sound of major tonality.
Then have them remove the bells C
and F♯ and play the remaining bells
to hear the sound of a pentatonic
scale. Point out: A pentatonic scale
is made up of five different tones
arranged in a specific pattern, giving
it its own special sound.

3. Have children sing "The Frog in
the Well" (major, p. 178) and "Harvesting Tea" (pentatonic, p. 216) with
the recording to hear the difference
in songs based on two different
kinds of scales.

4. Play the recording of "An Iroquois
Lullaby." Question: Is the tonality
major, like "The Frog in the Well," or
pentatonic, like "Harvesting Tea"?
(Pentatonic)

5. When children know "An Iroquois
Lullaby" (p. 234) have them sing it
with the recording while individuals
play the melody on recorder or bells.

There can be many arrangements of tones within an octave.

Play the major scale starting on G. Then play the pentatonic scale.

| MAJOR | G A B C D E F♯ G |
| PENTATONIC | G A B D E G |

Here are two songs that you know. Sing them to hear which matches the general sound of the major scale and which matches the general sound of the pentatonic scale.

"The Frog in the Well," p. 178

"Harvesting Tea," p. 216

Play this pentatonic melody on recorder or bells.

You will need these five tones.

Practice them before you play.

D E G A B

AN IROQUOIS LULLABY

IROQUOIS INDIAN SONG

FROM CANADA'S STORY IN SONG BY EDITH FOWKE AND ALAN MILLS. © GAGE PUBLISHING 1965. REPRINTED BY PERMISSION.

Ho, ho,___ wa - ta - nay, Ho, ho,___ wa - ta - nay,

Ho, ho,___ wa - ta - nay, Ki - yo - ke - na, ki - yo - ke - na.

234 Tonality—Atonality

REVIEW/REINFORCEMENT

Take time to have children sing other pentatonic songs
they know; for example:
• Harvest Time, p. 59
• Muje Mukesin, p. 207

TRY THIS

Using two sets of bells, or two xylophones with the appropriate bars marked with tape, have children play the D
major scale (diagram, p. 231), then the G major scale (diagram, p. 234). Point out: Although one scale is at a higher
pitch level than the other, both scales have the same general sound—the sound of major tonality.

This song from China is sung at New Year's celebrations.

The melody is based on the pentatonic scale. Sing it or play

it on recorder or bells. You will need these five tones.

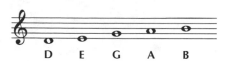

D   E   G   A   B

COLORFUL BOATS

FOLK SONG FROM CHINA   ENGLISH VERSION BY CAROL KERR

COPYRIGHT © 1979, WILLIAM M. ANDERSON. USED BY PERMISSION.   Piano acc., p. 254

Tsai lung chuan yia me yia wei yao,
See the bright col-ored har-bor boats,

Lai da mang yao___ yia he hei,
Dec-o-rat-ed for fes-ti-val,

Lai dau tze li bien yia wei tze yao,
Come to watch as they dance on the waves;

Lai bai nien yao hua tze,
Cel-e-brate the New Year,

Yai he hai hai yao he hei,
Sing to-geth-er, sing with joy,

Lai bai nien yao hua tze.
Cel-e-brate the New Year.

Tonality—Atonality 235

TONALITY—ATONALITY · Lesson 6

MATERIALS
Record 10, "Colorful Boats"; Pupil's Book, p. 235; recorders or bells

VOCABULARY
major, pentatonic, phrase, dotted rhythm

IDEAS FOR TEACHING
1. Play the recording of "Colorful Boats" and have children try to identify the general sound as major or pentatonic. (Pentatonic) Suggestion: If children have difficulty, have them play the major and pentatonic scales shown on p. 234 to discover which one matches the general sound of the melody. Point out: "Colorful Boats" is a New Year's song from China. Many Oriental melodies are based on the pentatonic scale.

2. Play the recording again as children follow the notation on p. 235. Help them analyze the melody to make it easier to learn. Questions: How many phrases are in the song? (Six) Which two phrases are exactly alike? (4, 6) Which two phrases are the same for the first measure, different for the second measure? (1, 2) Which phrase has a dotted rhythm at the beginning? (5) Which phrases have a dotted rhythm at the end? (1, 2)

3. When children are ready, have them sing with the recording. Suggestion: Choose five children and assign each a phrase of the music to learn to play on recorder or bells. Then, as the class sings, have each child play at the appropriate time. Note: The child assigned phrase 4 will play twice—after phrase 3 and after phrase 5.

TEACHER INFORMATION
The Chinese verse of "Colorful Boats" is pronounced as follows:

Tsai lung chuan yia me yia wei yao,
tsī long ch'ahn yah may yah way yah-oh

Lai da mang yao yia he hei,
lī dah-oh mang yah-oh yah huh hay

Lai dau tze li bien yia wei tze yao,
lī dah-oh tsoo lee ben yah way tsoo yah-oh

Lai bai nien yao hua tze,
lī bī nen yah-oh hwah tsoo

Yai he hai hai yao he hei,
yī huh hī hī yah-oh huh hay

Lai bai nien yao hua tze.
lī bī nen yah-oh hwah tsoo

TONALITY—ATONALITY • Lesson 7

MATERIALS
Pupil's Book, p. 236; bells

VOCABULARY
major scale, whole-tone scale

IDEAS FOR TEACHING

1. Choose someone to arrange the bells in the order of the C major scale as shown on p. 236. Then have individuals play the scale in an upward direction and in a downward direction. <u>Point out:</u> This scale has the same sound as the other major scales children have played—D (p. 231), G (p. 234)—but it begins at a different pitch level.

2. Have someone arrange the bells in the order of a whole-tone scale beginning on C as shown on p. 236. Then have individuals play the scale upward and downward. <u>Point out:</u> This scale begins like the major scale, but then changes so that the total sound is different from any of the other scales children have played—major, minor, or pentatonic.

3. Encourage individuals to learn to play "Frère Jacques" two ways— using the tones of the major scale, and using the tones of the whole-tone scale. The notation on p. 236 will help them. When they are ready, have them perform for the class. <u>Note:</u> Children will need to add the lowest G bell to the major scale and the lowest G# bell to the whole-tone scale in order to play the last phrase of the "Frère Jacques" melody. <u>Point out:</u> A melody that is based on the tones of the major scale has a different sound when played using the tones of the whole-tone scale. Each scale has its own special sound.

Look at these scale diagrams. Notice how they are alike and how they are different. Then play the scales on bells.

MAJOR	C D E F G A B C
WHOLE TONE	C D E F# G# A# C

Play "Frère Jacques" as a major melody, using the tones of the major scale.

FRERE JACQUES (Major)

Now play "Frère Jacques" as a whole-tone melody, using the tones of the whole-tone scale.

FRERE JACQUES (Whole Tone)

Each scale has a different general sound. A melody has the same general sound as the scale it is based on.

236 Tonality—Atonality

TRY THIS
Have children arrange the bells in the order of the C minor scale as follows: C   D   Eb   F   G   Ab   Bb   C
<u>Point out:</u> This scale has the same sound as the D minor scale (p. 231), but it begins at a different pitch level. Then have children add the lowest G bell and play "Frère Jacques" with the tones of the minor scale as follows.
(<u>Note:</u> This activity reinforces the concept that each scale—major, minor, whole tone—has its own special sound, and that the general sound of a melody depends upon the kind of scale it is based on.)

Frère Jacques (Minor)

Listen to this song. Is the melody based on a major scale, or a

whole-tone scale? Whole-tone scale

ND OF SUMMER MUSIC BY DAVID EDDLEMAN WORDS BY SUZANNE SCHMITT

Piano acc., p. 264

Swim-ming,___ Build-ing cas-tles Out___ of sand___ at the shore.

Till the tide comes wash-ing a-way Sum-mer,___

Sum-mer,___ Sum - mer.___

The lyrics of "End of Summer" form a five-line poem called a

cinquain. The lines of a cinquain follow this pattern of

syllables: 2-4-6-8-2.

END OF SUMMER

Swimming, (2)

Building castles (4)

Out of sand at the shore. (6)

Till the tide comes washing away (8)

Summer. (2)

Suzanne Schmitt

Make up your own whole-tone melody for the poem.

TONALITY—ATONALITY • Lesson 8

MATERIALS
Record 10, "End of Summer"; Pupil's Book, pp. 236 and 237; bells

VOCABULARY
whole-tone scale, cinquain

IDEAS FOR TEACHING
1. Take time for children to review the general sound of the major and whole-tone scales by playing each one on the bells, beginning on C (diagrams, p. 236).

2. Play the recording of "End of Summer." Question: Does this melody have the same general sound as the major scale, or the whole-tone scale? (Whole-tone scale)

3. Call attention to the lyrics of "End of Summer" in the notation on p. 237. Point out: The lyrics are written in the style of poetry called cinquain (sing-kayn'). Note: A cinquain is an unrhymed poem of five lines, with each line having a specified number of syllables—2, 4, 6, 8, 2.

4. Help children find the cinquain syllable pattern in the poem "End of Summer."

5. Encourage children to make up their own whole-tone melody for the cinquain "End of Summer." Have them refer to the scale diagram on p. 236 to know which tones to use. Suggestion: Allow children to experiment with the bells or at the piano during free time. When they are ready, have them perform their melodies for one another.

TRY THIS
1. Some children may wish to write their own poem in the form of a cinquain and create a melody for it based on the whole-tone scale.

2. Encourage children to learn to sing "End of Summer." When they know the song, have them compare it with a song based on a major scale, for example, "The Frog in the Well" (p. 178). Discuss how it feels to sing each kind of tonality.

MODULE 23

OBJECTIVES, p. XV

THE ARTS: Focus, No Focus

MATERIALS
Record 10, Webern: *Five Movements for String Quartet,* Op. 5, No. 3; Mozart: *Divertimento in D,* "Marcia"; Pupil's Book, pp. 238 and 239; flashlights

VOCABULARY
focus, no focus; center of interest, tonal, atonal, tonal center

IDEAS FOR TEACHING
1. To illustrate the concept of focus, no focus, have children experiment with flashlights as follows. A selected number of children stand anywhere in the room, each holding a flashlight. Each child moves his or her flashlight in a predetermined phrase of eight beats, then moves the light a different way for another phrase of eight beats. The children continue until they have each traced five phrases with their flashlights. The movements may be long or short; they may be high, focusing the light on the ceiling, or low, focusing on the floor. Lead others to see that as the children move, the lights move in many parts of the room. There is no one focus. Then have children experiment to find ways to give focus to the lights. One way is to designate a spot in the room where the children will all flash their lights at the beginning and end of each phrase. Another way is to have the children walk forward and backward, each flashing his or her light on the same center of interest. ⟶

THE ARTS: FOCUS, NO FOCUS

In some paintings your eyes travel to one important place—a center of interest, or focus.

Which of these paintings has such a focus? Which has not?

Georgia O'Keeffe. THE WHITE FLOWER. (1931.) Oil on canvas. 30 x 36 inches. Collection of the Whitney Museum of American Art.

238 MODULE 23: Focus, No Focus

TEACHER INFORMATION
Georgia O'Keeffe (American, 1887-   ) *The White Flower:* The paintings of this artist often emphasize enlarged details of flowers or dried bones or western barns or churches—like closeup camera photographs. The attention to detail in this painting gives the flower a lifelike quality.

James Brooks (American, 1906-   ) *Tondo:* Tondo is a term for paintings or sculptured reliefs in oval or circular form. This artist often uses it for his colorful, active paintings that combine improvisation with control.

Anton Webern (Austrian, 1883–1945) *Five Movements for String Quartet,* No. 3: Webern composed music of great concentration in which a profound sense of expression was contained in brief moments of sound. However "difficult" for the ear, his works have a compelling effect on the listener willing to become absorbed in their tiny world.

For biographical information about Mozart, see Teacher's Edition p. 66 (Teacher Information).

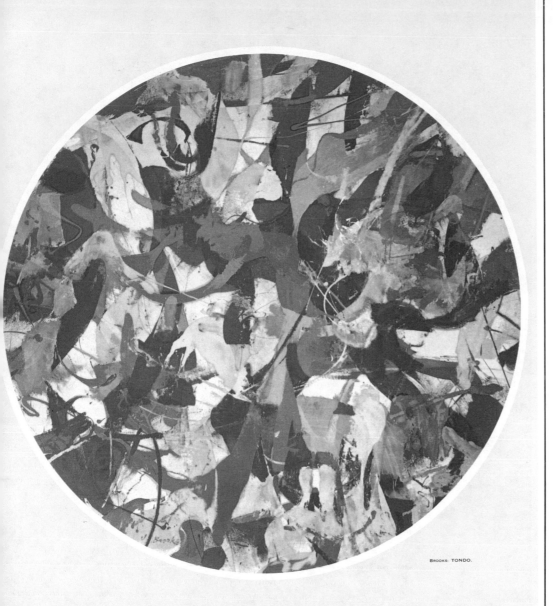

BROOKS: TONDO.

In some music your ears hear one tone as most important (tonal music).

The music comes to rest on that tone.

Some music does not have a tonal center (atonal music).

Listen to these pieces. Which is tonal? Which is atonal?

🔊 Webern: *Five Movements for String Quartet*   🔊 Mozart: *Divertimento in D*
10   10

Focus, No Focus 239

---

2. Give children time to look at the paintings on pp. 238 and 239. <u>Questions</u>: Which painting seems to draw your eyes to one important spot, to a center of interest? Which painting does not? <u>Note</u>: Help children discover that *The White Flower* has a strong focal point in the center, where the stamens, with their oval anthers and stemlike filaments, are highly textured and intensely white. The outer petals merely form an encircling background with no one strong point calling attention to itself. The painting *Tondo* (a term for any round painting) is spread evenly all over. No area of color or shape or line dominates. The eye travels over the painting without centering on any one focal point.

3. Play the recording of the Webern and Mozart pieces. <u>Questions</u>: Which piece has a tonal center, an important tone that the music comes to rest on? Which piece is atonal, with no one important tone toward which the other tones move? (The Mozart is tonal; the Webern, atonal.)

REVIEW/REINFORCEMENT
1. Play other recorded music from Book 4 for children to identify as tonal or atonal; for example:
• Babbitt: *Ensembles for Synthesizer,* p. 84 (atonal)
• Copland: *Billy the Kid,* p. 84 (tonal)
• Mozart: *String Quartet in D Minor,* p. 178 (tonal)
• Stravinsky: *Fanfare for Two Trumpets,* p. 230 (atonal)
• Varèse: *Poème électronique,* p. 202 (atonal)

2. Have children compare the Rose Window on p. 94 with the painting on pp. 156 and 157 to determine which has a strong center of interest (The Rose Window, with its center circle from which the rest of the window radiates).

TRY THIS
Have a small group of children perform movement activities that focus on a center of interest; for example:
(a) Children form a circle with one child in the center. While children in the circle perform one pattern of movement, the child in the center (the focal point) performs a different pattern.
(b) Children each find a space in the room. As one child (the center of interest) performs a fast, active movement, everyone else performs a slow, quiet movement. <u>Note</u>: The "active" child may move about among the "quiet" children. He or she will still be the center of interest.

MODULE 24

OBJECTIVES, p. XV

TEXTURE • Lesson 1

MATERIALS
Record 10, *Call Chart 9: Texture*; Pupil's Book, pp. 240 and 241

VOCABULARY
texture, melody alone, melody with countermelody, melody with chords, melody performed as a round

IDEAS FOR TEACHING
1. Call attention to the photograph of children wearing knitted garments on p. 240. <u>Point out:</u> In each garment, strands of yarn are knitted together to create a special look and feel called texture.

2. Take time to talk about the texture of the clothing children in the class are wearing—knitted textures, and woven textures in cotton, corduroy, wool, synthetic fabrics, etc. <u>Point out:</u> The way the threads are intertwined gives each fabric its own special texture. <u>Suggestion:</u> Have children bring in articles from home that illustrate various ways materials are woven or joined to create different textures— potholders children may have made, baskets, netting, examples of macrame, etc. <u>Mainstreaming Suggestion:</u> Pass around the articles so that children with visual and motor impairments can feel the similarities and differences in texture.

3. Tell children that just as threads and yarns are used to create texture in clothing, melodies and chords are used to create texture in music. →

TEXTURE

240 MODULE 24: Texture

CALL CHART 9: TEXTURE

Listen for the different textures in some music you know.

The chart will help you hear them.

1. MELODY ALONE

Amazing Grace

2. MELODY WITH COUNTERMELODY

Michael Finnegan

3. MELODY WITH CHORDS

Me and My Brother, Oliver Lee

4. MELODY SUNG AS A ROUND

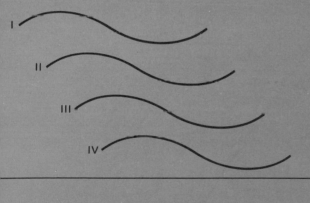

Up the Street the Band Is Marching Down

Texture 241

Point out: In clothing we see texture; in music we hear it.

4. Play the recording of *Call Chart 9* and have children listen to hear whether the texture is the same for all the examples, or different for each one (different). Note: Children have already experienced a variety of textures through playing, singing, and listening: melody alone, melody with countermelody, melody with chords, melody performed as a round. Even though call charts are intended to be directed listening experiences, encourage children to try to identify some of the specific textures they hear before they look at the chart (p. 241). Then have them check their answers by following the chart as they listen to the recording again. The words and symbols beside each number indicate the texture children are hearing.

TRY THIS

Assign groups of children to select a song they know and prepare a performance of it that illustrates any one of these textures:
- melody alone
- melody with countermelody
- melody with chords
- melody performed as a round

Over a period of time, have each group perform for the class. Ask the class to identify the texture they hear.

Suggestion: Take time to discuss the elements that make up the texture for each performance—e.g., vocal melody with countermelody played on bells, or three different voice parts sounding together in a round.

MATERIALS

Record 10, "This Land Is Your Land"; Pupil's Book, pp. 242 and 243; Autoharp

VOCABULARY

texture, melody alone, melody with countermelody, melody with chords

IDEAS FOR TEACHING

1. Have children look at the notation on p. 242. <u>Point out:</u> "This Land Is Your Land" has two sections—refrain and verses. Then ask children to listen for each section on the recording. Questions: How are the refrain and verses alike? (They use the same melody.) How are they different? (Each verse uses different words.) Invite children to join in singing the melody when they can.

2. Give some children time to practice the Autoharp part for "This Land Is Your Land." They will play the chords F, C_7, B^b. The letter names in the score tell when to change from one chord to another. Players may use the strumming pattern shown on p. 243, or a pattern that they create. When they are ready, have them play the Autoharp to accompany the class singing. <u>Note:</u> Players begin strumming on the first strong beat, on the word *your.*

3. When children know the melody, have them follow the notation on p. 243 to sing the countermelody with the recording. <u>Note:</u> On the recording, the countermelody is sung with the refrain after verses 2 and 3. <u>Mainstreaming Suggestion:</u> Have less capable children sing the melody of the refrain. ⟶

Use different textures when you perform "This Land Is Your Land."

1. Sing the melody alone.

THIS LAND IS YOUR LAND

WORDS AND MUSIC BY WOODY GUTHRIE COUNTERMELODY BY RUTH TUTELM

TRO—© COPYRIGHT 1956, 1958, & 1970 LUDLOW MUSIC, INC. NEW YORK, N.Y. USED BY PERMISSION. Piano acc., p. 317

242 Texture

TEACHER INFORMATION

<u>Mainstreaming Note:</u> An adaptation for "This Land Is Your Land" appears in *Silver Burdett Music for Special Education.*

2. I've roamed and rambled and I followed my footsteps
   To the sparkling sands of her diamond deserts,
   And all around me a voice was sounding,
   "This land was made for you and me." *Refrain*

3. When the sun comes shining and I was strolling
   And the wheatfields waving and the dust clouds rolling,
   As the fog was lifting a voice was chanting,
   "This land was made for you and me." *Refrain*

4. Have children plan a performance of "This Land Is Your Land" that includes these textures:
- melody alone
- melody with chords
- melody with countermelody

Note: Children may wish also to combine textures by continuing to play the Autoharp chords when the melody and countermelody are sung together.

2. Sing the melody with Autoharp accompaniment.

3. Add this countermelody when you sing the refrain.

COUNTERMELODY (Refrain)

This land is your land, this land is mine,

From Maine to Mon - ta - na, des - ert to the shore,

We sing that this land is your land, this land is mine,

Yes, it's made for you and me. _____

Texture 243

TRY THIS
Have small groups each choose one of the following songs and plan a performance that includes as many textures as possible (melody alone, melody with countermelody, melody with chords, melody performed as a round). When the groups perform, have the class identify each texture they hear.
- Evening, p. 189
- Hear the Rooster, p. 10
- I Love the Mountains, p. 60
- Joy to the World, p. 139
- Michael Finnegan, p. 30
- Sandy McNab, p. 9
- When Is a Door, p. 9
- When the Saints Go Marching In, p. 58

MATERIALS
Record 10, "The Ghost of John";
Pupil's Book, p. 244; bells or record-
ers

VOCABULARY
texture, density, thin, thick

IDEAS FOR TEACHING
1. Have children follow the notation
on p. 244 as they listen to the recording. Questions: Which staff begins with a long sound? (Staff 3)
Which staff begins with sets of repeated tones that move downward? (4)

2. When children know the song,
have them sing it as a round. Note:
Begin with a two-part round, increas-
ing to three and four parts only
when children are ready.

3. Call attention to the diagrams
below the notation on p. 244.
Point out: (a) When children sing
the melody alone, there is only one
sound at a time; the density of the
music is thin. (b) When they sing a
two-part round, there are two different sounds at once; the density is
thicker. (c) The density of the round
becomes thicker still when three,
then four different sounds occur together. Note: Be certain that children
do not confuse density with loudness. The density of music is thin or
thick depending upon the number of
different *parts* that occur simultaneously, not on the number of singers
or players performing each part.

4. Have children increase the density
by adding the parts for bells or recorder when they sing "The Ghost of
John." The more vocal and instrumental parts they perform together,
the thicker the density will be.

When you know this song, sing it as a round. This will make the density of the music thicker. For an even thicker density, add the parts for bells or recorder to your singing.

THE GHOST OF JOHN — WORDS AND MUSIC BY MARTHA GRUBB

I
Have you seen the ghost of John?

II
Long white bones with the skin all gone,___

III
Oo, oo,___

IV
Would - n't it be chil - ly with no skin on!

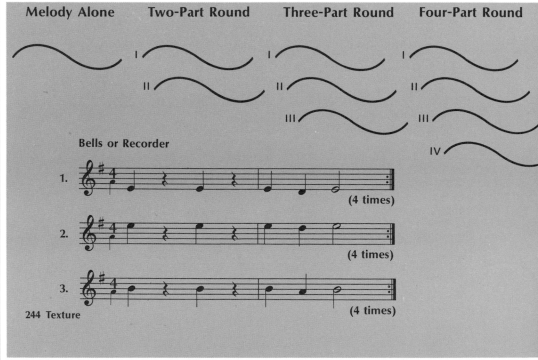

Melody Alone   Two-Part Round   Three-Part Round   Four-Part Round

Bells or Recorder
1. (4 times)
2. (4 times)
3. (4 times)

244 Texture

TRY THIS
Children can show texture through movement. Have them
practice the following movements to perform with "The
Ghost of John."
Phrase 1 (8 beats): Take four slow steps forward, crouching
lower with every step (each step lasts
two beats).
Phrase 2 (8 beats): Take four slow steps backward, gradually rising again to full height (each
step lasts two beats).
Phrase 3 (8 beats): Circle around in place, stepping the
steady beat (eight steps).

Phrase 4 (8 beats): Stand in place, shivering and shaking to
illustrate the words of the phrase.
When they know the movements, have some children perform them as a movement round while everyone else sings
with the round on the recording. Note: Give all children
an opportunity to participate in the movement activity as
well as to observe it. Point out: In music we hear texture;
in movement we see it.

TEACHER INFORMATION
Mainstreaming Note: An adaptation for "The Ghost of
John" appears in *Silver Burdett Music for Special Educa-
tion.*

erform this song using various textures. Is the density thin, or thick?

ALM OF THANKSGIVING
DAKOTA INDIAN HYMN   MUSICAL SETTING BY CARLTON YOUNG

ENGLISH WORDS BY PHILIP FRAZIER

COPYRIGHT © 1975 BY HOPE PUBLISHING CO. ALL RIGHTS RESERVED. USED BY PERMISSION.   Piano acc., p. 301

1. Man - y and great, O God, are Thy things, Mak - er of
2. Grant un - to us com - mu - nion with Thee, Thou star - a -

earth and sky;___ Thy hands have set the heav - ens with stars;
bid - ing One;___ Come un - to us and dwell with___ us

Thy fin - gers spread the moun - tains and plains.___ Lo, at Thy
With Thee are found the gifts of___ life.___ Bless us with

word the wa - ters were formed; Deep seas o - bey Thy voice.
life that has no___ end, E - ter - nal life with Thee.

ecorder

(6 times)

utoharp Drone (to be plucked an octave lower)

Texture 245

MATERIALS
Record 10, "Psalm of Thanksgiving"; Stravinsky: *Fanfare for Two Trumpets;* Record 8, M. Franck: *Intrada II;* Pupil's Book, p. 245; recorders or bells, Autoharp

VOCABULARY
texture, density

IDEAS FOR TEACHING

1. Have children look at the notation on p. 245. Help them observe that the melody uses many repeated tones, steps, and small leaps.

2. Play the recording of "Psalm of Thanksgiving" and have children follow the notation to find the place where there is an octave leap from a low tone to a high tone (staff 2—from low C to high C, measures 4 to 5).

3. When children know the melody, have them perform it as follows:
• melody alone
• melody with recorder counter-melody
• melody with Autoharp drone
Question: Which texture has the thinnest density? (Melody alone)
Suggestion: To experience the sound of the thickest density possible with the elements on p. 245, have children sing the melody with recorder and Autoharp parts played together.

4. Play the recordings of the Stravinsky and Franck works. Questions: Which piece has thin density throughout? In which one is the density sometimes thin, sometimes thick? (*Fanfare for Two Trumpets* has thin density throughout; *Intrada II* uses both thin and thick density.)
Point out: In *Intrada II,* children can hear thick density at both loud and soft dynamic levels.

MATERIALS

Record 10, "He's Got the Whole World in His Hands"; Pupil's Book, p. 246; Autoharp

VOCABULARY

texture

IDEAS FOR TEACHING

1. Play the recording and have children join in singing when they can (notation, p. 246).

2. Have children experience texture two ways: (a) by singing the melody alone; (b) by performing the melody with Autoharp chords. Note: Have as many children as possible play the Autoharp accompaniment. It uses only two chords, F and C₇. Children may use the strumming pattern on p. 246—playing long strums for the half notes (♩), short strums for the quarter notes (♩)—or a pattern that they create. Point out: Players begin strumming on the first strong beat, on the word *whole*.

3. Have children use what they know about music to observe the following in "He's Got the Whole World in His Hands":

• The song has four phrases, all the same length.

• Phrases 1 and 3 have the same melody.

• Phrases 1, 2, and 3 have the same rhythm.

• In each phrase there is syncopation on the words *in his hands*.

• The song has a range of six tones, from F to high D.

• The song uses mostly repeated tones and small leaps, all of which have tones that are an interval of a third apart.

Perform this song two ways: 1. **as a melody alone**

2. **as a melody with chords**

HE'S GOT THE WHOLE WORLD IN HIS HANDS

BLACK SPIRITUAL   Piano acc., p. 273   Orff-instrument acc., p. 343

1. He's got the whole world ____ in his hands, ____
2. He's got the wind and rain ____ in his hands, ____
3. He's got both you and me ____ in his hands, ____

He's got the whole world ____ in his hands, ____
He's got the wind and rain ____ in his hands, ____
He's got both you and me ____ in his hands, ____

He's got the whole world ____ in his hands, ____
He's got the wind and rain ____ in his hands, ____
He's got both you and me ____ in his hands, ____

He's got the whole world in his hands. ____
He's got the whole world in his hands. ____
He's got the whole world in his hands. ____

Autoharp

246 Texture

TEACHER INFORMATION

Encourage children to be aware of as many qualities as possible in music that they perform or listen to. The more they are aware of musical qualities, the more they will be able to react to them.

en to this music. Sometimes you will hear a melody with guitar accompaniment. The density of the sound will be thin. Sometimes you will hear a vocal or instrumental countermelody along with the melody and accompaniment. The density of the sound will be thicker. Each time a number is called, choose the answer that describes the texture you hear.

Makem: *Winds of Morning*

(MELODY WITH ACCOMPANIMENT)   COUNTERMELODY ADDED
THIN DENSITY   THICKER DENSITY

MELODY WITH ACCOMPANIMENT   (COUNTERMELODY ADDED
THIN DENSITY   THICKER DENSITY)

(MELODY WITH ACCOMPANIMENT)   COUNTERMELODY ADDED
THIN DENSITY   THICKER DENSITY

MELODY WITH ACCOMPANIMENT   (COUNTERMELODY ADDED
THIN DENSITY   THICKER DENSITY)

MELODY WITH ACCOMPANIMENT   (COUNTERMELODY ADDED
THIN DENSITY   THICKER DENSITY)

MELODY WITH ACCOMPANIMENT   (COUNTERMELODY ADDED
THIN DENSITY   THICKER DENSITY)

Texture 247

TEXTURE • Lesson 6

MATERIALS
Record 10, *What Do You Hear? 19: Texture*; spirit master

VOCABULARY
texture, thin density, thicker density

TEACHER INFORMATION
Suggestion: Give children an opportunity to listen to the recording again, outside of the What Do You Hear? experience. Have them identify the kind of countermelody they hear for numbers 2, 4, 5, and 6—vocal, or instrumental. (Numbers 2, 4, and 6 have a vocal countermelody; number 5, an instrumental countermelody.)
Point out: The density of the sound is thicker at numbers 2, 4, 5, and 6 because another part—a countermelody—has been added to the original melody and accompaniment, not because more voices are singing the melody. The additional voices change the dynamics of the sound, not the density.

These two paintings are by the same artist. What do you notice about the top part of each? What do you notice about the bottom part of each?

The density of what you see is an important part of how a painting feels.

OBJECTIVES, p. XV

THE ARTS: Density

MATERIALS
Record 10, Copland: *Statements*, "Cryptic"; Copland: *Music for a Great City*; Pupil's Book, pp. 248 and 249

VOCABULARY
density: thin, thick

IDEAS FOR TEACHING
1. Have children look at the paintings on pp. 248 and 249. Encourage comments. Note: (a) If children use words like *weird, crazy,* or *spooky* to describe the paintings, tell them that some painters like to express the "unreal world" of the imagination. These painters, called surrealists, depict things that are *above* or *beyond* realism. (b) Encourage children to comment on some of the following qualities in the paintings: color, shapes, lines, focus on a center of interest or lack of focus, direction, texture, the feeling of perspective (i.e., a feeling of depth from front to back). Questions: What do you see in the top part (or background) of each painting? What do you see in the bottom part (or foreground)? Note: Through discussion, help children discover that there are similarities and differences in density. In the first painting (p. 248), the top and bottom parts are thin, open, light, uncrowded. In the second painting (p. 249), the top part is thin and uncrowded like the first painting, but the bottom part is thick, full, heavy, busy, crowded. ⟶

Tanguy, Yves. MAMA, PAPA IS WOUNDED! 1927. Oil on canvas, 36¼ x 28¾". Collection, The Museum of Modern Art, New York.

248 MODULE 25: The Arts—Density

TRY THIS
1. Have children create a sound piece that has several sections—some with thin density, some with thick density. Children might follow this procedure:
(a) Make a plan or score showing which sections will have thin density, which ones, thick density; for example:

A (thin)	B (thin)	C (thick)	B (thin)	A (thin)
A (thick)	B (thin)	A (thick)	C (thin)	A (thick)

(b) Choose instruments for each section. Use one percussion instrument for sections with thin sounds, several instruments for sections with thick sounds.
(c) Decide what rhythm pattern(s) the instruments will play for each section. Note: For sections with thick density, several different rhythm patterns should occur simultaneously.
(d) Rehearse each section by itself.
(e) Put it all together by playing the piece from beginning to end, one section after another.
(f) Evaluate the sound piece. Was the contrast between thin and thick density clear? How could the piece or the performance be improved? ⟶

TANGUY, YVES. MULTIPLICATION DES ARCS. 1954. OIL ON CANVAS, 40 x 60". COLLECTION, THE MUSEUM OF MODERN ART, NEW YORK. MRS. SIMON GUGGENHEIM FUND.

Music has density, too. Listen to two pieces by the same

composer. What do you notice about the density of each one?

🔘 Copland: *Statements*　　　🔘 Copland: *Music for a Great City*
10　　　　　　　　　　　　　　　10

Density in painting can be made by having open spaces (thin)

or by crowding many things into a space (thick).

Density in music can be made by having only a few sounds

(thin) or by piling up sounds together (thick).

Each art creates a feeling of thin or thick in its own way.

The Arts—Density 249

2. Help children hear that sounds can also give a feeling of density. As others listen, have two children, one in the front of the room, one in the back, repeat their name over and over, both at the same time. Point out: The sound is thin or spread out. Then have all the children in the room simultaneously repeat their name over and over. Point out: Now the sound is thick, full, and heavy.

3. Play the recording of the two works by Copland—*Statements* ("Cryptic") and *Music for a Great City*. Question: What do you notice about the density of sound in each piece? Note: Help children articulate the idea that the sound of "Cryptic" has a thin, light, empty, "spread out" density; and that the sound of *Music for a Great City* has a thick, heavy, full, "bunched together" density.

REVIEW/REINFORCEMENT

Use the paintings on pp. 36 and 37 to reinforce the concept of thick and thin density. Lead children to observe that the first painting (p. 36) has extremely thick density: it is full of colorful, vibrant shapes and lines forcefully interacting with one another; there is no open space anywhere. Although the second painting also uses intense colors, it has a feeling of spaciousness, or openness. With the exception of the dark shading at the lower left and the strips of color at the top and right, the painting has a thin density. Suggestion: Encourage children to find other examples of thin and thick density in illustrations, photographs, etc.

Children are now ready to take Test 3 for Book 4. Additional information about Silver Burdett Music Competency Tests is found in the introduction of this book.

2. When children sing familiar songs, have them play an accompaniment that has a thin density or a thick density; for example:
Thin Density
• melody with recorder or bell countermelody
• melody with vocal countermelody
• melody accompanied by one or two percussion parts
Thick Density
• melody with countermelody and Autoharp chords
• melody accompanied by Autoharp chords and several percussion parts

TEACHER INFORMATION

Yves Tanguy (French, 1900–1955)　*Mama, Papa Is Wounded* and *Multiplication des Arcs:* Tanguy (pronounced Tahngee') was a master of surrealism—art that explores the superreality of dreams, fantasies, and wild imaginings. His works give a sense of vast, endless space on which weird, unrecognizable shapes exist. This fantasy world, captured with brilliant artistic technique, is found in no other works except those by this hypnotic painter.

For biographical information about Copland, see Teacher's Edition p. 83 (Teacher Information).

ALL HID

TRADITIONAL

ARRANGED BY DONALD KALBACH

PUPIL'S BOOK, PAGE 161

All hid, All hid, All hid,___ All hid,___ Five, ten,

fif - teen, twen - ty, all___ hid; Five, ten, fif - teen, twen - ty,

all ___ hid, All hid. Five, ten, fif - teen, twen - ty,

Twen-ty-five, thir - ty, thir-ty-five, for - ty, For - ty-five, fif - ty, fif - ty-five, six - ty;

Six - ty-five, seven-ty, seven-ty-five, eigh-ty, Eigh-ty-five, nine-ty, nine-ty-five, hun-dred.

*Omit cue notes when playing accompaniment.

AMAZING GRACE

EARLY AMERICAN MELODY

ARRANGED BY FRANK FOX

WORDS BY JOHN NEWTON

PUPIL'S BOOK, PAGE 192

1. A - maz - ing___ grace how sweet the sound That
2. 'Twas grace that___ taught my heart to fear, And

saved a ___ wretch like me!___ I once___ was___
grace my ___ fears re - lieved;___ How pre - cious___

250

lost, but now____ am__ found, Was blind, but__ now I
did that grace____ ap - pear The hour I__ first be -

see._____
lieved!_____

3. Through many dangers, toils, and snares,
   I have already come;
   'Tis grace has brought me safe thus far,
   And grace will lead me home.

4. The Lord has promised good to me,
   His word my hope secures;
   He will my shield and portion be
   As long as life endures.

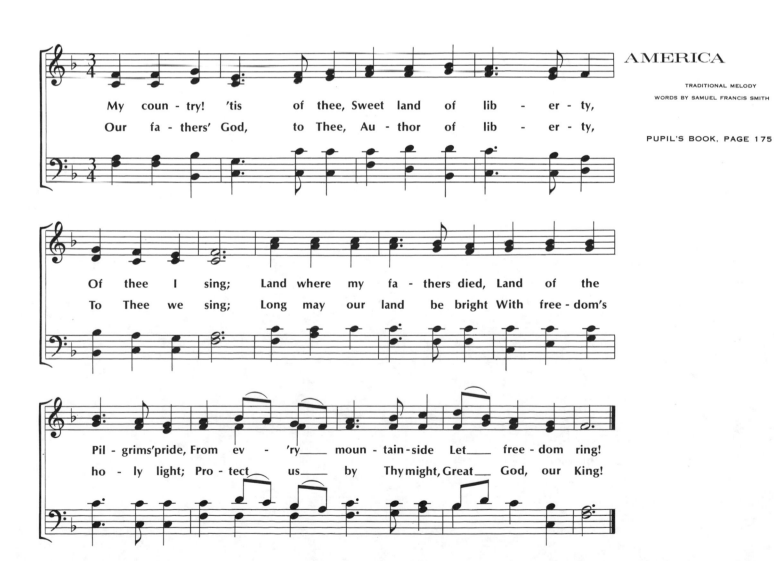

AMERICA

TRADITIONAL MELODY
WORDS BY SAMUEL FRANCIS SMITH

PUPIL'S BOOK, PAGE 175

My coun - try! 'tis of thee, Sweet land of lib - er - ty,
Our fa - thers' God, to Thee, Au - thor of lib - er - ty,

Of thee I sing; Land where my fa - thers died, Land of the
To Thee we sing; Long may our land be bright With free - dom's

Pil - grims' pride, From ev - 'ry____ moun - tain - side Let____ free - dom ring!
ho - ly light; Pro - tect____ us____ by Thy might, Great____ God, our King!

251

AMERICA, THE BEAUTIFUL

MUSIC BY SAMUEL A. WARD
WORDS BY KATHARINE LEE BATES

PUPIL'S BOOK, PAGE 153

O beau - ti - ful for spa - cious skies, For am - ber waves of grain, For
O beau - ti - ful for pa - triot dream That sees be - yond the years Thine

pur - ple moun - tain maj - es - ties A - bove the fruit - ed plain! A -
al - a - bas - ter cit - ies gleam, Un - dimmed by hu - man tears!

mer - i - ca! A - mer - i - ca! God shed His grace on thee And

crown thy good with broth - er - hood From sea to shin - ing sea!

Wistfully

CLOUDS

MUSIC BY HOAGY CARMICHAEL
ARRANGED BY W. W. SCHMIDT
WORDS BY CHRISTINA ROSSETTI

PUPIL'S BOOK, PAGE 55

White sheep, white sheep, high on a wind - y hill,

When the wind stops, you all stand still; But

when _____ the wind blows, you walk a - way slow. Oh,

white sheep, white sheep, Where do you go?

CLEMENTINE

AMERICAN FOLK SONG

ARRANGED BY W. W. SCHMIDT

PUPIL'S BOOK, PAGE 154

1. In a cav - ern, in a can - yon, Ex - ca - vat - ing for a
2. Light she was, and like a fair - y, And her shoes were num - ber
3. Drove she duck - lings to the wa - ter Ev - 'ry morn - ing just at

mine, Dwelt a min - er, for - ty-nin - er, And his daugh - ter, Clem-en -
nine, Her - ring box - es with-out top - ses, San - dals were for Clem-en -
nine, Hit her foot a - gainst a splin - ter, Fell in - to the foam-ing

REFRAIN

tine.

tine. Oh, my dar - ling, oh, my dar - ling, Oh, my dar - ling Clem-en -

brine.

tine, You are lost and gone for - ev - er, Dread-ful sor - ry, Clem-en-tine.

253

CHANUKAH SONG

HASIDIC FOLK SONG
ARRANGED BY NICHOLAS ZUMBRO
ENGLISH WORDS BY ALICE FIRGAU

PUPIL'S BOOK, PAGE 232

'Tis the week of Cha-nu-kah, Good cheer it is bring - ing. This hol - i - day we cel - e - brate in danc - ing and sing - ing. ___

Gath-er 'round to-geth - er, the ho - ra we'll do; Then join in a song that our

fore - fath - ers knew. But hush now and come now, The

can - dles we light one by one. Then hear the sto - ry of

God and His glo - ry And how pre-cious free - dom was won.

COLORFUL BOATS

FOLK SONG FROM CHINA
ARRANGED BY PHILIP LEE
ENGLISH VERSION BY CAROL KERR
COPYRIGHT © 1979. WILLIAM M. ANDERSON. USED BY PERMISSION.

PUPIL'S BOOK, PAGE 235

Tsai lung chuan yia me yia wei yao, Lai da mang yao ___ yia he hei,

See the bright col-ored har - bor boats, Dec - o - rat - ed for fes - ti - val,

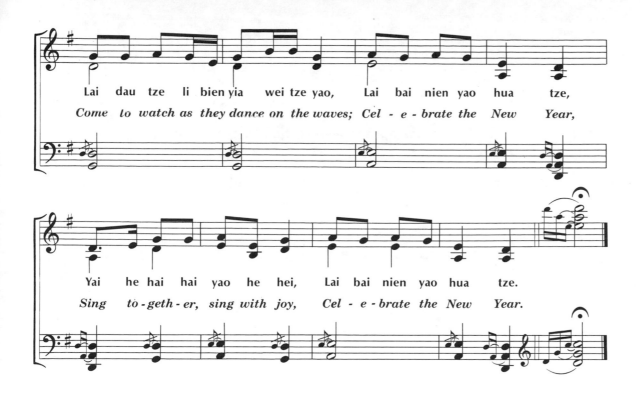

Lai dau tze li bien yia wei tze yao, Lai bai nien yao hua tze,
Come to watch as they dance on the waves; Cel - e - brate the New Year,

Yai he hai hai yao he hei, Lai bai nien yao hua tze.
Sing to-geth-er, sing with joy, Cel - e - brate the New Year.

DAYENU

HEBREW PASSOVER SONG
ARRANGED BY HARVEY HOLLMAN
ENGLISH WORDS BY ELIZABETH S. BACHMAN

PUPIL'S BOOK, PAGE 40

Happily

1. He has led us out of E - gypt, led His peo - ple out of E - gypt,
2. He has giv - en us the Sab - bath, giv - en us the ho - ly Sab - bath,
3. He has giv - en us the To - rah, giv - en us the bless - ed To - rah,

REFRAIN
Accelerando

He has led us out of E - gypt, *da - ye - nu.*
He has giv - en us the Sab-bath, *da - ye - nu.* *Da - da - ye-nu,___*
He has giv - en us the To - rah, *da - ye - nu.*

da - da - ye-nu,___ Da - da - ye-nu, da-ye-nu da-ye-nu da-ye-nu ye-nu da-ye-nu.

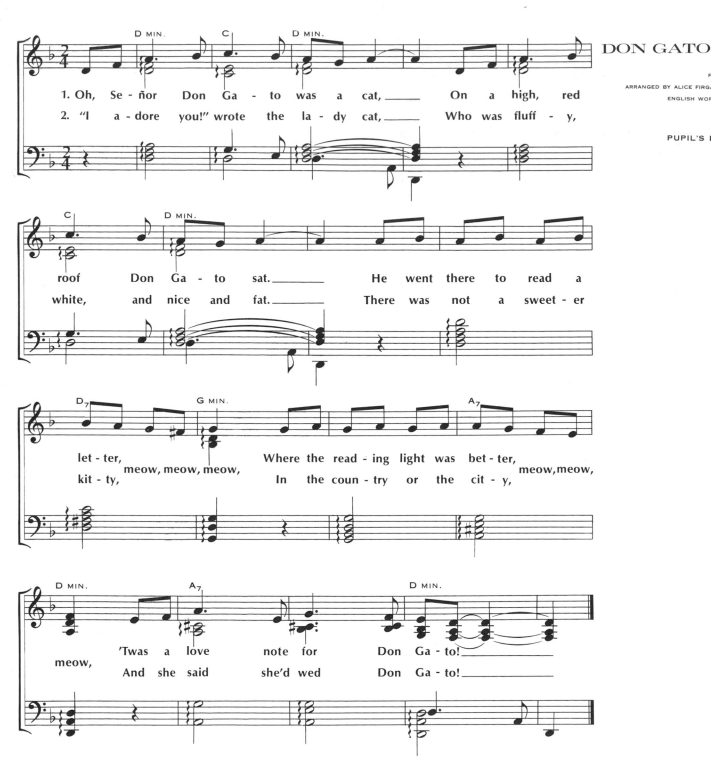

DON GATO

FOLK SONG FROM MEXICO
ARRANGED BY ALICE FIRGAU
ENGLISH WORDS BY MARGARET MARKS

PUPIL'S BOOK, PAGE 164

1. Oh, Se - ñor Don Ga - to was a cat, _____ On a high, red
2. "I a - dore you!" wrote the la - dy cat, _____ Who was fluff - y,

roof Don Ga - to sat. _____ He went there to read a
white, and nice and fat. _____ There was not a sweet - er

let - ter, meow, meow, meow, Where the read - ing light was bet - ter, meow, meow,
kit - ty, In the coun - try or the cit - y,

meow,
'Twas a love note for Don Ga - to! _____
And she said she'd wed Don Ga - to! _____

3. Oh, Don Gato jumped so happily
He fell off the roof and broke his knee,
Broke his ribs and all his whiskers, . . .
And his little solar plexus, . . .
"¡Ay carramba!" cried Don Gato!

4. Then the doctors all came on the run
Just to see if something could be done,
And they held a consultation, . . .
About how to save their patient, . . .
How to save Señor Don Gato!

5. But in spite of everything they tried
Poor Señor Don Gato up and died,
Oh, it wasn't very merry, . . .
Going to the cemetery, . . .
For the ending of Don Gato!

6. When the funeral passed the market square
Such a smell of fish was in the air,
Though his burial was slated, . . .
He became re-animated! . . .
He came back to life, Don Gato!

256

DON'T COUNT YOUR CHICKENS

WORDS AND MUSIC BY CARMINO RAVOSA
ARRANGED BY ROSEMARY JACQUES
© 1971 CARMINO RAVOSA

PUPIL'S BOOK, PAGE 100

Don't

count your chick-ens be - fore they hatch, Be - fore they hatch, be - fore they hatch. Don't count your chick - ens be - fore they hatch, Be - fore they hatch, (clap clap) they hatch! Don't you

plan a-bout to-mor-row, 'cause to-mor-row does-n't come un-til to-mor -

row; Have a lot-ta fun to-day be-cause to-mor-row may just bring a lot-ta

sor - row. Don't you sor - row. Don't

count your chick-ens be - fore they hatch, Be - fore they hatch, be -

fore they hatch. Don't count your chick-ens be - fore they hatch, Be -

fore they hatch, *(clap clap)* they hatch!

A GREAT BIG SEA

FOLK SONG FROM NEWFOUNDLAND

ARRANGED BY IAN LAPIERRE

From old time songs and poetry of Newfoundland. Reprinted by permission of Gerald S. Doyle Ltd.

PUPIL'S BOOK, PAGE 77

Jauntily
SOLO

1. A great big sea hove in Long Beach, Right fol - or - al
2. A great big sea hove in the Harbor,

tad - dle did - dle I - do. A great big sea hove in Long Beach And
A great big sea hove in the Harbor And

Gran - ny Snooks she lost her speech, To me right fol - di - dy fol - dee.
hove right up in Ke - ough's Parlor,

3. "Oh, mother dear, I wants a sack,"   With beads and buttons down the back,"

Right fol-or-al taddle diddle I-do.   To me right fol-didy fol-dee.

"Oh, mother dear, I wants a sack

JOY TO THE WORLD

WORDS AND MUSIC BY HOYT AXTON

ARRANGED BY POLLY CARDER

Copyright © 1970 by Lady Jane Music. Used by Permission.

PUPIL'S BOOK, PAGE 139

1. Jer - e - mi - ah was a bull - frog, Was a good friend of mine. Nev - er un - der-stood a sin - gle word he said, but we al - ways had a might - y fine time. Yes, we al - ways had a might - y fine time. Sing - ing joy to the world. All the boys and girls now. Joy to the fish - es in the deep blue sea.

2. If I were the king of the world, tell you what I'd do,
Throw away the fears and the tears and the jeers,
And have a good time with you.
Yes, I'd have a good time with you. *Refrain*

DRY BONES

BLACK SPIRITUAL
ARRANGED BY GEORGE WINSTON

PUPIL'S BOOK, PAGE 42

E - ze-kiel cried, "Them dry bones!" E - ze-kiel cried, "Them

dry bones!" E - ze-kiel cried, "Them dry bones!" Now

hear the word of the Lord. The foot bone con-nect-ed to the

jaw bone, The jaw bone con-nect-ed to the head bone, Now

hear the word of the Lord. Them bones, them bones gon-na

walk a-round, Them bones, them bones gon-na walk a-round, Them

getting slower last time

bones, them bones gon-na walk a-round, Now hear the word of the Lord.

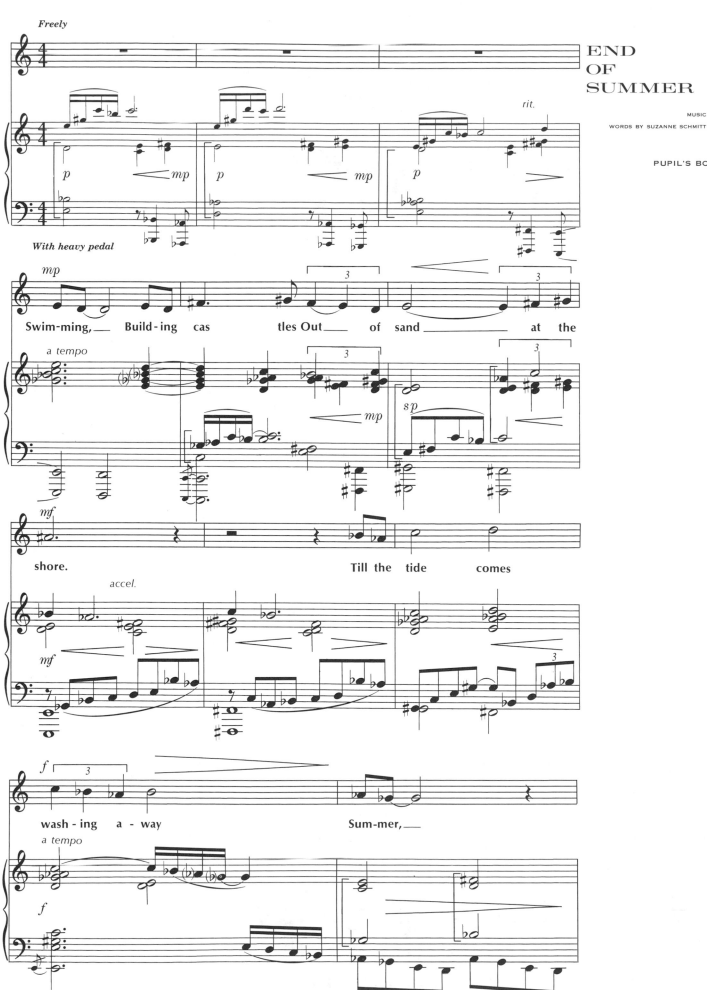

END OF SUMMER

MUSIC BY DAVID EDDLEMAN
WORDS BY SUZANNE SCHMITT

PUPIL'S BOOK, PAGE 237

264

FISHERMAN'S SONG

CALYPSO MELODY
WORDS BY WILLIAM ATTAWAY
ARRANGED BY SAMUELE MAQUÍ

WORDS FROM CALYPSO SONG BOOK BY WILLIAM ATTAWAY. COPYRIGHT
© 1957 BY REBUS PUBLISHING CO. COPYRIGHT ASSIGNED © 1957 TO CALYPSO
MUSIC, INC. USED BY PERMISSION.

PUPIL'S BOOK, PAGE 54

Sum-mer,___ Sum-mer.___

1. Fish-er-men sleep when the fish don't bite,___ Weigh up, Sus-i-an-na, Salt
2. Fish-er-man's la-dy don't use no comb,___ She

fish in the hold and we two ton light,___ Round the Bay of Mont-ser-ray.___
comb her___ hair with___ cod-fish bone,___

REFRAIN

Weigh up, Sus-i-an-na, Round the Bay of Mont-ser-ray.___

Fish all___ night and we sleep all day,___ Round the Bay of Mont-ser-ray.___

3. Fisherman's lady got a dimple knee,
   Weigh up, Susianna,
   She boil her porgy with rice and peas,
   Round the Bay of Montserray. *Refrain*

FOLK SONG FROM GREECE
ENGLISH WORDS BY MARIA JORDAN
ARRANGED BY MEL ALEGRIOU

PUPIL'S BOOK, PAGE 72

With a lilt

1. Find the ring, the ring that keeps mov - ing,
2. Find the ring, the ring that keeps mov - ing,

Find the ring, oh, where did it go?
Find the ring of sil - ver or gold.

The se - cret ring's in some - bod - y's hand, Some-
Pass it to me, I'll pass it to you, We

bod - y you know, come guess if you can!
must - n't get caught, what - ev - er we do!

Don't say a word if you are the one, Don't

give it a - way and spoil all the fun!

MANANA

FOLK SONG FROM SPAIN
COLLECTED AND ADAPTED BY BEATRICE LANDECK
ARRANGED BY SUZANNE ARTHUR
ENGLISH WORDS BY ROSEMARY JACQUES

PUPIL'S BOOK, PAGE 76

With motion

Ma - ña - na, por___ la ma - ña - na pa - sas - te,
Ma - ña - na, por___ la ma - ña - na I___ stood there,

Jua - na, por___ mi ta - ller, la ran le. Te
Look - ing down___ at the street, la ran le. When

ju - ro que___ ten - go ga - na de___ ver - te,
Juana passed by___ with her twin - kling eye,___ I just

Jua - na, la___ pun - ta el pie.
saw the toes___ of her feet.

DUNDAI

HEBREW FOLK SONG
ARRANGED BY W. W. SCHMIDT
ENGLISH WORDS BY HAROLD AKS

PUPIL'S BOOK, PAGE 90

Briskly

Ⓐ

Land of Is - ra - el, O land of mine, On you the sun and moon and stars do shine.

Ⓑ

Dun - dai, dun-dai, dun-dai, Dun-dai - dai, Dun - dai, dun-dai, dun-dai, Dun - dai - dai.

267

TINA, SINGU

FOLK SONG FROM AFRICA

ARRANGED BY LAWRENCE EISMAN

From CHANSONS de NOTRE CHALET. Courtesy of World Around Songs. Burnsville, N.C.

PUPIL'S BOOK, PAGE 104

Ti - na, Sing - u le - lu - va - tae - o. Wat - sha,___ wat - sha,___

wat - sha.___ Wat - sha,___ wat - sha,___

wat - sha,___ wat - sha,___ wat - sha.___ La, la - la - la - la - la -

la, la - la - la - la - la - la, la - la - la - la - la - la - la - la - la - la.

BILLY BOY

FOLK SONG FROM ENGLAND

ARRANGED BY CAROL KERR

PUPIL'S BOOK, PAGE 170

1. Oh,___ where have you been, Bil - ly Boy, Bil - ly Boy? Oh,___ where have you

2. Did she bid you to come in, Bil - ly Boy, Bil - ly Boy? Did she bid you to come

been, charm-ing Bil - ly? I have been to seek a wife, She's the

in, charm-ing Bil - ly? Yes, she bid me to come in, There's a

joy___ of my life,

dim -ple in her chin, She's a young thing and can-not leave her moth-er.___

3. Did she give you a chair, Billy Boy, Billy Boy?
   Yes, she gave me a chair, but there was no bottom there,

4. Can she make a cherry pie, Billy Boy, Billy Boy?
   She can make a cherry pie, quick as a cat can wink her eye,

5. Can she cook and can she spin, Billy Boy, Billy Boy?
   She can cook and she can spin, she can do most anything,

6. How old is she, Billy Boy, Billy Boy?
   Three times six and four times seven, twenty-eight and eleven,

269

GO, TELL IT
ON THE
MOUNTAIN

BLACK SPIRITUAL
ARRANGED BY JAMES ROOKER

PUPIL'S BOOK, PAGE 64

1. When I was a seek-er, I sought both night and day. I
2. He made me a watch-man Up-on the cit-y wall. And
3. In the time of Da-vid, Some said he was a king. And

asked the Lord to help me, And He shows me the way._____
if I serve Him tru-ly, I am the least of all._____
if a child is true born, The Lord will hear him sing._____

REFRAIN (IN RHYTHM)
CHORUS

Go, tell it on the moun - tain,

COUNTERMELODY

Go, tell it on the

Over the hills and ev'ry-where. Go, tell it on the
moun - tain,

moun - tain, Our heav'n - ly Lord___ is born.

Go, tell it on the moun-tain, our Lord is born.

Brightly

Hi-neh mah tov u-ma na - im, She-vet a-chim gam ya - chad.

Hi - neh mah___ tov, She-vet a-chim gam ya - chad. ya - chad.

HINEH MAH TOV

HEBREW FOLK SONG

ARRANGED BY FRANCIS GIRARD

PUPIL'S BOOK, PAGE 208

NINE
RED
HORSEMEN

FOLK MELODY FROM MEXICO
ARRANGED BY SAMUELE MAQUI
WORDS BY ELEANOR FARJEON

FROM ELEANOR FARJEON'S POEMS FOR CHILDREN. ORIGINALLY
PUBLISHED IN SING FOR YOUR SUPPER BY ELEANOR FARJEON. COPYRIGHT,
1938 BY ELEANOR FARJEON. RENEWED 1966 BY GERVASE FARJEON. BY
PERMISSION OF J.B. LIPPINCOTT, PUBLISHERS, AND HAROLD OBER ASSOCIATES,
INCORPORATED.

PUPIL'S BOOK, PAGE 219

HE'S GOT THE WHOLE WORLD IN HIS HANDS

BLACK SPIRITUAL
ARRANGED BY GEORGE WINSTON

PUPIL'S BOOK, PAGE 246

2. He's got the wind and rain . . .

3. He's got both you and me . . .

GRANDPA

WORDS AND MUSIC BY CHRIS DEDRICK

© 1972 ALMITRA MUSIC COMPANY, INC.

PUPIL'S BOOK, PAGE 151

man. And no one else re-mem-bers all the things that Grand-pa
him. His know-ledge has a beau-ty like the leaves up - on a

can. Sto - ries full of truth - ful - ness that time can - not e-
limb. Like the leaf, a pat - tern, _____ and like the branch, a

rase Are writ - ten out like gos - pel in the wrin - kles of his
strength, For, like the tree, he's breathed the wind and watched the world at

REFRAIN

face. Grand - pa, Grand - pa-pa, _____ Grand - pa-pa-pa,
length.

274

Grand - pa - pa - pa - pa.

3. Some-times___ you can sit with him___ and nev - er say a

word. You start to think of si - lence as a

sound that can be heard, And, hear-ing it, you're

led in - to a dif - f'rent place to live Where

noth - ing scares or hurts you, and there's noth - ing to for - give.

REFRAIN

Grand - pa, Grand - pa - pa, ___ Grand - pa - pa - pa, ___

Grand - pa - pa - pa - pa.

I'M
GONNA
WALK

WORDS AND MUSIC BY DAVID EDDLEMAN

PUPIL'S BOOK, PAGE 44

Not too fast

I'm gon-na put, put, put on my

walk-in' shoes,___ I'm gon-na but-, but-, but-ton up my coat, I'm gon-na

walk right a-cross the land, there's lots o' things to see, and if you wan-ta you can walk with me.

Oh, yes, I'm gon-na walk to the East, Walk to the West,

Walk to the North and South; The one thing that I love

the best Is walk-in' all a-bout. Well, I'm gon-na

IN BAHIA TOWN

FOLK SONG FROM BRAZIL

ARRANGED BY JAMES ROOKER

ENGLISH WORDS BY VERNE MUÑOZ

MELODY FROM FOLK SONGS AND DANCES OF THE AMERICAS, PUBLISHED BY THE GENERAL SECRETARIAT OF THE ORGANIZATION OF AMERICAN STATES.

PUPIL'S BOOK, PAGE 80

Happily

1. In Ba-hi-a town, So they say,
   In Ba-hi-a town, So they say,

They sell co-co-nuts for a pen-ny In the mar-ket place.
They sell fish that's bet-ter than an-y You will ev-er

taste. La la la la la la la la la, La la la la la
la la, la.

2. In Bahia town,   In Bahia town,
   So it seems,   So it seems,
   You can buy a sewing machine   You can buy a lamp made of glass
   That stitches like a dream.   In shades of blue and green.
                                  La la la la la . . .

ISLAND HOPPING

FOLK SONG FROM GREECE

ENGLISH WORDS BY MARIA JORDAN

ARRANGED BY MEL ALEGRIOU

PUPIL'S BOOK, PAGE 118

Brightly

Ⓐ

1. Bags are packed and all is read - y, can't wait___ to start;

2. Parents with their sons and daughters planned for this day;
   Now the boat glides 'cross the waters, we're on our way.
   Grecian islands lie before us—
   Hydra, Spetsai, lovely Poros
   Beckon us as, in a chorus, "Come," they all say, *Ahstoh kahloh,*
   "Come," they all say.

HAND ME DOWN

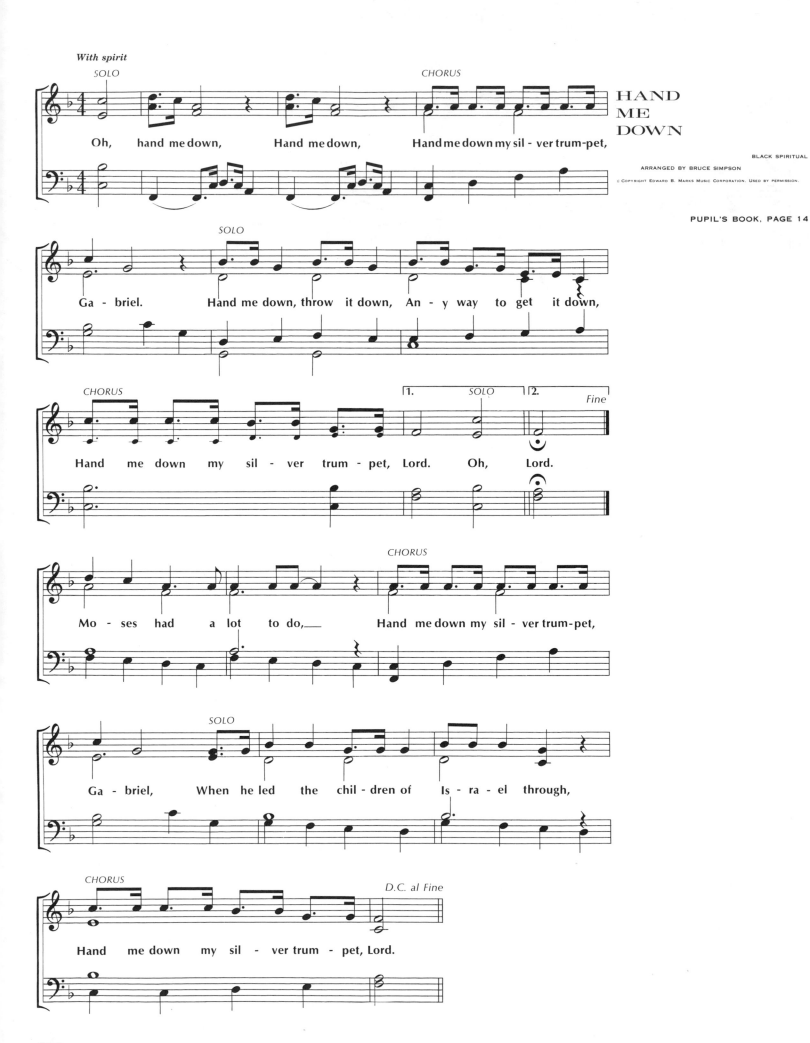

BLACK SPIRITUAL

ARRANGED BY BRUCE SIMPSON

© COPYRIGHT EDWARD B. MARKS MUSIC CORPORATION. USED BY PERMISSION.

PUPIL'S BOOK, PAGE 14

HARVESTING TEA

FOLK SONG FROM JAPAN
ARRANGED BY DONALD KALBACH
ENGLISH WORDS BY RAYMOND MATTHEWS

PUPIL'S BOOK, PAGE 216

1. When sum-mer comes up-on the moun-tains and the val - leys,
2. And as they pick each rip-ened leaf so ver-y gent - ly,

And cov-ers ev-'ry-thing with fresh and ten-der young, green leaves,
They sing a song of joy; the air is filled with mel-o-dy;

Then it is time for all the peo-ple of the vil-lage
Their hap-py song is car-ried on the sum-mer breez-es;

To gath-er in the fields to har-vest leaves for tea.
It says it's time a-gain to har-vest leaves for tea.

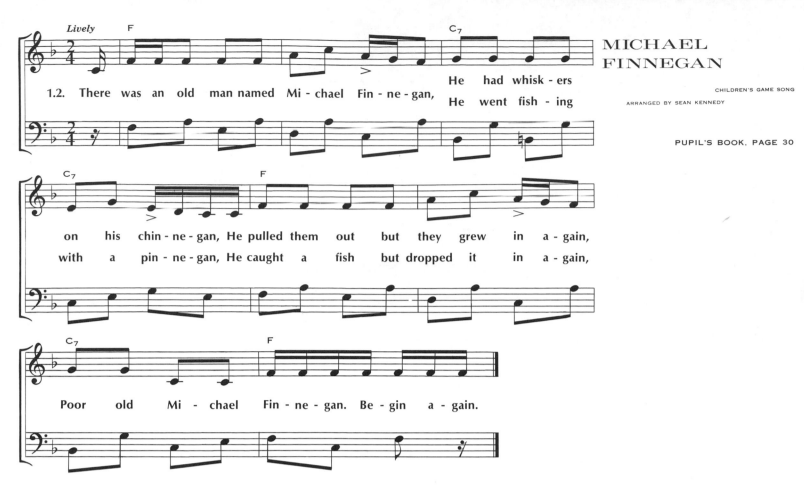

MICHAEL FINNEGAN

CHILDREN'S GAME SONG
ARRANGED BY SEAN KENNEDY

PUPIL'S BOOK, PAGE 30

1.2. There was an old man named Mi - chael Fin - ne - gan,
He had whisk - ers
He went fish - ing
on his chin - ne - gan, He pulled them out but they grew in a - gain,
with a pin - ne - gan, He caught a fish but dropped it in a - gain,
Poor old Mi - chael Fin - ne - gan. Be - gin a - gain.

3.   There was an old man named Michael Finnegan,
     Climbed a tree and barked his shinnegan,
     He lost about a yard of skinnegan,
     Poor old Michael Finnegan. Begin again.

4.   There was an old man named Michael Finnegan,
     He grew fat and then grew thinnegan,
     Then he died and that's the endegan,
     Poor old Michael Finnegan. Begin again.

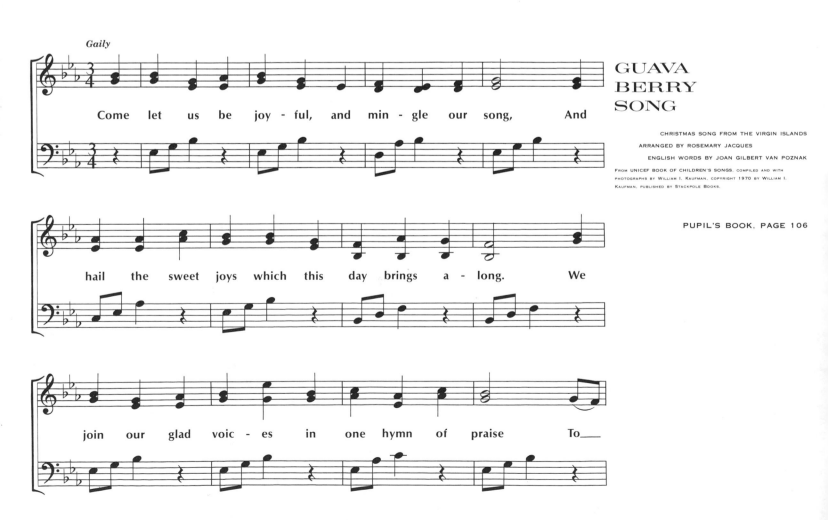

GUAVA BERRY SONG

CHRISTMAS SONG FROM THE VIRGIN ISLANDS
ARRANGED BY ROSEMARY JACQUES
ENGLISH WORDS BY JOAN GILBERT VAN POZNAK
From UNICEF BOOK OF CHILDREN'S SONGS, compiled and with photographs by William I. Kaufman, copyright 1970 by William I. Kaufman, published by Stackpole Books.

PUPIL'S BOOK, PAGE 106

Come let us be joy - ful, and min - gle our song, And
hail the sweet joys which this day brings a - long. We
join our glad voic - es in one hymn of praise To___

Him__ who has kept us, and__ length-ened our days.

A mer-ry Christ-mas to you all, A mer-ry Christ-mas to you all, A mer-ry

Christ-mas, A mer-ry Christ-mas, A mer-ry Christ-mas to you all!

Good morn - in', good morn - in', We wish you a mer-ry Christ - mas, Good

morn - in', good morn - in', We wish you a mer-ry Christ - mas, Good

morn - in', good morn - in', We've come for the gua-va ber - ry, Good

morn - in', good morn - in', Oh put it on the ta - ble.

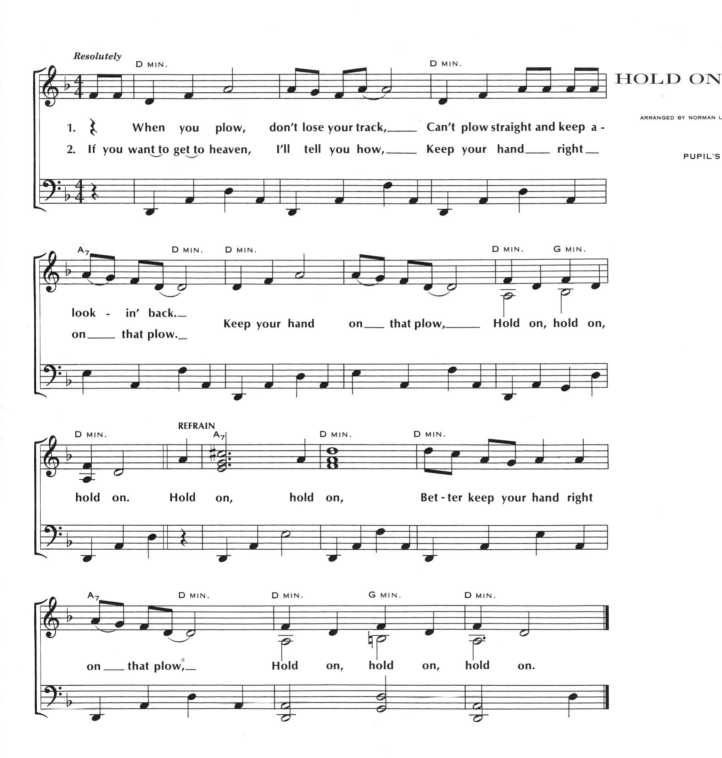

HOLD ON

AMERICAN FOLK SONG

ARRANGED BY NORMAN LLOYD

PUPIL'S BOOK, PAGE 122

1. When you plow, don't lose your track,____ Can't plow straight and keep a-
2. If you want to get to heaven, I'll tell you how,____ Keep your hand____ right____

look - in' back.____ Keep your hand on____ that plow,____ Hold on, hold on,
on____ that plow.____

REFRAIN

hold on. Hold on, hold on, Bet - ter keep your hand right

on____ that plow,__ Hold on, hold on, hold on.

3. Keep on plowin' and don't you tire,
Ev'ry row goes higher and higher.
Keep your hand on that plow,
Hold on, hold on, hold on. *Refrain*

4. If that plow stays in your hand,
Head you straight for the promised land.
Keep your hand on that plow.
Hold on, hold on, hold on. *Refrain*

EVENING

FOLK MELODY FROM HUNGARY
ARRANGED BY CAROL KERR
ENGLISH WORDS BY ROSEMARY JACQUES

PUPIL'S BOOK, PAGE 189

Voic - es fill the eve - ning air with their hap - py sing - ing,

Joy and laugh - ter ev - 'ry - where through the land are ring - ing.

Cast - ing all their cares a - way, Danc - ers whirl till break of day.

Hear the mu - sic play. Voic - es fill the eve - ning air

with their hap - py sing - ing, Joy and laugh - ter ev - 'ry-where through the land are ring - ing.

HURRY, GOOD SHEPHERDS

Pastores a Belén

CHRISTMAS SONG FROM PUERTO RICO
ARRANGED BY ROSEMARY JACQUES
ENGLISH VERSION BY VERNE MUÑOZ

PUPIL'S BOOK, PAGE 184

Oh, hur - ry on your way;_____ Good shep-herds, hur-ry to see Him. The
Pas - to - res, a Be - lén _____ Va - mos con a - le - grí - a; Que

Son of Mar - y waits;_____ Good shep - herds, hur-ry to greet Him. In
ha na - ci - do ya _____ El Hi - jo de ___ Ma - rí - a. A -

Beth - le-hem,_____ the bless - ed Ba - by lies. _____ In
lli, _____ a - llí, _____ Nos es - pe - ra Je - sús. _____ A -

Beth - le-hem,_____ the bless - ed Ba - by lies._____ Bring
lli, _____ a - llí, _____ Nos es - pe - ra Je - sús. _____ Lle -

hon - ey sweet for Mar - y's Son, And al - mond cakes for
ve - mos pues tu - rro - nes y miel Pa ra o - fre - cer al

ev - 'ry - one. Bring hon - ey sweet for Mar - y's Son, And
Ni - ño Man - uel, lle - ve - mos pues tu - rro - nes y miel Pa -

al - mond cakes for ev - 'ry - one. Hur - ry, hur - ry,
ra o - fre - cer al Ni - ño Man - uel. Va - mos, va - mos,

do not de - lay, Greet___ the Ba - by born___ this day,_____
va - mos a ver, Va - mos a ver al re - cién na - ci - do,

Greet___ the Ba - by born ___ this day.
Va - mos a ver al Ni - ño Man - uel.

LAZY
COCONUT
TREE

MUSIC BY DOUGLAS COOMBES
ARRANGED BY SAMUELE MAQUÍ
WORDS BY JOHN EMLYN EDWARDS
FROM TA-RA-RA-BOOM-DE-AY. PUBLISHED BY A & C BLACK LTD.
REPRINTED BY PERMISSION OF DAVID HIGHAM ASSOCIATES LIMITED.

PUPIL'S BOOK, PAGE 41

LOUIS MOVED
AWAY

MUSIC BY JIM HUNTER
ARRANGED BY ROSEMARY JACQUES
WORDS BY TOM PAISLEY

PUPIL'S BOOK, PAGE 56

290

al - ways had some bread to__ spend.__ His

dad - dy makes good__ pay; __ That's what they all__ say.

And now I'll nev - er have a__ friend,__ 'Cause

Lou - is moved a - way.__ 'Cause Lou - is moved a - way.

'Cause Lou - is moved a - way.__

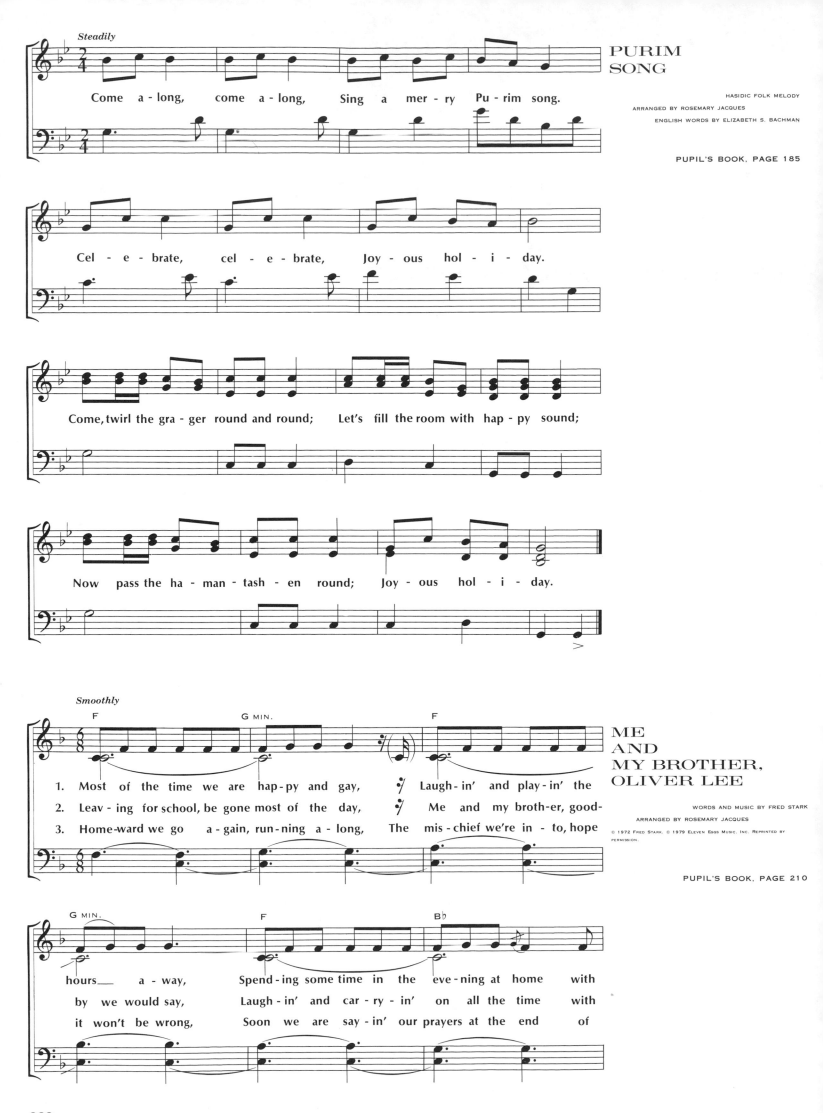

PURIM SONG

HASIDIC FOLK MELODY
ARRANGED BY ROSEMARY JACQUES
ENGLISH WORDS BY ELIZABETH S. BACHMAN

PUPIL'S BOOK, PAGE 185

Come a-long, come a-long, Sing a mer-ry Pu-rim song.

Cel-e-brate, cel-e-brate, Joy-ous hol-i-day.

Come, twirl the gra-ger round and round; Let's fill the room with hap-py sound;

Now pass the ha-man-tash-en round; Joy-ous hol-i-day.

ME AND MY BROTHER, OLIVER LEE

WORDS AND MUSIC BY FRED STARK
ARRANGED BY ROSEMARY JACQUES
© 1972 FRED STARK. © 1979 ELEVEN EGGS MUSIC, INC. REPRINTED BY PERMISSION.

PUPIL'S BOOK, PAGE 210

1. Most of the time we are hap-py and gay,   Laugh-in' and play-in' the
2. Leav-ing for school, be gone most of the day,   Me and my broth-er, good-
3. Home-ward we go a-gain, run-ning a-long, The mis-chief we're in-to, hope

hours___ a-way, Spend-ing some time in the eve-ning at home with
by we would say, Laugh-in' and car-ry-in' on all the time with
it won't be wrong, Soon we are say-in' our prayers at the end of

292

THE MOSQUITO

FOLK SONG FROM COLOMBIA
ARRANGED BY FRANCIS GIRARD
ENGLISH WORDS BY MARGARET MARKS

PUPIL'S BOOK, PAGE 142

Not too fast

1. I went to the Sie - rra Blan - ca To hunt with my dog, Pe -
2. So huge was this big mos - qui - to, A ti - dal wave swelled the

rri - to, When sud - den - ly I en - count - ered a
wa - ter, His head lay in Cá - diz har - bor, His

great o - ver - grown mos - qui - to. I dropped to my knees and
feet lay a - cross Gi - bral - tar. And then the or - deal was

fired,_____ And star - tled by that ex - plo - sion, The
o - ver, The bug ceased to make a mo - tion, I

an - i - mal lost his bal - ance And tum - bled in - to the o - cean.
called for a crane and der - rick, You've nev - er seen such com - mo - tion.

3. They made from his hide ten thousand
   High boots of the finest leather,
   And just from the bits left over,
   A hundred or so umbrellas;

   And even now, ten years later,
   Though nothing could seem absurder,
   The whole of the Spanish Army
   Is eating mosquito-burger!

294

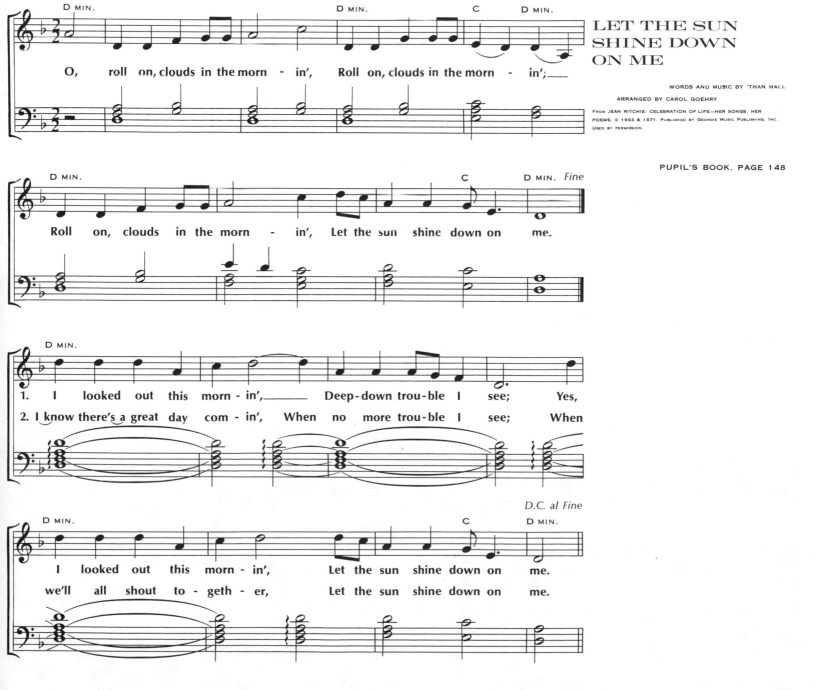

LET THE SUN
SHINE DOWN
ON ME

WORDS AND MUSIC BY 'THAN HALL
ARRANGED BY CAROL GOEHRY

FROM JEAN RITCHIE: CELEBRATION OF LIFE—HER SONGS, HER
POEMS. © 1963 & 1971. PUBLISHED BY GEORDIE MUSIC PUBLISHING, INC.
USED BY PERMISSION.

PUPIL'S BOOK, PAGE 148

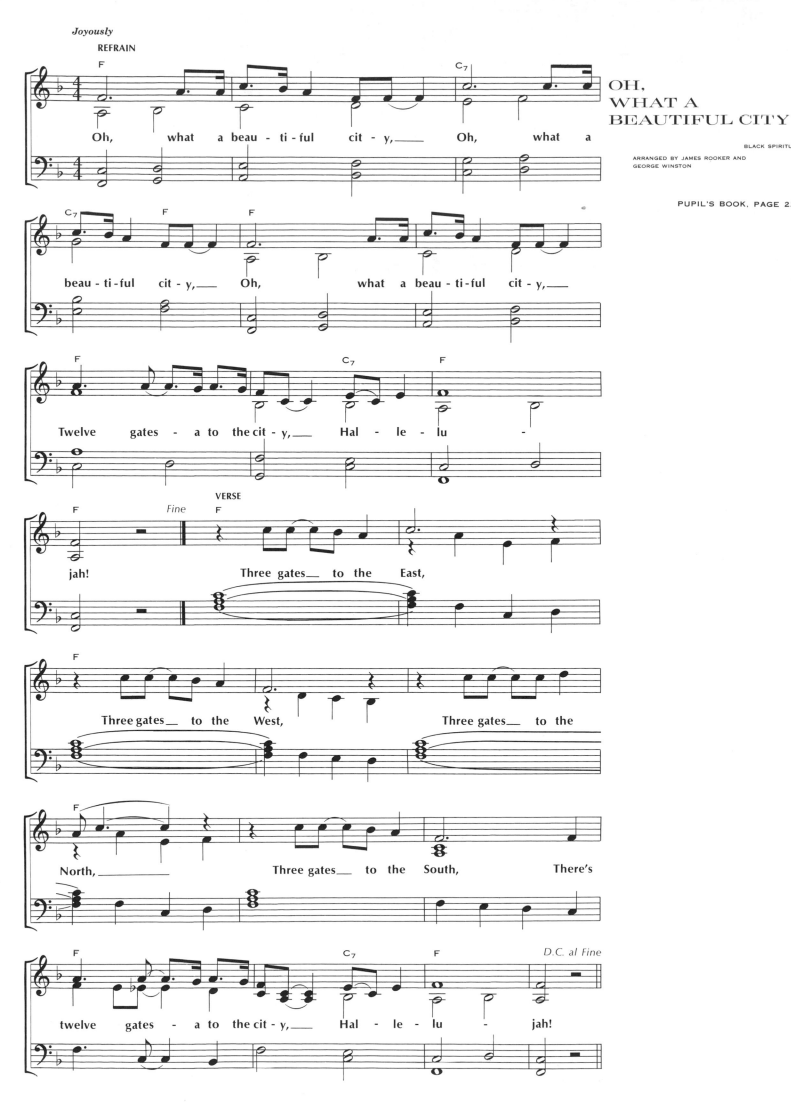

OH, WHAT A BEAUTIFUL CITY

BLACK SPIRITUAL

ARRANGED BY JAMES ROOKER AND
GEORGE WINSTON

PUPIL'S BOOK, PAGE 220

THREE WHITE GULLS

FOLK SONG FROM ITALY
ARRANGED BY ALBERT DE VITO
ENGLISH WORDS BY MARGUERITE WILKINSON

Original title "The Three Doves" by Marguerite Wilkinson from
Botsford Collection of Folk Songs—Volume 3. Copyright
© 1921, 1922 G. Schirmer, Inc. Used by Permission.

PUPIL'S BOOK, PAGE 218

1. There are three white gulls a - fly - ing; There are three white gulls a -
2. In the waves they dip their soft wings; In the waves they dip their

fly - ing; There are three white gulls a - fly - ing; By the sea they
soft wings; In the waves they dip their soft wings; Then soar to the

cry, By the sea they cry, By the sea they cry. There are three white gulls a -
sky, Then soar to the sky, Then soar to the sky. In the waves they dip their

fly - ing; By the sea they cry, By the sea they cry, By the sea they cry.
soft wings; Then soar to the sky, Then soar to the sky, Then soar to the sky.

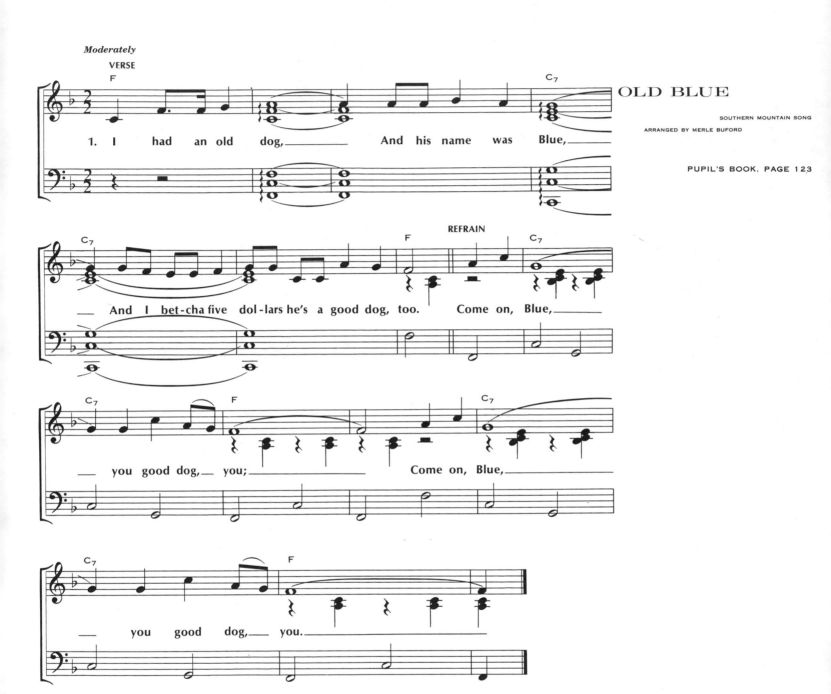

OLD BLUE

SOUTHERN MOUNTAIN SONG
ARRANGED BY MERLE BUFORD

PUPIL'S BOOK, PAGE 123

2. I grabbed my axe and I tooted my horn,
   Gonna git me a 'possum in the new-ground corn. *Refrain*

3. Chased that ol' 'possum up a 'simmon tree,
   Blue looked at the 'possum, 'possum looked at me. *Refrain*

4. Blue grinned at me, I grinned at him,
   I shook out the 'possum, Blue took him in. *Refrain*

5. Baked that 'possum all good and brown,
   And I laid them sweet potatoes 'round and 'round. *Refrain*

6. Well, Old Blue died, and he died so hard,
   That he shook the ground in my back yard. *Refrain*

7. I dug his grave with a silver spade,
   I let him down with a golden chain. *Refrain*

8. When I get to heaven, first thing I'll do,
   Grab me a horn and blow for Old Blue. *Refrain*

298

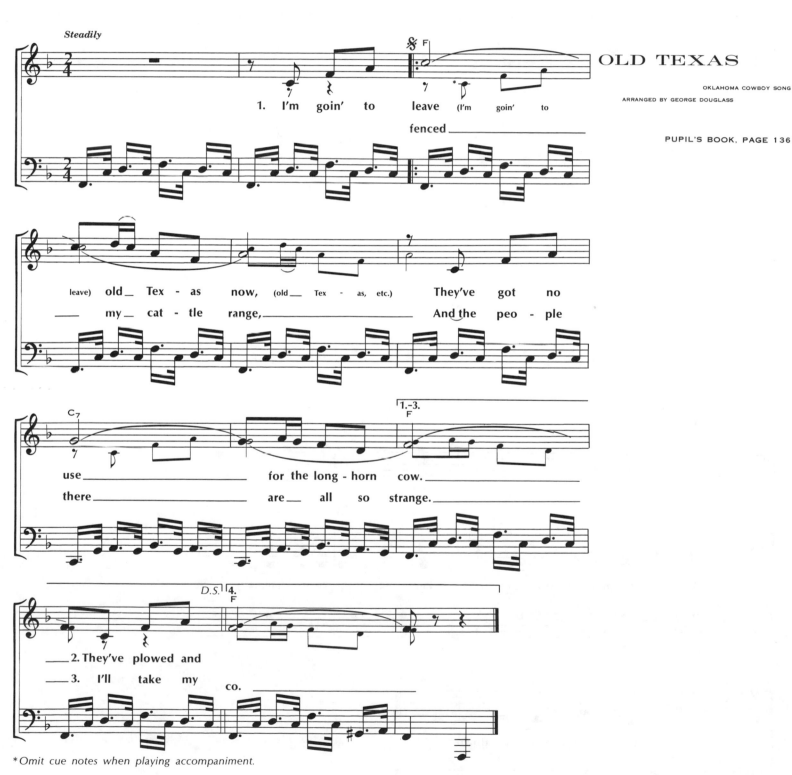

OLD TEXAS

OKLAHOMA COWBOY SONG
ARRANGED BY GEORGE DOUGLASS

PUPIL'S BOOK, PAGE 136

1. I'm goin' to leave (I'm goin' to leave) old Texas now, (old Texas, etc.) They've got no use for the long-horn cow.

fenced my cattle range, And the people there are all so strange.

2. They've plowed and

3. I'll take my co.

Omit cue notes when playing accompaniment.

3. I'll take my horse, I'll take my rope,
   And hit the trail upon a lope.

4. Say *adios* to the Alamo
   And turn my head toward Mexico.

PAY ME MY MONEY DOWN

SLAVE SONG FROM THE GEORGIA SEA ISLANDS
COLLECTED AND ADAPTED BY LYDIA A. PARRISH
ARRANGED BY FRANCIS GIRARD

TRO—® COPYRIGHT 1942 AND RENEWED 1970 HOLLIS MUSIC, INC. NEW YORK, N.Y. USED BY PERMISSION.

PUPIL'S BOOK, PAGE 4

Brightly

1. I thought I heard the cap - tain say,   "Pay me my
2. As soon as the boat was clear of the bar,   "Pay me my
3. Well, I wish I was Mr. Ste - ven's son,   "Pay me my

mon - ey down, — To - mor - row is our sail - ing day, —
mon - ey down," — He knocked me down with the end of a spar, —
mon - ey down," — Sit on the bank and watch the work done, —

REFRAIN

Pay me my mon-ey down."
"Pay me my mon-ey down."   "Pay me, oh, pay me,
"Pay me my mon-ey down."

Pay me my mon-ey down, — Pay me or go to jail, —

Pay me my mon-ey down." —

PSALM OF
THANKSGIVING

DAKOTA INDIAN HYMN

MUSICAL SETTING BY CARLTON YOUNG

ENGLISH WORDS BY PHILIP FRAZIER

ARRANGED BY GEORGE RAVENSONG

COPYRIGHT © 1975 BY HOPE PUBLISHING CO. ALL RIGHTS RESERVED. USED
BY PERMISSION.

PUPIL'S BOOK, PAGE 245

1. Man - y and great, O God, are Thy things,
2. Grant un - to us com - mu - nion with Thee,

Mak - er of earth and sky;
Thou star - a - bid - ing One;

Thy hands have set the heav - ens with stars;
Come un - to us and dwell with us;

Thy fin - gers spread the moun - tains and plains.
With Thee are found the gifts of life.

Lo, at Thy word the wa - ters were
Bless us with life that has no

formed; Deep seas o - bey Thy voice.
end, E - ter - nal life with Thee.

RED,
RED
ROBIN

WORDS AND MUSIC BY HARRY WOODS

ARRANGED BY OLLIE OLDAY

COPYRIGHT © 1921 BY BOURNE CO. COPYRIGHT RENEWED. THIS ARRANGEMENT
COPYRIGHT © 1981 BY BOURNE CO. ALL RIGHTS RESERVED. USED BY
PERMISSION OF BOURNE CO. AND EMI MUSIC PUBLISHING LIMITED.

PUPIL'S BOOK, PAGE 147

hours and hours._____ I'm just a kid a-gain,

do - in' what I did a-gain, Sing - ing a song, When the

red, red, rob - in comes bob, bob, bob-bin' a - long._____

Brightly

ROOKOOMBINE

FOLK SONG FROM JAMAICA

ARRANGED BY GEORGE DOUGLASS

MELODY AND WORDS OF FIRST VERSE FROM FOLK SONGS OF JAMAICA, EDITED AND ARRANGED BY TOM MURRAY. COPYRIGHT 1952 BY THE OXFORD UNIVERSITY PRESS, LONDON; WORDS OF SECOND VERSE FROM FOLK SONGS OF THE CARIBBEAN BY JIM MORSE. COPYRIGHT © 1958 BY BANTAM BOOKS. USED BY PERMISSION.

PUPIL'S BOOK, PAGE 190

1. Train top a bridge jus - a run like a breeze, An' a
2. Went King - ston town just to have me look a - roun', But in -

gal un - der-neath it a wash her che - mise. Oh, Roo-koom - bine ee - na
stead look a - roun', oh, me spent ev - 'ry poun'.

San - ta Fe, Roo-koom-bine ee-na San - ta Fe, Oh, Roo-koom-bine.___

303

PADDY WORKS
ON THE
RAILWAY

IRISH-AMERICAN RAILROAD SONG
ARRANGED BY W. W. SCHMIDT AND JEAN KUNST

PUPIL'S BOOK, PAGE 209

SOLO

1. In eigh - teen hun-dred and for - ty - one I put my cord - u - roy
2. In eigh - teen hun-dred and for - ty - two I left the old ___ world
3. It's "Pat, do this," ___ and "Pat, do that," with - out a stock - ing

breech - es on, I put my cord - u - roy breech - es on to
for the new, Oh, spare me the luck ___ that brought me through to
or cra - vat, And noth - ing but ___ an old straw hat, while

REFRAIN
CHORUS

work up - on the rail - way.
work up - on the rail - way. Fil - li - mee - oo - ree -
work - ing on the rail - way.

oo - ree - ay, Fil - li - mee - oo - ree - oo - ree - ay,

Fil - li - mee - oo - ree - oo - ree - ay, to work up - on the rail - way.

RUN, RUN, RUN

WORDS AND MUSIC BY CHRIS DEDRICK

PUPIL'S BOOK, PAGE 98

Lyrics: Run, run, run ___ through the sun-light, Run, run, run ___ through the snow. Run, run, run, ___ don't be up-tight, Run, run, run, ___ Free-dom, go. ___

SAMBALELE

FOLK SONG FROM BRAZIL
ARRANGED BY W. W. SCHMIDT
WORDS BY RUTH AND THOMAS MARTIN

PUPIL'S BOOK, PAGE 22

Gaily

Ⓐ VERSE

1. Hear how the mu - sic is play - ing, Dance to its light - heart - ed
2. Dance while the drum - beat is pound - ing, Mel - low gui - tars soft - ly

meas - ures, Clap - ping and stamp - ing and sway - ing,
strum - ming, And cas - ta - nets clear - ly sound - ing,

Ⓑ REFRAIN

Join in the car - ni - val plea - sures.
Join in the whis - tling and hum - ming.   Sam - ba, sam - ba,

sam - ba - la - le - le, While we are danc - ing and sing - ing so gai - ly,

Sam - ba, sam - ba, sam - ba - la - le - le, While we are danc - ing and sing - ing so gai - ly.

WORDS AND MUSIC BY ARTHUR CARTER
ARRANGED BY CAROL KERR
USED BY PERMISSION.

PUPIL'S BOOK, PAGE 96

SANDS GET INTO YOUR SHOES

1. You have - n't lived__ in the sum - mer - time__ Un - til you've gone__ to the
2. The sun comes beat - ing down on your head,__ The dust gets in - to your

beach,_____ And tast - ed ice - cream: the lem - on lime,__ Ba -
eyes,_____ Your feet they hurt,__ but the thing you dread's__ The

na - na, wal - nut and peach.
mos - qui - toes__ and the flies.

And sands, and sands, and

sands get in - to your o - pen shoes, And sands, and sands, and

sands get in - to your shoes.

3. You leave your things by the waterside,
   And then somehow you forget
   To move them back from the rising tide—
   Your towels and blanket get wet.
   And sands . . .

309

SCRATCH, SCRATCH

WORDS AND MUSIC BY HARRY BELAFONTE AND
LORD BURGESS
ARRANGED BY LAURA S. WENDEL

"SCRATCH, SCRATCH ME BACK" BY HARRY BELAFONTE AND LORD BURGESS
© COPYRIGHT 1957 BY CLARA MUSIC PUBLISHING CORPORATION
ALL RIGHTS RESERVED USED BY PERMISSION

PUPIL'S BOOK, PAGE 6

Not too fast

1. Oh, we went out to a par - ty, It was me and Ben and
I was quite em - bar-rassed, Till my two friends I did
scratch-ing was con - ta - gious, And it didn't take ver - y

Mac, And be - fore I knew what hap-pened, I got an
see, Well,_____ they were mad - ly itch - ing, And they were
long, Ev'ry - body there was itch - ing, As they_____

itch - in' on my back.
scream-ing louder than me. Scratch, scratch me back,
joined me in this song.

Scratch, scratch me back. It real - ly is a fact,_____ The less I

1., 2.
3.

itch, the more I scratch.
2. Well,_____
3. Now, this
scratch.

SILENT NIGHT

MUSIC BY FRANZ GRUBER

ARRANGED BY JAMES ROOKER

WORDS BY JOSEPH MOHR

PUPIL'S BOOK, PAGE 212

Gently

1. Si - lent night, ho - ly night, All is calm,
2. Si - lent night, ho - ly night, Shep - herds quake

all is bright Round yon Vir - gin Moth - er and Child.
at the sight, Glo - ries stream __ from heav - en a - far,

Ho - ly In - fant so ten - der and mild, Sleep in heav - en - ly
Heav'n - ly hosts __ sing "Al - le - lu - ia, Christ the Sav - ior is

peace, _____ Sleep __ in heav - en - ly peace. _____
born! _____ Christ __ the Sav - ior is born!" _____

*Left hand may be played alone as an accompaniment.

311

SHE'LL BE COMIN' ROUND THE MOUNTAIN

SOUTHERN MOUNTAIN SONG
ARRANGED BY DONALD KALBACH

PUPIL'S BOOK, PAGE 167

1. She'll be com - in' round the moun-tain when she comes, _____ She'll be com - in' round the moun-tain when she comes, _____ She'll be com - in' round the moun-tain, She'll be com - in' round the moun-tain, She'll be com - in' round the moun - tain when she comes. _____

2. She'll be driv - in' six white hor - ses when she comes, _____ She'll be driv - in' six white hor - ses when she comes, _____ She'll be driv - in' six white hor - ses, She'll be driv - in' six white hor - ses, She'll be driv - in' six white hor - ses when she comes. _____

3. Oh, we'll kill the old red rooster when she comes, . . .

4. Oh, we'll all have chicken and dumplings when she comes, . . .

5. Oh, we'll all go out to meet her when she comes, . . .

SONG OF THE ANGEL

MENNONITE MELODY
ARRANGED BY KARL SCHAUFUSS
© 1966 BY LAWSON-GOULD MUSIC PUBLISHERS, INC. USED BY PERMISSION.

PUPIL'S BOOK, PAGE 126

Not too slow

1. Fear not, fear not, good _ shep - herds _ all, Let faith your fear de - stroy; For

lo, this night I___ bring___ to___ you Good ti-dings of great joy,_____ Good

ti - dings___ of great joy.

2. Awake your ears and hark to me,
   To hear the glorious Word:
   For unto you is born this day
   A Saviour, Christ the Lord,
   A Saviour, Christ the Lord.

3. You'll find the Babe in Bethlehem,
   Born of the Mary maid;
   All wrapped in swaddling clothes is he,
   And in a manger laid,
   And in a manger laid.

4. So join us now with one accord
   To sing this wondrous birth:
   Give praise to God, our heav'nly King,
   And peace to men on earth,
   And peace to men on earth.

SKIP TO MY LOU

AMERICAN GAME SONG
ARRANGED BY CAMERON MCGRAW

PUPIL'S BOOK, PAGE 170

Gaily

1. Flies in the butter-milk, shoo, fly, shoo! Flies in the butter-milk, shoo, fly, shoo!

Flies in the butter-milk, shoo, fly, shoo! Skip to my Lou, my dar - ling.

2. Little red wagon painted blue, . . .

3. Lost my partner, what'll I do? . . .

4. I'll get another, better than you! . . .

SOURWOOD MOUNTAIN

AMERICAN FOLK SONG
ARRANGED BY BRUCE SIMPSON

PUPIL'S BOOK, PAGE 16

Well-accented

1. Chick - en crowin' on Sour - wood Moun - tain, Hey de - ing dang did - dle al - ly day.

So man - y pret - ty girls, I can't count 'em, Hey de - ing dang did - dle al - ly day.

My true love, she lives in Letch - er, Hey de - ing dang did - dle al - ly day.

She won't come and I won't fetch her, Hey de - ing dang did - dle al - ly day.

2. My true love's a blue-eyed daisy, . . .
   If I don't get her, I'll go crazy, . . .
   Big dog bark and little one bite you, . . .
   Big girl court and little one slight you, . . .

314

THE STAR-SPANGLED BANNER

MUSIC BY JOHN STAFFORD SMITH
WORDS BY FRANCIS SCOTT KEY

PUPIL'S BOOK, PAGE 62

Oh,—say! can you see, by the dawn's ear - ly light, What so proud-ly we

hailed at the twi - light's last gleam-ing, Whose broad stripes and bright stars, through the

per - il - ous fight, O'er the ram - parts we watched were so gal - lant - ly

stream-ing? And the rock - ets' red glare, the bombs burst-ing in air, Gave

proof through the night that our flag was still there. Oh, say, does that — Star - Span-gled

Ban-ner — yet — wave — O'er the land — of the free and the home of the brave.

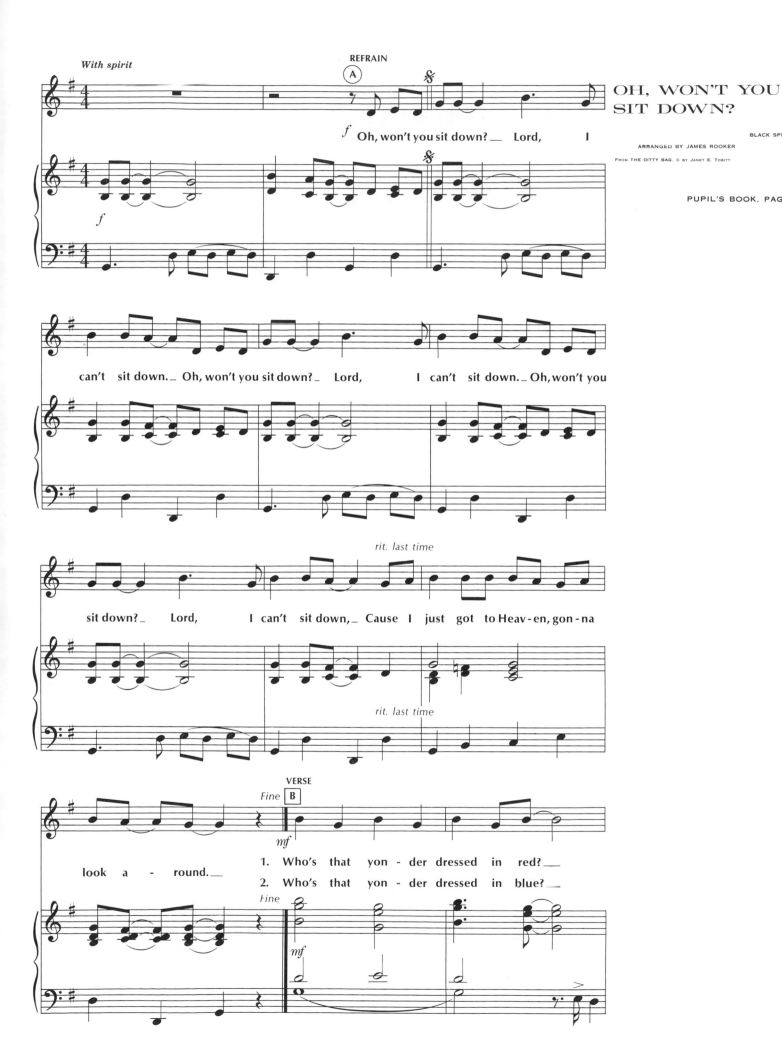

OH, WON'T YOU
SIT DOWN?

BLACK SPIRITUAL

ARRANGED BY JAMES ROOKER

FROM THE DITTY BAG. © BY JANET E. TOBITT

PUPIL'S BOOK, PAGE 24

Must be the chil-dren that_ Mo - ses_ led._ Who's that yon - der
Must be the chil-dren that are com - in'_ through._ Who's that yon - der

dressed in white? _ Must be the chil-dren of the Is - rael - ite._ Oh, won't you
dressed in black? _ Must be the hyp - o -crites a - turn-in'_ back._

D.S. al Fine

THIS LAND IS YOUR LAND

WORDS AND MUSIC BY WOODY GUTHRIE
ARRANGED BY JAMES ROOKER
COUNTERMELODY BY RUTH TUTELMAN

PUPIL'S BOOK, PAGE 242

Briskly
REFRAIN
COUNTERMELODY

This land is your land, this land is

MELODY

This land is your land,_ this land is my land,_

mine, From Maine to Mon - ta - na,

_ From Cal - i - for - nia_ to the New York

des - ert to the shore, We sing that this land is
is - land;_____ From the red - wood for - est_____

your land, this land is mine, Yes, it's
_____ to the Gulf Stream wa - ters;_____

made for you and me._____
This land was made for you and me._____

8va

VERSE

1. As I was walk - ing _____ that rib - bon of
2. I've roamed and ram - bled_____ and I fol - lowed my
3. When the sun comes shin - ing_____ and I____ was

high - way, _____ I saw a - bove me _____
foot - steps _____ To the spar - kling sands of _____
stroll - ing _____ And the wheat - fields wav - ing _____

_____ that end - less sky - way. _____ I saw be -
_____ her dia - mond des - erts, _____ And all a -
_____ and the dust clouds roll - ing, _____ As the fog was

low me _____ that gold - en val - ley, _____
round me _____ a voice was sound - ing, _____
lift - ing _____ a voice was chant - ing, _____

This land was made for you and me. _____
"This land was made for you and me." _____
"This land was made for you and me." _____

POLLY WOLLY
DOODLE

AMERICAN FOLK SONG
ARRANGED BY NICHOLAS ZUMBRO

PUPIL'S BOOK, PAGE 171

1. Oh, I went down South for to see my Sal, Sing - ing

Pol - ly Wol - ly Doo - dle all the day; My Sal, she is a

spunk - y gal, Sing - ing Pol - ly Wol - ly Doo - dle all the day. Fare thee

well, fare thee well, Fare thee well my fair - y fay, For I'm

goin' to Loui-si-an-a, for to see my Su-sy-an-na, Sing-ing Pol-ly Wol-ly Doo-dle all the day.

2. Oh, my Sal, she is a maiden fair,
Singing Polly Wolly Doodle all the day;
With curly eyes and laughing hair,
Singing Polly Wolly Doodle all the day.

3. The partridge is a pretty bird,
It has a speckled breast,
It steals away the farmer's grain,
And totes it to its nest!

4. The raccoon's tail is ringed around,
The 'possum's tail is bare,
The rabbit's got no tail at all,
Just a little bitty bunch of hair!

5. The June bug, he has golden wings,
The lightning bug totes a flame,
The caterpillar's got no wings at all,
But he gets there just the same!

GING GONG GOOLI

FOLK SONG FROM BRITISH GUIANA
ARRANGED BY LAURA S. WENDEL

From SECOND FUN AND FOLK SONG PROOF BOOK. © 1962
COOPERATIVE RECREATION SERVICE, INC. USED BY PERMISSION

PUPIL'S BOOK, PAGE 18

Ging gong goo-li goo-li goo-li goo-li wat-cha, Ging gong goo, ging gong goo. Ging gong goo. Hai-la, hai-la shai-la, Shai-la hai-la shai-la ho-la-ho! hai-la shai-la ho!

NAUGHTY LITTLE FLEA

WORDS AND MUSIC BY NORMAN THOMAS
TRANSCRIBED FROM THE RECORDING BY
MIRIAM MAKEBA AND HARRY BELAFONTE
ARRANGED BY ROSEMARY JACQUES

© 1957 PINEBROOK MUSIC CORP. C/O H/B WEBMAN & COMPANY
USED BY PERMISSION

PUPIL'S BOOK, PAGE 140

Where did the naught-y lit-tle flea go? Won't some-bod-y tell me? Where did the naught-y lit-tle flea go? Won't some-bod-y tell me?

1. There was a naught-y lit-tle flea; He climbed up on the dog-gie's knee; He climbed some here, he climbed some there; He___ was climb-ing ev-'ry-where. Tell me,

2. He climbed some here, he climbed some there; He___ was climb-ing ev-'ry-where. And now at last he's found a nest Where he can get some food and rest. Tell me, Where did the naught-y lit-tle flea go?

3. He bit him here, he bit him there; He bit him al-most ev-'ry-where. When he was done he want-ed more; He nev-er tasted such a dog be-fore. Tell me,

Won't some-bod-y tell me? Where did the naught-y lit-tle flea go? Won't some-bod-y tell me? tell me?

WHEN THE SAINTS GO MARCHING IN

BLACK SPIRITUAL
ARRANGED BY DONALD KALBACH

Not too fast

1. Oh, when the saints go march-ing in,

Oh, when the saints go march-ing in,

Oh, Lord, I want to be in that num-ber

When the saints go march-ing in.

PUPIL'S BOOK, PAGE 58

2. Oh, when the stars refuse to shine, . . .   3. Oh, when I hear that trumpet sound, . . .

THE
WISE MAN
BUILT
HIS HOUSE

ORIGIN UNKNOWN
ARRANGED BY WILLIAM ARMENTI

PUPIL'S BOOK, PAGE 21

1. Oh, the wise man built his house up-on the rock, Oh, the wise man
2. Oh, the rains came down and the floods came up, Oh, the rains came

built his house up-on the rock, Oh, the wise man built his
down and the floods came up, Oh, the rains came down and the

house up-on the rock, And the rains came tum-bling down.
floods came up, But the house on the rock stood firm.

3. Oh, the silly man built his house upon the sand, (*3 times*)
   And the rains came tumbling down.

4. Oh, the rains came down and the floods came up, (*3 times*)
   And the house on the sand went swisssssssssssh.

SEE,
CAN'T YOU
JUMP FOR JOY

BLACK-AMERICAN RING SHOUT
ARRANGED BY LAURA S. WENDEL

PUPIL'S BOOK, PAGE 150

My Lord calls me, See, can't you jump for joy,_____

See, can't you jump for joy,_____ See, can't you jump for joy.___

My Lord calls me, See, can't you jump for joy,___

Broth - er, can't you jump for joy. ___

Lively—not fast

I KNOW AN OLD LADY

MUSIC BY ALAN MILLS

ARRANGED BY FRANK FOX

WORDS BY ROSE BONNE

Copyright 1952 and 1960 by Peer International (Canada) Ltd. Sole Selling Agent Peer International Corporation. Used by permission.

PUPIL'S BOOK, PAGE 52

1. I know an old la - dy who swal-lowed a fly; I don't know why she

swal-lowed a fly! I guess she'll die!_____ 2. I

know an old la - dy who swal-lowed a spi - der that wrig-gled and wrig-gled and

tick - led in - side her; She swal - lowed the spi - der to catch the fly, But

I don't know why she swal - lowed the fly. I guess she'll die!_____ I

bird! Now, how ab - surd, to
cat! Now, fan - cy that, to
know an old la - dy who swal - lowed a dog! My, what a hog, to
goat! Just opened her throat and
cow! I don't know how she

No repeat first time

swal - low a bird! 3. She swal - lowed the bird to catch the spi - der
swal - low a cat! 4. She swal - lowed the cat to catch the bird,____ *(To 3)*
swal - low a dog! 5. She swal - lowed the dog to catch the cat,____ *(To 4)*
swal - lowed a goat! 6. She swal - lowed the goat to catch the dog,____ *(To 5)*
swal - lowed a cow! 7. She swal - lowed the cow to catch the goat,____ *(To 6)*

that wrig-gled and wrig-gled and tick-led in-side her, She swal-lowed the spi-der to

catch the fly, But I don't know why she swal-lowed the fly;

Verses 3-6.   *D.S.* | *Verse 7.*

I guess she'll die!_____ I die!_____ 8. I

(Spoken)

know an old la-dy who swal-lowed a horse; She's dead, of course!

327

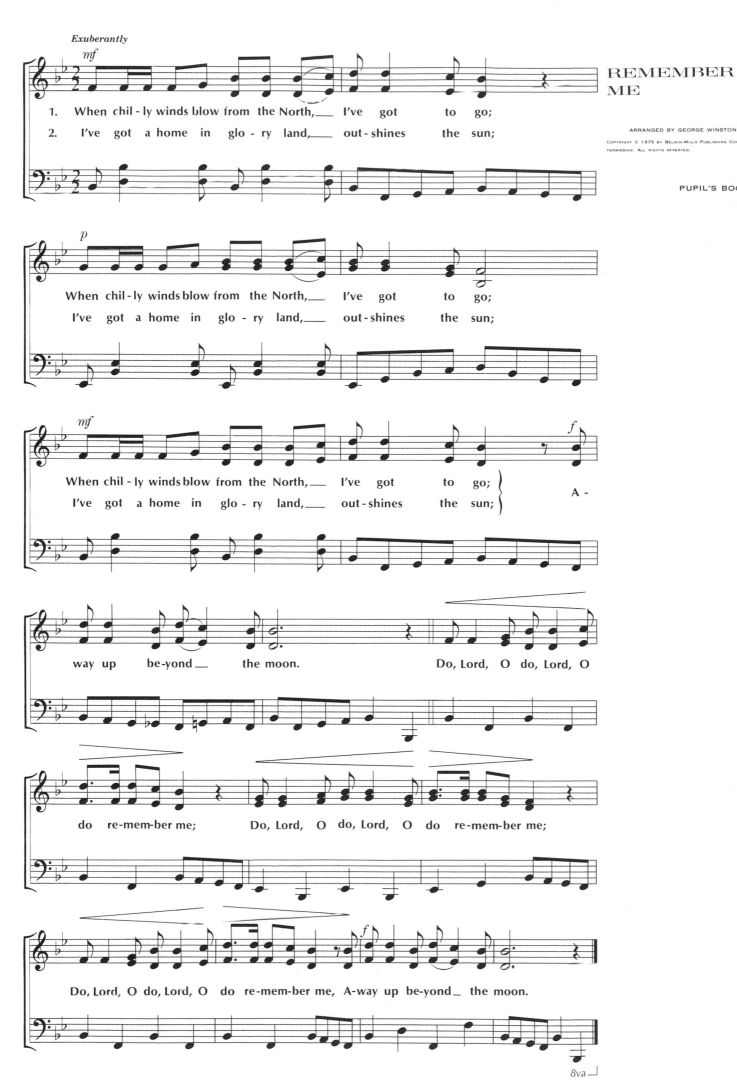

REMEMBER ME

BLACK SPIRITUAL

ARRANGED BY GEORGE WINSTON

PUPIL'S BOOK, PAGE 92

Exuberantly

mf

1. When chil - ly winds blow from the North, __ I've got to go;
2. I've got a home in glo - ry land, __ out - shines the sun;

p

When chil - ly winds blow from the North, __ I've got to go;
I've got a home in glo - ry land, __ out - shines the sun;

mf　　　　　　　　　　　　　　　　　　　　　　　　　　*f*

When chil - ly winds blow from the North, __ I've got to go;
I've got a home in glo - ry land, __ out - shines the sun;　A -

way up be-yond __ the moon.　　　　Do, Lord, O do, Lord, O

do re-mem-ber me;　　Do, Lord, O do, Lord, O do re-mem-ber me;

f

Do, Lord, O do, Lord, O do re-mem-ber me, A-way up be-yond_ the moon.

8va

328

AIN'T
GONNA
RAIN

AMERICAN FOLK SONG
ARRANGED BY ROSEMARY JACQUES

PUPIL'S BOOK, PAGE 171

3. I'll tune the fiddle, you get the bow,
   It ain't gonna rain no more.
   The weatherman just told me so,
   It ain't gonna rain no more. *Refrain*

4. Oh, what did the blackbird say to the crow?
   "It ain't gonna rain no more.
   It ain't gonna hail, it ain't gonna snow,
   It ain't gonna rain no more." *Refrain*

TWO LITTLE PIECES, NO. 1

MUSIC BY ANTON BRUCK

FROM 44 ORIGINAL PIANO DUETS AS EDITED BY WALTER ECKARD. © 1962
THEODORE PRESSER COMPANY. USED BY PERMISSION.

SECONDO

PUPIL'S BOOK, PAGE 1

TA-RA-RA BOOM-DE-AY

WORDS AND MUSIC BY HENRY SAYERS
ARRANGED BY OLLIE OLDAY

PUPIL'S BOOK, PAGE 146

Ta - ra - ra boom - de - ay, Ta - ra - ra boom - de - ay,

Ta - ra - ra boom - de - ay, Ta - ra - ra boom - de - ay,

TINGA LAYO

CALYPSO FROM THE WEST INDIES

ARRANGED BY DARRELL PETER

ENGLISH VERSION BY MARGARET MARKS

PUPIL'S BOOK, PAGE 149

Tin - ga Lay - o! Run, lit - tle don-key, run! Tin - ga

¡Ven, mi bu - rri - to, ven!

Lay - o! Run, lit - tle don-key, run! run! 1. My don - key

¡Ven, mi bu - rri - to, ven! ven! 1. Bu - rri - to

yes, my don - key no, My don-key stop when I tell him to go!

si, bu - rri - to no. ¡Bu - rri - to co - me con te - ne - dor!

2. My donkey hee, my donkey haw,
   My donkey sit on the kitchen floor! *Refrain*

3. My donkey kick, my donkey balk,
   My donkey eat with a silver fork! *Refrain*

THE FROG IN THE WELL

FOLK SONG FROM THE SOUTHERN APPALACHIANS
ARRANGED BY GEORGE DOUGLASS

FROM ENGLISH FOLK SONGS FROM THE SOUTHERN APPALACHIANS BY CECIL SHARP. USED BY PERMISSION OF THE OXFORD UNIVERSITY PRESS.

PUPIL'S BOOK, PAGE 178

1. There was a frog lived in the spring,
2. The frog went swim-ming 'cross the lake,

Sing song Kit-ty can't you ki-mey O; He

was so fat he could not swim,
He got swallowed by a big, black snake,

Sing song Kit-ty can't you ki-mey O.

Kee-mey O ma ki-mey O ma dir-ey O ma wear, Me hi, me ho, me

in come Sal-ly Sin-gle, Some time Pen-ny Win-kle, In stepped nip cat,

Hit him with a brick bat, Sing song Kit-ty can't you ki-mey O.

ORFF-INSTRUMENT ACCOMPANIMENTS

The accompaniments on the following pages are arranged for pitched and nonpitched instruments. The names of the instruments are abbreviated at the beginning of each line of music.

Sop. Gl.	Soprano Glockenspiel	Timp.	Timpani
Alto Gl.	Alto Glockenspiel	Cast.	Castanets
Sop. Xyl.	Soprano Xylophone	Cym.	Cymbal
Alto Xyl.	Alto Xylophone	F.C.	Finger Cymbals
Bass Xyl.	Bass Xylophone	Tam.	Tambourine
Sop. Met.	Soprano Metallophone	Tri.	Triangle
Alto Met.	Alto Metallophone	W.B.	Woodblock
Bass Met.	Bass Metallophone		

The pitches to be played on each pitched percussion instrument are indicated at the beginning of the score. (If the instrumentation is changed within a composition, the new instrument is listed and pitches are indicated at the appropriate entrance.) Capital letters are used for the pitches in the lower octave of the instrument; small letters for the upper octave. Bars that are not used may be removed from the instrument.

All instrument parts (except timpani) are notated in the treble clef. This allows greater flexibility in substituting one instrument for another if necessary.

Notes with a down-stem are played with the mallet in the left hand; notes with an up-stem are played with the mallet in the right hand. When two instruments are notated on one staff, one is indicated by up-stems, the other by down-stems.

USING THE TEACHING SUGGESTIONS

The teaching suggestions at the top of each page are designed as ways to "get to" the instruments. These suggestions are not the only method possible, but offer one approach to the music.

The first step in learning each accompaniment is to *know the song*. Do not attempt to add instruments until the children are confident with at least one verse of the song. Whenever possible, all children should practice the chants and rhythm exercises so that they are involved in the music, whether or not they are playing an instrument.

Allow portions of several class sessions to learn each accompaniment. Some may be mastered in two or three sessions; some may require several.

Although learning the accompaniments is primarily an aural experience, notation may be helpful. When appropriate, notate or have children notate the rhythm and melody patterns as they learn them.

The recordings of these Orff arrangements are literal reproductions of the notation. As children work with the accompaniments, they should be encouraged to improvise introductions, interludes, and melodies of their own.

MALLET TECHNIQUES FOR ORFF INSTRUMENTS

1. Sit or stand with good posture. Hold the arms slightly away from the body. Bend the elbows so the forearms are several inches above the instrument keyboard.

2. The correct feel of holding the mallets is like holding bicycle handle bars. Hold the mallets between the thumbs and curved index fingers, lightly wrapping the other fingers around each handle. The ends of the handles should be visible. Thumbnails face each other; palms "look at" the floor. *Note:* Don't let the index fingers straighten to point down the mallet.

3. To avoid hitting the mallet sticks against each other, hold one mallet slightly farther away from the body than the other. Also, the mallet sticks should slant toward each other at a 45° angle. This helps keep the arms and hands in position for good wrist action.

4. Whenever possible, alternate left and right hands. This helps coordination, playing fast passages, and playing both hands simultaneously.

5. Play in the center of the bar.

6. Play with a flexible wrist, Begin from a "ready" position above the bar and return to this position after each stroke. Think of pulling the tone out of the bar, not beating it in.

OH, WON'T YOU SIT DOWN?

1. Tambourine: Teach this part to the entire class. When the children know the tambourine part, have them sing the song along with it.

2. Sop. Xyl. and Alto Xyl.: Pat legs and chant one of the following patterns. Notice the two notes in a row played by the right hand.

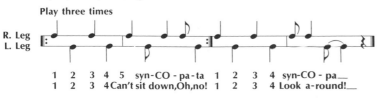

Play three times

| 1 | 2 | 3 | 4 | 5 | syn-CO - pa-ta | 1 | 2 | 3 | 4 | syn-CO - pa__ |
| 1 | 2 | 3 | 4 | Can't sit down, Oh, no! | 1 | 2 | 3 | 4 | Look a-round!__ |

Transfer these parts to the instruments. If the children have difficulty, they may try stepping the patterns.

3. Bass Xyl.: Have the children learn this part by patting their legs and singing pitch names. They may chant the last two measures on page 334 with the other xylophone parts (with appropriate left/right patting).

4. Sop. Gl. and Alto Gl.: Add improvisation in the second section of the song. Questions and answers in the glockenspiel parts correspond to the questions and answers in the song. Encourage the glockenspiel players to relate their answers to the questions, perhaps by playing the same rhythm as the beginning or the ending of the question.

Practice the second section of the song. The tambourine will play tremolos with the Sop. Xyl. and Alto Xyl. Then it will play the cadence "punctuation marks" with the Bass Xyl.

OH, WON'T YOU SIT DOWN?

BLACK SPIRITUAL   ARRANGED BY MARILYN COPELAND DAVIDSON

Pupil's Book, p. 24   Alternative piano acc., p. 316

Voice

SOLO   CHORUS

1. Who's that yon-der dressed in red?___ Must be the chil-dren that___ Mo-ses led.___
2. Who's that yon-der dressed in blue?___ Must be the chil-dren that are com-in' through.___

Sop. Gl.
and
Alto Gl.

Sop.   Alto

Improvised "question" ending on D   *Improvised "answer" ending on D*
using these pitches.   *using these pitches.*

Sop. Xyl.

Alto Xyl.

Bass Xyl.

Tam.

Voice

SOLO   CHORUS   SOLO   D.S.

Who's that yon-der dressed in white?___ Must be the chil-dren of the Is-rael-ite.___
Who's that yon-der dressed in black?___ Must be the hyp-o-crites a-turn-in' back.___ Oh, won't you

Sop. Gl.
and
Alto Gl.

Sop.   Alto

"question"   *"answer"*

Sop. Xyl.

Alto Xyl.

Bass Xyl.

Tam.

PAY ME MY MONEY DOWN

Write the basic chant on the board. As you play the recording, have the children chant in rhythm.

Pay it to me now, oh please, sir; Pay it now, oh please!

Teach the rhythm of the instrument parts by playing only on words given below. Transfer the rhythms to the

instruments. Add the introduction after the song is learned. (3x means to play three times.)

1. Sop. Xyl./Alto Xyl.: Clap or pat the rhythm.

Pay to me, oh please, Pay!

PAY ME MY MONEY DOWN
SLAVE SONG FROM THE GEORGIA SEA ISLANDS

COLLECTED AND ADAPTED BY LYDIA A. PARRISH   ARRANGED BY MARILYN COPELAND DAVIDSON

TRO—© COPYRIGHT 1942 AND RENEWED 1970 HOLLIS MUSIC, INC. NEW YORK, N.Y. USED BY PERMISSION.

Pupil's Book, p. 4   Alternative piano acc., p. 300

336

2. Cowbell and Drum

Cowbell
Drum

Pay me, please, Pay it now, oh please!

(The cowbell plays only on the first beat every fourth measure—once through the complete pattern.)

3. Bass Xyl.: Pat legs.

Side of R. Leg
R. Leg
L. Leg
Side of L. Leg

Pay now, please, Pay.   Pay now, please, Pay.

REFRAIN

Voice — Pay me my mon-ey down."— "Pay___ me,___ oh, pay___ me,___ Pay me my

Recorder

Alto Gl

Sop. Xyl.
or
Alto Xyl.

Bass Xyl.

Cowbell
Drum

Maracas

(Last time)

Voice — mon-ey down,___ Pay me or go to jail, ___ Pay me my mon-ey down."—

Recorder

Sop. Xyl.
or
Alto Xyl.

Bass Xyl.

Cowbell
Drum

Maracas

2. As soon as the boat was clear of the bar,
    "Pay me my money down,"
    He knocked me down with the end of a spar,
    "Pay me my money down." *Refrain*

3. Well, I wish I was Mr. Steven's son,
    "Pay me my money down,"
    Sit on the bank and watch the work done,
    "Pay me my money down." *Refrain*

4. Alto Gl. and Recorder:

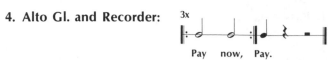

Pay now, Pay.

5. Maracas: Snap fingers.

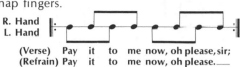

(Verse) Pay it to me now, oh please, sir;
(Refrain) Pay it to me now, oh please.___

HOLD ON

1. Sop. Xyl. and Alto Xyl.: Pat the rhythm of the Alto Xyl. part starting with the right hand, then starting with the left hand.

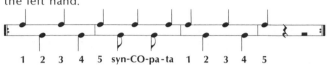

1 2 3 4 5 syn-CO-pa-ta 1 2 3 4 5

Transfer this to the Alto Xyl. The part may be played by two players. Add the Sop. Xyl. This instrument plays the steady quarter notes on the second "1 2 3 4 5." Point out that the syncopated rhythm pattern in this song is the same as the pattern in both "Oh, Won't You Sit Down?", page 334, and "Pay Me My Money Down," page 336.

2. Bass Xyl.: Practice the counting pattern above, playing only the notes indicated. The left hand will cross over the right on the syllable "pa" when this part is transferred to the instrument. Have children practice:

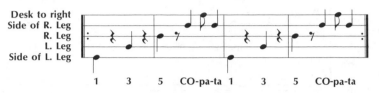

Desk to right
Side of R. Leg
R. Leg
L. Leg
Side of L. Leg

1 3 5 CO-pa-ta 1 3 5 CO-pa-ta

3. Glockenspiels and Metallophones: In the refrain and coda have the soprano instruments play the top two

HOLD ON

AMERICAN FOLK SONG   ARRANGED BY MARILYN COPELAND DAVIDSON

Moving   **Pupil's Book, p. 122   Alternative piano acc., p. 286**

Glockenspiels may improvise a four- or eight-measure introduction/interlude using bells from D to d.

notes and the alto instruments play the bottom note. During the interludes between verses, glockenspiels or recorders may improvise questions and answers in D minor. Children may relate the two sections by imitating rhythms or melodic ideas.

4. Choke Cymbal: Add the cymbal part on beats 2 and 4. Keep the two cymbals close to each other, like a dance band "high-hat" cymbal.

2. If you want to get to heaven, I'll tell you how,
   Keep your hand right on that plow.
   Keep your hand on that plow,
   Hold on, hold on, hold on. *Refrain*

3. Keep on plowin' and don't you tire,
   Ev'ry row goes higher and higher.
   Keep your hand on that plow,
   Hold on, hold on, hold on. *Refrain*

4. If that plow stays in your hand,
   Head you straight for the promised land.
   Keep your hand on that plow,
   Hold on, hold on, hold on. *Refrain*

OH, WHAT A BEAUTIFUL CITY

BLACK SPIRITUAL   ARRANGED BY MARILYN COPELAND DAVIDSON

Teaching notes, p. 341   Pupil's Book, p. 220   Alternative piano acc., p. 296

OH, WHAT A BEAUTIFUL CITY

1. Sop. Gl. and Alto Gl.: The glockenspiel parts move in parallel motion. While the children sing, have them place both hands on parts of the body as indicated.

In the second section of the song the Sop. Gl. plays whole notes as the Alto Gl. continues the pattern. Have the two glockenspiels practice together, the Sop. Gl. joining for the last four measures in the second section.

Transfer to the instruments with two players on each part. Each player must learn his starting pitch to play the stepwise pattern.

Three gates___ to the South, There's twelve gates - a to the cit - y,___ Hal - le - lu - jah!

MICHAEL FINNEGAN CHILDREN'S GAME SONG ARRANGED BY MARILYN COPELAND DAVIDSON
Teaching notes, p. 342 Pupil's Book, p. 30 Alternative piano acc., p. 284

1. There was an old man named
was an old man named

2. Sop. Xyl. and Alto Xyl.: Have children sing section B facing the direction they are singing. Have them finish each phrase with the syncopated pattern.

Side of R. Leg
R. Leg
L. Leg
Side of L. Leg

(East) syn-CO-pa-ta (West) And o-ver there.

Transfer to the instruments. Have the children tap their mallets together during the rest to feel the downbeat.

MICHAEL FINNEGAN

1. Nonpitched percussion: Divide the class into three groups to learn these parts. Assign one instrument part to each group. Have children chant only the words for their instrument.

Guiro
Woodblock
Triangle

Poor old Mi-chael, Mi-chael Fin-ne-gan

Voice: Mi-chael Fin-ne-gan, He had whis-kers on his chin-ne-gan, He pulled them out but they grew in a-gain, Poor old Mi-chael
Mi-chael Fin-ne-gan, He went fish-ing with a pin-ne-gan, He caught a fish but dropped it in a-gain, Poor old Mi-chael

Sop. Xyl.

Alto Xyl.

Bass Xyl.

Guiro

W.B. Tri.

D.S. three times **CODA**

Voice: Fin - ne - gan. Be - gin a - gain. 2. There
Fin - ne - gan. Be - gin a - gain. 3. There

Sop. Xyl.

Alto Xyl.

Bass Xyl.

Guiro

W.B. Tri.

3. (There) was an old man named Michael Finnegan,
Climbed a tree and barked his shinnegan,
He lost about a yard of skinnegan,
Poor old Michael Finnegan. Begin again.

4. There was an old man named Michael Finnegan,
He grew fat and then grew thinnegan,
Then he died and that's the endegan,
Poor old Michael Finnegan. Begin again.

Poor old Mi-chael Fin-ne-gan, Fin-ne-gan.

Have children learn the last two measures of the song. (The introduction is the same as the first pattern above.)

2. Xylophones: Divide the class into two groups. As one group pats the steady Bass Xyl. rhythm (alternate hands starting with R.H.) have the other group lightly clap eighth notes. To teach the Alto Xyl. changes, have children clap and snap with both hands. (Clap the F–A interval, snap the F–B♭ interval.) Transfer the xylophone parts to the instruments.

HE'S GOT THE WHOLE WORLD IN HIS HANDS BLACK SPIRITUAL

ARRANGED BY MARILYN COPELAND DAVIDSON

Teaching notes, p. 344   Pupil's Book, p. 246   Alternative piano acc., p. 273

HE'S GOT THE WHOLE WORLD IN HIS HANDS

Practice each instrument part with the class singing in the order below. Do not add more than one or two parts each class session.

1. Bass Xyl.: Pat legs to the steady beat. Alternate hands starting with the left hand. Have children learn the left hand part to the verse of the song. Add the introduction and ending after the children are secure with the verse.

2. Sop. Met. and Alto Met.: These instrument parts have the same rhythm. Children may learn them both in the same class period. Practice the patterns below to learn the pitch changes in each part. Children may chant the rhythm as they pat legs.

3. Alto Xyl.: Pat both legs to the steady beat. To learn the pitch changes, children may practice moving one hand at a time while the other hand pats the steady beat.

After the children have practiced the parts above, have them put them together and transfer to the instruments.

4. Alto Gl.: Practice the exercise below to develop the "feel" of the instrument part. Use both hands. Then transfer to the instrument.

5. Sop. Gl.: This instrument plays the introduction and the ending section. Children may pat legs to the steady beat, alternating hands, starting with the right hand. They will play a descending and ascending pentatonic scale.

KOOKABURRA

1. Bass Xyl.: Pat legs.

2. Sop. Xyl. and Alto Xyl.: Divide the class into two groups. As one group practices the Bass Xyl. ostinato, have the second group snap fingers to the left, then to the right.

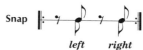

2. He's got the wind and rain in his hands,
    He's got the wind and rain in his hands,
    He's got the wind and rain in his hands,
    He's got the whole world in his hands.

3. He's got both you and me. . . . . .

3. Castanets: Have children clap and chant.

He sim-ply sits.

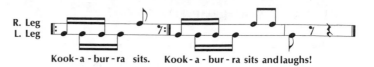

Kook-a-bur-ra sits.   Kook-a-bur-ra sits and laughs!

4. Woodblock: The woodblock and xylophone sixteenth-note rhythm patterns are the same and can be taught at the same time. Have children pat legs.

5. Recorder: Recorder players may learn the rhythm of their part by playing with the Bass Xyl. for the first four measures and with the woodblock as above.

KOOKABURRA

WORDS AND MUSIC BY MARION SINCLAIR   ARRANGED BY MARILYN COPELAND DAVIDSON

FROM THE DITTY BAG. COMPILED BY JANET E. TOBITT. USED WITH PERMISSION.

Pupil's Book, p. 144   Teaching notes, p. 344

SEE, CAN'T YOU JUMP FOR JOY

1. Bass Met.: Pat legs.

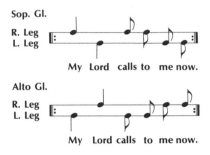
Side of R. Leg
R. Leg
L. Leg
My Lord calls.

Children may sing the moving tones (D E D) with letter names, numbers, syllables, or the chant above. Hand motions in the patting exercise should be very smooth and sustained.

2. Sop. Gl. and Alto Gl.: Both instrument parts have the same rhythm pattern. Pat legs and chant.

Sop. Gl.
R. Leg
L. Leg
My Lord calls to me now.

Alto Gl.
R. Leg
L. Leg
My Lord calls to me now.

3. Sop. Xyl. and Alto Xyl.: Divide the class into two groups. Each group will chant the rhythm of one of the instruments, either the Sop. Xyl. or the Alto Xyl.

See, can't you jump.   I can real - ly jump.
(Alto)   (Sop.)

As one group chants and pats legs, the other group will chant and snap fingers or clap. The children can listen for the contrasting rhythm patterns of each part.

R. Leg
L. Leg
See, can't you jump.   I can real - ly jump.

4. Body percussion: The finger snap and hand clap may be performed by two groups, one group for each sound. Also, children may suggest other sounds to use for special effects. Use these sounds on the word *jump* when it occurs in the song.

5. Recorder: This part moves with the melody. Add it to the ensemble after the other instrument parts have been learned.

Teach the last measure of the song. Chant *Jump for joy* on the last three notes (beats 3 and 4) of each part.

SEE, CAN'T YOU JUMP FOR JOY   BLACK SPIRITUAL   ARRANGED BY MARILYN COPELAND DAVIDSON

Pupil's Book, p. 150   Alternative piano acc., p. 324

*Experiment with a sound on the word "jump." Use a slide whistle, a cymbal, or other sound effect.

Voice: See, can't you jump for joy, _____ See, can't you jump for joy, _____ Broth-er, can't you jump for joy. _____

HINEH MAH TOV

Teach the instrument parts for this song a section at a time. Begin with the first section, then the second, and end with the introduction and final note. Children may wish to clap the rhythm pattern of their instrument as they sing to get the "feel" of the ensemble. Add only one instrument at a time, assigning two or three children to learn each part.

Section A

1. Alto Xyl.: Pat legs and chant.

2. Sop. Xyl.: Pat legs and chant.

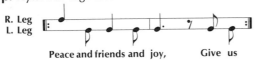

3. Alto Met., Bass Xyl., and Bass Met.: Pat legs and chant.

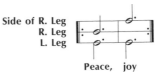

4. Alto Gl. and Sop. Met.: Pat legs and chant. Sop. Gl. has the same rhythm.

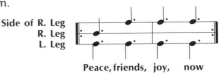

5. Finger Cymbals: Clap and chant.

HINEH MAH TOV

HEBREW FOLK SONG   ARRANGED BY MARILYN COPELAND DAVIDSON

Pupil's Book, p. 208   Alternative piano acc., p. 271

6. Tambourine: Clap and chant.

Peace,   oh now give us peace   and joy to all, Now give us

Section B

1. Alto Xyl.: Pat legs and chant.

Hi - neh mah tov   u - ma

2. Sop. Met. and Alto Met.: Pat legs and chant.

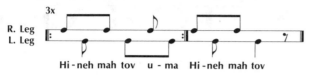

Hi - neh mah tov   u - ma   Hi - neh mah tov

3. Bass Xyl. and Bass Met.: Pat legs and chant. Children silently think the syllable *neh* of *hineh*.

Hi-(neh) mah tov   u   ma   Hi-(neh) mah tov

4. Sop. Gl. and Alto Gl.: Pat legs and chant. In the third measure, have the children move their hands slightly to the left, bringing them back for the fourth measure.

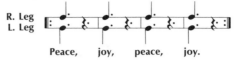

Peace,   joy,   peace,   joy.

5. Finger Cymbals: Clap and chant.

Peace,   joy,   peace, friends, joy.

6. Tambourine: Clap and chant.

Peace,   give us joy,   give us

Children may wish to combine two or three parts to practice. Be sure they are secure with one section before trying another. When they are ready to play the song, add the introduction. It uses the first four measures of the first section played by the Sop. Xyl., Bass Xyl., Bass Met., and the tambourine.

TUNING THE AUTOHARP

It is essential to keep the Autoharp in tune. Factors such as weather and frequency of use may necessitate tuning the Autoharp occasionally. Unless you have had a great deal of experience in hearing chords, you may need to request the help of your music teacher or a local music store.

SUGGESTED TUNING PROCEDURE

Since the Autoharp is a chording instrument, it should be tuned by chords rather than by consecutive tones of the scale.

1. Start with the F-major chord. Press the F button and check all F, A, and C strings with the corresponding tones on a well-tuned piano or a set of tuned bells. (Tighten the string to raise its pitch; loosen it to lower its pitch. To be certain that you are tuning the correct string, trace your finger along the string to its tuning peg.)

2. Press the C-major button and tune the C chord (C—E—G). If you have tuned all C's carefully (in the F chords), you have only the E and G strings to tune.

3. Continue, as above, tuning chords in the following order:

   —G-major chord (G—B—D). Only the B and D strings remain to be tuned as the G strings were tuned in the C chord.

   —G_7 chord (G—B—D—F) should now be in tune as the F strings were tuned earlier.

   —D_7 chord (D—F$^{\#}$—A—C). Only the F$^{\#}$ strings remain to be tuned.

   —B$^{\flat}$ chord (B$^{\flat}$—D—F). Only the B$^{\flat}$ (A$^{\#}$) strings remain to be tuned.

   —E_7 chord (E—G$^{\#}$—B—D). Only the G$^{\#}$ strings remain to be tuned.

   —A_7 chord (A—C$^{\#}$—E—G). Only the C$^{\#}$ strings remain to be tuned.

   —E$^{\flat}$ chord (E$^{\flat}$—G—B$^{\flat}$). Only the E$^{\flat}$ strings remain to be tuned.

4. All members of the following chords belong to other chords which have already been tuned: C_7, A min., D min., G min., D, F_7.

DO 🤙 RE 🤚 MI 🤚 FA ✋ SOL 🤚 LA ✊ TI 👆 DO¹ 🤙

KODALY GUIDE

Listed below are basic melody patterns found in the song materials in SILVER BURDETT MUSIC, Book 4. The list is intended as a resource for teachers who incorporate Kodály techniques in their teaching. The headings (S–M, M–S, etc.) indicate the melody patterns. The numbers in parentheses indicate the measures that contain the patterns. (Note: For songs with har-mony parts, measure numbers always refer to the melody.) The letter u before a number means that the pattern begins with the upbeat to the measure.

To give children experience with reading rhythm, see Note-Reading Index, Reading Rhythm (p. 352).

S-M
America, the Beautiful, 153 (u 1, u 5)
Find the Ring, 72 (1–2)
Hear the Rooster, 10 (17–18, 21–22)
Hurry, Good Shepherds, 184 (25)
Kookaburra, 144 (2)
Red, Red Robin, 147 (11–12)
Three White Gulls, 218 (u 5, u 9)

M-S
Amazing Grace, 192 (u 9)
Dayenu, 40 (1, 2)
He's Got the Whole World in His Hands, 246 (2, 6)

S-L-S-M
Hand Me Down, 14 (u 1, u 9 10)
Naughty Little Flea, 140 (1, 5)
Silent Night, 212 (1–2)

S-L
Naughty Little Flea, 140 (u 13)
Sourwood Mountain, 16 (11, 15)

S₁-L₁
Jane, Jane, 217 (4, 8, 12, 16, 20, 24, 28, 32)

S-L-S
Hurry, Good Shepherds, 184 (u 9–10, u 13–14)

S-M-L-S-M
Pay Me My Money Down, 4 (u 1–2, 9–10)

M-S-L-S
Tinga Layo, 149 (u 1–2, u 5–6)

L-S-M
Joy to the World, 139 (1, 3–4, 5)

L-M
Dundai, 90 (1–2)
Let the Sun Shine Down on Me, 148 (9, 13)
Rally Song, 120, 133 (3–4)

D-M
All Hid, 161 (1–2)
Dundai, 90 (5, 7)
Sambalele, 22 (9, 13)

D¹-M¹
Remember Me, 92 (u 7, u 15)

M-D
Clementine, 154 (u 2, u 10)
Dry Bones, 42 (2, 4, 6, 28, 30, 32)
Kookaburra, 144 (4, 7–8)
Oh, Won't You Sit Down? 24 (9–10, 13–14)
Red, Red Robin, 147 (13–14)
Sourwood Mountain, 16 (1, 5)

S-M-D
He's Got the Whole World in His Hands, 246 (u 1, u 5)
Star-Spangled Banner, The, 62 (u 1, u 9)
Ta-ra-ra Boom-de-ay, 146 (3, 7, 15–16)

D-S
Song of the Angel, 126 (u 1, u 5)

M-S-D
Mañana, 76 (2–3, 4–5)

D-M-S-M
Guava Berry Song, 106 (u 25–27, u 33–35)

M-R-D
All Hid, 161 (Section B)
Chanukah Song, 232 (u 2)
Flea! 39 (5)
Sourwood Mountain, 16 (4, 8, 12, 16)
Tina, Singu, 104 (3–4)

M¹-R¹-D¹
Purim Song, 185 (9, 13)
Remember Me, 92 (2, 6)

D-R-M
Evening, 189 (6, 8)

D-R-M-R-D
Chanukah Song, 232 (3, 5)
Red, Red Robin, 147 (u 1, u 5, u 29)
Tina, Singu, 104 (12)

D-R-D
Hand Game Song, 7 (7–8, 13–14)

D¹-R¹-D¹
Purim Song, 185 (1–2)

R-M
Don Gato, 164 (u 12)

D-M-S
Clementine, 154 (u 3, u 11)
Ging Gong Gooli, 18 (u 2, u 6)

In Bahia Town, 80 (1–2, 9–10)
Oh, What a Beautiful City, 220 (1–2, 5–6)
Sambalele, 22 (1, 5)

M-R-M
Don Gato, 164 (3–4, 7–8)

D-R-M-S
Sourwood Mountain, 16 (3, 7)

D-S₁
Clementine, 154 (u 1, u 9)

R-D
Colorful Boats, 235 (1, 3, 7, 11)

D¹-L-S
Hotsia! 168 (u 2–3, u 5–6, u 8–9, u 17–18, u 20–21)
Namane Kare, 196 (1, 9)

D-L₁-S₁
All Hid, 161 (3–4)

D¹-L
Hotsia! 168 (1, 4, 7, 10, 13, 16, 19, 22, u 23–24, 25)

D-L₁
Harvest Time, 59 (5, 7)
He mele o ke kahuli, 215 (1, 3)
Hold On, 122 (7–8, 13–14)
Jane, Jane, 217 (u 6–7)

S₁-D
Amazing Grace, 192 (u 1, u 5, u 13)
Great Big Sea, A, 77 (u 1, u 9)
Michael Finnegan, 30 (u 1, u 5)
Rookoombine, 190 (u 5, u 9)

S-D¹
Star-Spangled Banner, The, 62 (u 25, u 29)

S₁-D-S₁-L₁-S₁
Frog in the Well, The, 178 (u 1–2, u 5–6)

S₁-D-R-M
Sands Get into Your Shoes, 96 (u 1, u 5)

S-L-D¹
Remember Me, 92 (1, 5, 9, 13)

S₁-L₁-S₁-D
Oh, Won't You Sit Down? 24 (u 1, u 3, u 5)

NOTE-READING INDEX

The following information is intended for teachers who wish to develop their own music-reading program using materials in SILVER BURDETT MUSIC, Book 4. It is divided into two sections as follows.

Reading Rhythm: This section lists songs according to the note values that make up the rhythm, and (beginning with the heading ♪ ♩ ♪) according to specific note combinations (patterns) that occur in the songs. When the note values or rhythm patterns apply only to part of a song, specific measures are identified in parentheses. (Note: For songs with harmony parts, measure numbers always refer to the melody.) The letter *u* before a measure number means that the upbeat to the measure is included. Note: The numeral before each song title indicates the meter of the song (6 equals $\frac{6}{8}$ meter).

Reading Melody: This section lists songs according to the pitches they use. When the pitches apply only to part of a song, specific measures are identified in parentheses. (Note: For songs with harmony parts, measure numbers always refer to the melody.) The letter *u* before a measure number means that the upbeat to the measure is included. Note: The headings are organized according to scale degrees, from lowest to highest—e.g., D, R, M; D, R, M, F; D, M; R, M, F, S. Some teachers may wish to use numbers instead of the pitch syllables (do, re, mi, etc.) to designate scale degrees—D = 1, R = 2, M = 3, etc.

Reading Rhythm

♩ ≀, ♫
4 He mele o ke kahuli, 215 (1-4)
3 Nine Red Horsemen, 219 (Section B)

♩, ♫
4 Evening, 189 (1-4, 10-13)
2 Hand Game Song, 7 (1-7)
4 Iroquois Lullaby, An, 234

♩, ≀, ♫, ♩
2 Jane, Jane, 217 (29-32)
3 Nine Red Horsemen, 219 (Section A)
3 When Is a Door? 9 (1-8)

♩, ≀, ♩
2 Jane, Jane, 217 (1-8)

♩, ♫, ♩
3 Amazing Grace, 192 (1-4)
4 Dayenu, 40 (1-4)
4 Dundai, 90 (Section B)
4 Evening, 189 (5-9)
4 Ghost of John, The, 244 (1-4, 7-8)
3 Guava Berry Song, 106 (Section A)
4 Guava Berry Song, 106 (Section C)
2 Here I Go, 8
2 Purim Song, 185 (Section A)
3 Sandy McNab, 9

♩, ♩
4 Namane Kare, 196 (5-8)

♫, ♩
2 Hear the Rooster, 10 (17-24)

♫, o
4 Harvest Time, 59

♩, ≀, ♫, ♩.
4 Don't Count Your Chickens, 100
  (u 15-22)

♩, ≀, ▬, ♩.
4 Run, Run, Run, 98 (Section B)

♩, ♫, ♩, ♩.
3 Clouds, 55 (1-4)
4 Ghost of John, The, 244

♩, ♫, ♩.
4 Song of the Angel, 126 (u 1-4, u 9-10)

♩, ♩, o, ♩.
4 Psalm of Thanksgiving, 245 (1-4, 9-12, 18-24)

♩, ♩, ♩.
3 Find the Ring, 72

♩, ♩.
4 For Health and Strength, 127

♩ ♪, ♫♫, ♩.
6 Hineh mah tov, 208
6 I Know an Old Lady, 52 (u 1-4, u 7-14, u 17-28)
6 Paddy Works on the Railway, 209

♩ ♪ ♩ ≀, ♫♫, ♩.
6 Hurry, Good Shepherds, 184 (u 17-30)

♪ ♩ ♪
4 Dayenu, 40 (Section B)
2 Hear the Rooster, 10 (1-16)

♫ ♫
4 Lazy Coconut Tree, 41 (10-12, 14-16)
4 Oh, What a Beautiful City, 220 (11-14, 17-18)

♩ ♩ ♩
4 Go, Tell It on the Mountain, 64 (Section A)

♬♬
2 Ging Gong Gooli, 18 (Section A)
2 Island Hopping, 118 (19-22)
2 Kookaburra, 144 (5-8)

♩. ♪
3 Amazing Grace, 192 (u 9-12)
3 America, 175
4 America, the Beautiful, 153
4 Don't Count Your Chickens, 100 (u 5-8, u 25-28)
4 Dundai, 90 (Section A)
4 Great Big Sea, A, 77
4 Harvesting Tea, 216
2 Seasons of the Year, The, 127
3 Star-Spangled Banner, The, 62 (u 17-32)

♫♫
2 Chanukah Song, 232 (7-14)
2 In Bahia Town, 80 (5-8, 13-16)
2 Kookaburra, 144
2 Purim Song, 185 (Section B)

≀, ♫♫
4 Naughty Little Flea, 140 (Section A)

♫♫
2 Michael Finnegan, 30 (1-8)

♫
3 Clementine, 154
2 Colorful Boats, 235
4 Dry Bones, 42 (Section B)
4 Flea! 39 (7-10)
3 Guava Berry Song, 106 (Section B)
2 Hand Game Song, 7 (9-14)
4 Hand Me Down, 14 (Section A)
4 I Love the Mountains, 60 (1-10)
2 Sasa Aberewa, 70
4 Song of the Angel, 126 (u 7-10)
3 Star-Spangled Banner, The, 62 (u 1-16)
2 Ta-ra-ra Boom-de-ay, 146
4 Up the Street the Band Is Marching Down, 87
4 Wise Man Built His House, The, 21

♪ ♪
3-2 Muje Mukesin, 207

CLASSIFIED INDEX

364

INDEX

PICTURE CREDITS

1 2 3 4 5 6 7 8 9 10—RRD—88 87 86 85 84 83 82 81 80